GOOD GOVERNING

Good Governing: The Police Power in the American States is a deep historical and legal analysis of state police power, examining its origins in the founding period of the American republic through the twentieth century. The book reveals how American police power was intended to be a broad, but not unlimited, charter of regulatory governance, designed to implement key constitutional objectives and advance the general welfare. It explores police power's promise as a mechanism for implementing successful regulatory governance and tackling societal ills, while considering key structural issues like separation of powers and individual rights. This insightful book will shape understanding of the neglected state police power, a key part of constitutional governance in the United States. This title is also available as Open Access on Cambridge Core.

Daniel B. Rodriguez is the Harold Washington Professor of Law at Northwestern University Pritzker School of Law. In addition to Northwestern, Professor Rodriguez has held tenured positions at the University of Texas, the University of San Diego, and the University of California, Berkeley and has held visiting positions at Harvard, Stanford, and Columbia. His scholarship focuses on public law, including constitutional law, administrative law, and regulation.

Good Governing

THE POLICE POWER IN THE AMERICAN STATES

DANIEL B. RODRIGUEZ
Northwestern University Pritzker School of Law

Shaftesbury Road, Cambridge CB2 8EA, United Kingdom

One Liberty Plaza, 20th Floor, New York, NY 10006, USA

477 Williamstown Road, Port Melbourne, VIC 3207, Australia

314–321, 3rd Floor, Plot 3, Splendor Forum, Jasola District Centre, New Delhi – 110025, India

103 Penang Road, #05–06/07, Visioncrest Commercial, Singapore 238467

Cambridge University Press is part of Cambridge University Press & Assessment, a department of the University of Cambridge.

We share the University's mission to contribute to society through the pursuit of education, learning and research at the highest international levels of excellence.

www.cambridge.org
Information on this title: www.cambridge.org/9781009123051

DOI: 10.1017/9781009127370

© Daniel B. Rodriguez 2024

This publication is in copyright. Subject to statutory exception and to the provisions of relevant collective licensing agreements, with the exception of the Creative Commons version the link for which is provided below, no reproduction of any part may take place without the written permission of Cambridge University Press & Assessment.

An online version of this work is published at doi.org/10.1017/9781009127370 under a Creative Commons Open Access license CC-BY-NC-ND 4.0 which permits re-use, distribution and reproduction in any medium for non-commercial purposes providing appropriate credit to the original work is given. You may not distribute derivative works without permission. To view a copy of this license, visit https://creativecommons.org/licenses/by-nc-nd/4.0

When citing this work, please include a reference to the DOI 10.1017/9781009127370

First published 2024

A catalogue record for this publication is available from the British Library

Library of Congress Cataloging-in-Publication Data
NAMES: Rodriguez, Daniel B., 1962– author.
TITLE: Good governing : the police power in the American states / Daniel B. Rodriguez, Northwestern University, Illinois.
DESCRIPTION: Cambridge, United Kingdom ; New York, NY : Cambridge University Press, 2024. | Includes bibliographical references and index.
IDENTIFIERS: LCCN 2023054656 (print) | LCCN 2023054657 (ebook) | ISBN 9781009123051 (hardback) | ISBN 9781009127370 (ebook)
SUBJECTS: LCSH: Police power – United States. | Police regulations – United States. | Constitutional law – United States.
CLASSIFICATION: LCC KF4695 .R59 2024 (print) | LCC KF4695 (ebook) | DDC 342.73/0418–dc23/eng/20231204
LC record available at https://lccn.loc.gov/2023054656
LC ebook record available at https://lccn.loc.gov/2023054657

ISBN 978-1-009-12305-1 Hardback
ISBN 978-1-009-12421-8 Paperback

Cambridge University Press & Assessment has no responsibility for the persistence or accuracy of URLs for external or third-party internet websites referred to in this publication and does not guarantee that any content on such websites is, or will remain, accurate or appropriate.

Contents

Acknowledgments		*page* vii
	Introduction	1
	PART I POWER FOR THE PEOPLE: CREATING THE MODERN POLICE POWER	
1	State Constitutions and the Governance Project	17
2	The Police Power in Our Republic's First Century	42
3	"The Power to Govern Men and Things": The Police Power Evolves to Meet New Conditions	84
4	The Shape of the Police Power in the Modern Era	133
	PART II STRUCTURAL CONSIDERATIONS	
5	Separating and Distributing Powers and Functions	173
6	Constitutional Rights	200
7	Turning Inside Out: Resolving Conflicts over the Scope of the Police Power	237
8	The Police Power and Federalism	261

PART III THE POLICE POWER'S PROMISE

9   Spheres of Regulatory Governance   283

10 Techniques of Regulatory Intervention: New Legal
    Tools to Solve Wicked Problems   318

    Conclusion   331

Index   333

Acknowledgments

This book reflects a deep dive into one key constitutional principle and power, but it reflects a wider amount of thinking about state constitutionalism and its form and function. Some of this thinking has resulted in published research, some has been sketched in various public lectures at law schools, and the rest has emerged rather organically from discussion in courses with terrific law students at various law schools where I have taught. And yet most of it is new with the work on this book. A number of prominent academics and judges, most recently the Hon. Jeff Sutton of the US Court of Appeals, have urged the academy to look beyond the US Constitution and federal constitutional law, to the myriad issues that arise in the context of state constitutions and state constitutional law. Hopefully this book responds to this call. State constitutions are at center stage of the most difficult debates and controversies in modern American politics, and I am hopeful that this book will be joined by a growing number of works to go onto the proverbial state constitutional law bookshelf.

In developing the book's central ideas, I have drawn upon earlier presentations and lectures. In 2020, I gave the Victor Johnson Lecture at Vanderbilt Law School, and that helped me in organizing many of the themes in this book. Before that, I had given a number of endowed lectures that helped to develop and sharpen various ideas here. These include the Jefferson Memorial Lectures at the University of California, Berkeley, the William Brennan Lecture on State Constitutional Law at Oklahoma City University Law School, the Rutgers State Constitutional Law Lecture, and the Nathaniel Nathanson Memorial Lecture at the University of San Diego. Thanks to the colleagues who invited me to give these lectures and to the participants who contributed their thoughts. I am thankful for good comments at faculty workshops and symposia at the law schools at New York University, University of San Diego, Texas A&M University, the University of Kentucky, and the University of Bologna. Late in the life of this manuscript, I had the benefit of a roundtable on this book, organized by Northwestern's Center on Law and Business, under the direction of my colleague Alex Lee, and with the valuable help of Derek Gundersen. A number of leading scholars participated in this meeting and made this book appreciably better. They include Bridget Fahey, Lee Fennell, Tom Gaylord, Joanna Grissinger, Jamila Jefferson-Jones, Anthony Michael Kreis, Alex Lee, Gregory Mark, Jonathan Marshfield, Ajay Mehrotra, Jim Rossi, Nadav Shoked, and Justin Weinstein-Tull.

Special thanks to early mentors at University of California, Berkeley, where I began my academic career and where my interest in issues of federalism, structural constitutional law, and state constitutional law was stoked. They include Jesse Choper, Robert Cooter, Robert Post, Ed Rubin, Harry Scheiber, Martin Shapiro, and Jan Vetter. Two other great scholars deserve mention. Mat McCubbins (who passed away in the summer of 2021) and Barry Weingast, my teachers, good friends, and frequent co-authors, have both helped me to better understand puzzles in American constitutional politics and regulation and have modeled for me and others what first-rate interdisciplinary scholarship is.

Thanks to a great group of Northwestern research assistants, including Abigail Kuchnir, Paul Piazza, Christian Flowers, Adam Hitti, Quinn Bessette, and Immer Chriswell, for help at various stages. Tom Gaylord of our wonderful law library has been, and continues to be, an excellent resource in many ways. I appreciate the support of the two deans who have been at Northwestern during the duration of this book's work, Jim Speta and Hari Osofsky. Thanks to the great editorial and production team at Cambridge University Press, including Matt Galloway, a champion of this project from the early stages, and also Jadyn Fauconier-Herry.

Last but not least, I am incredibly grateful for the support of my wife (and colleague), Leslie Oster, in various ways, including as an occasional editor, and also to my growing Texas family. This book is dedicated to my parents, living and deceased, whose support and impact has been immeasurable.

Introduction

The state police power – in essence, the power of the state government to protect the health, safety, morals, and general welfare of its citizens – is a modern constitutional curiosity. As an historical matter, vigorous debates over the existence, nature, and scope of the police power were common in the early years of our republic. The power was mentioned first by the Supreme Court in the 1827 case of Brown v. Maryland,[1] but, even before that, it was a familiar part of state constitutions in the Revolutionary period and in the years following. Indeed, the police power was (and still is) the fulcrum of the state's regulatory authority, and much of ordinary regulation of various objects and situations emerged from the police power, seen as a central element of a sovereign government under the rule of law.

Despite the persistent interest in the police power by courts, state and federal, and also by commentators (no less than three treatises were devoted to the topic in the late nineteenth and early twentieth centuries),[2] the police power steadily faded from interest and attention. A law student in an American law school today will spend no appreciable time looking at the police power, except maybe as part of a discrete historical inquiry into how the Supreme Court used notions of liberty of contract and substantive due process during the Lochner era of the early twentieth century to restrict state regulatory authority over economic matters.[3] It is a concept whose desuetude is rather obvious, but still puzzling. Legal historian Harry Scheiber would describe the police power as "one of the most important concepts in American constitutional history,"[4] but as a matter of deep theory or practical reflection, few would pause to wonder why it is of so little consequence in discussions of contemporary American constitutionalism.

The very obscurity of the police power reveals tendencies in the academic discourse around American constitutionalism that ought to be highlighted in their own right. One is the lack of serious and sustained attention in the American legal academy, including both teaching and scholarship, to matters of state constitutional law.[5] The police power is an essential part of state constitutions and, with a little focus on state constitutions, we might expect that a rich understanding of the power would suffer from the same remoteness from concern. The other reason for its irrelevance, a bit more complex to unpack, is that issues of constitutional power lose their centrality in a period in which the most concrete issues for constitutional adjudication – whether at the national or state level – are whether and to what extent official power is limited by certain individual rights. Take an ordinary case in which an individual is asserting that a state statute limits her ability to express certain content on the grounds that her expression would disrupt the moral sensibilities of a community. Maybe she wins, maybe she loses; but the court's inquiry will focus less on the status and structure of the government's power to protect the public's morals and more on whether she has a fundamental First Amendment right that is being compromised by the state regulation. You can conjure up a thousand hypotheticals of constitutional conflict and you will find that most of the focus will be on the *right*, not on the *power*.[6] This situation was not nearly as common in much earlier eras, when the courts were less intensely preoccupied with questions of fundamental rights and tiers of review and more on whether the government had the power to act in the first instance. Insofar as the scope of the police power is less central to the structure of constitutional adjudication, attending to this power has declined as a priority in scholarship and also in the caselaw.

Good Governing is an effort to reconsider the police power, and for reasons that are important for understanding state constitutionalism in the United States, as well as the architecture and potential of regulation at the state and local level. The basic argument is that the police power is a core component of the state constitution – that is to say, every state constitution, even acknowledging state-to-state differences – and emerges as a technology to enable the government, acting on behalf of the people as sovereign, to fulfill our most essential constitutional objectives. These objectives can be considered at various granular levels, and so we can speak of the role of law in addressing the imperatives of securing public safety, protecting state citizens from threats to their public health, maintaining good order, protecting individual liberty and private property, and ensuring the education of its citizens and a clean environment (these last two goals part of more modern constitutional understandings, connected to notions of positive rights). At a more global level, we can see as a principal objective of state constitutionalism the empowerment of state and local institutions to engage in what we call here good governing – good governing in a twin sense, of effective regulatory decision-making and of official choices for the public good. The police power, in its standard locution and its interpretation by courts, refers to some specific goals (health, safety, and morals) and a larger, more overarching goal (general welfare, the common good). So long as we take seriously the role and function of state constitutions in our scheme of American governance, we should, too, account for the shape and function of the police power.

While the principal subject of this book is the police power in the American states, this broad and deep inquiry is situated in a larger inquiry into the nature and theory of American state constitutionalism. It is from the vantage point of a richer understanding of state constitutions that we can gain a nuanced and, in some important ways, novel understanding of the police power. After all, the power emerges directly from these fifty documents, not from the United States Constitution; it is one of those classic powers reserved to the states via the Tenth Amendment. State constitutions are the foundation of the power, providing it with shape and scope. And yet state constitutions often get a bad rap in discussions of American constitutionalism and its foundations. When they are not neglected in whole or in part, they are often regarded as clumsy, cumbersome vessels for instantiation of current policy fads. James Gardner famously described state constitutional as a "failed discourse,"[7] highlighting, as others have, the jumble of state constitutional provisions and the lack of a tradition of truly independent state constitutional interpretation.

Whatever misgivings scholars and citizens have about the content of particular state constitutions, it remains true that these documents govern official action and wide swaths of political and social life in American life. Their puzzles are, to be sure, close to the surface. Robert Post wrote in a book about constitutional reform in California the following: "State constitutions face a fundamental challenge: They must constitute a polity within a polity. They must establish a distinctive political culture within the confines of the encompassing and transcendent political culture of the nation."[8] However distinctive be these cultures, state constitutions are also instruments of governance that share some common properties, and common goals and should be viewed for some of their cohesive elements in establishing unique (from the US Constitution) methods and theories of governance.[9] In short, we can talk sensibly about American state constitutionalism, without descending into a Tower of Babel where we are talking only about our state constitutions in isolation. That said, we need also attend to the particular institutional context – let us call it the positive political theory of state constitutional design and performance[10] – to understand how instruments of governance are formed and how to enable and impede officials to implement purposive goals. Indeed, we cannot sensibly speak of constitutional objectives without attending to the fact that these constitutions are forged in the crucible of political compromise and strategies. "A written constitution," political scientist Donald Lutz writes, "is a political technology."[11] It is with an eye or two attending to the matters, distinct to individual constitutions in one respect, but a common practice across states in another, that we can unpack and understand the objectives of constitutions. In the end, the police is a principle, but it is also a tactic. This study aims to illuminate its contents and logic from both dimensions.

This is not principally a work of history, but of constitutional theory and normative argument. However, the history of the police power is important, as it provides the frame within which struggles over its identity, its purpose, and ultimately its limits can be understood. The story of the police power begins at the beginning, that is, with the enactment of the first Revolutionary-era constitutions and the early interpretations of those constitutions, along with developments in the common law and legislative interpretation. The Supreme Court's role was important in the nineteenth century in acknowledging the state police power, when its place in our new constitutional republic might have been precarious, given the creation of a US Constitution and the emergence of a strong federal role in managing and regulating our new nation. Yet even more important to the evolving shape of the police power were key state cases in the nineteenth and early twentieth century, cases which grappled with the state's role as a guardian of the public's welfare and, moreover, with the place of government regulation in a system in which both liberty and private property were important, even if never sacrosanct. Litigation over the police power was part of an admixture of doctrinal developments and controversies involving private property owners (individuals and businesses) and those who made claims on government to redress wrongs and to promote the general welfare. In the critical period beginning in the Jacksonian era, continuing in antebellum America, through the Civil War and Reconstruction, and then into the Progressive era, the courts developed important doctrines, not coincidentally with "public" usually in the title, including public rights, public trust doctrine, public purpose, and public use in eminent domain, that sought to balance property rights with the commands of a government that was active, progressive, and stunningly ambitious. Ultimately, from these legal decisions, both state and federal, there emerged a police power that was capacious, but with constitutional guardrails, and, importantly, not limited to addressing private harm.

There were twists and turns in this story, as could be expected in the long arc of American legal and political history, and the contours of the police power were shaped and reshaped in various ways through the nineteenth century and into the twentieth century, a century that began with the experiment of what has been called "laissez faire constitutionalism." This critical episode in American constitutional history can become a bit overheated in its retelling, but it is nonetheless a focused event that captures important parts of our American constitutional history in a period of grand turbulence. Moreover, it is as much about the evolving conceptions of regulatory power and notions of property and sovereignty as it is about the birth of so-called substantive due process.

The story of the police power's evolution has no ending point, of course, and the period after the end of the New Deal, despite the fact that the police power faded into almost complete obscurity as the century wore on, is an important, if neglected, part of the story. In the second half of the twentieth century especially, constitutional rights emerged as significant constraints on official power, including power wielded by state and local governments under their respective constitutions. And while the focus, as mentioned above, was on the content of the rights, the basic logic of the police power was nonetheless a key part of the mix. Courts, and especially state courts, cared to consider whether and to what extent state and local regulation was arbitrary, the product of animus or self-dealing, and so in some broad sense unreasonable. These were components of police power doctrine in an earlier era, as the treatise writers taught us, but they persisted, albeit in ways somewhat more latent (and for that reason somewhat confusing) and complex. In the time of the Covid-19 pandemic, courts were asked to consider anew challenges to the assertion of authority by governors, legislatures, and agencies to regulate, in often draconian ways, in order to protect public health and safety. Questions involving the police power remerged, but often without a coherent vocabulary to resolve intense, and powerfully partisan, controversies. An earlier essay on the topic by this author describes the police power as simultaneously inscrutable and irrepressible.[12] It is also indispensable, and the development of constitutional adjudication involving some of the major issues of American public policy illustrate these elements.

Beyond the historical perspective on the police power, there are some key structural issues about the operation of this power, issues that help illuminate broad themes in both state constitutional performance and in regulatory strategy at both the state and local level. Whereas the police power was seen in its origins as strictly a legislative power – an implication of the legislature's plenary power established under state constitutions from the beginning of our republic – it evolved into a power exercised by other governmental institutions, including municipalities, special purpose governments, and administrative agencies. In short, it shape-shifted just as American regulatory institutions did over the expanse of our history. Yet the police power was no *deus ex machina*. Its use and utility, and the institutions who deployed it, were the product of intentional political choices and strategies. Moreover, these choices often generated controversies, some rising to the level of constitutional conflicts. Recurring to the Covid pandemic again, we saw in 2020 and 2021 complaints that state constitutions were being stretched too far in giving governors and agencies power to limit freedom and the use of property. The nondelegation doctrine in state constitutional law, unlike its cousin in the federal constitutional context, is alive and well, as are other doctrines unique to state constitutional law, and so state courts struggled with these issues. The configuration of the police power is ultimately not just about drawing boundaries around what power is or is not too much; it is, as well, about the sensible design of institutions, rules, and procedures that enable it to function and to not be used. Indeed, very much the same could be said about constitutions writ large. How we think about the police power is how we think about constitutional structure and performance. That is a prime theme in this book's analysis of the police power.

The effort to rescue the police power from its obscurity is warranted by its capacity as an idea and a doctrine that illuminates wide themes in the study regulation and constitutional governance. We might say, albeit with some equivocation, that a closer look at the history, logic, and function of the police power might contribute to better interpretations of that power in instances of conflict. Equivocal because to a great degree this depends upon one's favored method of constitutional interpretation. In the focus on the content of rights and on the dimensions of power, method matters. And so commentators may and do urge on courts that they approach these issues in, say, an originalist or "living constitutionalist" manner. Whatever method one favors, however, it will be fruitful to consider, as courts have for decades, perhaps even centuries, the basis of the regulation – that is, the constitutional power from which it emanates and its rationale. So, for example, when a state court considers whether a regulation violates equal protection principles, it will typically look at whether the statute is a reasonable exercise of governmental power and, with that, whether the law is arbitrary or irrational. Occasionally such an inquiry will lead to further questions of whether the law truly is grounded in general welfare rather than, say, animus or corruption. The doctrine evolves to be sure, but the century inquiry has long been: "Is this law permissible? Is it a rational (or, when the scrutiny standard is strict, compelling) exercise of governmental power?" In this respect, the police power's logic remains an important, often ambient, legal construct, one that provides an important window into the nature and structure of state constitutional law.

A note on constitutional interpretation and interpretive method: a sophisticated view of the police power necessitates a close look at its origins, its history, but it need not rely on the ability of a judge to discern the original public meaning of this phrase or state constitutions generally. This book will be unlikely to warm the heart of a committed constitutional originalist. Not only is the evidence of the meaning that the framers of the US Constitution and these myriad documents, enacted over a long time period, gave to the police power elusive, but this author is skeptical about the originalist project on the whole, and sustained attention to the history of this power has not eroded this skepticism.

Beyond constitutional theory, the police power is important for deeply practical reasons. We live in a world in which many of our most difficult problems as experienced at a state or even local level and in which the capacity and resolve of the government is frequently in question. Issues involving housing affordability, gun violence, pedestrian safety, environmental quality and equity, and threats from emerging technologies require creative government intervention. They require the right institutions and openness to imaginative agendas; and yet, as a constitutional matter, they also require the right amount of regulatory power. The police power can be a necessary (even if in no way sufficient) condition for well-intentioned governments to develop strategies and techniques to solve some of our most wicked problems. The connection between problem-solving and governmental power is hardly a new insight. Indeed, the police power in its original contents was intended to be a means by which the government could promote the general welfare. What is new is the increasing severity of the puzzling problems which plague us. This book has a practical mission, along with its analytical one, and that is to describe how the police power might be a vehicle for good governing, for enabling actions to improve the quality of life for all.

To this point, the reader might be expecting what amounts to long encomium to this vital power in the hands of a well-intentioned government. A celebration of the police power's tradition and potential of improving our life and welfare. Not so fast. Official decision-making through the police power over the complex expanse of American legal history has included some of the most troubling episodes of overweening public power. The law upheld by the Supreme Court in Plessy v. Ferguson was a police power law.[13] In that same spirit, so were a large number of laws characteristic of the Jim Crow South. In more modern times, zoning regulations that had the effect and perhaps also the purpose of segregating America, in all regions of the USA, were enacted under the police power. And the history of morals regulation, laws proscribing many aspects of social behavior and interfering in some of the most intimate matters of human behavior, is a history of the police power and its use to regulate in the name of what the government in this time considered good moral order. Nor do we need to see this as all behind us. Regulatory efforts are emerging as part of our current culture wars that would roll back commitments to equality by limiting access and opportunity for communities of color and the LBGTQ+ community – these, again, enacted under the rubric of the modern police power. The story of the police power is a normatively complicated one, and so the effort here is not necessarily laudatory, but analytical. As with all such powers, it can be used and misused.

In a similar vein, scholars who did not get the memo about the avowed irrelevance of the police power have highlighted the ways in which the police power is attached to notions of government power as a means of *policing*, of exercising social control in a way that can be, if not totalitarian, then overbearing and threatening. Markus Dubber and Chris Tomlins, in particular, have written thoughtfully in this century about the connections between the police power and highly contestable conceptions of legal autonomy and limitless public power.[14] Social thinkers such as Michel Foucault lurk closely in the background of these interesting perspectives, perspectives that can be viewed also as warnings about the ominous origins and careless use of the police as a mechanism of control rather than opportunity. While this account risks looking through a glass, darkly, at the police power, it is nonetheless important in reminding us that the awesome character of the police power should encourage close examination and thoughtful interrogation.

In this exegesis on the police power, and particularly the interrogation of the history, the author has benefited enormously from the seminal work of two leading American legal historians. William J. Novak has authored the single most important book on the history and function of the police power, *The People's Welfare: Law and Regulation in Nineteenth-Century America*.[15] He has written widely and powerfully on this subject in other writings and in a recent book, a magnum opus by any measure, he draws upon the police power and other key legal doctrines and ideas from the Progressive era especially to support a broad and bold thesis about the emergence and sustenance of truly progressive vision of democracy and governance in America.[16] In these various works, Novak describes how the police power was forged from evolving views among courts and commentators in the nineteenth and early twentieth centuries concerning questions of what constitutes a well-ordered society and how the government can regulate in order to promote these objectives.[17] The point made frequently in *The People's Welfare* is that the police power emerged from a *sic utere* (harm-reducing) conception of the role of government in enacting prescriptive legislation to become steadily transformed into a strategy for promoting the *salus populi* (public welfare). Further, he makes the connection between broad regulatory power, initially at the state level and later including the federal government, in implementing an "overruling necessity" and the rule of law.[18] He thus reveals through this dense historical analysis an idea of the police power that is distinct from, and in many ways contradictory to, the Schmittian idea of a rights-suspending, emergency constitution, and also inconsistent with the message that the police power is a limitless mechanism for establishing control.

The analysis here is likewise indebted to the great legal historian, Harry Scheiber, who has impacted the thinking of all who are interested in the development of American public law and regulatory governance during the nineteenth and twentieth centuries. His insights on property rights, governance, and the police power are influential generally and on the themes of this book in particular. Focusing mainly on the period leading up to and including the Progressive era, Scheiber illuminates the key patterns of legal doctrine involving regulation and property rights and how scrupulous attention by lawyers and courts to the general welfare is a basis not only for specific judicial doctrines but for a wider interrogation of the formalist underpinnings of property and contract.[19] Scheiber, following some of the pathbreaking work of J. Willard Hurst[20] and others working in this broad tradition of American legal history, describes how private property was long situated in a well-established and widely recognized conception of public rights and the public interest. He illustrates how long before the decision in the leading case of Munn v. Illinois (decided just after Reconstruction) myriad legal doctrines already recognized the power of the government to limit individual and social harm and, more meaningfully, implement important welfare goals, including the imperatives of infrastructure and public works. Therefore, there are deep connections among hoary legal doctrines including the public purpose requirement in state constitutional law, the public use requirement in eminent domain, public trust doctrine, public rights, and, finally, the police power.

For both Novak and Scheiber, the creation and persistence of the police power is fundamentally transformative; transformative in that it underwrites an exceptionally broad use of public power to implement ambitious goals of governance. Although their emphases and objectives as legal historians are distinct in many ways from the focus in this book, their shared view that the police power is tied ineluctably to the emergence of progressive regulatory governance in the United States influences meaningfully much of what follows here.

An overview of the argument herein: In the classical rendering of the police power, measured by how judges and early American legal scholars viewed the concept, what kept the power from becoming a hopelessly open-ended and unconditional grant of power to the state (or local) government to act for whatever reason and for whatever purposes was the notion that the safeguarding of the general welfare was essentially congruent with the protection of individuals from the misuse of one's property or some other actions that were violative of the social fabric. The formal division between public and private law captured, if sometimes clumsily, the idea that the government can protect against encroachments on private interests through the creation and enforcement of liability law, such as through actions in trespass or in nuisance. *Sic utere tuo ut alienum non laedes*, translated basically as "use your own property in such a way that you do not injure that of another." Where, for whatever reason, private law was inaccessible or adequate to secure these protections, the government could and should step in and enact positive law that would address private harms and ensure adequate compensation. And so far as impositions on the interests of a wider group of citizens, it was a fairly straightforward step to redressing harms through the law of public nuisance (the private law strategy) or through positive law that regulated certain conduct – again, under the *sic utere* principle.

In short, much of the police power, in its conception and in its operation, could be captured in this early period by ideas familiar to classic legal theory as explicated in the great engineers of the common law, Blackstone and others. A key step in the direction of widening governmental power while protecting the basic architecture of private property rights as they were defined in classic common law, including in its natural law underpinnings, was the development of the idea of the *jus publicum*, the notion that certain rights were given to the public and that the *in rem* rights so embedded in the very idea of ownership and the bundle of sticks in traditional private rights were qualified by the obligations of property owners and others to respect the *jus publicum*.

The police power, as we will delve into in more detail in the early chapters of this book, evolved considerably from this classic *sic utere* notion. In key interpretations by state courts,[21] the police power moved away from the formalistic, private law grounded idea of *sic utere*, with the government acting as more or less the trustee of individuals whose rights were being trampled, including individuals who made up the general public and so could trust that the government would proscribe public nuisances. It developed into an idea reflected in creative doctrine over a century's period that was much more (again, crediting Novak for the best explication of this development) in the spirit of *salus populi*.[22] We could and should expect our government to look after the public welfare, with mechanisms and for reasons quite separate from the more narrow obligation to redress discrete wrongs and to bring, for instance, an owner and her neighbor into balance through injunctive and compensatory relief. It evolved as well into a means of realizing goals and objectives that can be traced to the origins and foundations of state constitutions in the United States, in the founding period and afterward. In expanding the charge to state and local governments to protect health, safety, and the general welfare, the police power was a legal construct that would create the conditions (and, even more ambitiously, the obligations) of public officials for good governing. Our state constitutions are instruments of governance that reflect our high expectations of our governments and the officials who act on the appropriate authority (likewise the US Constitution, although this is not the focal point of our topic here). The police power, as it evolved, albeit unsteadily, over the expanse of our republic's history, was a key tool in the pursuit of these objectives.

A good part of the analysis of the police power, including especially the historical exegesis in the first four chapters, builds on the rich tradition of police power scholarship that was long ago in vogue, gradually faded, but has become more prominent as scholars have urged a reconsideration of our progressive legal traditions.[23] Though seldom pointing to the police power, they argue cogently for a more robust approach to constitutional interpretation, but also change and even fundamental reform to our institutions, and maybe the documents themselves.[24] The focus on themes of democratic constitutionalism reflects a movement, perhaps competing for influence with public meaning originalism as an approach to constitutional understanding in a divided polity. While it would a stretch to describe the effort in *Good Governing* as a work of democratic constitutionalism, it has as a more modest mission the bringing into the picture of constitutional theory and praxis the pertinent, if often peculiar, features of this neglected instrument of ambitious governance, the state police power.

Viewed from 10,000 feet, the story of the police power – not just the historical story, but our normative picture as well – is a steady, if not entirely linear, march from common law and constitutional formalism that kept the government's role in a discernible lane to a purposive expansion of the government's power to regulate individual behavior, private property, and businesses affected with a public interest. To be sure, this expansion accompanied an extraordinary growth in federal authority, a story in and of itself important, and frequently told. But this is not to take away from the persistent use by state and local governments, in various forms and fashions, of regulation through the police power on behalf of the *salus populi*.

To get to a complete understanding of the police power, we need to explore its nature as a concept defined by the widening of authority to govern, limited by constitutional rights at the federal and state level and also by its internal structure. But we also need to explore some of the very specific uses of this regulatory power, and so we look at such matters as zoning, morals regulation in various forms, occupational licensing, gun control, environmental protection, and other policy settings in which the police power matters. As to the matter of legal control, we look not only at the rules of the road that are conventionally seen as constitutional in origin and structure, but also the important set of legal constraints that emerge from administrative law, a source of law whose relevance can be matched only by its seeming neglect when the subject of constitutional powers and rights are under the spotlight.

It is in the struggle of defining an ample, ambitious power to govern and also setting guardrails around that power that we see the police power's dialectic. And in this study we can see anew the challenges embedded in configuring schemes and systems of regulation, of governing, that is progressive in its pursuit of the common good and the needs and wants of a complex society with many problems, but also respects individual liberty and private property.

This struggle has a very practical valence in the present day. The last several years has brought a renewed attention – for some, this comes with grave concern, for others optimism – to the responsibility of administrators and courts to protect private property and liberty rights against a threatening government. Many doctrinal examples abound. In the relatively few years between the Supreme Court's Kelo decision,[25] in which a narrowly divided court gave a broad interpretation of "public use" in takings cases, and the Cedar Park Nursery decision from two years ago,[26] the federal courts have been more receptive to property rights arguments that would not be unfamiliar to courts in the pre-New Deal area. Scholars have called some contemporary First Amendment decision-making an exercise in "First Amendment Lochnerism."[27] And as we saw in the spate of cases involving government restrictions during the Covid pandemic, there is a considerable amount of skepticism, often rather close to the surface, about the government's authority under the police power to restrict individual liberty by various mitigation measures. While no claim is being made here that we are on the verge of returning to Lochner, it is worth noting that the jurisprudential world is, when viewed on the whole, turning in a direction that demands a more measured response than saying with force and feeling that the New Deal and Great Society solved once and for all the question of how far the government can go to protect health, safety, and the general welfare. In these times, it is especially important to look at the conceptual and doctrinal components of the police power as a struggle among various forces, often opposing, rather than as an illustration of the fundamentally and impenetrably progressive nature of our modern system of constitutional government.

This book is in three Parts. Part I begins by situating the police power in the broad project of state constitutionalism. Three chapters follow, each looking at the police power in distinct historical periods, the first from the republic's beginning through the end of Reconstruction, the second from Reconstruction through the end of World War II, and the third up to the present time. In Part II, we look at important structural issues involving the police power. Chapter 5 looks specifically at the institutional architecture of the police power's use, including the separation of powers, local governance, and the emergence of administrative agencies as agents of the government's myriad authorities, including the police power. Chapters 6 and 7 look at the role of rights in police power controversies and at the internal structural limits that emerge from notions of reasonableness in constraining the police power. A final chapter in this Part explores the police power and American federalism. The final Part is more avowedly normative, looking at the potential of the police power as an engine for problem-solving, focusing on specific problems which are susceptible to innovative government regulation. The last chapter follows on this subject-matter analysis to look at specific, and in some cases quite novel, regulatory techniques, each more or less capable of addressing our wicked problems.

NOTES

1. 25 U.S. 419 (1827).
2. Ernst Freund, *The Police Power: Public Policy and Constitutional Rights* (1904); Christopher Tiedeman, *A Treatise on the Limitations of the Police Power in the United States* (1886); Thomas J. Cooley, *A Treatise on the Constitutional Limitations Which Rest on the Legislative Power of the States of the American Union* (1871).
3. See generally Barry Cushman, *Rethinking the New Deal Court: The Structure of a Constitutional Revolution* (1998); Howard Gilman, *The Constitution Besieged: The Rise and Demise of Lochner Era Police Power Jurisprudence* (1993).
4. Harry Scheiber, "The Police Power," in 4 *Ency. of American Constitution* 1744 (Leonard Levy et al. eds., 1986).
5. As hard as it is to provide a citation for a negative proposition, this neglect of attention to state constitutional has been noticed. See, e.g., Jeffrey S. Sutton, 51 *Imperfect Solutions: States and the Making of American Constitutional Law* 191–202 (2020) (describing the lack of attention in the legal academy on state constitutional law and proposing ideas that remedy this imbalance). The call for a renaissance of interest in state constitutional law has been associated with two lions of the bench, William Brennan and Hans Linde, both of which wrote about the importance of state constitutional law in American constitutionalism. See, e.g., Hans A. Linde, "E Pluribus – Constitutional Theory and State Courts," 18 *Ga. L. Rev.* 165 (1984); William J. Brennan, Jr., "State Constitutions and the Protection of Individual Rights," 90 *Harv. L. Rev.* 489 (1977). Despite the continuing neglect when viewed holistically, there are many scholars working productively on state constitutional law issues, more than at any time in the recent past, and throughout this book there is discussion of, and citation to, this important, and often new, work.
6. The exercise is isolating issues of constitutions rights from powers remains elusive, at least judging from both the constitutional law canon and also from scholarly commentary. A good essay that sheds valuable light on these issues from a comparative constitutional perspective is Stephen A. Gardbaum, "The Comparative Structure and Scope of Constitutional Rights," in *Research Handbook in Comparative Constitutional Law* (Rosalind Dixon et al. eds., 2011).
7. See James A. Gardner, "The Failed Discourse of State Constitutionalism," 90 *Mich. L. Rev.* 761 (1982).
8. Robert C. Post, "The Challenge of State Constitutions," in *Constitutional Reform in California: Making State Government More Effective and Responsive* 45, 46 (Bruce E. Cain & Roger G. Noll eds., 1995).
9. Se Daniel B. Rodriguez, "State Constitutional Theory and Its Prospects," 28 *N. M. L. Rev.* 271 (1998).
10. In a valuable essay on state constitutionalism, James Rossi describes well the positive political theory approach to studying state constitutionalism, an approach that is reflected in this study. See James Rossi, "Assessing the State of the State Constitutionalism," 109 *Mich. L. Rev.* 1145, 1158–60 (2011). On positive political theory more generally, see William H. Riker & Peter C. Ordeshook, *An Introduction to Positive Political Theory* (1973); John Ferejohn, "Law, Legislation and Positive Political Theory," in *Modern Political Economy* (Jeffrey S. Banks & Eric A. Hanushek eds., 1995).
11. See Donald Lutz, "The Purposes of American State Constitutions," 12 *Publius: J. Federalism* 27, 31 (1982). On this metaphor of constitutions as technology, Adrian Vermeule has an appealing description: "A successful constitution must not only be the

sum of its various functions, but should be understood as a complex piece of machinery in which the parts should work effectively in tandem." Adrian Vermeule, *Mechanisms of Democracy: Institutional Design Writ Small* (2007).
12. Daniel B. Rodriguez, "The Inscrutable (Yet Irrepressible) State Police Power," 9 N.Y.U. J. L. & Lib. 662 (2015).
13. 167 U.S. 537 (1896).
14. See Markus Dirk Dubber, *The Police Power: Patriarchy and the Foundations of American Government* (2005); Christopher Tomlins, "The Supreme Sovereignty of the State: A Genealogy of Police in American Constitutional Law, from the Founding Era to Lochner," in *Police and the Liberal State* (M. Dubber & M. Valverde eds., 2008); C. Tomlins, "To Improve the State and Conditions of Man: The Power to Police and the History of American Governance," 53 *Buff. L. Rev.* 1215 (2005).
15. Published by University of North Carolina Press in 1996.
16. William J. Novak, *New Democracy: The Creation of the Modern American State* (2022).
17. See, e.g., William J. Novak, "The American Law of Overruling Necessity: The Exceptional Origins of State Police Power," in *States of Exception in American History* 95 (G. Gerstle & J. Isaac eds., 2020); William J. Novak, "Police Power and the Hidden Transformation of the American State," in *Police and the Liberal State*, at 54.
18. See Novak, "Overriding Necessity".
19. Most of the citations to Prof. Scheiber's large body of work are in the later chapters.
20. See, e.g., J. Willard Hurst, *Law and the Conditions of Freedom in Nineteenth-Century America* (1956).
21. One judicial decision looms especially large, Commonwealth v. Alger, 7 Cush. 53 (Mass. 1851). This case, much analyzed by everyone who writes about the police power, will be discussed in depth in Chapter 2.
22. The full phrase, attributed to Cicero: "Salus populi suprema lex euro." Meaning that the welfare of the people is the supreme law.
23. See, e.g., Robert C. Post & Reva B. Siegel, "Democratic Constitutionalism," in *The Constitution in 2020* 25 (J. Balkin & R. Siegel eds., 2009). For an interesting and ambitious recent book squarely in this tradition, see Joseph Fishkin & William E. Forbath, *The Anti-Oligarchic Constitution: Reconstructing the Economic Foundations of American Democracy* (2022).
24. See, e.g., Sanford Levinson, *Framed: America's 51 Constitutions and the Crisis of Governance* (2012).
25. In Kelo v. City of New London, 545 U.S. 469 (2005), a narrowly-divided Court upheld the use of eminent domain to transfer a piece of land to a private company as an acceptable "public use" under the takings clause. See generally Ilya Somin, *The Grasping Hand: Kelo v. City of New London and the Limits of Eminent Domain* (2016).
26. 594 U.S. __ (2021). In that decision, the Court held that a law that entitled union organizers to come onto a landowner's property to engage in certain union-related activities was a physical invasion and therefore a taking under the eminent domain clause of the Constitution.
27. See Jeremy K. Kessler, "The Early Years of First Amendment Lochnerism," 116 *Colum. L. Rev.* 1915 (2016).

PART I

Power for the People: Creating the Modern Police Power

1

State Constitutions and the Governance Project

> The polis was a way of life, and the politeia, or constitution, was the plan for a way of life. The constitution describes what that life should be like, and the institutions by means of which will be achieved that way of life.
>
> Donald S. Lutz, *The Origins of American Constitutionalism*, 13

From the beginning of our republic through the present day, the constitutions of the American states have defined the structure and strategies of governance in the relevant polities. To understand the foundational power of state regulation, the police power, we need to understand how this power emerges from the ideas and designs of the state constitutions. Allowing for the particulars of individual state constitutions, we can resort to some general lessons and principles that will help define the scope of the project of state constitutionalism in the United States and, with it, the connection between that continuing project and the police power in the American states.

So far as the creation and sustenance of these documents are concerned, state constitutions span a wide spectrum in time, from the period before the establishment of our constitutional republic in the 1780s, as the first state constitutions were adopted, continuing throughout the gradual admission of additional states to the union and through the profound constitutional changes throughout the nineteenth and twentieth centuries.[1] Constitutions were hardly static: State constitutions would be frequently amended, sometimes soon after their original adoption,[2] and this reform project continues to the present day.[3] Despite the vast temporal expanse of this project of state constitution-making, we can still draw some useful lessons from the processes of constitution creation and reform beginning in the revolutionary era and continuing in the decades afterward.[4]

The states' powers to govern were shaped around choices made by the framers of the first and later state constitutions. As to the specific content of these powers, the Tenth Amendment of the US Constitution reserves powers not granted to the national government to the states respectively, or to the people.[5] Yet this amendment says nothing meaningful about what these state powers were to consist of.

Therefore, the basic idea and contours of the powers reserved for the states respectively, or to the people, including the police power, became the sole province of the state constitutions. Those constitutions would come to define the nature and scope of that power, as we will explore in more depth and detail in later chapters. What we want to consider here, drawing upon the history and logic of state constitutional development, is how choices in state constitutions reflect ultimate choices about how best to govern their communities. The core question of state constitutionalism is how to use fundamental law as architecture and as materials to implement the common good and, simultaneously, how best to safeguard individual and group interests and values in the preservation of liberty and private property. In short, state constitutionalism and the state police power are concerned with common matters.

REVOLUTIONARY STATE CONSTITUTIONALISM AND ITS CONSEQUENCES

As the esteemed historian Gordon Wood has taught us, revolutionary-era constitutions delivered what was an essentially new approach to governance in the new republic, an approach that would resonate not only in the creation of the US Constitution, but also in the early evolution of our scheme of American constitutionalism more generally.[6] The period of revolutionary constitutionalism marked a great advance in Americans' conception of the purpose and function of their new government.[7] Naturally, the most urgent task at hand was the colonists' severing of the connection with Great Britain. The efforts to disconnect through structural-formal mechanisms began before the Declaration of Independence and the Revolutionary War. "Prior to independence," writes Alan Tarr, "some colonies viewed the framing of constitutions as a mechanism for promoting a dissolution of ties with Great Britain."[8] This divorce was reflected in the hothouse of constitution-making that took place between the signing of the Declaration of Independence and the Constitutional Convention. Influential leaders worked tirelessly during this period to formulate constitutional structures and techniques.[9]

To be sure, many of these first documents were short and underdeveloped. As James Madison describes them in Federalist No. 47, state constitutions "carry strong marks of the haste, and still stronger of the inexperience, under which they were framed."[10] Whether this haste contributed to a skepticism about the status of the documents as fundamental law is difficult to assess. "In the states," Tarr writes, "reverence for the founders of state constitutions and their handiwork was notably lacking, as the orgy of nineteenth-century constitution-making attests."[11] And yet, when examining these earliest efforts at constitutional creation closely, we can see within them the emergence of a post-independence ideological framework aimed at balancing liberty and governance. As Donald Lutz writes: "Complete foundation documents in their own right, the state constitutions each produced a political system that could deal with the collective problems of their respective peoples .... The early state constitutions thus stand as the fulcrum in American constitutional history."[12]

What "problems" were these early framers trying to solve? Two stand out: First, what structures could they create that would enable good governing, that is, governance that would promote the general welfare of these new American citizens?[13] Second, how could they best ensure that the instruments of good governing would behave in the *public's* interest and, moreover, would not interfere unnecessarily with individual liberty and with private property rights? These goals were prominent not only because liberty and property were worthy objectives in their own right, but because their colonial experience – as well as other matters connected to the forging of new institutions and assumptions about individual and collective behavior (as Madison and other framers wrote about) – had inspired a real fear of potential tyranny and expropriation.[14]

Looking back at this critical period in the formation of constitutions and governmental power, it is important to note that the framers could not have known what was to follow in the few years after these first revolutionary-era constitutions were created. While they were not drafting these constitutions on a blank slate, they could not have expected the deterioration of the confederation and the weakness of the structures and institutions that the framers of the initial Articles of Confederation had constructed.[15] It is commonplace to observe that the framers of the US Constitution, deliberating in the heat of the Philadelphia summer, had learned powerful lessons from watching both the conduct of the states and the processes of constitution-making through which those states' conduct had been enabled.[16] However, it is rarer for historians to probe deeply into questions of how the framers of the state constitutions could have thought about the nature and scope of state legislative and executive powers, not knowing what governance powers the national government would come to have under the US Constitution and, moreover, what the processes and ideas that brought forth the historic and transformative document of 1787 would mean for the exercise of state power on the ground.

Still, there are important lessons we can draw from the dynamic of state and federal constitution-drafting. First, the drafters of the state constitutions expected that the state legislature would have the principal authority, and indeed the main burden, of governing in the interest of their respective state's citizens.[17] They knew also that the primary protector of liberty and property would be the states.[18] However, it is clear from what they said and what they did that they saw the state legislature as the supreme source of legal authority under the state constitution to help implement a well-ordered society and, also, as the prime mechanism for ensuring that the rights of their free people would be protected against encroachment.

The framers of these early constitutions dwelled on – perhaps even obsessed over – the perils of overbearing executive control and the danger it posed to individual liberty, and indeed much of their rhetoric that we have recovered over more than two centuries focuses on these issues.[19] "The evisceration of executive power," historian Jack Rakove writes, "was the most conspicuous aspect of the early state constitutions."[20] However, they were also faced with what was fundamentally a set of practical issues and were tasked with devising a way to carry out the functions of government to improve the lives and conditions of their state citizens. Improving social and economic conditions was imperative in these revolutionary and post-revolutionary states. The conditions for these improvements could be realized through "the beneficent hand of the state as reaching out to touch every part of the economy."[21]

From this idea of active governance in the pursuit of the common welfare, American historians in the republican tradition have concluded that the revolutionary-era constitutions reflected a distinct theory of government, one that departed from the liberal theory that is so often associated with the forging of the US Constitution.[22] State government power, Gary Gestle has recently written, "derived from a different political principle – one that held the public good in higher esteem than private right."[23] Gordon Wood writes in a similar vein: "The sacrifice of individual interests to the greater good of the whole formed the essence of republicanism and comprehended for Americans the idealistic goal of their Revolution."[24] Pennsylvania, it has been noted, made this objective explicit in its Declaration of Rights, declaring that "government is, or ought to be, instituted for the common benefit, protection, and security of the people, nation or community; and not for the particular emolument or advantage of any single man, family or set of men, who are a part only of that community."[25] In order to implement this greater good, the "state governments possessed a staggering freedom of action" and these powers "could be deployed progressively."[26] The essential idea, expressed in these myriad ways by scholars and contemporary observers, was that the state constitutions reflected an active, public-spirited conception of governing, one that echoed Whiggish political theory as translated into the distinctly American context by the ambitious framers of our first state constitutions and drawing upon the emerging theories of governing.[27]

The challenge for state constitution-makers was to create these broad powers while ensuring that the government would not devolve into a monarchy. Different states tackled these challenges in different ways, with Pennsylvania, for example, going to the extreme of not including the position of governor, New Hampshire not providing a chief executive of any kind, and the inclusion in all early constitutions of some system of separation of powers.[28] Framers were understandably worried about the concentration of power in the executive branch and undertook structural strategies to ameliorate these problems.

In addition to their ambient fear that broad constitutional power would create a roadmap toward a return to monarchical rule, the framers of the first constitutions worried also about the interests of their community members in preserving their prerogatives as free men, including the ability to accumulate and use private property and to enjoy the fruits of liberty, something obviously connected to their quest for independence from Great Britain.[29] Constitutional historiography of this period emphasizes the wide sphere of government regulation and activist governance, but this was only part of the context of this constitution-making. The rendering of broad state governance power does not mean that the framers were ambivalent or agnostic about protecting private property and individual liberty. The opposite was the case. "The safety of private property from arbitrary governmental requisition," Kruman writes, "was part of the whig culture colonial Englishmen shared with most inhabitants of the realm."[30] Likewise, individual liberty was treasured by colonial citizens, albeit a conception of liberty that was tied to the understandings of the times. The framers cared about property and liberty and, indeed, viewed the state constitutions – along with the US Constitution – as structural bulwarks against evisceration of these valuable rights. The public good and the preservation of private property and ordered liberty were not irreconcilable, at least as viewed by the eighteenth-century constitutional framers. What *was* required were mechanisms to assure the protection of liberty and property, while also investing in state governments the means of governing effectively.[31] Revolutionary-era constitutional framers were therefore aligned around the need to create constitutions as effective governance mechanisms, as means of protecting against the aggrandizement of power by a would-be king and the consolidation of power by factions in and out of government, and also as mechanisms to ensure that the government could function effectively and do the various "things of the utmost importance to the happiness of their respective citizens."[32]

We can draw three conclusions from this fertile period of state constitution-making during the revolutionary era. The first conclusion is that state constitutions "became instruments of government rather than merely frameworks for government."[33] This was reflected in how state constitutions evolved from parchments, sometimes eloquently forged by their creators, to discernible and meaningful governance instruments. Second, and relatedly, they were deeply concerned with issues of power, its nature, and its contours. They could not credibly expect that the national government would have adequate power under the Articles of Confederation to protect health, safety, and the general welfare. And so they looked inward, to their own constitutional structures and legal tools, to ensure that government would have adequate power to govern. Third, they were not content to borrow from their previous British masters the idea of a royal prerogative, however familiar this was to them, and so they worked hard to formulate an idea of governance that would be robust but not unlimited. In their drafting and the accompanying explanations of their project, they pursued twin goals: enabling the government, and especially the stage legislature, to govern effectively; and protecting individual liberty and private property. They faced the dilemma of how to construct mechanisms of power and how to restrain power once assigned, a dilemma, of course, that had become a persistent topic of consideration for political theorists over the centuries and in the lead-up to the creation of the American republic.[34]

In reflecting on the legacy of the state constitution-makers in the revolutionary era, our leading historian of this period writes: "Not only did the formation of the new state constitutions in 1776 establish the basic structures of our political institution, their creation also brought forth the primary conceptions of America's political and constitutional culture that have persisted to the present."[35] Neither the process nor the ultimate designs of these revolutionary-era constitutions were mechanical or even particularly tentative. They expressed the founders' instincts and preferences for governance strategies in this early, ambitious period. A full understanding of American constitutionalism cannot be accomplished without a close look at state constitution-building in the beginning years of the republic.

SUBORDINATION, CONSENT, AND POPULAR SOVEREIGNTY

The quest to escape from the bootheel of the monarch and to create mechanisms to protect against a reprise in control was paramount to the framers' goals in creating these new constitutions. "Madison's definition of tyranny was the one standard at the time, the arbitrary use of power, that is, contrary to the community's permanent, aggregate interest."[36] Thomas Paine made this point explicit as he "condemned as an arbitrary human invention the division of mankind into kinds and subjects."[37] Bloodied and battered by British domination, the framers thought of strategies to implement new forms of government that would be resistant, if not impervious, to capture by power-hungry individuals acting under asserted authority. As a consequence, "[t]he state constitutions of the 1770s and early 1780s also brimmed with provisions aimed at dismantling the aristocratic elements of the colonial social order."[38]

From this experience, the framers looked to structural mechanisms that would protect against the risk of subordination. These efforts presaged Madison's famous statement in Federalist No. 51: "If men were angels, no government would be necessary. If angels were to govern men, neither external nor internal controls on government would be necessary.... A dependence on the people is, no doubt, the primary control on the government; but experience has taught mankind the necessity of auxiliary precautions."[39] To be sure, Madison's principal auxiliary precaution, the establishment of a national veto on all disfavored state legislation, failed to garner adequate support.[40] However, Madison and his allies' (including Alexander Hamilton) forceful expressions of concern about state legislative power did succeed in fueling the effort in the Constitutional Convention to create suitable mechanisms for federal power.[41] This was the point, after all, in replacing the Articles of Confederation with a new constitution, one that would have sufficient means to empower a national government to undertake useful tasks on behalf of this nascent nation and manage a group of previously sovereign states.[42] Despite this profoundly important and novel effort at creating a constitution that would ensure a successful United States, there remained risks to private property and individual liberty. After all, the incentives to self-deal and the opportunities for factions to prosper did not disappear with the creation of the US Constitution, so long as individuals lived and worked in their respective states, and were subject to the authority of state governments. Indeed, the scale of state government made factions especially formidable and therefore threatening.

State constitutions remained essential in preserving and nurturing popular sovereignty. They created various structural mechanisms, supplemented as time passed by national structures and, later, by rights made enforceable by courts. These structures are rightly highlighted when the question is asked, "How did the framers ensure that power would be diffused and managed?" What undergirded these practical components was an idea – a novel idea that was essential to the forging of a new constitutionalism that would be compelling and sustainable. This was the idea of popular consent to government: the idea of popular sovereignty as the foundation of all constitutionally appropriate power.[43] Popular sovereignty was the foundational element in the emergence of a post-revolutionary constitutional ideology. At its core, the emerging constitutionalism of the post-revolutionary era was committed to popular sovereignty as the fulcrum of public authority. Here, the People rule. This was the boldest, most coherent manifestation of America's break from Great Britain's hegemony over the colonies and their prerogatives over the British scheme of constitutional governance. And so, for example, Delaware's Bill of Rights proclaimed: "All Government of Right originates from the people, is founded in Compact only, and instituted solely for the Good of the Whole."[44] Virginia: "All power is vested in, and consequently derived from, the people."[45]

The first state constitutions, and later the US Constitution, embodied the idea that the power lodged in government, at whatever level, was entirely conditional on popular consent. As Donald Lutz writes, "the state constitutions evolved and extended a step in consent theory begun in the colonial charters by blending societal consent with governmental consent. The ratification of a constitution not only established a form of government, but also affirmed the essential sociocultural base upon which the government rested."[46] This logic was radical in important respects. Colonialists had fought hard to secure independence from Great Britain on grounds that were focused on the abuses meted out to them and, relatedly, the burdens imposed without consent or meaningful participation in the activities of government ("taxation without representation").[47] However, it would not have been illogical for the framers to embrace existing sets of government institutions, and especially an elected legislature, but with added mechanisms designed to ensure that it would be more representative and more attuned to the will of the people. More novel was the idea that all power would derive directly from the power of the people, that the government was forged from the idea of popular sovereignty. No colonialist had direct experience with such a scheme, and thus they had to look beyond their experience – to the leading thinkers of government and constitutionalism – to assemble the logic and the strategy. It is in this principal respect that we can speak of the American revolutionaries as developing a new science of government.[48]

In describing popular sovereignty and citizen consent as fundamental ideas in eighteenth- and nineteenth-century American constitutionalism, we generally emphasize the function that these ideas serve in guarding against abuse of power and attacks on well-ordered liberty. However, there is another function that popular sovereignty performs, one that is important for any comprehensive analysis of constitutionalism and public power. **The framers saw popular sovereignty and consent** as improving the capacity and promise of government to advance the common good. Popular sovereignty is not only about checks on oppressive, arbitrary power, but also about good governing. "Majority will and the common good were inextricably linked" by our constitutions' framers.[49] The people's will in creating governmental institutions to act in their name was a means of advancing the people's welfare. Representative democracy was not just an abstraction that assured that citizens' consent would be respected, but a new structure of governance that would fuel law-making for the public good.[50] These constitutions would ensure "not only that everyone enjoy equality before the law or have an equal voice in government, but also that everyone have an equal share in the fruits of the common enterprise."[51]

The most obvious association between popular sovereignty and good governance is that the people in their manifest choices and in their delegation of responsibility to elected representatives to act in their name and on their behalf could decide ultimately whether and to what extent public officials were acting appropriately. In this sense, the structure of representative government, reflected through the prism of a strong separation of powers, enables citizens to monitor their representatives, thereby assuring that legislators are acting in the public interest and are working effectively to govern in their behalf.[52]

The commitment to popular sovereignty as the fundamental principle undergirding state constitutionalism continued long after the founding period. As a number of state constitutions were amended in the late nineteenth and early twentieth centuries to provide for mechanisms of direct democracy, the connection between popular sovereignty, public-spirited law-making, and accountability was made ever more manifest.[53] Moreover, the relative ease of amendment, and even total reconstruction, was indicative of the enduring commitment to popular sovereignty as a critical component of state constitutionalism, from its origins to the present day.[54]

DEMOCRACY AND REPRESENTATION

With popular sovereignty as the main source legitimizing public authority under the state constitutions, the framers of these documents looked to develop institutions that would implement their vision of good governing and the securing of individual liberty and private property, goals that they understood as compatible, not contradictory.[55] The new constitution had to, as Jennifer Nedelsky writes, "solve the pressing problem of legislative injustice."[56] And later state constitutional reformers looked to sustain these mechanisms through various safeguards and incentive-compatible arrangements. The goal of protecting against subordination and ensuring fidelity to popular sovereignty and the people's will was most clearly manifest in the commitment to an elected legislature – and to the principle that such a legislature would be supreme in the exercise of public power. As Wood writes:

> It was neither the widespread suffrage nor the institution of the electoral process throughout the governments but the appropriation of so much power to the

people's representatives in the legislatures that made the new governments in 1776 seem to be so much like democracies .... The real importance of the legislatures came from their being the constitutional repository of the democratic element of the society or, in other words, the people themselves.[57]

The principle of legislative supremacy reflected the framers' commitment to democracy as a guiding light around which governmental power was structured. To be sure, the framers were concerned throughout the revolutionary period and for many years afterward with cabining the excesses of democracy.[58] And so we see myriad statements of concern and even opprobrium about democracy as a means of governance.[59] Nonetheless, democracy had more than an ambient influence on how the colonists thought about their new experiment with governance and well-ordered liberty, and it likewise had an influence on some of the design mechanisms in the original constitutions. Efforts to keep the executive branch restrained in its influence over legislative choice found their origins in a commitment to democratic rather than aristocratic decision-making; so, too, did the commitment to rotation in office.

Ultimately, the framers looked to design a mixed government, with different spheres of power, a set of checks and balances, and, significantly, different kinds of electoral mechanisms in order to accomplish multiple ends and objectives in government design.[60] And yet the purpose of this mixed government was not to diminish democracy, but to temper its excesses and organize democratic processes in a way that maintained the best features and aims of a system of governance in the public interest.[61]

SKEPTICISM, STRUCTURE, AND CONSTITUTIONAL RESETS

The creation of new institutions (and adaptations of old ones) to carry out the objectives of good governance and restraints on the exercise of arbitrary power did not usher in a seamless and wholly successful scheme of constitutional governance in the post-revolutionary era. Our framers were imaginative and prodigious constitutional designers, but they were neither oracles nor magicians.

Difficult matters of democracy and representation would come to the center of the stage after the founding period and at various critical junctures in the century that followed. In the Jacksonian period, reformers sought to ameliorate the Whigs' carefully constructed architecture of legislative representation and expertise by introducing distinct checks on government power as well as structural schemes meant to limit the discretion and flexibility of legislators.[62] Emboldened democrats brought to the table a more powerful chief executive and also more conspicuous popular control of governmental institutions, including, significantly, the courts.[63] Such reforms reflected emerging skepticism with the idea expressed by the eighteenth-century Rhode Islander, quoted by Gordon Wood, that "[i]t is in their legislatures ... that the members of a commonwealth are united and combined together into one coherent, living body. This is the soul that gives form, life and unity to the commonwealth."[64]

During this period, the role and function of the state legislatures were under particular scrutiny. The framers' resolute faith in the legislatures as instruments of representative democracy faced challenges in the decades following the adoption of the US Constitution and the constitutions of the various states. "As the supposedly representative legislatures drifted away from the people," Wood writes, "men more and more spoke of the legislators' being just other kinds of rulers, liable to the same temptations and abuses rulers through history had shown – all of which made comprehensible the intensifying desire to make the representatives more dependent on the opinion of their constituents and the increasing invocations of 'the collective body of the people' to set against the legislatures."[65]

The concerns with the elected legislatures – in what they did and what they did not do – grew steadily from the time of their creation through to the first decades of the next century. "[W]e now see," wrote Ben Franklin, "that quite as much mischief, if not more, may be done, and as much arbitrary conduct acted, by a legislature."[66] Criticisms of the early state legislatures came from many quarters. Edmund Randolph thought the constitutions too democratic. He wrote that "[o]ur chief danger arises from the democratic parts of our state constitutions .... None of the constitutions have provided sufficient checks against the democracy."[67] Further, as Robert Williams noted in his depiction of early state constitutionalism, "Madison, Randolph, Wilson, and Morris, who were among the most influential delegates at the Constitutional Convention, saw the existing state constitutions, with Pennsylvania's as the most extreme example, as unable to provide checks against wide-ranging assaults on liberty and property by the relatively unfettered state legislatures."[68] "The people's will," writes Wood, "as expressed in their representative legislatures and so much trusted throughout the colonial period suddenly seemed capricious and arbitrary."[69]

Caretakers of these first revolutionary-era constitutions had basically three choices available to them to ensure that the state government would not abuse power and undermine the goal of popular sovereignty and citizen welfare. One was to directly impose a strict limit on the state legislative power, something that could be accomplished by restricting state powers to those explicitly granted and, following that limitation, granting precious few powers. This was, of course, the option taken with the federal government under the US Constitution. A second option was to develop a meaningful scheme of checks and balances to control legislative excess. A final option was to establish a bevy of individual rights designed to restrict official power by interposing suitable bulwarks against government overreach.[70]

In key ways, options one and three relied on a judiciary that could enforce such constraints – a reliance nearly impossible to contemplate at a time when no serious consideration had yet been given to judicial review as an awesome power through which the judiciary could invalidate duly enacted legislation.[71] Moreover, the very idea that legislative power would be limited by resort to external enforcement was hard to square with the principle of plenary legislative power and, perhaps even more, with the trust citizens had placed in their elected representatives to govern well on behalf of the public interest.[72]

For the time, the most sensible strategy was the middle one, to construct and design governmental institutions that would limit power and, especially, to establish a formal separation of powers. Distributing powers, as Publius would insist at the time that the US Constitution was being debated,[73] would have the effect of erecting barriers that would impede any accumulation of power that might threaten liberty. The separation of powers was truly the sort of "auxiliary precautions" that the framers designed to cabin and channel governmental power away from abuse toward salutary aims. Later, there would be debate about whether and to what extent maintaining this separation of powers would require judicial intervention.[74] But the question of how involved the judiciary would be in the quest for an effective scheme of checks and balances would remain opaque in this era. It was enough to describe the separation of powers as an important mechanism for accomplishing the state constitutions' aims of protecting against subordination, realizing popular sovereignty, and energizing government to govern on behalf of the general will and welfare.

The separation of powers was one of the brilliant and essential contributions of the framers to this new constitutional design.[75] This separation was one element in the larger matter of distribution of powers and the creation of a mixed government system. This was intended to improve the performance of government. There would be, as well, a relationship between this separation of powers and a broad authority given to the government to act. This wide compass, necessary to carry out the core purposes and functions of governance, required guardrails; and, especially before the development of individual rights as judicially enforceable checks on official action, these guardrails were furnished by the separation of powers.

Despite the faith the framers and other theorists put into these structural mechanisms of controlling and channeling power, concern about legislative power and its scope remained. It is important to remember that one of the core precepts of state constitutionalism was that state constitutions, unlike their federal brethren, were documents of limit.[76] This meant that limits would have to be forged from within the structure of governance or from rights and other rules exogenous to the plenary power that was embedded in the document.[77] Broad, indeed awesome, legislative power went hand in glove with this precept.

The most significant efforts to reset the objectives of democracy and connect these objectives to the schemes and structures of representation came during the Progressive era, a period in which reformers were successful in cabining legislative power and in creating rules and institutions to limit, and in some instances reconfigure, legislative power. These reform efforts, which began in the early nineteenth century and continued through the early twentieth, were born of a tension that persisted between the goals of democracy and the goals of representation, of the need to maintain the integrity of popular sovereignty through consent, not only metaphorical (as with the elected legislature) but actual.[78]

Notwithstanding these strong reform efforts and what might appear in the hot gaze of the Jacksonian period and its aftermath to be a withering of legislative power, law-making through elected state legislatures remained resilient – even in the face of serious concern about the performance of state legislatures. Political leaders spent a remarkable amount of time tweaking and repairing legislative structures, but none of this effectively disrupted the view of legislatures as the most promising institutions for safeguarding health and safety and for promoting the people's welfare – a view that we will see supported by the evolution of the police power in the nineteenth century, the subject of Chapter 2. To be sure, this project of legislature improvement and constitutional repair is an important part of the story, especially in our republic's first century. Political officials, acting in a way consistent with the idea of popular sovereignty, developed creative constitutional rules to facilitate good governing and public-regarding initiatives.[79] These include requirements that legislators act for a public purpose and that they not enact special legislation.[80] Later in the century, reformers added balanced budget requirements, the line item veto, and other structural mechanisms that had both the purpose and effect of checking legislative power. Related doctrines developed by courts, such as the public rights doctrine (which was mainly embedded in social constructivist accounts of private property and its protection)[81] and the public trust doctrine,[82] were fashioned to improve legislating. But more than that, it is important to see these doctrines and initiatives as a means of promoting democracy and maintaining the conditions for democratic decision-making. In sum, the state constitutions' framers aspired to create institutions to implement popular will and safeguard popular sovereignty: **It's not only about giving the *state* the power, it is about power to the people.**

LIBERTY AND PROPERTY RIGHTS

The concern with circumscribing threats to liberty and, especially, to private property loomed large in the minds and agendas of revolutionary-era constitutional framers, and it persisted to a large degree afterward. "'Wherever the real power in a Government lies,' [Madison] told Jefferson, 'there is the danger of oppression. In our Governments the real power lies in the majority of the Community, not from acts of Government contrary to the sense of its constituents, but from acts in which the Government is the mere instrument of the major number of the constituents.'"[83]

In modern historical literature in the republican tradition, much is made of the rejection of the standard view that our American constitutionalism – here speaking of both the US Constitution and the state constitutions – unequivocally embodied classical liberal theory.[84] In embracing this historical revisionism, we risk neglecting the myriad concerns the framers had with overweening state power and inadequate safeguards of property and liberty.[85] This is even more true of nineteenth-century historiography, where the emphasis is on the progressives' triumph over a static, mechanical view of individual rights through the embrace of active governance and a wide remit for the police power.[86] Nonetheless, when we look at the construction of state constitutions in the early republic, we see a consistent concern with protecting individual rights,[87] albeit accompanied by some deep uncertainty about the proper institutional mechanisms for undertaking this protection.[88] As new constitutions were introduced and existing constitutions substantially reformed, the concerns with assuring a suitable measure of protection for individual rights, including property and contract and also individual liberty, persisted. While no state constitution forged anything resembling a libertarian vision of sharply limited government and the preservation of sacrosanct individual dominion over real and personal property, state constitutions from the beginning were preoccupied with maintaining an adequate sphere of freedom. These concerns were both ideological and instrumental.[89] They would ensure that individuals be able to develop and utilize the instruments of commerce that would enable them and society to prosper.

With regard to internal constraints on governmental power, the framers were in a dilemma born of the fact that, as individuals whose lived experience was with British constitutionalism, they had a limited structural vocabulary available to them. They could imagine a scheme of rights, although not necessarily enforceable against validly enacted acts of the sovereign. They could imagine a system of separated and divided powers, as described by Montesquieu and other influential thinkers.[90] However, it was hard to envision limits on legislative power built into their constitutional system. Insofar as the state constitutions were always understood as documents of limit, not grant, where then would the limits come? The answer to this persistent question would remain somewhat elusive in the coming decades.

The early and later state constitutions did include various rights provisions.[91] Interestingly, the state police power was included in the declarations in the Pennsylvania constitution of 1776,[92] a choice that may seem structurally clumsy, given the intuitive distinction between a right and a power, but the framers may have done so to make crystal clear that the health, safety, and general welfare of its citizens was an elemental principle of state government and could be expressed as a right of individuals to good governance. After all, rights in this formative era of American constitutionalism commonly focused on the community, rather on the individual.[93]

However conspicuous or inconspicuous rights were in these early constitutions, there remained as an open question whether these rights would be enforceable against governments, either through the judiciary or some other mechanism.[94] For some of the rights delineated, the prospect of external enforcement through judicial review seemed problematic, if not impossible, to contemplate, and there are good reasons to expect that revolutionary-era state citizens and public officials who acted on their behalf saw it as such. Nonetheless, writes, Tarr, "the insusceptibility of various provisions to judicial enforcement was not a flaw, because the declarations were addressed not to the state judiciary primarily but to the people's representatives, who were to be guided by them in legislating, and even more to the liberty-loving and vigilant citizenry that was to oversee the exercise of governmental power."[95]

More robust and meaningful structural safeguards would await Americans' experience with the constitutions and the judiciary, the latter of which would prove vital in maintaining these safeguards by nurturing what inevitably grew from them, as well as maintaining the rights that would function as side constraints on the exercise of legislative and administrative power.

If the framers were so skeptical about including a full collection of rights in their state constitutions, what explains their steadfast effort to include a Bill of Rights in the US Constitution? The juxtaposition between the national and state constitutions in this realm reflects two different approaches to implementing the principle of popular sovereignty. For the national Constitution, the limits on the federal government's powers were sensible from the perspective of the framers (at least those framers whose views prevailed in these debates) because they knew that the residuum of the people's powers and thus their sovereignty would come from powers reserved to the states or to the people respectively. With respect to state constitutions, popular sovereignty would be ensured through careful attention to the structure of representative democracy, that is, to the design and functioning of the legislature; and it would also be protected through a diligent design of separation of powers and also of individual rights. In short, it was the design of the overall structure of the state constitutions that would work to protect popular sovereignty.[96] Moreover, the relative ease of amendment of state constitutions, whether through legislation or plebiscites or through the extraordinary mechanism of constitutional conventions, was a key means of ensuring that popular sovereignty would be safeguarded.

As we can consider the unsteady state of judicial intervention in protecting the people against legislative abuse and excess on the one hand and against legislative weakness on the other, we should focus on the modes of reasoning the courts used to interrogate legislative power. Despite the advent of written constitutions as fulcra of governmental power, federal and state courts were much more comfortable in using the common law as the lodestar source of their decisions. The force of common law reasoning in the first several decades of the nation's history was important in shaping our constitutional discourse, especially before we accumulated a large number of decided cases that could be described accurately as our emerging constitutional law.

The reliance on common law to scrutinize governmental power and interpret individual rights had at least two important effects in the developing constitutionalism of the republic's early years. First, common law reasoning viewed the judge as essentially discovering the law rather than interpreting text, much less making law in any discernible way.[97] Moreover, this discovery looked backward to principles and precedents in the common law as it had developed in merry old England. "Constitutional provisions were better understood as reminders than as enactments."[98] Looking to English law to discern the contents and limits of governmental power was a difficult, if not impossible, task, as, after all, there was no coherent notion of judicial review that would have supported an American court's finding that legislation violated the fundamental law and should thus be struck down. Yet,

State Constitutions and the Governance Project

even after judicial review was well established in state constitutionalism, as happened fairly early in the process and before <u>Marbury v. Madison</u>,[99] fidelity to a discovery model of judicial decision-making rendered problematic the courts' constitutional decisions in cases where precedent was lacking and in which questions of power and rights were prominent.

A second feature of the common law was also pertinent to early examinations of power and rights, and that is the reliance on considerations of natural rights and natural law.[100] This modality of reasoning was important in shaping how courts examined structural and (especially) rights issues.[101] Accordingly, it became part of the courts' police power jurisprudence, at least until the <u>Lochner</u> era passed into oblivion.

Judicial intervention in constitutional disputes has followed some discernible patterns across the history of state constitutionalism. In his two important books on state constitutional law, Judge Jeff Sutton has described in illuminating detail the ways in which state and federal courts have used (and should use) state constitutional arguments to resolve disputes about power and rights.[102] He reminds us that while judicial review emerged early in our state constitutional history, there was considerable skepticism about the practice, for "[e]arly Americans did not trust judges and preferred that their liberty and other rights rest in the hands of their peers or what was then perceived as the next-best option: legislatures."[103] And yet matters changed over time. Ultimately, Sutton writes, "[t]he country became increasingly comfortable with empowering judges to resolve constitutional cases and with perceiving them as trustworthy agents of the people."[104]

A wealth of scholarship has been devoted to the question of how judicial review and, more specifically, searching scrutiny of legislative action evolved and took hold in the American political culture and in the legal system.[105] Moreover, this is even before we get to the even more voluminous normative scholarship on whether this has been a mainly salutary development.[106] There is little on offer here in this book on this larger question. But one point that is pertinent to this chapter's analysis of state constitutionalism and what we call the good governing project is this: Judicial interventions by the state and federal courts into matters of governmental power and of rights have been shaped in important ways by the fact and the consequences of having written constitutions and, furthermore, having, at the state level, relatively prolix written constitutions. Not only do these long constitutions provide much to grapple with, both at the level of implementation institutions (including legislators, governors, agencies, municipalities, etc.) and at the level of judicial interpretation, but the structure and strategies of judicial intervention are the natural outgrowth of the fact that our government functions within the parameters of written constitutions. Despite the copious amount of modern commentary in the legal literature emphasizing the indeterminacy of text and the ideological sources of judicial decisions,[107] only the most hardcore cynic (or realist, if one prefers) can insist that there is no connection between the fact that we live in a system of written constitutions and the phenomenon of persistent judicial scrutiny of exercises of official power and inquiries into individual rights and their role as trumps.

GOVERNING STEADILY, AND STURDILY

Foundational principles of state constitutionalism (e.g., popular sovereignty, plenary legislative power) and pragmatically valuable structural mechanisms (e.g., separation of powers, direct democracy, limits on legislative power) are all part of the project of balancing the need for an active state government – active, that is, in its pursuit of the public good – with the need to preserve and safeguard interests essential to the well-being on individuals in the wider community, including the various sticks in the bundle of property rights and individual liberty, in both its positive and negative dimensions. When we measure the success of state constitutions by looking closely at constitutional performance and failure, we should consider how effective these operational principles and structures are in negotiating this balance between common good constitutionalism and individual freedom. This is in essence the measure of what we have called the project of good governing under a state constitutional framework.

A functioning state constitution will also be resolutely attendant to the perturbations of politics, coming from within the state, and also nationally. For a constitution to function well on behalf of the people subject to it, it must be stable. As political scientist Adam Brown writes in a recent book on the relationship between constitutional length and stability:

> Democratic constitutions must balance opposing ideals of democratic responsiveness and constitutional stability. As for stability, constitutions establish the boundaries and rules governing the governing process, providing a sure arena for the otherwise unsure game of politics. To provide this sure arena, constitutions must be so written as to ensure their own permanence.[108]

In recent work that emerges from the insights of modern rational choice political theory, Barry R. Weingast and various co-authors have emphasized key features of constitutional design and performance that are relevant to our discussion here. First, Weingast et al. point out the reasons for having constitutional constraints on political activity. Individuals will reasonably fear that their assets will be expropriated by others and worry, therefore, about subjecting their property and liberty to majoritarian political processes.[109] Enter constitutions. Constitutions create governance instruments that will respond to this rational fear and will guard against unrestricted majoritarianism.[110] Rights are perhaps the clearest and most essential type of such restraints; but so too are structural safeguards, including various checks and balances hardwired into constitutions.

Furthermore, it is important that these countermajoritarian instruments be self-enforcing, that is, not rely on politics or even principally on adjudication to assuage concerns of the populace. Constitutions create stability in governance, and, likewise, stability in public behavior.[111] It is important to avoid coups and disruptions that would happen if individuals, ever fearful, felt that they needed to act purposively to protect their interests.[112] Ideally, constitutions forge what Weingast et al. call a "self-enforcing equilibrium,"[113] that functions as a means of social insurance to secure the durability of the governing regime and provides for a fertile arena in which commercial transactions and other forms of community intercourse can function. Other institutions (e.g., a system for contracting; an orderly scheme of property rights) are important as well. But constitutions are a necessary condition for the operation of a state that remains efficacious and stable.[114] Without the constitution and its manifest countermajoritarian mechanisms, citizens will view politics as high stake affairs. They will fear, and not without basis, the government and also their fellow citizens. Even short of descending into a Hobbesian state of nature,[115] they will be limited in their willingness to create the conditions and structures for a successful economy; and they will find the establishment of a system of ordered liberty highly problematic. When we look at stakes in particular, the possibility of voice and even visit are not fanciful. States can be expected to compete with one another with institutional architecture. We can expect (and even hope) that this will lead to a race to the top; at the very least, the incentives are directed toward constructing meaningfully stable and efficacious constitutional arrangements.

Key constitutional powers, along with carefully configured rights, are part of the edifice of these constitutional arrangements that aspire to facilitate good governing. This is a normative ideal, but is also explicable on the positive political theory of governmental choice. This is an old idea, going back to ancient thinking about constitutionalism and carrying through the forging of American constitutionalism and our new science of government in the eighteenth century. It is also a *new* idea, as we think systematically about the capacity and potential of state constitutions in safeguarding liberty, facilitating democracy, and promoting the common good through sensible regulation and, in particular, the protection of health, safety, and morals.

To say, then, that the constitution aspires for government to act steadily and sturdily is just a homely way to represent the insight that good governing is a fundamental element of the project of state constitutionalism more generally. These are aspirations. Constitutional developments in the real world well frequently disappoint. To see these constitutions as too-malleable reflections of discrete policy choices or as unstable in that they are buffeted to and fro as the winds of political change blow is to distort the project of state constitutionalism in both a positive and a normative sense. State constitutions matter precisely because they are instruments of governance (albeit incomplete), not just museum pieces that contain an ultimately thin description of governmental ambition, a charge often levied at the US Constitution and many constitutions of other countries.

STATE CONSTITUTIONS AND THE PROJECT OF GOOD GOVERNANCE

In creating the state constitutions and also in reforming them in key respects over the republic's first two centuries, political leaders and ordinary citizens have forged three elements that are critical in understanding the nature and scope of the police power. First, they created in constitutional form an idea of governance that has persisted across political struggles, a Civil War, and a reset in the relationship among levels and institutions of government, and that is that the role and responsibility of state governments is to promote the general welfare. These new constitutions would, as Willi Paul Adams wrote, ensure that "everyone have an equal share in the fruits of the common enterprise."[116] Representative democracy would be in service of popular sovereignty and, further, in the aim of good governing, and, accordingly, the legislature was front and center, in power and in role.[117] This key idea found common ground in Whigs and Federalists, in Jeffersonians and Jacksonian Democrats. And, to telegraph a discussion in a later chapter in this Part, it proved incredibly resilient in the face of a sustained efforts on the part of conservative judges to undermine it through a particular approach to individual liberty and limited government. Second, state constitutions were perhaps most impactful on patterns of American constitutionalism and political choice, most generally in their experimentation with myriad mechanisms of governance structures, both with respect to enabling and limiting public power. By contrast to the US Constitution, where the basic template for government power was set in the terms of the original document (which is not to say that there has not been profound evolution in the actual performance of institutions in exercising this power over 235 years), state constitutions have given us imaginative, albeit occasionally chaotic, mechanisms of governance.[118] We will see as this book proceeds the ways in which these mechanisms have affected the structure and the functions of the police power. But we can say generally that these mechanisms of design have affected state and local governance in many fascinating ways. Third and finally, the actual functioning of governmental actors, wherever they are located, has been a consequence of how the state constitution has framed and shaped governmental power and conduct.[119] Government decision-making can undermine constitutional objectives, as we see when we take a close look at government performance in operation. However, it can also be true in a different context that bad governing derives from poor decisions made in the forging and framing of a state constitution. Garbage in, garbage out.

In any event, good governing as a goal is not a free-floating, politics-less concept. It is teleological, and the relevant governmental purposes that emerge from our constitutional objectives give us the best measure of success or failure. Discerning these objectives is a project of state government, acting in the name and interest of "we the people" of our respective states. And this is the project of national constitutionalism as well. The government here is not limited to courts, but includes all relevant branches and institutions working collaboratively, and through processes that we view as broadly democratic.[120] As these choices are being made, first in constitutional design and next in implementation, we can and should measure our policies, and the procedures that yield such policies, by reference to these summative objectives. We can then speak coherently of the quality of constitutions and constitutional arrangements; likewise, we can assess constitutional failure. The criteria are forged in the processes of state constitutional development. What it means to say that governing is good or bad is that such governing serves or deserves state constitutional objectives. The police power, as we will explore in more detail, has a general purpose and that is the promotion of good governing consistent with the objectives of state constitutionalism.

A good portion of the analysis of state constitutionalism in this chapter has focused on historical episodes and the political-historical context of choices made in the forging and reforming of state constitutions. Viewed from 10,000 feet, we should see these stories as part of a fundamental governance project. State constitutions grow out of ideas of how public officials should best govern on behalf of we the people; and, as well, ideas of how best to maintain our freedoms and liberties in the face of circumstances in which authority might be invoked, and maybe to our detriment. As an ideal, state constitutions are designed to facilitate good governing. The police power, in its evolution from the beginning to its present, is an instantiation of this basic idea, as we examine in the remainder of this book.

NOTES

1. See generally John Dinan, *State Constitutional Politics: Governing by Amendment in the American States* (2018).
2. For example, the New Jersey Constitution, adopted in 1776, was amended in 1777; the Oklahoma Constitution, adopted in 1907, was amended on the same day it was ratified.
3. The frequency of change – generally, and relative to the US Constitution – confounds serious efforts to warrant an "originalist" approach to state constitutions. We need not dwell on the matter of how exactly the history of state constitutions should specifically impact judicial interpretations or even whether anything like an original public meaning of the police power is possible. It is enough to say here that the very enterprise of originalist state constitution is rendered more problematic than a similar enterprise in interpreting the US Constitution because of the especially dynamic character of state constitutions. For an illuminating discussion of historical evidence in state constitutional law, see Maureen Brady, "Use of Convention History in State Constitutional Law," *Wisc. L. Rev.* 1169 (2022).
4. See Christian Fritz, "Fallacies of American Constitutionalism," 35 *Rutgers L. J.* 1327, 1327 (2004) ("Fundamental assumptions made about our early constitutional experience are inaccurate [in] denying us the capacity to see that the history of American constitutionalism is dynamic, not an elaboration of a static idea from 1787").
5. US Const., *Tenth Amendment*.
6. See generally Gordon S. Wood, *The Creation of the American Republic, 1776–1787* (1998). See also Gordon S. Wood, "Foreword: State Constitution-Making in the American Revolution" 24 *Rutgers L. J.* 911 (1992–93).

7. See generally Willi Paul Adams, *The First American Constitutions: Republican Ideology and the Making of the State Constitutions in the Revolutionary Era* (2001).
8. G. Alan Tarr, *Understanding State Constitutions* 60 (1998).
9. We speak here of state constitution-making as a general enterprise, keeping in mind that the decisions were being made in separate states. However, there were common concerns that animated the framers' efforts. "Some of the similarities," Alan Tarr writes, "found among state constitutions of the era can be traced to the states' common experience of British tyranny, which they understood in terms of a shared republican theory." Tarr, *Understanding State Constitutions*, at 66. This common experience was reflected in similar approaches to a set of common problems. "[A] concern for and consensus on basic issues of political principle did exist, and this contributed to the similarities among the constitution-makers in various states as they sought to give shape and authority to new governments that were consistent with republican principles, protective of rights, and committed to the public good." Ibid., at 91. See also Donald S. Lutz, *The Origins of American Constitutionalism* (1988), at 104 ("the documents display considerable inventiveness, but there are nevertheless strong institutional similarities and a political culture … basic to them all").
10. The Federalist No. 47. Tarr, *Understanding State Constitutions*, at 97. Other commentators give this formation period a more optimistic rendering. Daniel Hulseboch, in his influential account of New York and its role in the transformation of constitutionalism in the colonial era, notes that these documents "contained more than the nuts and bolts of administration. Each constitution also conveyed a vision of how the government related to its citizens and expressed the rights and duties of the people." Daniel Hulseboch, *Constituting Empire: New York and the Transformation of Constitutionalism in the Atlantic World, 1664–1830* 260–61 (2005). This was not undermined by the frequency of amendment in the post-revolutionary period for, as to these documents, "the people revised to reflect changing notions of how government should function each day on the ground." Ibid., at 260.
11. Tarr, *Understanding State Constitutions*, at 97.
12. Lutz, *Origins*, at 97.
13. See Wood, *Creation*, at 53 ("The sacrifice of individual interests to the greater good of the whole formed the essence of republicanism and comprehended for Americans the idealistic goal of their Revolution").
14. Ibid., at 410 ("Wherever the real danger in a government lies," Madison wrote, "there is a danger of oppression").
15. See ibid., at 391–467 (describing the "critical period before the Articles of Confederation were supplanted by the new constitution").
16. The concerns that the citizenry, echoed by the framers in various statements and writings, had with the behavior of state governments was palpable during this period. Despite the persistent and enduring place of the states in the competition of our constitutional republic in this first critical phase leading up to the enactment of the US Constitution, citizens of the new nation remained skeptical about state functioning in this new system. Jack Rakove notes the caution that framers expressed about state governance even while preserving state powers and limiting the national government. "Wilson and Madison," Rakove writes, "held that the states should be confined to their 'proper orbits' around a national 'sun' that they would neither 'warm [n]or enlighten'." Jack Rakove, *Original Meanings: Politics and Ideas in the Making of the U.S. Constitution* 170 (1996). He continues: "Nothing in these arguments suggested that they regarded the states as laboratories of liberty or nurseries of republican citizenship." Ibid. See also ibid., at 165 ("Because

the states bore the brunt of the final and economic problems that the Revolution created, they also offered the most conspicuous target for popular disenchantment with all government").

17. See, e.g., Marc. W. Kruman, *Between Authority & Liberty: State Constitution Making in Revolutionary America* 4 (1997) ("Americans wrote constitutions that enfeebled governors and situated virtually governmental power in the hands of enlarged legislatures more entirely representative of the people").
18. See ibid., at 155 ("Revolutionaries easily combined their understand of the common good with a belief in the inviolability of least at a few individual rights").
19. See generally M. J. C. Vile, *Constitutionalism and the Separation of Powers* (1967).
20. Rakove, *Original Meanings*, at 250.
21. Oscar & Mary Flug Handlin, *Commonwealth: A Study of the Role of Government in the American Economy: Massachusetts, 1774–1861* 52 (1969).
22. See Wood, *Creation*, at 50.
23. See Gary Gerstle, *Liberty and Coercion: The Paradox of American Government* 56 (2015).
24. Wood, *Creation*, at 53.
25. Pennsylvania Constitution of 1776, Declaration of Rights, art. 5. See generally Harvey C. Mansfield, Jr., *Taming the Prince: The Ambivalence of Modern Executive Power* (1989).
26. Wood, *Creation*, at 57.
27. For a good discussion of eighteenth-century Whiggish political theory, see Donald Lutz, *Popular Consent and Popular Control: Whig Political Theory in the Early State Constitutions* (1980).
28. See generally Robert E. Williams & Lawrence Friedman, *The Law of American State Constitutions* 268–74 (2d. 2023). See also Kruman, *Authority & Liberty*, at 132 ("In the eighteenth century, colonists worried about and sought to reduce the governors' executive formal powers"). One rather unusual example illustrating state efforts to prevent monarchical rule comes from New York, a state which was especially struggling with ongoing British presence and military battles at the time and sought to resist encroaching monarchy by vesting in its constitution exceptionally great power into their executive, who retained the right to dismiss the legislature.
29. See generally Jennifer Nedelsky, *Private Property and the Limits of American Constitutionalism: The Madisonian Framework and its Legacy* 6 (1989) ("property was not just an abstract symbol. It was a right whose security was essential to the economic and political success of the new republic").
30. See ibid., at 134.
31. See Adams, *First American Constitutions*, at 311 ("The safety of private property from arbitrary governmental requisition was part of the whig culture colonial Englishmen shared with most inhabitants of the realm").
32. Quoted in Rakove, *Original Meanings*, at 192.
33. See Lutz, *Origins*, at 29.
34. See Vile, *Constitutionalism and the Separation of Powers*.
35. See Wood, "State Constitution-Making," at 911.
36. Wood, *Creation*, at 84.
37. See Adams, *First American Constitutions*, at 103.
38. Joseph Fishkin & William E. Forbath, *The Anti-Oligarchic Constitution: Reconstructing the Economic Foundations of American Democracy* (2022), at 38.
39. The Federalist No. 51, at 269 (James Madison) (Sheridan Books, 2001).
40. On this ill-fated experiment, see Alison LaCroix, "What if Madison Had Won? Imagining a Constitutional World of Legislative Supremacy," 45 *Indiana L. Rev.* 41 (2011).

41. See Gordon S. Wood, *Power and Liberty: Constitutionalism in the American Revolution* 54–73 (2021).
42. See ibid., at 94–99. See also Pauline Maier, *Ratification: The People Debate the Constitution, 1787–1788* (2010).
43. See generally Bernard Bailyn, *The Ideological Origins of the American Revolution* (1967). The framer most closely identified with the fashioning of popular consent as the fulcrum of constitutional authority was Thomas Jefferson. However, the theme animated most of the framers, including John Adams, James Wilson, Madison, and even most of the antifederalist skeptics.
44. Del. Bill of Rts., § 1.
45. Va. Declaration of Rts. of 1776, § 2.
46. Lutz, *Popular Consent* at 69.
47. A phrase identified with colonialist James Otis. See Daniel A. Smith, *Tax Crusaders and the Politics of Direct Democracy* (1998).
48. See generally Wood, *Creation*, at 53–57.
49. Lutz, *Origins*, at 29.
50. See Fishkin & Forbath, *Anti-Oligarchic Constitution*, at 37–39.
51. Adams, *First American Constitutions*, at 188.
52. In an interesting reexamination of the separation of powers in state constitutions, state constitutional scholar Jon Marshfield emphasizes the utility of such formal separation of spheres of authority in enabling the citizens to hold their governmental accountable, the idea being that if they knew who were responsible for the particular decisions they would be able to exercise their democratic right to control their government. See Jonathan L. Marshfield, "America's Other Separation of Powers Tradition," 73 *Duke L. J.* (2023).
53. See generally Thomas Goebel, *A Government by the People: Direct Democracy in America, 1890–1940* (2002).
54. For an extended critique of the notion of sovereignty, including a discussion of how limits to authority and mechanisms of accountability make sovereignty conceptually meaningless, see Don Herzog, *Sovereignty RIP* (2020). On popular sovereignty in particular, see ibid., at 269–77 ("We don't have to locate sovereignty somewhere and we needn't pride ourselves on our genius in assigning it to the people. We can instead abandon it").
55. See Jennifer Nedelsky, *Private Property* ("property was not just an abstract symbol. It was a right whose security was essential to the economic and political success of the new republic"). The protection of private property was not motivated by purely libertarian motives. The framers understood that property was necessary to participate with equality in the democratic project. For an especially bold statement of this view, see Fishkin & Forbath, *Anti-Oligarchic Constitution*, at 32–33. "For the revolutionary generation," they write, "political liberty … depended on economic equality… [I]t is no wonder that the revolutionary generation believed republican governments had essential distributional tasks, and that they inscribed such precepts in their founding charters…"
56. Nedelsky, *Private Property*, at 23.
57. Wood, *Creation*, at 163. See also Lutz, *Origins*, at 105: The strong inclination to legislative supremacy is not surprising … The legislature was their protector against governmental tyranny, and they saw it as much more effective than were bills of rights and courts."
58. See generally Richard Hofstadter, *The American Political Tradition* (1957).
59. "Hence it is, that such democracies have ever been spectacles of turbulence and contention; have ever been found incompatible with personal security, or the rights of property; and in general have been as short in their lives as they have been violent in their deaths." The Federalist No. 10, at 46 (James Madison) (Sheridan Books, 2001).

60. Tarr writes: The founders "emphasis on majority rule, together with their use of the less emphatic ought in delineating rights, might seem to indicate a lack of commitment to individual rights ... But this conclusion fails to distinguish between violations of rights and legitimate restrictions on them. It also assumes a fundamental incompatibility between majority rule and the protection of rights, as well as between individual rights and the common good." Tarr, *Understanding State Constitutions*, at 80.
61. See, e.g., Jessica Bullman Pozen & Miriam Seifter, "The Democracy Principle in State Constitutionalism," 119 *Mich. L. Rev.* 859 (2021). See also Daniel J. Elazar, "The Principles and Traditions Underlying State Constitutionalism," *Publius*, Winter 1982, at 11–12.
62. On Jacksonian democracy, see Daniel Feller, *The Jacksonian Promise: America, 1815–1840* (1995).
63. See Alexis de Tocqueville, *Democracy in America* 93 (H. C. Mansfield & D. Winthrop trans. 2002). See also Jeffrey S. Sutton, *Who Decides? States as Laboratories of Constitutional Experimentation* 15 (2022).
64. Wood, *Creation*, at 162.
65. Ibid., at 409.
66. Quoted in ibid., at 432.
67. Ibid., at 67, quoting from I Farrand at 26–27.
68. Williams & Friedman, *American State Constitutions*, at 67–78.
69. Wood, *Creation*, at 405.
70. See Rakove, *Original Meanings*, at 289–90.
71. "The notion that judges could invalidate all governmental actions inconsistent with their interpretation of the constitution was simply unknown in the 1770s and early 1780s and would have been considered far beyond the scope of legitimate judicial power." Tarr, *Understanding State Constitutions*, at 72. See also Sylvia Snowiss, *Judicial Review and the Law of the Constitution*, Ch. 2 (1990).
72. See Rakove, *Original Meanings*, at 297–302 (discussing Montesquieu and the role of English political thought in developing early ideas of judicial review). See also Wood, *Creation*, at 454 ("Once the reaction to legislative supremacy had set in ... a new appreciation of the role of the judiciary in American politics could begin to emerge").
73. See, The Federalist No. 51.
74. See, e.g., Jesse Choper, *Judicial Review and the National Political Process: A Functional Reconsideration of the Role of the Supreme Court* (1980). See also Z. Payvand Ahdoubt, "Enforcement Lawmaking and Judicial Review," 135 *Harv. L. Rev.* 937 (2022).
75. See Williams & Friedman, *American State Constitutions*, at 267–78. See also Jim Rossi, "Institutional Design and the Lingering Legacy of the Antifederalist Separation of Powers Ideals in the States," 52 *Vand. L. Rev.* 1167 (1999).
76. See Williams & Friedman, *American State Constitutions*, at 281–82. See Client Follow-Up Co. v. Hynes 390 N.E. 2d 847, 847–50 (Ill. 1979).
77. This is referring just to constraints internal to the state. National oversight would be secured through the supremacy of the federal government under the powers granted to them by the US Constitution.
78. See Adams, *First American Constitutions*, at 260: "A pessimistic view of human nature was part of the argument for a system of checks and balances. A carefully thought out scheme of opposing and cooperating institutions could, perhaps, counteract the ill effects of human weakness."
79. On nineteenth century constitutional reforms, see Dinan, *State Constitutional Politics*.
80. See Williams & Friedman, *American State Constitutions*, at 312–14; Sutton, *Who Decides?* at 249–56.

81. See, e.g., James L. Huffman, "The Public Interest in Private Property Rights," 50 *Okla. L. Rev.* 377 (2020).
82. See Erin Ryan, "The Public Trust Doctrine, Property, and Society," in *Handbook of Property, Law, and Society* (Graham, Davies, & Godden eds., 2022).
83. Wood, *Creation*, at 410.
84. See ibid.
85. See, e.g., Nedelsky, *Private Property*, et seq.
86. See Gerstle, *Liberty & Coercion*; Fishkin & Forbath, *Anti-Oligarchic Constitution*; William J. Novak, *New Democracy: The Creation of the Modern American State* (2022).
87. See Wood, *Power & Liberty*, at 36 ("In these new republic constitutions, the Revolutionaries' central aim was to prevent power ... from encroaching on liberty").
88. See Tarr, *Understanding State Constitutions*, at 60–63
89. See James W. Ely, Jr., *The Guardian of Every Other Right: A Constitutional History of Property Rights* 42–58 (2008).
90. See generally Vile, *Constitutionalism and the Separation of Powers*.
91. See Tarr, *Understanding State Constitutions*, at 75–82
92. See Penn. Const. of 1776, Declaration III.
93. See Tarr, *Understanding State Constitutions*, at 77–78.
94. See Jason Mazzone, "The Bill of Rights in the Early State Courts," 92 *Minn. L. Rev.* 1 (2007).
95. See Tarr, *Understanding State Constitutions*, at 78.
96. See generally Gordon S. Wood, "State Constitution-Making."
97. See generally Melvin Eisenberg, *The Nature of the Common Law* (1991). See also John M. Finnis, "Natural Law and Legal Reasoning," 38 *Clev. St. L. R.* 1 (1990).
98. See Stuart Banner, *The Decline of Natural Law: How American Lawyers Once Used Natural Law and Why They Stopped* 22 (2021).
99. 5 U.S. 137 (1803).
100. See Banner, *Natural Law*, at 18–45.
101. See, e.g., Randy Barnett, "The Intersection of Natural Rights and Positive Constitutional Law," 25 *Conn. L. Rev.* 853 (1993).
102. See Sutton, *Who Decides?* at 34.
103. See ibid., at 59.
104. Ibid.
105. See Sai Prakash & John Yoo, "The Origins of Judicial Review," 70 *U. Chi. L. Rev.* 887 (2003).
106. See, e.g., Jeremy Waldron, "The Core of the Case Against Judicial Review," 115 *Yale L. J.* 1346 (2006); Larry D. Kramer, "Foreword: We the Court," 115 *Harv. L. Rev.* 4 (2001); Herbert Wechsler, "The Political Safeguards of Federalism: The Role of the States in the Composition and Selection of the National Government," 54 *Colum. L. Rev.* 543 (1954).
107. See, e.g., Lee Epstein, et al., *The Behavior of Federal Judges: A Theoretical and Empirical Study of Rational Choice* (2013); Jeffrey Segal & Harold A. Spaeth, *The Supreme Court and the Attitudinal Model* (1993).
108. See, e.g., Mark Tushnet, "Following the Rules Laid Down: A Critique of Interpretation and Neutral Principles," 96 *Harv. L. Rev.* 781 (1983). For a comprehensive survey of the debate, see Brian Leiter, "Legal Indeterminancy," 1 *Legal Theory* 481 (1995).
109. See Barry R. Weingast, "The Political Foundations of Democracy and the Rule of Law, 91 *Amer. Poli. Sci. Rev.* 245 (1997). See also Douglas C. North & Barry R. Weingast, "Constitutions and Commitment: The Evolution of Institutions Governing Public Choice in Seventeenth Century England," 44 *J. Econ. Hist.* 803 (1989).

110. See Barry R. Weingast, "High Stakes to Low Stakes Politics: Should Majoritarians Embrace Countermajoritarian Constitutional Provisions?" (ms. 2022).
111. See, e.g., Rui de Figueiredo & Barry R. Weingast, "Self-Enforcing Federalism," 21 *J. L. Econ. & Org.* 103 (2005).
112. See generally James L. Buchanan & Gordon Tullock, *The Calculus of Consent: The Logical Foundations of Constitutional Democracy* (1962); Peter C. Ordeshook, "Constitutional Stability," 3 *Const. Pol. Econ.* 137 (1992).
113. See Sonia Mittal & Barry R. Weingast, "Self-Enforcing Constitutions: With an Application to Democratic Stability in America's First Century," 10 *J. L. Econ. & Org.* 1 (2011). See also Adam Przeworski, *Democracy and the Market* (1991); Russell Hardin, "Why a Constitution?" in *The Federalist Papers and the New Institutionalism* (Bernard Grofman & Donald Wittman eds., 1989).
114. The idea that a state, with certain characteristics, is necessary to ensure an optimal level of security and liberty is a familiar one in the political theory literature. Indeed, variations of this theme go back to Hobbes and Machiavelli. A valuable recent treatment of some of these general issues is Philip Pettit, *The State* (2022). See also Daren Acemoglu & James Robinson, *Why Nations Fail: The Origins of Power, Prosperity, and Poverty* (2013).
115. See Thomas Hobbes, *The Leviathan* (C. B. MacPherson ed. 1968).
116. Adams, *First American Constitutions*, at 188. See also Daryl J. Levinson, "Parment and Politics: The Positive Puzzle of Constitutional Commitment," 124 *Harv. L. Rev.* 657 (2011).
117. See Wood, *Creation*, at 163; Lutz, *Origins*, at 105.
118. As to the common mission across diverse states, Tarr summarizes the framers' accomplishments thusly: "[A] concern for and consensus on basic issues of political principle did exist, and this contributed to the similarities among early state constitutions. So too did the sense of common purpose among the constitution-makers in various states as they sought to give shape and authority to new governments that were consistent with republican principles, protective of rights, and committed to the public good." Tarr, *Understanding State Constitutions*, at 91.
119. See generally Daniel B. Rodriguez, "State Constitutional Failure," 2011 *U. Ill. L. Rev.*
120. See Michael C. Dorf & Charles F. Sabel, "A Constitution of Democratic Experimentalism," 98 *Colum. L. Rev.* 267 (1998).

2

The Police Power in Our Republic's First Century

The basic insight from the previous chapter is that the nature and scope of the police power is revealed by a coherent account of state constitutionalism, with attention to both the constitutions' ideologies and their practices. To judge whether and to what extent the police power "works" as an instrument of public policy, we must assess its performance in light of what the constitution expects of public authorities acting under this power. Such an assessment includes a deep dive into how courts have thought about the police power when they have considered conflicts raised by individuals objecting to the government's use of the police power.

As we will see in this and subsequent chapters, the police power is made up of an admixture of legal constructs, toggling between judicial interpretations and legislative and administrative practice.[1] Yet at its core is constitutional authority and direction, each drawn from state constitutions' designs and objectives. Insofar as the connection between the police power and state constitutionalism has long been neglected among scholars, a full chapter devoted to that subject was important to set the table. For the remainder of this book, we focus on the development and evolution of the police power and to its potential as a strategy to improve governance in the contemporary United States. This chapter examines the police power from the early republic to the end of Reconstruction.

There are four intersecting ideas that emerge from a close look at the police power over the course of our republic's history, especially in this critical first era. First, the police power reflects a deliberate and fairly consistent commitment to an ambitious approach to governance, one that focuses on the capacity and obligation of public officials to protect and promote the general welfare of the states' citizens.[2] This view is broadly congruent with leading scholarship on the police power, going back to writers of the late nineteenth century including Justice Thoms Cooley, Christopher Tiedemann, and Ernst Freund, each authors of major treatises on the police power, and up to the present, with the seminal historical work of William Novak and Harry Scheiber. It is also congruent, albeit in a more indirect sense, with a wealth of contemporary scholarship on democracy and American constitutionalism.[3] This scholarship emphasizes the deeply and broadly democratic character of constitutionalism in America, distinguishing this in key ways from the familiar logic of constitutions as fundamentally countermajoritarian, and, *a fortiori*, anti-democratic governance instruments. As we explore the awesome scope of the police power as a fulcrum of American governance, we should orient this conversation around influential depictions of state governance and constitutional development over the expanse of, at first, two centuries. Although this book is not a work of legal history, the historical context is important to understanding what the police power has become and how it has evolved. Second, the police power was originally understood and continues to be understood as a power that is in some constructive tension with the protection of individual rights. These protections form important cornerstones of American constitutionalism and risk being neglected in scholarship that emphasizes the plasticity of these and other negative rights and steady expansion of the government's regulatory powers.[4] We will see, in our focus in this chapter on the republic's first century and in the next chapter covering the critical half century between Reconstruction's end and the end of World War II, the major ways in which the police power developed alongside the evolution and shifting terrain of private property and liberty rights. In contrast to the libertarian idea of property rights as rigid constraints on the power of government to govern, legislatures and courts came to see property rights in a broader social context, one that viewed rights as subject to public exigencies and social imperatives and as critical to the fundamental goal of promoting the people's welfare.

The centrality of property and contract rights to our well-ordered liberty in our American constitutional scheme did not wither away as the imperatives of active governance grew. While the balance shifted in important ways toward broad governmental authority, tensions between the public interest and the prerogatives of individual property owners persisted. Third, although it would be accurate to say about the police power at the end of Reconstruction that it is an essential attribute of the regulatory authority of state governments under state constitutions and an element of popular sovereignty in our American constitutional tradition, this power was never intended to be limitless. Nor truly can it be, if it is to be consistent with our best constitutional understandings. A comprehensive account, therefore, of the police power must account for and explain the reasons for and the character of these limits. Fourth and finally, the police power has proved incredibly adaptive to changing conditions and also to the need to create new implementation mechanisms for regulation, such as administrative agencies and municipal governments. The evolution of the power from a means by which the legislature could assert its plenary authority to govern to a more institutionally dynamic method of governance is a neglected, but important, part of the police power story.

As we discussed in Chapter 2, there is necessarily a strong connection between the police power and American state constitutionalism. This power exists not as some free-floating attribute of governance or as a mechanism deriving its character and contents from the common law, but instead as a power embodied in the state constitutions. Moreover, insofar as it is a power reserved by the states through the US

Constitution's Tenth Amendment, it is part of our American constitutional scheme more generally. With that in mind, we first will situate our discussion within the debate over how and why it matters that the police power is an embedded constitutional power. What specific consequences follow from the fact that the source of the police power is and has always been the constitution, frequently explicit in the document's test, but always central in its overall context and ideology?

THE POLICE POWER AND CONSTITUTIONAL MEANING

The framers of the first state constitutions in the eighteenth and early nineteenth centuries were engaged in two struggles simultaneously, the outcomes of which would define the governance structure of the new nation for the critical first decades. One struggle was how to create effective frameworks of government through these constitutions – this in order to get the people's work properly done. We can characterize this is a struggle, rather than merely an effort, because these framers were developing essentially new ideas about governance, public power, and individual rights as they crafted these documents, all against the backdrop of a persistent fear that they might substitute one tyranny for another. The other struggle was how best to define the sustain the relationship between the national and state governments. A theme prominent in both of these struggles was how to ensure that all spheres of government had power adequate to fulfill the functions of government, to promote the general welfare and secure the blessings of liberty. Likewise, the framers resolved to maintain sufficient protection of individual liberty and property.[5] That this strong commitment was inchoate was not because these values were not prized. Rather, these founders were acting within the conditions and circumstances of their times. They developed strategies before the emergence of a more robust understanding of constitutional rights and the role of the courts in safeguarding these rights and well before the incorporation of the Bill of Rights to the states and before the establishment of rights distinctly held by citizens of the states through the transformative impact of the Fourteenth Amendment of the US Constitution a century after the republic's creation.[6] Moreover, they did so in a time when they had invested great faith in the state legislature as an instrument of democracy and as a protector of certain vested interests.

Essential to the resolution of these questions of authority and its limits was the predicate question of who would be able to wield power in the name of We the People and, in addition, who would govern the governors? "The overriding issue Americans confronted before and after the independence," writes G. Edward White, "was the nature and location of sovereignty in government."[7] The framers' answer, as we discussed in the previous chapter, was popular sovereignty, that is, *rule by the people* and thus the derivation of all governmental power from the people in its choice to assemble constitutions and the appropriate institutions of government to carry out the people's will.[8] Although the framers were not without their doubts and fears about the muscular exercise of public authority by state and local governments,[9] they ultimately cast their lot with a vision of government in this new republic that embraced strong state power.[10] To put it another way, the framers understood that one of the consequences of reserving power to the states was that the states would possess a broad range of powers. This was not a bug, but a positive feature of the developing American constitutionalism.

The very best example of the framers' commitment to capacious state power was the police power itself. This was the instantiation of the idea that state constitutions were documents of limit, not grant, and that state governments would manage their fair share of duties under our overall scheme of governance.[11] Moreover, the police power, like all other elements of the constitution, sprung from the fundamental function and obligation of the government to protect and promote the public welfare. While the framers were certainly preoccupied with fashioning sufficient checks and balances to limit power, we should see these efforts as ultimately derivative of the effort to create structures of governance that would implement our common good and in the name of the people who consented to this approach to good governing.[12] Government would protect our health, safety, and welfare, and would implement policies to advance the public welfare.

What do we make of the fact that this power was labelled a "police" power rather than, say, a "regulatory" or a "governance" power? Policing was a concept with an ancient lineage, tracking the activities of social control in the Roman and medieval periods. A number of scholars have noted that the concept of the police power comes into English law through the idea of the *patria potestas*, with the King's solemn duty to manage the affairs of the household at its core.[13] In his *Commentaries on the Laws of England*, Blackstone described the function of the public police as "the due regulation and domestic order of the kingdom, whereby the inhabitants of the State, like members of a well-governed family, are bound to conform their general behavior to the rules of propriety, good neighborhood, and good manners, and to be decent, industrious, and inoffensive in their respective stations."[14] While this rendering shared much in common with the conception of government obligation articulated by other rough contemporaries, including Vattel[15] and Adam Smith,[16] we can trace this large description of the constitutional power to ensure "domestic order" and the mechanisms necessary to enable a population to flourish all the way back to Aristotle.[17] The police power was the power to govern well and for the common good.

The revolutionary-era thinkers were surely attentive to these themes and could readily imagine that state governments under state constitutions would have as their critical goal protecting the public welfare as an obligation to look after the "household." However, what they thought of as the household is more associated with the idea of the common good and general welfare as defined by constitutional understandings and objectives of the times, not by monarchs acting through the royal prerogative. Policing may have been associated with powerful mechanisms of control, as it was understood by Blackstone and, if one wants to look deep into the etymology of all this, in the notion of *policizia* or *parens patriae*,[18] but this understanding was not buttressed by constitutional theory in the early American republic. That the colonists did not expect to be managed and subject to ubiquitous social control was obvious from seeing the lengths to which they went to secure limits on government power and general executive power in particular. To be sure, American constitutional choices were not made in a vacuum and certainly the framers learned much from Blackstone with regard to situating a broad governance power in constitutional frameworks.[19] However, they pushed back hard against the idea that underlay the king's prerogative and the benevolent goal of safeguarding the household. Instead, they wanted bold, broad power tethered to constitutional guardrails.[20] Therefore, paying inordinate attention to Blackstone and related conceptions of the police as a social control mechanism risks confusing the issue of what British constitutionalists expected from the king and what new Americans demanded of those who were exercising power in the people's name. In the end, Blackstone's formulation "serves badly as a guide to constitutional doctrine and governmental realities in the United States in the 1790s or the early nineteenth century."[21]

If organizing our thinking of the police power around antediluvian notions of household management and social control is misleading as a framing of what the founding fathers aspired to achieve in creating this power, what then do we see as these central aspirations and, further, why ought we to care?

Let us start with the big objective: The framers of the revolutionary constitutions and the leaders who would follow in their steps in constructing new constitutions and in reforming the original documents were committed to energetic governance that would realize important public objectives, including the expansion of the economy and widening opportunities for prosperity for their citizens.[22] They also were concerned to reduce harms to citizens, harms that were ubiquitous in an era in which health and safety were at risk from various threats.[23] These goals necessitated ambitious public powers, including a broad police power. At the same time, the framers worried, for reasons we described in Chapter 1 in our larger discussion of constitutional objectives, about the threat by ambitious governments to our individual liberty and private property.

To best understand the solutions at which they arrived, we need to see both parts of the equation: the part that emphasizes, with the revolutionary spirit of state constitution-making, that the authority of state governments would be enormously capacious, this in order to implement key needs and wants of the citizenry of this new nation, but also the part that is concerned with ensuring that elected representatives would not simply reinforce the efforts of the British monarch by using the police power as essentially a king's prerogative.

The issues cut even deeper than concerns with government capaciousness. They were likewise concerned with rapaciousness. The framers' vision of energetic regulatory governance was in tension from the beginning with the objective of protecting liberty and private property, protections necessary to a well-ordered society. In highlighting the ubiquitous commitment of early and later constitution makers to advancing the public welfare through regulations that would supercharge the economy and address myriad social problems, we should not ignore the tensions that emerged from our strong commitment to protecting liberty and property. Our American public law, constitutional law and administrative law included, insists that the government act with regard to our cherished liberty and property rights in a way that is neither arbitrary nor unreasonable. We have always had limits on the exercise of governmental power; and these limits are built on a dual edifice, the first borne of an informed skepticism about the incentives and temptations of lawmakers, reflected cogently in Madison's views on factions in Federalist No. 10,[24] and the second born of a view that a principal function of the government to which we consent as a people is to protect our liberty and property.[25] It is in the tension between activist government and safeguarding of our liberties, between what would come to be called public rights and our classic and evolving private rights that we can learn much about the development of the police power.

To understand how the framers understood the balance between broad authority to protect the common good and the need to check the government and to protect citizen liberties, we should look at what they viewed as the principal threat. From one important perspective, the principal concern was the anemic quality of the central government under the Articles of Confederation and its inability to control "the centrifugal tendency of the States."[26] They needed to construct a system that would address the myriad threats to this fledgling nation; and so the preoccupation with creating a suitably strong federal government, one whose powers could evolve to meet emerging conditions, made very good sense given the immediate relevant history.[27] They were concerned as well with the various needs of its citizens to prosper and they knew that an active government was essential to meet these current and future needs.[28] Such governance would be critical to securing "the blessings of liberty" and to "promote the general welfare," themes at the heart of the framers' description of, and hopes for, these new constitutions, and also very much on the mind of the various thinkers whose views would play such a central role in the framers' approach to the subject.

The framers' commitment to individual liberty in the US Constitution is revealed in expressions and in structural choices, and yet the large claim that the document and its framing history underwrote a liberty-forward vision of American constitutionalism has come under strong criticism as the so-called republican tradition of constitutional historiography has taken strong root over the last four decades.[29] However strong were the framers' commitments to a liberal idea of governance in the US Constitution, the overall structure and ideology of the state constitutions reflected a studied concern with enabling government to exercise wide authority to protect citizen welfare and secure the common good. So far as the states were concerned, "[the police power] underwrote an American theory of governance that was collectivist and majoritarian rather than liberal."[30]

From this, we might conclude that "the states were the original architects of Progressivism, not the federal government, and they drew their justification at least in part from a reinvigorated conception of the states' police power."[31] However, this dichotomy between the progressive state governments and the libertarian national government proves too much. At the center of our revolutionary constitutional tradition, forged in a struggle against monarchical governance, is the safeguarding of individual liberty and property, while enabling effective governance in the name of We the People. The states may have been the original engines of progressivism, but what progressivism meant in the post-framing period was surely different than what it would come to mean seven decades later, as society and the market economy evolved, the meaning of citizenship was redefined after a bloody war, and we the people enacted transformative constitutional amendments. Ultimately, it would become untenable to maintain, both as a practical and theoretical matter, two competing ideologies of regulatory governance, one aiming at liberty and the other at equality and social welfare. Rather, American constitutionalism has long aspired to mechanisms that reconciled the demands of social welfare governance and individual liberties, of energetic regulation and private property.

Still, the state constitutions had from the beginning of the republic purposes different than the US Constitution, and the framers thus choose constitutional structures that would allocate principal responsibility and prerogative to different levels of government, one illustration of which was the establishment of the police power as a *state*, and not a *federal*, power. This was the central genius of American constitutional federalism.[32] The overarching objective, as we should remember, was to facilitate the abilities of both levels of government to pursue what were ultimately common objectives, that of promoting the general welfare and securing the blessings of liberty to ourselves and to our posterity. The Constitution's preamble declares that this is the fundamental objective of the federal Constitution. But this same surpassing elegance of the overarching goals of governance are contained in state constitutions as well.

MEANING, PURPOSE, AND STRATEGY

The ascription of a coherent constitutional vision to the framers of the state and federal constitutions risks falling into the trap of supposing that there is one true story here, a story revealed in the creation of, and advocacy for, the US Constitution and the various state constitutions adopted at roughly the same time. This framing of these events might support an originalist argument that we should interpret the police power in accordance with the will of the framers to accomplish these two objectives.[33] Such a view, to put it in the right contemporary jargon, is in alignment with the original public meaning of the police power.[34] And yet the original public meaning of the police power remains elusive – or, at the very least, incorrigible, as a basis for interpreting it fruitfully in matters of dispute.

As to the matter of original public meaning, we cannot say beyond extracting some important themes from the statements and actions of the founding fathers about the shape and scope of regulatory governance what exactly they would have wanted from the police power as it was applied in circumstances that would emerge as the needs of states and the nation evolved in various directions. The history here matters, and much more than a little, even if the framers' intentions and the original public meaning of a phrase so capacious and complex as "the police power" matters less.[35]

We can nonetheless extrapolate from their expressions and their actual tactics, including the structural decisions they made in these constitutional texts, what they aimed for as a matter of strategy. The meaning of this power can be understood by considering the larger context of political strategy and choice in a constitutional republic. Makers of state constitutions created institutions and spheres of power in order to accomplish deliberate goals. As we discussed in the previous chapter, these goals include creating structures to cabin executive influence (which revolutionary constitutionalists equated with the royal prerogative) and, later, to limit the risks of legislative excess. They include mechanisms to facilitate energetic and public welfare-enhancing governance. Further, citizens were also concerned to reduce the likelihood that government would turn away from the general welfare and toward opportunistic methods of expropriation. Hardwiring individual rights into these constitutions, as the framers did with the Bill of Rights in the US Constitution, assisted in reducing these risks and in creating this self-enforcing equilibrium.

Mobilizing their state and local governments to protect the general welfare meant establishing a clear set of powers, powers that were not dependent upon the federal government's choices under the US Constitution. The framers could not forecast the future, of course, but they could well imagine the challenges faced at the time the constitutions were forged and also the need for flexibility and discretion in light of what they surely could see would be changing circumstances and conditions. The quest was for an equilibrium that would ensure stability while accounting for adaptation.

The framers were also concerned about maintaining schemes that would ensure that private property would be adequately protected. A police power without limit would represent a continuing threat to individual liberty and prosperity and would therefore be deeply problematic; it would trigger fear and would sap the new nation of the consent it needed from key constituencies in order to ensure cooperation and acquiescence in important governmental choices. Therefore, proper limits were not merely desirable, but were necessary. The main veins of contemporary police power scholarship emphasizes the incredible breadth of the police power, the "staggering freedom of action" the states possessed.[36] However, a comprehensive account of the power needs to see both sides, to reconcile this awesome power with the concern with the appropriate limits on this power. Constitutions, to be self-enforcing in the sense just described, need to reach an equilibrium, one in which powers and limits are in alignment and in a way that can reassure fearful citizens.

Ultimately, matters of constitutional meaning, purpose, and strategy are inextricably linked. State constitutions were created to be instruments of governance; they were designed to facilitate the efforts of public officials on behalf of the governed. They were designed not as monuments to the public's fundamental values, but as instruments designed to work. In order to function as effective instruments, the framers needed to have a shrewd sense of the dynamics of state-level politics, not to mention the complexities of federalism, given that these states were embedded in a constitutional system that involved actors at multiple levels of governance. In understanding these dynamics, the framers incorporated views about human nature and the motivations of actors under conditions of constraint and uncertainty.[37] Attention to strategy, and to intended and unintended consequences, was not a new insight, but a manifestation of the new science of politics that took individuals as they found them and understood that both citizens and officials would design institutions and procedures in order to achieve certain purposes.[38] James Madison not only understood this well, but also gave us perhaps the most famous declaration about the nexus between individual behavior and structural solutions in Federalist No. 10 and elsewhere in the Federalist Papers, where he wrote about factions, democracy, and representative government and the ways to address key impediments to representative democracy under a constitutional framework.[39] While these timeless statements were made in the context of the ratification debates over the US Constitution, the overall analysis was important to an understanding of American constitutionalism more generally, and so was pertinent to choices made in state constitutions as well.

The nexus between purpose and strategy is a complicated one and implicates issues broader than what can be captured here; however, the essential point is that constitutions have purposes that we can learn about from a dense and broad inquiry into the text, context, and ideas embedded in these documents and contemporary political practice. Historical exegesis of the sort that has shed important light on our American constitutional tradition has been essential in exposing some of these key purposes, a point central to interpretive methodologies of various stripes, including, but not limited to, originalism. Moreover, we can learn some probative things about political strategy as constitutional designers and other relevant officials thought about such matters at the time. This enables us to understand better the design and performance of certain governmental institutions and how they might facilitate political purposes and objectives. For example, certain executive powers given to the governor can assist interest groups within the political process with protecting against legislative threats that will undermine their interests.[40] This is illustrative of the deliberate, purposive choice of constitutional architects to create mechanisms of power that can effectuate present and future objectives by anticipating responses and tactics from other government officials with different, and occasionally competing, objectives.[41] All of this is to say that there are connections we can draw between constitutional purpose and strategy, and, when we do so, we can get a better picture on the overall framework of constitutions as documents that help citizens and elected representatives accomplish their objectives by setting out the rules of the game and constructing the institutions that will exercise authority and implement policy. Such information helps us in better understand the police power. We can say, albeit in a fairly abstract way here, that this power helps public officials accomplish certain strategies associated with the people's welfare. At the same time, this power is not free-floating, as some sort of extra-constitutional emergency power in the sense that, say, Carl Schmitt might have imagined,[42] but is embedded in constitutions that have internal and external limits on its use as an instrument of governance.

*

From this framing of the question, we explore next how the police power helped to accomplish key objectives in state constitutionalism. The focus in the remainder of this chapter and the final two chapters in this Part I, is on specific dilemmas and challenges faced by government authorities and also the courts in dealing with the content, scope, and limits of the police power.

NASCENT FEDERALISM: THE POLICE POWER/ COMMERCE POWER PUZZLE

From the adoption of the US Constitution, the overall system of American constitutionalism took on a fundamentally different valence. The question was no longer one of defining and structuring governmental power, as was the principal function of constitution-making in the revolutionary period. Rather, another fundamental question emerged, and that was how to reconcile constitutionally established state power with the power and authority of the national government.[43] This was the core issue of constitutional federalism that preoccupied the framers and later the Supreme Court.[44] A thorough understanding of the framers' purposes and of their achievements with respect to the distribution of powers in the US Constitution remains elusive, even as generations of constitutional historians and legal scholars have analyzed this critical period of American history. One prosaic point is that the contours of federalism were not made explicit in the document and indeed that term was nowhere used in the document explicitly. The appropriate lines between state and federal authority were not self-evident, to say the least. Ultimately, the distribution of authority between the federal government and the states would evolve in light of practice and also key judicial interpretations.

One of the central federalism controversies in the new republic was the relationship between the police power of state governments and the enumerated powers of Congress in Article I. To what extent could a broad state power to protect health, safety, and the general welfare coexist with Congressional power to tackle major issues that, as the framers had quickly discovered in the early years of the nation's history, called for national action? One particular puzzle concerned the interaction between the police power to regulate certain business activity, such as transportation, and Congress's power in Article I, Section 8 to regulate interstate commerce.[45] The US Constitution accorded Congress an exclusive power to regulate interstate commerce; at the same time, among the reserved powers the states had under the Tenth Amendment was the state constitutional authority to protect health, safety, and welfare. It would not take great imagination to see the potential for these two powers to come into conflict. What would ensure that state governance strategies would not undermine the objectives of our new nation?[46]

Such conflict emerged in the second decade of the nineteenth century, first in the dispute that gave rise to the Court's decision in Gibbons v. Ogden.[47] New York had granted a monopoly for steamboat traffic to Messers. Fulton and Livingston. This was challenged on the grounds that this interfered with interstate commerce and therefore impeded the national government's power under the Commerce Clause.[48]

Chief Justice John Marshall spelled out the basic structure of national governance and state prerogative in circumstances in which the demands of an unobstructed interstate commerce required limiting state control. "The genius and character of the whole government," Marshall writes,

> seem to be that its action is to be applied to all the external concerns of the nation, and to those internal concerns which affect the States generally, but not to those which are completely within a particular State, which do not affect other States, and with which it is not necessary to interfere for the purpose of executing some of the general powers of the government.[49]

Acknowledging the secure existence, after the adoption of the US Constitution, of the states' taxation and police powers, Marshall's objective is to sort out where the exercise of such powers interfere with the plenary power of Congress to regulate commerce (which, early in the opinion, Marshall explains includes navigation and all the necessary instrumentalities of commerce).[50] To the Marshall Court, the solution to the puzzle of reconciling police power of the states and the commerce power of the federal government was to view these powers as involving two different imperatives, one that was scrupulously connected to local goals and needs and the other that was a structural mechanism to ensure that our nation could function effectively, that is, without balkanization and interference with common purposes.

Importantly, Marshall acknowledged the broad police powers of the states and also that these powers would be used in myriad contexts when the need arose to protect state citizens' public health and safety.[51] Noting "the acknowledged power of a State to regulate its police, its domestic trade, and to govern its own citizens,"[52] he gives the example of quarantines, an action that surely affected transportation and therefore commerce, as an example of such health-related powers.[53] However, these powers must be exercised consistent with the purpose and logic of Article I of the US Constitution, to ensure that the state was not interfering with the free flow of commerce. According special navigation privileges to Livingston and Fulton was an example of such an interference.

A point largely taken for granted, then and now, was that if and insofar as there was a clash between national and state interests, national interests would undoubtedly prevail.[54] The US Constitution explicitly reserved broad powers to the states, but simultaneously ensured that national objectives would prevail where there were conflicts. This is essentially what they meant by federal supremacy. State and national interests could be symmetrical, but they would occasionally come into conflict. Where so, it would fall to the courts to determine whether the states were, in advancing their interests, acting inconsistently with a power vested in the national government. The police power would only pertain to state decisions made within the proper domain of state authority. This would be made more clear by the Court in McCulloch v. Maryland[55] and other lodestar federalism cases. But there was precious little disagreement on the point that the federal government could constrain the states' exercise of the police power, that is, so long as these powers came into conflict with legitimate federal interests under the Constitution. The Supremacy Clause made crystal clear that the federal government's will would prevail.

As to the matter of police power and interstate commerce, the Court further elaborated on this conflict and its consequences in Brown v. Maryland.[56] The needs of a commercial republic, the Court in Brown reasoned, required restrictions on the balkanization that would happen if states could make their own decisions for their own purposes.[57] In addition to reinforcing the logic of Gibbons, Brown was interesting in that it was the first instance in which the Supreme Court specifically mentioned the police power.[58] Without defining it comprehensively, the mention of the power made what might have been a wholly abstract idea of state prerogative to govern on behalf of its people into an actual power with a constitutional source, and a power that survived the adoption of the US Constitution.

The case in which the Supreme Court in the early years of the republic worked out most thoroughly the nexus between the police and commerce powers was New York v. Miln.[59] This case involved a statute enacted to protect the public health of the community by requiring that a ship's captain, within twenty-four hours after docking at the port, report in writing the names, ages, and last legal settlement of every person who has been on board the vessel. That this was an exercise of the state's police power, and not the assertion of a power over commerce, was revealed, said Justice Barbour for the Court, by the state's rationale for the law, focusing on the town's purpose, ends, and means of implementation of this law. "It is apparent," wrote Barbour,

> from the whole scope of the law that the object of the legislature was to prevent New York from being burdened by an influx of persons brought thither in ships, either from foreign countries or from any other of the states, and for that purpose a report was required of the names, places of birth, &c., of all passengers, that the necessary steps might be taken by the city authorities to prevent them from becoming chargeable as paupers."[60]

This purpose set this law apart from the laws considered in both Gibbons and Brown. In those cases, the states were asserting power – to regulate commerce – that were exclusively Congress's under the US Constitution. With this clear conflict in view, the Court held in both Gibbons and Brown, that the federal government's power is exclusive and thus the assertion that the states had a police power to regulate was of no consequence. In Miln, by contrast, there is no equivalent federal interest and therefore no power that could be squared with the commerce clause. Given that the Constitution is a document of grant, meaning that the federal government has only those powers enumerated in the document, the state's actions under the police power could not be supplanted by the federal government.

There is no new constitutional law made in Miln, but instead the case nonetheless illuminates the principle from Gibbons and Brown, that where state laws do not impose burdens on commerce, they are not inconsistent with the US Constitution but are, rather, part of the ordinary public health regulations, equivalent to quarantines and the like, that Chief Justice Marshall in Gibbons had said are part of "[t]he completely internal commerce of a state [and therefore] may be considered as reserved for the state itself."[61] While none of these cases provide a good definition of the police power, such a definition was unnecessary to decide the outcomes. What was ultimately at stake in all three cases was what we might call pure federalism. Was there a conflict? Who would prevail in such conflicts under principles of US constitutional law? Tacit in these early decisions in our history of constitutional federalism was it that fell solely to the states to determine what powers they had under their own constitutions. In these early watershed commerce clause cases, the great chief justice acknowledged the police power, but did not endeavor to define it.

Nonetheless, these cases, decided over a decade and a half period, were important in reinforcing the power of the states to act locally and with respect to the "internal commerce" of the states, while also curtailing state actions which interfered with commerce that was external. This key move could not be regarded as inevitable at the time these controversies were brewing. After all, the Court had two other roads available to them. One involved weighing the interests of the federal and state governments and making a determination of whether and when state interests were superior to national interests. A second road was to view the Tenth Amendment as creating a safe harbor for states when it was acting under its police powers, even if state actions interfered with commerce. This would involve drawing a line between state efforts to regulate interstate commerce directly and state actions which were aimed toward other objectives but, at least indirectly, interfered with interstate commerce. The affirmation of exclusive federal power over matters of commerce in these and other key cases, would ultimately settle the matter of whose will would triumph once and for all.[62] It became plausible that the courts would second-guess state legislatures and impose more substantial guardrails on the assertion of state power over economic activity in individuals and firms where it might bump up against national concerns. What we learn from the early commerce power cases is that the state police power is reserved power and in that regard is undisturbed by the enactment of the US Constitution. However, the power is not unlimited and cannot be exercised in ways that would interfere with the free flow of commerce. It makes sense, therefore, that the state police power would, from the Supreme Court's perspective, remain intact even in the face of the steadily growing imperative of exerting national influence and control over various issues that implicated interests of the United States.[63]

*

There were three developments in the first decades after the republic's creation that shaped the emergence of the police power as a significant force in state governance. The first was the need to conscript the state legislature into the project of helping to solve the problems of interference with individuals and communities' safety and health by others. This was the classic issue of *sic utere*, one that was reflected in our private law of torts as developed and implemented principally through the common law.[64] Governments at both the state and local level began to intervene more actively, through legislation and regulation, in order to address issues that were characteristic of a society with greater risk, economic needs, and more compassion and sense of obligation to the common welfare. The police power was a key element in this enterprise. The second development was the increasing need for infrastructure and public works projects, this to address the important needs of a growing population and ever more interdependent economy. While the national government would play an important role in these efforts, and a profoundly more important role in the twentieth and twenty-first centuries, the fulcrum of these infrastructure efforts was at the state level. The police power functioned here as a mechanism of improving "the people's welfare."[65] Third and finally, just as the legislative power was evolving in distinct ways, so too there emerged new notions of legislating. At the time of the framing and for many years afterward, the common law reigned supreme as a mechanism of addressing conflicts involving property and personal harm and, more broadly, in defining the scope and contents of legal duties and rights. However, as the nineteenth century continued, there were changes in how we thought about the role and functions of common law adjudication and, in addition, how we thought about the province of legislation.[66]

RIGHTING WRONGS, PROTECTING THE GENERAL WELFARE

As the first state constitutions were forged, and for many years thereafter, common law was in the ascendancy, with positive legislation interstitial.[67] Tort law had steadily developed mechanisms to combat harms to the general welfare, in addition to redressing various types of person-to-person wrongdoing (including threats to one's property rights, as with traditional trespass and nuisance actions). And so, to consider a counterfactual, the police power might have developed as a mere adjunct to the common law of torts and property and the emergent criminal law. For instance, it could have been focused narrowly on abating nuisances, that is, the improper exercise of one's property to cause injury to a neighbor, and about redressing public nuisances and wrongs that represent threats to public health and safety.

Early police power cases suggested that it would play this limited role, essentially a public law version of the *sic utere* principle. After all, the earliest of American police power cases typically involved redress for wrongdoing and, in that sense, legislation (state or local) was more often than not described by the court as a supplement to the common law.[68] However, we will see that the police power expanded considerably over the decades of the nineteenth century, so as to develop a quite different, and considerably bolder, rationale for proper regulation.

Let us first consider what this earlier and more narrow construction of the police power revealed. One of the most elemental concepts in the study of American torts and property law, introduced to law students early their first-year study and drawing upon several centuries of caselaw and commentary, is the notion of *sic utere tuo ut alienum non laedus*, roughly translated into the expressed limit on the ability of one to exercise his liberty or use his property so as to interfere with the rights of his fellow man.

The law of nuisance captures this idea well, albeit in the rather wooly way this body of law has developed over its lifetime. The theory of classical nuisance law encapsulates four basic principles that are important to our understanding of the police power as a mechanism for enforcing the *sic utere* principle. First, there is the idea that individual rights, including property rights, are "relational and qualified."[69] The right to use and enjoy one's property is a fundamental stick in the bundle of the owner's rights, but it is conditional on society's judgment that this use and enjoyment must not interfere with others' freedom and interest.[70] Second, there is the wider view that builds from the *sic utere* notion that individuals should use their property in a peaceful way and in due accord with the society's general welfare.[71] Third, this "should" extends from something akin to the Golden Rule to an obligation imposed by edict of the government, either through the common law of torts and property or through positive law that limits the actions of individuals so as to maintain the peace and common good.[72] Fourth and finally, the task inevitably falls to the judge to make the difficult assessment of whether one's use of property is reasonable or unreasonable; after all, it is not the interference that the law proscribes, it is the unreasonable interference, taking account of the standards that the common law or statutory law delineates in measuring the propriety of the conduct under survey.

Property rights were viewed in these early cases as including the freedom to use. The room for restriction was narrow, principally limited to circumstances involving private or public nuisances. Where such harm-causing activity occurred, however, this matter would warrant public regulation as well as a recovery under traditional principles of tort law. A good illustration of this principle in an early police power case is <u>Brick Presbyterian Church v. Mayor of New York</u>, decided in 1826.[73] There the plaintiff claimed that a restriction imposed by the city on his ability to use this land as a cemetery would interfere with his use of the property, more specifically, their covenant of quiet enjoyment. The operation of a cemetery in this community would, argued the plaintiff, impose a distinct harm on the public. Accepting such a claim, said the New York high court, would run afoul of the *sic utere* principle. Viewed from a public harm perspective, it is "unreasonable in the extreme to hold that plaintiff should be at liberty to endanger … [the lives] of the citizens generally."[74]

Likewise, in evaluating one year later a municipal regulation limiting a boat owner's right to connect their boat to a dock in a dangerous manner, the court in <u>Vanderbilt v. Adams</u> insisted that this statute was "passed for the preservation of good order in the harbor"[75] and was "essentially necessary for the purpose of protecting the rights of all concerned."[76] The law protects property owners' interests only when the owner can be said to suffer an injury, but under the *sic utere* principle "this is not considered as an injury."[77] After all, the property owner benefits reciprocally, if indirectly, as a member of the general public. A law enacted therefore under the *sic utere* principle is "constitutional and obligatory."[78] "Every public regulation in a city may and does, in some sense, limit and restrict the absolute right that existed previously, but this is not considered an injury. So far from it, the individual, as well as others, is supposed to benefit."[79]

These strong statements of governmental roles and responsibilities under the police power are characteristic of a time in which the public law of government regulation existed alongside the common law as a complementary means to redress private harm.[80] Government regulation supplemented tort law in this regard. Courts could and occasionally did declare a certain act to be a public nuisance.[81] But the duly enacted ordinance or statute accomplished the same objective in declaring (nay, discovering!) that certain threats to the health and safety of the public were properly addressed through positive law.

To the extent that the police power began principally as an instrument to safeguard the *sic utere* principle, this was principally because the kinds of regulations created were designed to limit public nuisances and other sorts of threats to individual well-being. Even within this structure, it is important to understand, as Novak wrote, that nuisance law in this time "was neither trivial nor timid"[82] and "nineteenth-century jurists were quite explicit about both the overarching significance and the public power of the law of nuisance."[83] Ordinary nuisance law focuses on comparing competing private property claims. One's use of property, so the rule goes, should not interfere with the use of property by another. This use might simply mean quiet enjoyment, and that stick in the bundle is protected against interruption or intervention. Courts saw the police power as protecting against public nuisances, nuisances which reflected threats to the general welfare and not merely violations of discrete duties in the classic tort law sense. In essence, the courts were broadening the meaning of what represented a harm worthy of redress.

Did the redressing of wrongs exhaust the basis and content of the police power?[84] Not according to the collection of state cases dealing with the police power, especially as we get later into the century. The courts moved steadily away from the strict *sic utere* idea in considering the scope of its power toward a broader conception of what this power means. While it was easier to capture many of the early safety and health regulations in some sort of "redressing harm" notion, state regulations took on a somewhat different shape as social conditions evolved.[85] The government became focused on implementing regulations that advanced public purposes. This was not lost on the leading treatise writers of the time,[86] or on the leading historian of the police power, William Novak, who, looking closely at these developments, sees the development of a *salus populi* (people's welfare) sensibility in the rendering of the police power in the early period of its development in state and federal jurisprudence.[87] He labels this in a recent essay, "The American law of overruling necessity," and views its principal consequence for constitutional interpretation as "the idea that public right was always supreme, trumping private right."[88] Although we will interrogate in subsequent chapters this depiction of the power in the wider context of state constitutionalism and the promise of good governing, it captures crisply and compellingly the basic point that the police power was understood as a means of realizing wider social aims than the vindication of natural rights and compensating for specific harms.[89]

The shift from redressing wrongs, the classic tort law ideal, to embracing the social good was reflected in the phrase "Good order," a reference to the general welfare of the community, which was a common phrase in the early cases. In an 1835 case from Maine,[90] the court upheld severe restrictions on the construction of wood buildings, declaring that such a regulation "shall be needful to the good order of [the] body politic."[91]

The evolution of the police power toward a more public welfare-enhancing instrument of active governance is revealed well in the case most widely associated as the foundational state police power case, Commonwealth v. Alger.[92] As a preliminary aside, it is striking that Alger is viewed as the central case in the development of the police power given that it was decided in 1851, by which time the state courts had roughly thirty years of experience of deciding police power controversies, and had written literally dozens of decisions on this subject. Nonetheless, Alger is considered iconic for its bringing together of perhaps the greatest antebellum-era state court judge, Lemuel Shaw, with a classic dispute over the reach and scope of governmental power to limit private property.[93] Chief Justice Shaw writes an elaborate opinion excavating the purpose of the police power and in doing so constructs a framework that is at once powerfully supportive of the government's broad ambitions in this area, but frequently misunderstood, as we will see, in its depiction of the police power's true nature and provenance.

Alger involved a municipal ordinance that restricted the prerogative of the defendant Mr. Alger to build a wharf on his property. This wharf, according to the city of

Cambridge, interfered with navigation along the Charles River, an imposition properly redressable by the government in its decision to regulate the use of this owner's property. For the court, the question was essentially this: "Are the prohibitions contained in this statute consistent with every right embraced in the grant?"

At a higher level of generality, the court was confronted with the question of whether this law was within the scope of the city's discretion under the police power. The court thus had to decide on what basis the government can interfere with one's use or enjoyment of one's private property as a means of redressing of a distinct harm and violation of a duty. As to the matter of the appellant's property right, this was a somewhat unusual case. Critically, the fact that this is a matter involving property in a seabed and, further, involves navigation makes this an easier case for the government in its exercise of power.[94] "[W]hether this power," writes Shaw, "be traced to the right of property or right of sovereignty as its principal source, it must be regarded as held in trust for the best interest of the public, for commerce and navigation, and for all the legitimate and appropriate uses to which it may be made subservient."[95] Therefore, the government's power to regulate the property's use is not only capacious, it is obligatory.[96] It is part of the government's role in securing the navigation servitude, a public right that predates the advent of all the state constitutions and is sourced in English common law.[97]

What we remember, however, about *Alger* is not necessarily the holding, which was unremarkable, given the well-established navigation servitude, but what Chief Justice Shaw says more extravagantly about the nature and scope of the government's police power taken as a whole:

> This principle of legislation is of great importance and extensive use, and lies at the foundation of most enactments of positive law, which define and punish *mala prohibita*. Things done may or may not be wrong in themselves, or necessarily injurious and punishable as such at common law; but laws are passed declaring them offences, and making them punishable, because they tend to injurious consequences; but more especially for the sake of having a definite, known and authoritative rule which all can understand and obey. In the case already put, of erecting a powder magazine or slaughterhouse, it would be indictable at common law, and punishable as a nuisance, if in fact erected so near an inhabited village as to be actually dangerous or noxious to life or health. Without a positive law, every body might agree that two hundred feet would be too near, and that two thousand feet would not be too near; but within this wide margin, who shall say, who can know, what distance shall be too near or otherwise? An authoritative rule, carrying with it the character of certainty and precision, is needed.[98]

However certain or precise a particular ordinance or statute is, a duly authorized legislature can (and surely must) develop strategies to protect and promote the public interest through laws that are fashioned ex ante to confront social problems that may emerge ex post. This is an important shift from a conception of positive law as mostly an act of discovery, as embedded in notions of natural right,[99] to a view of legislation as confronting contemporary social conditions and the needs of a dynamic economy and society. This view would persist largely unabated from the antebellum period in which Alger was decided to the present.

Unfortunately, Alger is occasionally seen as auguring an idea of the police power as an outgrowth of the unlimited monarch, as an exemplar of a conception of governance that sees the police power as mostly tautological, as a restatement of the basic point that the legislature can undertake regulatory strategies for any reason it sees fit. At first glance, perhaps, Chief Justice Shaw's opinion seeks to hold two irreconcilable ideas in its hands at the same time, the idea that it is no more nor less than the full power of the sovereign and is an American iteration of the idea of the royal prerogative and the idea that it is grounded in American state constitutionalism. The conventional way that scholars square the circle is to read the opinion as the font of the basic idea that the police power cannot truly be defined; it is, as this view goes, a statement that the state government's power to regulate in the name of the general welfare is subject to no serious structural limits. And so it can be cabined only in two ways, either by the actions of the federal government under the edicts of the US Constitution or by invoking individual rights from either the national or the state constitutions.

This idea of the police power was reinforced memorably by Chief Justice Taney in The License Cases.[100] There he said:

> [W]hat are the police powers of a state? They are nothing more or less than the powers of government inherent in every sovereignty to the extent of its dominions. And whether a state passes a quarantine law, or a law to punish offenses, or to establish courts of justice, or requiring certain instruments to be recorded, or to regulate commerce within its own limits, in every case it exercises the same powers – that is to say, the power of sovereignty, the power to govern men and things within the limits of its dominion. It is by virtue of this power that it legislates, and its authority to make regulations of commerce is as absolute as its power to pass health laws except insofar as it has been restricted by the Constitution of the United States.[101]

In his book on the police power, Marcus Dubber dwells on the connection Shaw draws between the police power and the limitless executive power instantiated in British law. Although Shaw mentions the term "police" just once, Dubber emphasizes the dichotomy critical to Blackstone's formulation between police regulation and the protection of private right through "justice" (here quoting Ernst Freund, author of an influential early twentieth-century treatise on the police power).[102] Dubber sees in Shaw's Alger opinion the insistence that "[p]olice is an executive matter, as opposed to a legislative or judicial one" and, from that, obliterates the obligation of all exercises of governmental power to the state constitution whose design constructs not only official power, but the offices themselves.[103] Dubber collapses the constitutional subject into the royal prerogative, claiming, amazingly, that "there is nothing about the formulation of the police power in the Massachusetts constitution that is inconsistent with the derivation of the power from the king's prerogative."[104]

However, this can only be right if the police power is purely executive by nature or design and, further, if the exercise of executive power cannot be limited in any way by constitutional commands, whether through structure or rights. This cannot be right as a matter of ordinary constitutional construction, even in the 1850s, nor is there any evidence that Justice Shaw thought it so. The source of the power to abate public nuisances through a clear prohibition on wharf building as in this case may well be the *jus publicum*, an idea growing out of the royal prerogative and the government's obligation to look after the general welfare. Shaw articulates well the history of this obligation and its role in creating the navigation servitude (and, later, the public trust doctrine). But in the recounting of the origins of public trust, there is nothing that points to the notion that a necessary component of the executive's obligation is that this power be unlimited. Rather, constitutional government emerges in the American context precisely in order to separate government duty from unalloyed discretion. By mid-century, it simply was not a credible view of constitutionalism in America that the police power is a species of executive prerogative, a power whose "defining characteristic became its very undefinability."[105]

There is another flaw in this account. In minimizing the impact of state constitutions and ideas of constitutionalism emerging with a force in and after the revolutionary era, the view that Shaw's signal contribution was in looking backward to the pre-American sources of police and regulation, we not only risk reifying the increasingly anachronistic dichotomy between private and public law, but also begin to lose the thread of the continuity between common law and new notions of lawmaking. Nineteenth-century lawmakers and legal scholars, following in the footsteps of the revolutionary era constitutionalists, fashioned an approach to lawmaking that was principally prescriptive, not declarative, and was ambitious in creating new structures of public policymaking for society's emerging wicked problems. The common law was not abolished or abandoned, as Shaw and his contemporaries make clear, but nor was it to be maintained as the one true source of law. Blackstone's shadow loomed large in the Jacksonian and antebellum periods to be sure,[106] but not so large that it obscured the emerging approach to legislation characteristic of Americans in the post-framing period, an approach that would continue to be reshaped throughout the nineteenth and twentieth centuries. Ultimately, Shaw's description of the royal prerogative is best understood as a narrow, if shrewd, paean to the navigation servitude and the important notion that much land is imprinted with a public purpose, so sayeth the common law. Shaw noted the continuity of the idea of submerged land being part of the public's birthright and being an exemplar of the public rights that citizens had in ensuring that such land would be maintained to their benefit, even if it inconvenienced private property ideas.[107]

Shaw's brilliance in <u>Alger</u> is in weaving together myriad themes in the police power to come to the conclusion, and that is that our constitutional culture had come to understand by mid-century that public rights undergird "the release of energy" that Willard Hurst memorably wrote about in describing the pragmatic foundations of state power in that period.[108] At the same time, Shaw acknowledges with remarkable foresight that American constitutionalism requires limits, even judicially imposed ones, and even ones that would need to be crafted in concrete cases through a sort of constitutional common law.[109] Courts would come to shape these limits through their scrutiny of the legislation to ensure that it revealed a public purpose, and not an arbitrary assertion of power.[110]

Alger was not decided in an historical vacuum. By the time of the Massachusetts decision mid-century, state courts had grappled frequently with the question of the police power as a constitutionally grounded authority in government and also with the question of whether it was limited. In 1838, for example, the Chancery Court of New York struck down a law prohibiting the erection of a hay press, holding that, despite the breadth of the police power, "all by-laws must be reasonable."[111] Here the law was clearly unequal in its operation, privileging individuals who had already assembled these contraptions over those who had not yet done so. The concern with arbitrary laws – not just the arbitrary application of laws, something that would come to sound in procedural due process notions emerging later in the nineteenth and into the twentieth century – would persist during the entire history of the police power, from distant past to present, as we will explore in later chapters. For now, the essential point is that the power was not understood either in Alger or in the commentary at the time as a limitless executive power, sprouting directly from Blackstonian notions of policing and the prerogatives that were necessary to maintain the order of the household.

By the time of Alger, *sic utere* was fading as a foundational basis for the establishment and exercise of the police power.[112] While the police power was and would always be limited in its exercise, it was not restricted to the redressing of discrete and identifiable private harms.

We should recall the nexus between rights and social welfare, and the larger connection to the police power in the nineteenth century.[113] Rights were seen as relational from the very beginning of our Republic's existence and for a good while before. "A natural or legal right was not something to be exerted against society, but was intimately connected to the duties and moral obligations incumbent on social beings."[114] Rights and liberties were embedded in social obligations. This is not the same as saying that rights were always defeasible in the case of government regulation. We need to give context to social obligation. After all, we can turn that back around say that an essential social obligation was to protect the rights and liberties of citizens. Two things were true, or at least plausible: First, rights were relative and were connected strongly to public obligations; second, rights, including property rights, occasionally functioned as trumps, in order to limit the government's use of the power of the state to place reasonable constraints on liberty. Note that before there was a *salus populi* conception of the police power, there was the hoary concept of *sic utere*. Our common law, including our tort, contract, and property law, was critical in redressing wrongs to individuals, and we could conceptualize that as part of a project to protect one's liberty to be free from injury.

Early police powers cases occasionally capture in interesting ways this idea that the function of regulation under this power is to protect rights. In <u>Vanderbilt v. Ames</u>, the wharf tying case referred to earlier, the court focused on "protecting the rights of all concerned," going so far as to the say that this law is not only constitution but is "obligatory."[115] In an 1823 Massachusetts case in which the government had prohibited digging, therefore incurring the ire of a property owner, the court insisted that they were protecting the public's rights. A couple of decades later, the court upheld a law on the argument that the legislature was prohibiting "a use of property which would be injurious to the public." One might be tempted to refer to the *sic utere* idea that these (and other) cases were just about prohibiting public harms.[116] However, in invoking the language of rights, the courts were urging upon readers a larger idea, namely that there was an agenda at work in regulatory governance. Protecting the public meant not merely safeguarding individuals' valued personal and economic interests, but the protection of the public's rights, and these were rights to health, safety, and good morals. In short, the emerging use of the police power illustrated by Shaw's analysis in <u>Alger</u> and other nineteenth-century cases underwrote a view of what would later come to be called positive rights, an idea that previewed in no small measure what state constitutions would come to look like in the twentieth century.

A collection of state cases in the early nineteenth century and into the antebellum period brought together the *sic utere* and *salus populi* notions under a broader framework. The shift from one to the other was hardly a sharp one; after all, the common law remained dominant in this period, with state legislation, to say nothing of regulatory administration, often used in a more interstitial than comprehensive way. The expressed rationale in judicial cases upholding the use of the police toggled between these two conceptions, at least until well into the Progressive era. In this early police power framework, the regulatory power of government was seen principally as securing public rights through the responsible use of the police power. Later cases would focus more conspicuously on the matter of public purpose and the common good. In the nation's first century, the courts would look deeply at how the government implemented its obligations to protect citizen interests and rights, while also developing notions of public rights under the rubric of *jus publici* concepts.

One of the more interesting illustrations of the judiciary's focus on the matter of individual harm-creating conduct as the fulcrum of the power is a Vermont case from 1855, <u>Thorpe v. the Rutland & Burlington Railroad Co</u>.[117] The state legislature had enacted a statute requiring railroad companies to compensate cattle owners for all cattle killed whenever the company had failed to put up a cattle guard. The state's authority over railroads companies was established by the time of the decision, as the Supreme Court had held in the <u>Dartmouth College</u> case that states had plenary power over corporations, power subject to the usual limits of state constitutions.[118] (Recall that federal constitutional rights were not enforceable against the states at that time.)[119] However, this case did not answer the question of the state's particular obligation under its police power. As to this, Justice Redfeld notes that breadth of the power to protect harm and do social good: "This police power of the state extends to the protection of the lives, limbs, health, comfort, and quiet of all persons, and the protection of all property within the state."[120] The regulation of the railroads in this instance, which requires cattle guards and obliges the company to compensate cattle owners if they do not put up guards, is grounded in two elements of the police power: First, "the police of the roads," well suited of course to the conduct of the railroads; and, second, the general police power, by which Redfeld says, extravagantly, "persons and property are subjected to all kinds of restraints and burdens, in order to secure the general comfort, health, and prosperity of the state, of the perfect right, in the legislature to do which no question ever was, or, upon acknowledged general principles, ever can be made, so far as natural persons are concerned."[121] Just as this law brings together the matter of compensating for harm-causing conduct with prospective regulation, the formulation of the power in <u>Thorpe</u> and many other cases of this era highlights the police power's concern with both *sic utere* and *salus populi* principles.

The nature of what a public harm entailed or, better yet, a kind of social problem that required governmental intervention, evolved over the first century of the American law and thus so did the contents of the police power. In this subsection, we have explored the critical ways in which the police power undergirded an evolving vision of energetic government, one that was increasingly decoupled from an antediluvian conception of public law as a mere implementation mechanism for private law ideas of harm reduction and righting wrongs. But, in doing so, they connected their objectives to a plausible model of constitutional rights, one that emphasized democracy and the public good over autonomy and private interest.

INFRASTRUCTURE AND PUBLIC WORKS

By the time the country had reached the age of a quarter century, pressures built on the state governments to make important improvements in their infrastructure.[122] As William Novak writes with regard to public rights in roads, rivers, ports, & squares, "Today public powers and rights in such locales seem self-evident. But the outcome of nineteenth-century policy was more in dispute. There was, after all, nothing inherently public about a highway or riverway."[123] Progress in the new nation requires considerable energy and initiative in matters of infrastructure and public works. [Therefore,] "[ro]ads, rivers, and ports were singled out early as territory for the extension and elaboration of state powers of police."[124]

These projects were tied not only to the welfare of the states as states, but also to the larger goal of facilitating commerce and transportation among the states. Madison foresaw this imperative when he wrote in Federalist No. 14:

> [T]he intercourse throughout the Union will be facilitated by new improvements. Roads will everywhere be shortened, and kept in better order; accommodations

for travelers will be multiplied and meliorated; an interior navigation on our eastern side will be opened throughout, or nearly throughout, the whole extent of the thirteen States. The communication between the Western and Atlantic districts, and between different parts of each, will be rendered more and more easy by those numerous canals with which the beneficence of nature has intersected our country, and which part finds it so little difficult to connect and complete."[125]

The building of the Erie Canals and Ohio, as Harry Scheiber has taught us, was a central part of the strategy of ambitious steps to address infrastructure deficiencies and to expand practically the reach and scope of their economy at a time when such expansion was essential to realizing the citizens' objectives.[126] Other great infrastructure projects followed. However, it is not only the building of public works that was extraordinary; also remarkable was how the law accommodated the choices of legislators and administrators to undertake this big and medium-size projects when to do so was to impact, and in some cases recreate, extant property and contract rights.[127]

The literature on this period in a way begins in the middle of the story, emphasizing the continuity between an ambitious conception of public authority and a welcoming of energetic governance and the confirmation of public power to do what is necessary to advance the well-being of a rapidly industrializing society. Some scholars view this as more or less inevitable, given the imperatives of the times, while some of the critical history views with skepticism the motivations of courts and legislatures and sees these developments in what are ultimately deterministic accounts.[128] Both of those views are illuminating, but they do not begin early enough in the story to help us see the tensions and the consequences.

Governmental strategy to create and implement these projects took place in the shadow of important property rights claims. We need not necessarily call these rights "vested," so as to follow the tradition that would lead to a hypercritical view of the wisdom and ultimately the constitutionality of state and local regulation.[129] But we can at least note that there were established private rights, coming from contract and property law, that were to be protected and could not be interfered without an adequate basis. Indeed, it would be impossible to make any sense of the inclusion of a contract clause and an eminent domain clause in the US Constitution, as well as the inclusion of specific rights provisions dealing with contract and property, if we did not see the framers of these documents as concerned with the basic integrity of liberty and property.[130]

Robust regulatory powers, including police, taxation, and eminent domain powers, emerged out of a need to address these individual rights and to entrust to legislatures, under limits, the discretion to make decisions that would enhance the public interest, even though it inconvenienced individuals or businesses.[131] In a leading case involving the construction of the Contract Clause where a private corporation complained that Massachusetts had extinguished their rights by providing for a new public bridge, the Court remarked that "[t]he object and the end of all Government is to promote the happiness and prosperity of the community by which it is established, and it can never be assumed that the Government intended to diminish its power of accomplishing the end for which it was created."[132] This strong declaration of the states' power and prerogatives to make infrastructure choices in what they viewed as the public interest was especially important, coming as it did in an era in which states were building and improving with extraordinary energy and resolve.[133] Both the Supreme Court and the state courts were to give a very broad construction to state power and almost no cotton to individual complaints. At the state level, the choice was generally made in favor of state authority.

As public authorities displaced the interests of private property owners and occasionally entire communities in order to accomplish public work projects, courts acknowledged that these choices reflected tradeoffs that represented very bad news for those displaced. Eminent domain would later provide one form of redress in circumstances in which property was taken, but where the impact was destruction not confiscation, property owners would be compelled to endure sacrifice. As a Pittsburgh court wrote in a case involving the cutting down of a valuable tree on church property:

> The constitutional provision for the case of private property *taken* for public use, extends not to the case of property *injured* or *destroyed*; but it follows not that the omission may not be supplied by ordinary legislation. No property was taken in this instance; but the cutting down of the street consequent on the reduction of its grade, left the building useless, and the ground on which it stood worth no more than the expense of sinking the surface of it to the common level. The loss to the congregation is a total one, while the gain to holders of property in the neighborhood, is immense. The legislature that incorporated the city, never dreamt that it was laying the foundation of such injustice; but, as the charter stands, it is unavoidable.[134]

Many of the expressed rationales for sacrificing individual and community interests to government goals, and indeed the reasoning in these cases more generally, were thin and largely unilluminating; they did not furnish anything helpful in understanding where the limits to such governmental choice lie. The frequent references to eminent domain, as we will discuss in more detail in the next chapter, provided guidance with respect to the category of intrusion – taking versus regulation that destroyed or substantially reduced value – but this would not be helpful in shaping any limits on governmental action in this latter category until the Court developed a regulatory takings doctrine.[135] What could be gleaned from these cases at most was an articulation of the increasingly accepted view that choices undertaken to regulate the use of private property must be understood as part of the larger context of government progress and the imperative that state and local governments have ample discretion to make policy choices, especially given the important infrastructure needs of this rapidly growing nation.

What is especially interesting about infrastructure as a category of public policy here in the nineteenth century is that these decisions were not about addressing distinct public harms, but were about improvements. They were progressive in the literal sense that they were fundamentally about progress. Moreover, the government, in the pursuit of these bold initiatives required of its citizens sacrifice: sacrifice in the form of both economic contribution (taxes) and restricting the use of private property for the public good. In all, the government asked the citizenry to adjust their expectations about the nature of property and the dominion of ownership, and in ways that were vital in providing governments with the versatility to carry out essential infrastructure projects and programs.

NEW NOTIONS OF LEGISLATING

There is a key point underlying the early police power cases, one that might be considered more prosaic than the vision reflected in Shaw's famous opinion in <u>Alger</u>. It is that the state's interest in acting to protect health, safety, and welfare emerged from a distinctive view of the nature and role of state government in implementing public policy through legislation and other forms of regulation. In the nineteenth century lawmakers were working through these new schemes of legislating and the police power helped support a vision of public power that was ambitious, proactive, and centered on improving public welfare.

The police power was shaped in the first decades of the American republic by the evolving character of legislative lawmaking. In the early years of the republic, public officials thought of legislating in ways different than today. In early America, the legislature was seen as an organ acting alongside the courts in developing a common law, one connected to principles of natural law. "Natural law," legal historian Stuart Banner writes, "formed a backdrop against which the legislation was enacted, a set of background principles from which the legislature was presumed not to wish to deviate."[36] Statutory lawmaking was seen as essentially declaratory, much like the constitutional provisions from which the legislature derived its power.[37] It would take many years, and serious shifts in the understanding of the nature of legislating as a form of distinct positive law, for the American legal system to see regulation and legislation for what it was: the product of specific policy choices made by public officials.

As to whether this declaratory view of lawmaking was tied inextricably to natural law concepts and therefore all the legislature was tasked to do was to discover what the law of nature commanded or was nested in a more complex and multifaceted view of the connection between legislation and the common law, remains uncertain. This was the fulcrum of the famous debate between William Blackstone and Jeremy Bentham.[38] So far as the police power is concerned, the question is interesting, but is not ultimately fundamental. After all, the choices of how best to protect the general welfare could emerge from many different views of what good public policy demanded. The common good could be, and many citizens and officials at the time thought it *should* be, embedded in natural law. This would not make any special difference in the efficacy or the authority of the legislation; rather, this was a matter of determining where courts looked to determine whether the constitution authorized governmental action in the first instance. To be sure, a key questioned loomed as to whether the constitution was fundamental law or else was binding only insofar as it was consistent with natural law precepts.[139] However, by the time that police power controversies came before the state and federal courts, it had long been resolved that the question of power and of rights would be centered by state constitutional analysis and not by natural rights thinking or, in Holmes's reference to the common law, "the brooding omnipresence in the sky."[140]

Still unsettled in the late eighteenth and early nineteenth centuries was the question of what kind of lawmaking was best designed to protect health and safety. And, more generally, what was the purpose of lawmaking by legislatures as the functions and objectives of state government were just beginning to take shape in the early decades of this new republic? From one perspective, the legislature should undertake initiatives through legislation to implement policy that advanced the cause of social welfare and the public interest. Legislation was the manifestation of the lawmakers' goal of good governing. From another perspective, however, the legislature should be concerned principally with methods to address particular or general harms. Legislation was a form of positive law to be sure, but as a species of public law that exists in parallel with the common law, is basically intended to recognize and redress individual wrongs. Just as the state's criminal law exists side by side with tort law as complementary mechanisms to address and punish wrongs, the act of legislating is an act of redressing wrong.

This view of legislating goes along with the *sic utere* principle. Legislating to protect the public health and safety can be seen as essentially declaratory of specific harms or wrongs that have been committed by, say, property owners and, in its declaration, embody the proactive effort to stop these harms before they occur. This perspective gives the power an anchor to the *sic utere* principle. Likewise, it effectively narrows the scope of its coverage.

Where notions of lawmaking start to shift later in the century, so too does the framework of the police power. The classic debate between William Blackstone and Jeremy Bentham played out principally in the context of British political thought. However, the themes in this contest illuminated emerging American notions of lawmaking in the federal state context. Under classic views of the law, judges were oracles whose comparative advantage was in discovering legal principles and applying them to concrete cases. The province of legislation remained to be determined as the contours of the police power were likewise being constructed through statutes and judicial decisions. We should see these developments as in a parallel orbit.[141]

JUDICIAL REVIEW, INDIVIDUAL RIGHTS, AND THE SUPREME COURT

The police power in the nation's first century was embodied in a vision of active governance, an idea of legislatures acting on behalf of the *salus populi*, and the cases in the state court cases in the antebellum period and continuing through the Civil War and in its aftermath reflected this commitment to progressive public policy. The challenge was to configure appropriate limits to the exercise of these powers. State courts met those challenges through mainly close interrogations of the rationale for the exercise of these powers, looking also to the security of individual liberties and private property rights protected through the common law and through the state constitutions. Judicial review was well established in the states, and so a close review of the many state cases involving the police power in the period from the enactment of the original constitutions through the antebellum period indicates that state courts were reasonably comfortable with examining state actions to assess whether they were consistent with the fundamental law of the state. That said, the methods of judicial review shifted over this period. Early cases looked like explorations typical of common law reasoning. As the century continued, courts took more seriously the ideas that it was a constitution they were interpreting, and adjusted their approaches to judicial review accordingly.[142]

Individual rights played a limited role in the period before Reconstruction. In Barron v. Baltimore, the Supreme Court held that the bill of rights did not apply to the states.[143] To a significant degree, this made the matter of judicial review simpler in practice, as neither federal or state courts would be troubled to consider whether the exercise of the state's police power trampled on the rights delineated in the Bill of Rights.[144] Despite Barron, the Court did have occasions to consider constitutional matters involving the exercise of state regulatory power and possible constitutional limits on this power. In Calder v. Bull,[145] decided a half decade before Marbury v. Madison and so before the Court's foundational judicial review decision, the Court's justices engaged in an interesting discussion in dicta about whether or not a state law could be rendered nugatory because it conflicts with the constitutional authority of the state to act. Chief Justice Chase offers the example of "a law that takes property from A. and gives it to B," insisting that "It is against all reason and justice for a people to entrust a legislature with such powers, and therefore it cannot be presumed that it has done it. The genius, the nature, and the spirit of our state governments amount to a prohibition of such acts of legislation, and the general principles of law and reason forbid them."[146] In Fletcher v. Peck,[147] the Court read the Contract Clause of the Constitution to limit the ability of a state to redefine contractual obligations so as to escape what would have been a breach under the standards set at the time. This rule would effectively shape the police power in a small, but not inconsequential fashion, in that it created a limit on the state's prerogative to define contract rights in a way that obviated any guardrail on state power. The full-throated notion of vested rights and its impact on the police power would come to the fore later in the century, but Fletcher did indeed preview the idea that contract and property rights were insured by the Constitution against destruction. It "began a long line of cases in which the Court used the Contracts Clause to prevent stage legislatures from interfering with 'vested' property rights."[148] It would be much later before the eminent domain power would be read in a similar fashion to constrict the maneuvering room of the state.

In Charles River Bridge v. Proprietors of Warren Bridge,[149] the Court upheld a Massachusetts decision to grant a second franchise to build a bridge over the river, despite a contractual agreement with the corporation operating the Charles River bridge that their franchise would be exclusive. Chief Justice Roger Taney, writing for all but one of the justices, described how the property rights of the incumbent bridge builder were subject to modification as an ordinary part of the evolution of such rights. "While the rights of private property are sacredly guarded," he wrote, "we must not forget that the people also have rights, and that the happiness and well-being of every citizen depends on their faithful preservation."[150] This broad paean to the *salus populi* notion of the police power would be echoed by Taney in his opinion in The License Cases referred to above.[151] In that case upholding a restriction on who may be a liquor distributor in the state, Taney wrote:

> But what are the police powers of a state? They are nothing more or less than the powers of government inherent in every sovereignty to the extent of its dominions. And whether a state passes a quarantine law, or a law to punish offenses, or to establish courts of justice, or requiring certain instruments to be recorded, or to regulate commerce within its own limits, in every case it exercises the same powers – that is to say, the power of sovereignty, the power to govern men and things within the limits of its dominion. It is by virtue of this power that it legislates, and its authority to make regulations of commerce is as absolute as its power to pass health laws except insofar as it has been restricted by the Constitution of the United States.[152]

The enactment of the Fourteenth Amendment signaled a new era in the Constitution's development as a check on official action, or at least that was the basic idea.[153] It would seem that individuals would now enjoy the privileges or immunities of citizenship and this would presumably include the equal protection and due process of law. However, the Court's decision in The Slaughterhouse Cases[154] reduced significantly the role of the Constitution in limiting state action under the police power. Here the Court declined to hold against Louisiana's butcher monopoly, essentially rejecting in whole cloth the normative arguments propounded over hundreds of pages by Thomas Cooley just a few years earlier. Justice Miller addressed the issue of whether and to what extent the privileges or immunities of citizens clause of the newly enacted Fourteenth Amendment provides a meaningful constraint on the exercise of the police power, writing that citizens within the states "must rest for their security and protection where they have heretofore rested," and therefore the Fourteenth Amendment adds nothing by way of new protections.[155] This basic approach to understanding the Fourteenth Amendment, including not only privileges or immunities, but also due process – what one scholar labelled a "minimalist interpretation,"[156] under the Fourteenth Amendment – approach would go unmodified throughout the remainder of Reconstruction and thereafter. Indeed, not until the next century would the federal courts look to notions of due process as an independent constraint on the exercise of the police power.[157]

The main focus of scholars who have written about the *Slaughter-House Cases* has been on what the Court did not do, with respect especially to the privileges or immunities clause of the Fourteenth Amendment, and also with the equal protection and due process clauses. However, what the Court did do was to reinforce "the enduring power of the antebellum map of federal and state powers, with its emphasis on the primacy of states to define and to limit the civil rights of their citizens."[158] This meant that the onus remained on state constitutions to define and, through judicial review, implement constraints on the exercise of the police power, whether through state-level due process protections or other mechanisms.

Questions nonetheless persisted during the Reconstruction period over how the US Constitution limited the states' use of the police power. Some of these issues grew out of the felt urgency, in Southern states and elsewhere, to enact measures to limit the rights of freedmen. This effort would culminate in Plessy v. Ferguson,[159] considered more fully in the next chapter, and would be echoed in other federal, and some state, cases. The more global question concerned whether and to what extent certain regulatory measures that impacted the prerogatives of businesses and their use of their property would be limited by the Constitution.

The principal decision during this era was Munn v. Illinois, decided by the Supreme Court in 1877.[160] Munn gave the Court the opportunity to examine the so-called Granger laws, and specifically the constitutionality of maximum rates for grain warehouses and elevators. With the Fourteenth Amendment establishing the rights to equal protection and due process of the laws, an establishment that the Court had narrowly limited four years earlier in the Slaughter-house Cases, and also in other key cases involving civil rights at or around that same time, the Court in Munn was not writing on a blank slate. On the contrary, this was an occasion to revisit in a controversial policy setting the question of whether and to what extent a state's regulatory powers over business conduct would be newly limited by this major constitutional amendment.

Chief Justice Waite, writing for the Court, acknowledged early in his opinion the broad reach of the police power, noting that "the government regulates the conduct of its citizens one towards another, and the manner in which each shall use his own property, when such regulation becomes necessary for the public good,"[161] and as to the history of constitutional limitations on such powers, Waite observed that "statutes are to be found in many of the States upon some or all these subjects; and we think it has never yet been successfully contended that such legislation came within any of the constitutional prohibitions against interference with private property."[162] Having dispensed rather quickly with the claim that the Fourteenth Amendment's guarantees of equal protection and due process limit the police power, the Court returns to the familiar issue of whether the state has properly acted within the scope of its police power. Here the Court repairs to classic common law notions of public property, invoking Lord Chief Justice Hale in his seventeenth-century treatise, *De*

Mortibus Maris.[163] For businesses whose private property is "affected with a public interest," the power – and indeed the obligation – exists in the legislature to create all regulations appropriate to safeguard the public's interest by restricting the owner's use over such property.

The "affected with a public interest" rationale has been much maligned, with Oliver Wendell Holmes calling it "little more than a fiction" and Felix Frankfurter "an empty formula,"[164] but the ultimate rationale, as Harry Scheiber has explained at length,[165] is unremarkable once you see the connection drawn by Chief Justice Waite to notions of public rights well entrenched in English common law and described by no less than authority than Lord Hale.[166] Moreover, the secret sauce in <u>Munn</u> is not only this framing of the property as public rather than private, but in its exploration of the economic conditions in this industry, conditions that protected, said the Court, <u>Munn</u>'s monopoly over grain warehouses and elevators in this region of the country. The Court explained that the legislature was owed enormous deference in enacting regulations designed to limit the ability of this company to take advantage of their monopoly rents.[167] An important fact in <u>Munn</u> is that Illinois had, just seven years earlier, specifically amended its constitution "to make it the duty of the general assembly to pass laws for the protection of producers, shippers, and receivers of grain and produce"[168] and to carry out further actions to tackle this monopoly situation. For this reason, the legislature would enjoy enormous discretion. Notwithstanding the risk that the legislature would abuse this discretion, the Court concludes that on the equal protection and due process matters, for "protection against abuses by legislatures, the people must resort to the polls, not to the courts."[169]

<u>Munn</u> makes clear that the wide berth states enjoy in enacting police power regulations is largely undisturbed by the enactment of the Fourteenth Amendment. We should say "largely" and not "totally" because neither this case nor other cases decided in the federal courts in the first years after the enactment of this amendment declare that state regulations enjoy some sort of constitutional safe harbor by virtue of the fact that they are enacted under the police power. The skepticism about the states' invocation of the police power to restrict private property rights would be expressed loudly by Justice Cooley in his treatise,[170] and by other commentators. Moreover, we would see the emergence a quarter century later of a vigorous doctrinal adventure by the Court to restrict significantly the scope and reach of state government under its police powers. And so <u>Munn</u>'s blow to the emerging constitutional protections of individual liberty and private property augured by the Fourteenth Amendment was an important one, but it was hardly the last word.

THE POLICE POWER AT THE END OF RECONSTRUCTION

The combination of Supreme Court jurisprudence with regard to state police power and individual rights and the voluminous body of state court cases decided by the time that our republic came close to its hundredth birthday revealed a police power that was broad in scope, decoupled from a narrow objective of redressing private harms, and responsive to key considerations involving our rapidly growing and changing economy. The power, like state constitutions generally, was ambitious and progressive. At the same time, skepticism about governmental motives and strategies persisted. Such skepticism was famously animate during the Jacksonian period, and various reforms to the system, including important constitutional reforms, were illustrative of these democratic, and even anti-legislative, impulses.[171] While the Jacksonian period morphed into the antebellum period which ended in conflict, dissolution, and a terrible civil war, there were continuing controversies over the proper scope of state regulation, both in its agendas and in its impact on civil liberties and especially private property rights. As courts dealt with these controversies, the awesome police power of the states was reinforced and, where necessary, redeemed.

Concern with the extent to which the police power was undermining individual rights would become most prominent in the early twentieth century, as the Supreme Court began to intervene with a vengeance in controversies involving the police power and contract and property rights. But this concern existed long before this movement and we should account for the difficult position that the courts were in the antebellum period and throughout the Civil War and Reconstruction. Two important considerations motivated these concerns. One was the persistence of natural law and natural rights as an influence on judicial thinking in constitutional adjudication. "Natural law," notes Stuart Banner, "loomed large in discussions of property. Lawyers often spoke of 'property as a natural right – as a right derived from the law of nature.'"[172] Such thinking proved remarkably resilient throughout the nineteenth century, and, even after the Reconstruction era legislative debates and the enactment of the Reconstruction amendments, natural law reasoning could commonly be seen in cases involving property and liberty rights.

These modes of reasoning created obstacles to a more progressive approach to regulating, where such regulation implicated established rights, established not only through positive law (which, would have rendered them more amenable to change with legislative action) but through natural law refracted through the lens of classical legal thinking.[173]

Another important consideration was the growing skepticism about legislatures and legislative lawmaking. This skepticism began, early after the framing period and caught fire during the Jacksonian era. Legislatures were viewed as feckless and even corrupt. The critique came from distinct directions. For progressives, state legislatures frequently acted in ways that reflected preference for certain factions or castes. The critique that the public interest was often subordinated to private interest continued to have resonance through much of the nineteenth century. Indeed, state constitutions were reformed in important ways during the Progressive era, most notably to restructure legislative power by narrowing its latitude to act. Legislative skeptics were not content, however, with these structural reforms. They insisted as well on judicial intervention to implement significant checks on the legislature.

From a very different perspective came the state governments of the old South, led by officials who, as Reconstruction proceeded and as Southern states were readmitted to the Union with their new constitutions, worried with good reason that Congress would encourage the states' use of the police power and would fashion new civil rights in order to impose desegregation, equality safeguards, and other unwelcome restrictions on their way of life. To be sure, the Court's Plessy decision would ultimately give them reassurance on that score, but that case wouldn't come until nearly the end of the century. So there would be a quarter century between Munn and Plessy in which White Southerners fretted about the prospects that the police power would facilitate radical change.

Finally, the many individuals and small businesses whose property was at risk from government regulation – remembering that at this time eminent domain was not yet much of a bulwark against property regulation – were skeptical about the legislatures' commitment to protecting their property and liberty. Even those who could and would concede that property rights needed to be balanced against social need had concerns that state legislators determined to make their mark as agents of major change in urbanizing communities and in states reeling from economic disruptions, such as the panics of 1873 and 1893, would not strike the right balance. Legislatures acting in the shadow of their constitutional frameworks had a rational fear of government intrusion.

Like so many other aspects of American public law and governance strategies in the initial decades of the republic, judges, legislators, and executive officials engaged in experiments. The problems identified above, the principal one being how to balance a broad police power with individual rights, began to be solved in two distinct ways. First, courts, and especially state courts, developed new approaches to deciding cases, relocating private property rights in a wider social mission. The objective was not to diminish them, but to configure them as part of the common good, with a social purpose. Novak summarizes the earlier cases as having "laid the groundwork for a wider assertion of state power throughout the society and economy."[74] This wider assertion reflected not only a mechanical broadening of power, but "new, creative, and perfectionist (as opposed to old, negative, and preservationist) dimensions of the well-regulated society."[75]

Second, states amended their constitutions (or, in the case of the later-admitted states, deliberately drafted their constitutions) to create new structural rules and arrangements to channel governmental power in a way that they viewed as sensible for this era. They imposed significant checks on legislation action through balanced budget requirements and debt limits. They empowered governors and also municipalities, in order to counteract legislative hegemony. These reforms did not do so much to weaken the regulatory power of state governments as to disperse power through these imaginative checks and balances.

A third aspect of the courts' approach to the police power as viewed from the vantage point of Reconstruction's end is worth noting as we look in subsequent chapters. This is the development and evolution of the notion of public property rights, the correlative idea of public purpose, and the burden of showing that the regulation is reasonable. These doctrines reflected a sort of alchemy of good governing, available to courts of the time to examine with an accommodating eye the use of broad and bold governmental power to implement social policies even where private rights would be compromised.

Finally, we should note as one of the central features of the police power during our first century that it was part of the legal underpinnings of a vast deployment of regulatory actions and activity. It is one thing to point to a constitutional authority to act boldly. It is another to describe the many ways in which state and local governments put this authority to work in decisions to protect health and safety through creative regulatory strategies and to facilitate the common good through targeted and general strategies. The progressive era of the late nineteenth century is generally associated with expansive governance and regulatory ingenuity, as also is the New Deal. However, we should not neglect the widespread and sustained use of the police power at the state level during the decades prior to the Progressive era. The result of these efforts was a tangible increase in various health and safety measures, increased regulations of public morals, and extraordinary progress on matters of infrastructure. New predicaments emerged as governments tackled long-simmering problems. But the ledger of regulatory activity reveals an active government pursuing pragmatic goals, availing themselves of the opportunities that the police power provided, and doing so as part of the omnibus project of constitutional governance.

NOTES

1. See Gary Gerstle, *Liberty and Coercion: The Paradox of American Government* 61 (2015) ("Police power allowed state governments to engage in extensive regulation of the economy, society, and morality"). See also Max M. Edling, *Perfecting the Union: National and State Authority in the U.S. Constitution* 89 (2021) ("[I]nformed Americans ... used the term police to designate a range of government activities intended to create a specific socioeconomic outcome: the rational, well-ordered, and opulent society"); Christopher L. Tomlins, *Law, Labor, and Ideology in the Early American Republic* 56 (1993) ("'internal police' appears [to the framers] to comprehend governmental power to regulate in the pursuit of peace, order, and justice in the community ... and the constitutional structures through which the concerns of the community gained articulation and were translated into action").
2. See generally Robert C. Palmer, "Liberties as Constitutional Provisions 1776–1791," in *Liberty and Community: Constitutional Rights in the Early American Republic* 61 (William E. Nelson & Robert C. Palmer eds., 1987).
3. On democratic constitutionalism, see Larry D. Kramer, *The People Themselves: Popular Constitutionalism and Judicial Review* (2004); Mark Tushnet, *Taking the Constitution Away from the Courts* (1999); Robert C. Post & Reva B. Siegel, "Democratic Constitutionalism," in *The Constitution in 2020* 25 (J. Balkin & R. Siegel eds., 2009).
4. See, e.g., William J. Novak, *The People's Welfare: Law and Regulation in Nineteenth-Century America* 6 (2000) ("Changes in the meaning of liberalism in American history

are much more complicated and compelling than the one-dimensional tale of a shift from negative to positive definitions of liberty and freedom").
5. See generally James W. Ely, Jr., *Guardian of Every Other Right: A Constitutional History of Property Rights* (3rd ed. 2007).
6. See generally Michael Kent Curtis, *No State Shall Abridge: The Fourteenth Amendment and the Bill of Rights* (1986).
7. G. Edward White, *Law in American History, Volume 1: From the Colonial Years through the Civil War* 187 (2012).
8. See Donald Lutz, *Popular Consent and Popular Control: Whig Political Theory in the Early State Constitutions* 17–19 (1980).
9. Colonialist Benjamin Austin would write "[i]t has become absolutely necessary, that the 'majority of persons' should be cautioned against acquiescing in the sentiment of placing implicit confidence in their Representatives." Quoted in Gordon S. Wood, *The Creation of the American Republic, 1776–1787* 257 (1998).
10. See generally Gerstle, *Liberty and Coercion*, at 21 ("The Constitution established a federal system in which a great deal of authority was left to the states").
11. See Daniel B. Rodriguez, "The Inscrutable (But Irrepressible) State Police Power," NYU J. L. & Liberty 662 (2015).
12. "More than the central government, state governments were thought of as embodiments of the people, and from this it followed that the people would not ordinarily require protection against themselves." Gerstle, *Liberty and Coercion*, at 67.
13. Markus Dirk Dubber, *The Police Power: Patriarchy and the Foundations of American Government* 47–62 (2005). See also William J. Novak, "The American Law of Overruling Necessity: The Exceptional Origins of State Police Power," in *States of Exception in American History* 109–10 (G. Gerstle & J. Isaac eds., 2020). Novak's observation that "[t]he American police power flows directly from these early legal conceptions of overruling necessity," with particular reference to Blackstone, is somewhat in tension with his analysis of the police power's origin in his The People's Welfare. While noting there "the substantive roots of state regulatory power in early modern notions of police or Polizei," Novak observes, rightly in my view, that "police power has little do with our modern notion of a municipal police force. the triumph of this particular legal terminology was part of a late nineteenth-century effort to reign in, constitutionalize, and centralize the disparate powers of states and localities." Ibid., at 13.
14. William Blackstone, 1 *Commentaries on the Laws of England*, at 64.
15. See Emerich de Vattel, *Le droit des gens. Ou principes de la loi naturelle*, 1740–1750, reprinted in *The Classics of International Law* (J. Brown Scott ed., 1916).
16. Adam Smith, *Lectures on Jurisprudence* 5 (R. Meek et al. eds., 1978 (1896)).
17. See 3 Aristotle, *Politics* 1280B 10–11 (T. J. Sanders ed. 1981). See generally Santiago Legarre, "The Historical Background of the Police Power," 9 J. Con. Law. 745 (2007).
18. See Legarre, "Historical Background," at 764.
19. See Albert Alschuler, "Rediscovering Blackstone," 145 U. Penn. L. Rev. 1 (1996); Dennis Nolan, "Sir William Blackstone and the American Republic: A Study of Intellectual Impact," 51 NYU L. Rev. 731 (1976).
20. Wood, *Creation*, at 56.
21. Harry Scheiber, "The Police Power," in 4 *Ency. of American Constitution* 1744 (Leonard Levy et al eds., 1986).
22. See, e. g. Calvin C. Jillson, *Constitution-Making: Conflict and Consensus in the Federal Convention of 1787* (1988); Charles Beard, *An Economic Interpretation of the Constitution* (1913).

23. John Fabian Witt, *American Contagion: Epidemics and the Law from Smallpox to Covid 19* (2020).
24. The Federalist No. 10. Not to mention a legion of pre-revolutionary thinkers going back at least to Hobbes. On the connection between Hobbes view of politics and the framers, see Gary L. McDowell, "Private Conscience & Public Order: Hobbes and 'the Federalist'," 25 *Polity* 421 (1993).
25. It is hard to know exactly what to make of legal historian Ted White's observation that "the ideas of liberty and property were not central concerns to the framers of the Constitution; they served more as background ideas that helped underscore the vital importance of sovereignty issue." White, *Law in American History, Volume 1*. This is an oversimplification of a more complex history. See, e.g., Jennifer Nedelsky, *Private Property and the Limits of American Constitutionalism: The Madisonian Framework and its Legacy* (1989).
26. See Forest McDonald, *States' Rights and the Union: Imperium in Imperio, 1776–1876* (2000).
27. See generally Edling, *Perfecting the Union*, at 35–74.
28. Gerstle, *Liberty and Coercion*, at 61.
29. See, e.g., Gordon Wood, *The Radicalism of the American Revolution* (1991). See also J. G. A. Pocock, *The Machiavellian Moment: Florentine Political Thought and the Atlantic Republican Tradition* (1973). See also Robert Shallope, "Toward a Republican Synthesis: The Emergence of a Understanding of Republicanism in American Historiography," 29 *Wm. & Mary Q.* 49 (1972).
30. Gerstle, *Liberty and Coercion*, at 61.
31. Ibid., at 81.
32. See Jack Rakove, *Original Meanings: Politics and Ideas in the Making of the U.S. Constitution* 161–202 (1996).
33. On originalism, see, e.g., Lawrence B. Solum, "Originalism and Constitutional Construction," 82 *Fordham L. Rev.* 453, 510 (2013).
34. "Original public meaning asserts that the meaning sought is that revealed by the text as reasonably understood by a well-informed reader at the time of the provision's enactment." John O. McGinnis & Michael Rappaport, "Unifying Original Intent and Original Public Meaning," 113 *Northw. U. L. Rev.* 1371 (2019). See also See, e.g., Randy E. Barnett, *Restoring the Lost Constitution: The Presumption of Liberty* 92 (Updated ed. 2014) ("'[O]riginal [public] meaning' originalism seeks the public or objective meaning that a reasonable listener would place on the words used in the constitutional provision at the time of its enactment.").
35. For an originalist explanation of the police power, see Randy Barnett, "The Proper Scope of the Police Power," 79 *Notre Dame L. Rev.* 429 (2004). See also Barnett, *Restoring the Lost Constitution*, at 322–37. Barnett looks at the original meaning of the Ninth Amendment and the Fourteenth Amendment, both constructed in the shadow of a strong devotion to natural rights, and suggests that the framers of these two amendments, separated of course by several generations in time, intended to limit the exercise of the police power through the inclusion of due process, equal protection, and privileges or immunities. What remains missing in this well analyzed originalist account is what exactly the framers of both the US constitution and the various state constitutions intended to achieve by giving state legislatures such broad powers to regulate health, safety, and welfare in the first instance. Focusing on the origins of the limits without accounting for the wide expanse of regulatory power leaves the analysis, taken on its own originalist terms, out of balance.
36. See Gerstle, *Liberty and Coercion*.
37. See generally Robert Cooter, *The Strategic Constitution* 103–25 (2000); William H. Riker, *Federalism: Origin, Operation, Significance* (1964).

38. See generally David Epstein, *The Political Theory of the Federalist* (1984).
39. Federalist No. 51.
40. See Kanol Direnc, "Interest Groups and Lobbying in Political Executives," in *The Oxford Handbook of Political Executive* 608 (2020).
41. See McDonald, *States' Rights and the Union*, at 1–25 (2000) (describing the problem of divided sovereignty and the framers' solution).
42. On Schmitt, see Michael Head, *Emergency Power in Theory and Practice: The Long Shadow of Carl Schmitt* (2016).
43. See generally Edling, *Perfecting the Union*.
44. See Rakove, *Original Meanings*, at 161–202. See also <u>McCulloch v. Maryland</u>, 17 U.S. 316 (1819).
45. U.S. Const. Art. I, Sec. 8.
46. See Christopher Tomlins, "To Improve the State and Condition of Man: The Power to Police and the History of American Governance," 53 *Buffalo L. Rev.* 1215, 1236 ("[T]he Commerce Clause became the decisive arbiter of which government got to exercise a de facto police").
47. 22 U.S. (19 Wheat.) 1 (1824).
48. For a thorough description of the case, its context and its resolution, see White, *Law in American History Volume I*, at 237–40.
49. 22 U.S. at 195.
50. Ibid., at 190.
51. Ibid., at 203.
52. Ibid., at 208.
53. Ibid., at 205 ("quarantine and health laws ... are considered as flowing from the acknowledged power of a State to provide for the health of its citizens").
54. But see White, *Law in American History Volume I*, at 239 ("[Marshall] seems to be conceding, without acknowledging it, that the states had some power to regulate activities that had some effects on interstate commerce").
55. 17 U.S. (4 Wheat.) 316 (1819).
56. 25 U.S. 419 (1827).
57. Ibid., at 448.
58. "The power to direct the removal of gunpowder is a branch of the police power, which unquestionably remains and ought to remain with the states." Ibid., at 443.
59. 36 U.S. (11 Pet.) 102 (1837).
60. Ibid., at 133.
61. 22 U.S. at 195.
62. See White, *Law in American History Volume I*, at 193–244.
63. See generally Alison L. LaCroix, *The Ideological Origins of American Federalism* (2011).
64. See, e.g., William A. McRae, "The Development of Nuisance in the Early Common Law," 1 *U. Fla. L. Rev.* 27 (1948).
65. See Novak, *People's Welfare*.
66. See David Lieberman, *The Province of Legislation Determined* (1988).
67. See Novak, *People's Welfare*, at 38 ("The common law rather than natural law, positivism, or constitutionalism was the foundation for the well-regulated society").
68. See generally Robert G. Bone, "Normative Theory and Legal Doctrine in American Nuisance Law: 1850 to 1920," 59 *So. Cal. L. Rev.* 1101 (1986).
69. See Novak, *People's Welfare*, at 34. "A natural or legal right was not something to be exerted against society, but was intimately connected to the duties and moral obligations incumbent on social beings"). Ibid., at 33.

70. See Joseph W. Singer, *Entitlement: The Paradoxes of Property* (2000).
71. See Gregory Alexander, *Property and Human Flourishing* (2018); Laura Underkuffler, "On Property: An Essay," 100 *Yale L. J.* 127 (1990).
72. See Jeremy Waldron, *The Right to Property* (1988).
73. 5 Cow. 538 (NY 1826).
74. Ibid., at 542.
75. Vanderbilt v. Adams, 7 Cow. 349, 350 (NY 1827).
76. Ibid., at 351.
77. Ibid., at 352.
78. Ibid.
79. Ibid. See Novak, *People's Welfare*, at 143–44.
80. See generally Harry N. Scheiber, "Public Rights and the Rule of Law in American Legal History," 72 *Cal. L. Rev.* 217 (1984).
81. See Horace C. Wood, *A Practical Treatise on the Law of Nuisances* (2nd ed., 1883).
82. Novak, *People's Welfare*, at 62.
83. Ibid., at 61.
84. "For judges deciding police power cases in the 1870s, the law of nuisance provided the categories for determining when it was legitimate for the state to regulate on behalf of the health, safety, and morals of its citizens." Morton J. Horwitz, *The Transformation of American Law 1870–1960* 28 (1992).
85. See Novak, *People's Welfare*, at 60–71 ("Nineteenth-century jurists were quite explicit about both the overarching significance and the public power of the law of nuisance").
86. See Christopher Tiedeman, *A Treatise on the Limitations of the Police Power in the United States* (1886); Thomas J. Cooley, *A Treatise on the Constitutional Limitations Which Rest on the Legislative Power of the States of the American Union* (1871).
87. See Novak, *People's Welfare*.
88. Novak, "Overruling Necessity," at 96, 98.
89. One good example of this is the regulation of streets. "The public power to remove and abate nuisances and encroachments on highways as a crucial instrument of sovereignty and an important development in early American law." Novak, *People's Welfare*, at 123–24. "The policing of the streets was but a prelude to a general extension of police powers throughout American economy and society." Ibid., at 125. He concludes: "As streets and highways became increasingly public, the regulatory powers of the state were enhanced. State control of streets, rivers, ports, and other public places involved not only the power to keep them free and open to public access but a more general duty to police them." Ibid., at 147–48. Maureen Brady has a somewhat different account of the situation, focusing on the street grading cases from this same early period. See Maureen Brady, "Property's Ceiling: State Courts and the Expansion of Takings Property," 102 *Va. L. Rev.* 1167 (2015).
90. Wadleigh v. Gilan, 12 Me. 403 (Maine 1835).
91. Ibid.
92. 61 Mass. (7 Cush) 53 (1851). "The most influential American discussions of the police power appeared in judicial opinions written by state judges … And Alger was the most influential of the lot." Dubber, *The Police Power*, at 104.
93. Alger is covered extensively in all of the major analyses of the police power, modern and older. See Dubber, *The Police Power*, at 104–14; Novak, *People's Welfare*, at 19–25; Tomlins, "The Supreme Sovereignty of the State: A Genealogy of Police in American Constitutional Law, from the Founding Era to Lochner," in *Police and the Liberal State*, 36–38 (Markus D. Dubber and Mariana Valverde eds., 2008). "Perhaps the most

important step in the practical evolution of police regulation came in the 1851 case Commonwealth v. Alger, which analytically linked the common law doctrines that formed the basis of early American police regulations to the broad conception of government power reflected in the term "police power" as defined by the Supreme Court.'" Benjamin Barros, "The Police Power and the Takings Clause," 58 *U. Miami L. Rev.* 471 (2004). On Justice Shaw and Alger, see Leonard Levy, *The Law of the Commonwealth and Chief Justice Shaw* 229, 241–54 (1997).

94. See Scheiber, "Public Rights," at 222 ("In Alger, Shaw derived from the common's law riparian doctrines a set of long-accepted, well-demarcated distinctions as to the character of property rights in lands under navigable waters as bordering such waters").
95. 61 Mass. at 83.
96. Ibid., at 85.
97. On Hale, see 1 *Collection of Tracts Relative to the Law of England* (F. Hargrave ed. 1787).
98. 61 Mass. at 96.
99. See Gerald J. Postema, *Bentham and the Common Law Tradition* 4 (2d ed. 2019) ("Common Law theory reasserted the medieval idea that law is not something made either by king, Parliament, or judges, but rather is the expression of a deeper reality which is merely discovered and publicly declared by them").
100. 46 U.S. 504 (1847).
101. Ibid., at 583.
102. See Dubber, *The Police Power*, at 110.
103. See ibid., at 113.
104. See ibid., at 106.
105. Dubber, *The Police Power*, at 120.
106. See, e.g., Alschuler, "Rediscovering Blackstone."
107. Legal historian Christopher Tomlins seemingly effaces the nexus between constitutional structure and this legislature power with respect to the police power's origins, noting that "Alger underscored the essential irrelevance of the sovereign popular claim to a constitutional point of origin when it came to the police power." This statement could have two distinct meanings. It could mean that the police power comes to the United States as a species of the royal prerogative, before becoming domesticated by constitutional structure. Or it could mean that the police power has no foundation in constitutional authority, but was and is a form of constitutional exceptionalism. This is less plausible, and not in serious accord with Tomlins's other writings on the police power.
108. See James Willard Hurst, *Law and Social Order in the United States* (1977).
109. Alger, 61 Mass. at 83–85
110. Ibid.
111. Mayor of Hudson v. Thorne, 7 Paige ch. 261 (NY 1838).
112. See Novak, *People's Welfare*, at 30.
113. Ibid., at 32–35.
114. Ibid., at 33.
115. 7 Cow. at 352.
116. In other exercises of this power, the connection between harm and general welfare was more attenuated. In Forbes' Case, for example, the New York court considered the constitutionality of a state statute prohibiting vagrancy. This was held as appropriate within the police power, as part of the government's will to advance the general welfare of the community. It could be styled as an effort to head off discernible threats to public safety

117. 27 Vt. 140 (1855).
118. Dartmouth College v. Woodward, 4 Wheat. 518 (U.S. 1819).
119. Mayor of Hudson v. Thorne, 7 Paige ch. 261 (NY 1838).
120. Ibid.
121. Ibid.
122. See generally Daniel T. Rodgers, *Atlantic Crossings: Social Politics in a Progressive Era* 117 (1998) ("Growing at every edge, cities were eager for technological improvement and expanded services").
123. Novak, *People's Welfare*, at 117.
124. Ibid.
125. The Federalist No. 14.
126. See Harry Scheiber, *Ohio Canal Era: A Case Study of Government and the Economy, 1820–1861* (1969).
127. See Scheiber, "Public Rights"; Harry Scheiber, "The Road to Munn: Eminent Domain and the Concept of Public Purpose in the State Courts," in *Perspectives in American History, Volume V: Law in American History* 329 (D. Fleming & B. Bailyn eds., 1971).
128. See generally Morton Horwitz, "The Emergence of an Instrumental Conception of Law, 1780–20" in *Perspectives in American History, Volume V: Law in American History* 287 (D. Fleming & B. Bailyn eds., 1971).
129. On the idea of vested rights, see Edward Corwin, "The Basic Doctrine of American Constitutional Law," 12 *Mich. L. Rev.* 247 (1914).
130. See generally William Treanor, "The Original Understanding of the Takings Clause and the Political Process," 95 *Colum. L. Rev.* 782 (1995).
131. See Calder v. Bull, 3 U.S. 386 (1798).
132. Charles River Bridge v. Warren Bridge, 36 U.S. (11 Pet.) 420 (1837).
133. See J. Willard Hurst, *Law and the Conditions of Freedom in the Nineteenth-Century* (1986); Morton Keller, *The Affairs of State: Public Life in Late Nineteenth Century* (1977).
134. O'Connor v. Pittsburgh, 18 Pa. St. Rep. 187, 190 (1851).
135. Nor would it persist after the Supreme Court developed a regulatory takings doctrine in the late 1920s.
136. Stuart Banner, *The Decline of Natural Law: How American Lawyers Once Used Natural Law and Why They Stopped* 18 (2021). As Morton Horwitz describes natural rights in this regard: "[N]atural rights discourse structured legal argument by suggesting starting points, background assumptions, presumptions, or first principles in the law." Morton J. Horwitz, *The Transformation of American Law, 1870–1960* 158 (1992).
137. See Postema, *Bentham*, at 14–17 (describing declaratory basis of statutory law under the common law tradition).
138. See Postema, *Bentham*, at 262–94.
139. Ibid.
140. Southern Pacific Co. v. Jensen, 244 U.S. 205, 222 (1917) (Holmes, J., dissenting).
141. See Lieberman, *Legislation Determined*.
142. See Daniel B. Rodriguez, "State Constitutional Common Law" (ms. 2024).
143. Barron v. Baltimore, 32 U.S. 243 (1833).
144. Whether and to what extent judicial review would supply an important check on the exercise the state police power in the early years after the adoption of the state constitutions and into the antebellum period was unclear for a long while. None of the original

thirteen constitutions spoke to this issue explicitly; nor does it appear that the matter of judicial review was a major part of the debate in the constitution-making process. Although judicial review was not referenced in Article III of the US Constitution nor in the Bill of Rights, the framers understood that issues of judicial scrutiny would become prominent.

145. 3 U.S. 386 (1798).
146. Ibid., at 388.
147. 10 U.S. 87 (1810). See also Tony A. Freyer, *Producers v. Capitalists: Constitutional Conflict in Antebellum America* 17 (1994) ("The overall trend of decision making under both the Marshall and Taney Courts was toward constitutional interpretations that generally sanctioned a broad police power").
148. White, *Law in American History Volume I*, at 229. One of the most important cases in this line was Trustees of Dartmouth College v. Woodward 17 U.S. 518 (1819). There the Court held that the chartering of a private corporation created a contract that was vested and thereby subject to the Contracts Clause. This was consequential in that corporations control and use private property in myriad ways and the states would need to be cognizant in undertaking regulations that impaired certain contract rights and restricted the use of property that it was not modifying the contract in a way that would run afoul of the Contract Clause.
149. 36 U.S. 420 (1837).
150. Ibid., at 470.
151. 46 U.S. 504 (1847).
152. Ibid., at 583.
153. See generally Kate Masur, *Until Justice Be Done: America's First Civil Rights Movement, from the Revolution to Reconstruction* 303–41 (2021) (describing the origins of the Fourteenth Amendment).
154. 83 U.S. 36 (1873).
155. Ibid., at 75.
156. See G. Edward White, *Law in American History Volume II: From Reconstruction through the 1920s* 37 (2016).
157. See Freyer, *Capitalists*, at 32.
158. White, *Law in American History Volume II*, at 38.
159. 163 U.S. 537 (1896).
160. 94 U.S. 113 (1877).
161. Ibid., at 125.
162. Ibid.
163. Ibid., at 126–28.
164. Ibid., at 129.
165. See Scheiber, "The Road to Munn."
166. 94 U.S. at 126–28.
167. Ibid., at 128–30.
168. Ill. Const. Art. 13, Sec. 7.
169. 94 U.S. at 134.
170. Cooley, *Constitutional Limitations*.
171. See generally John Dinan, *State Constitutional Politics: Governing by Amendment in the American States* (2018).
172. Banner, *Natural Law*, at 44. (quoting from "Property and its Origin," United States Jurist 2 (1872): 324). Professor Banner reminds us that this natural law thinking was not limited to judicial decisionmaking, but was found in large measure in the text and context of the

state constitutions. He notes the language of the New Hampshire Constitution of 1784, in providing that "all men have certain natural, essential, and inherent rights [including the] acquiring, possessing and protecting property ...." Banner, *Natural Law*, at 73 (quoting N.H. Const. 1784, Part, I, arts. II, V).
173. On classical legal thought and its connection to emerging American constitutionalism, see William M. Wiecek, *The Lost World of Classical Legal Thought: Law and Ideology in America, 1886–1937* 24–27 (1998). On its connection to the police power in particular, see Horwitz, *Transformation II*, at 27–31. On the classical legal thought generally, see Duncan Kennedy, *The Rise and Fall of Classic Legal Thought* (1975).
174. Novak, *People's Welfare*, at 116.
175. Ibid., at 115.

3

"The Power to Govern Men and Things"

The Police Power Evolves to Meet New Conditions

As Americans moved from Reconstruction toward the Progressive era, the hunger for a more activist government grew.[1] The demands of a rapidly expanding economy, and one that was integrated in important way, drove regulatory change and expansion, especially with regard to federal initiatives. While a main focus in the academic literature on the Progressive era emphasizes the ways in which the federal government's role expanded,[2] the last quarter of the nineteenth and first quarter of the twentieth centuries was an era in which regulatory activity was focused at the state and local level.[3] As Susan Pearson writes in connection with state regulation: "If we turn our eyes from the arenas usually privileged in stories of statebuilding – social welfare provision and labor regulations – and look to the regulation of morals, sexuality, marriage, and race relations, then the postbellum years appear as an era of expanded government."[4] To be sure, the architecture of constitutional federalism was reconfigured in important ways by the Reconstruction amendments and attendant statutes,[5] and it was further reshaped as the imperatives of a national economy emerged. However, the impact of regulatory power remained state-centered, from the end of Reconstruction into deep into the twentieth century.

We will focus in this chapter on the evolution of the police power in the half century from Reconstruction to the aftermath of the Second World War. During this period, the courts looked more closely – and often skeptically – at the state police power, considering whether and to what extent the scope of government authority should be curtailed. This happened most famously in the twenty-plus years defined as the Lochner era, named after the famous 1905 case, Lochner v. New York.[6] However, we should not neglect what the courts did both before and after Lochner to map out the terrain of the police power. So-called "laissez faire constitutionalism" casts a big light on the subject of governmental authority and property rights during this time and it is generally identified with the period bookended by Lochner and key deal cases, including Nebbia v. New York[7] and West Coast Hotel v. Parrish in 1937.[8] Thus laissez faire constitutionalism is indeed a "thing," a thing whose moment was critical to an understanding of state regulatory power in the first two decades or so of the twentieth century.[9] But a more complete story of how the police power was shaped by courts and other governmental actors during the half century between Reconstruction and the 1940s requires a more nuanced appraisal. We should see the ways in which the police power itself – and not just the negative rights that were advanced to curtail the power's scope – took shape as a legal construct and foundational constitutional principle during this long period. Its shape was affected by decisions of legislators and administrators, by the movements in American constitutional development and politics, and, last but not least, through state and federal court decisions.

In this period, we see struggles in the courts and elsewhere over the police power's scope and its limits. One important aspect of this story is the continuing impact of natural law thinking and the way in which such thinking drove forward the idea that individuals have vested rights that were to be safeguarded against overreach by government.[10] However, the main event, as it were, was not natural law and vested rights, nor Lochner and its progeny, although both of these episodes were important to the story. Rather, it was two developments that supported the general cause of defining the police power, developments that came mainly from separate quarters. First, there was the relentless call for more active government, one that would drive economic progress and would also protect safety and health from the threats that emerged from industrialization and the often dangerous modern world and would also protect public morals from threats. At the heart of the Progressive era was a faith, not lost as the country moved into the twenties and thirties and finally into the Depression and World War II, in the capacity of government to govern for the people's welfare. The ways in which government actors developed meaningful regulatory strategies to aspire to a well-ordered society is the principal story of the police power in this period.

Second, courts worried with good reason that this faith in activist government would yield power that could not and would not be effectively checked and channeled. Legislative and administrative activism generated strong efforts at counterbalance. The Reconstruction amendments provided an important part of the toolkit, especially in its establishment of due process and equal protection as protections applicable across the nation. Scholars looking at the rise of administrative governance worried about this emerging approach to governance and advocated for greater control.[11] But it would be a long time into the future until the federal courts gave full force to these mechanisms of control.[12] Meanwhile, while the federal courts experimented with laissez faire constitutionalism, state courts attended to the risks of excessive public power by close interrogations of the police power's excesses. Sometimes this was accomplished through the resort to individual rights, such as liberty of contract and private property, as in Lochner, other times it happened through a close look by judges at the justification for state regulation. Key questions were: Was this a reasonable exercise of the police power? Was it arbitrary? That is, based upon little more than prejudice and without process that is due to individuals who would have had their property confiscated or their liberty restricted?

Moreover, in one important new area of law, regulatory takings, the Court developed requirements that obligated government to pay those who were harmed in discernible ways by decisions involving their property and its use. Takings law was a fairly minor part of the police power and governance story in the half century following Reconstruction. However, starting with Pennsylvania Coal v. Mahon,[13] decided in 1922, and continuing for a century afterward, the federal courts' approach to determining when and to what extent compensation was owed because of ruinous regulation became an increasingly important part of the effort to balance active government with individual rights.

The struggle never disappeared during this period, nor was the puzzle of how to balance activist governance with individual liberty and property ever truly solved. The picture painted in this chapter is one that highlights these tensions and struggles and situates these conflicts in larger debates about governance, property, and liberty.

We should emphasize as well the growing skepticism toward the legislature as an institution managing governance in Reconstruction's aftermath. Anti-legislative thinking did not begin in this era, to be sure. The Jacksonian period saw constitutional reformers and ordinary citizens turning the light on legislatures and fretting about lawmakers' ability to act democratically and responsibly so far as both efficacious governance and protection of liberty were concerned. But the Progressive era was notable in the ways in which reformers adjusted constitutional rules to limit legislative power and, moreover, pushed for regulatory innovations such as greater use of administrative agencies and of municipal governments to implement the police power's objectives.

One important lesson to be drawn from the exercise of the police power in this half century is that the police power was not limited to actions of state legislatures.[14] During this time, we saw meaningful regulation undertaken by administrative agencies, and the emergence of a significant amount of administrative law. Much is written about the rise of national administrative agencies and struggles about their legitimacy and control.[15] However, this development was mirrored, and even presaged, by administrative decision-making on the part of state-level agencies and bureaus. Likewise, regulatory activity under the police power was a common strategy of municipal governments. A good chunk of public policy, including zoning, which we will examine in some detail later in the chapter, was carried out by local governments under the rubric of delegated police power. These phenomena were controversial; they may have troubled the framers of the various early state constitutions, to the extent that matters to the enterprise of figuring out what the police power means. But, in any event, it was a commonplace by the time of the 1920s and 1930s. Any comprehensive treatment of the police power ought to account for these important developments.

The emphasis in the standard literature on judicial intervention during this period has been on Lochner and the emerging libertarian constitutionalism, an approach that drove more searching judicial scrutiny of economic and social welfare legislation in the name of protecting individual liberty and property rights.[16] The movements that give rise to the fabled Lochner era were part of a growing effort on the part of myriad institutions of government, not limited to the courts, to examine closely the structure and output of legislatures and agencies. The push for progressive legislation grows at the same time that there emerged skepticism about the behavior and conduct of legislatures. To the extent that powerful interest groups and common citizens saw their situation becoming out of balance, efforts at reconciling an expansive police power with individual rights became more prominent. Lochner era cases and other instances of activist judicial review illustrated the countermajoritarian elements of this skepticism, while on the other side was an equivalent concern with maintaining democracy in the face of what was seen as regulatory capture and influence by factions and special interests. Indeed, constitutional reformers were able to express skepticism in both directions, and so forged both majoritarian and countermajoritarian solutions. As a result of these developments, the police power emerged from the era considered in this chapter with a new shape.

PROGRESSIVE LEGISLATION EMERGES

The development of legislation and administrative policy during the Progressive era was largely a consequence of expanding needs of a republic, considered both at the state and at the federal level. Looking back on this period in 1932, Ernst Freund wrote of the extraordinarily widening scope of legislative intervention in the preceding half century, complex but essential, and notable for how it transformed not only regulation as such, but also the role of the state in dealing with more modern exigencies.[17]

As to whether the main contents of legislative regulation were supplied by the national government or the state governments, the answer was both. At the federal level, that was an enormous pressure to respond to the condition of an increasingly integrated economy.[18] Transportation was radically transformed, and something that we now take largely for granted – a railroad system that spans many states in order to efficiently ship goods and transport citizens on the move – was in a precarious position, especially given state political interests that tilted toward protectionism.[19] The federal government was called upon to solve problems created by private businesses operating on their own initiative in the marketplace and by state and local governments looking after their own interests. In the Progressive era, the national government enacted legislature that created a large regulatory infrastructure – and a major federal agency, the Interstate Commerce Commission, to deal with these and related issues.[20]

Likewise, massive public investment, including federal resources and resources collected from the states, was necessary to support a nascent, but then quickly growing, communications infrastructure.[21] The invention and spreading use of the telegraph was one important technology. Afterward, the building of utility poles and their placement throughout the country was a credit to federal government foresight, and of course it came along with considerable investment. The expansion of communications technologies, the nature of which required support for its use across borders without disruption by individual states or communities, required significant federal intervention.[22] As with transportation, the infrastructure of national regulation was changed. Indeed, with the creation of the Federal Communications Commission in 1934, the central role of the federal government in our cross-state transportation scheme became entrenched.[23]

Some of the consequences of the rapid integration of the economy are dealt with by simultaneous federal and state action. So, for example, the feds stepped into the matter of safety in agriculture by the creation, in 1884, of the Bureau of Animal Industry,[24] tasked with addressing livestock disease, a consequence of the shipment of livestock to distant places – a new development, as previously farmers basically raised their own cows for their personal consumption or for a very nearby market. The states were also active in addressing food safety issues, and had various regulatory rules that dealt with adulterated food products within their borders. Similarly, labor laws were emerging in this era and both the federal and state governments needed to deal with not only the general protection of labor, through, for example, regulation on hours and conditions in the workplace, but also needed to reduce the chances of labor violence.[25] Such violence was not uncommon in this period and, after all, a comprehensive national approach would await the enactment of the National Labor Relations Act in 1935.[26]

The bottom line was that national regulation grew significantly during this period, as the conditions and consequences of a much more integrated market grew. At the same time, state regulation was persistent, and indeed the requirements of state intervention to ensure a modicum of order, including acceptable safety and health, expanded, not contracted, during this period. The steady increase in urban populations, and the attendant health and safety hazards of crowded cities, required new state and local laws. Moreover, an increase in infectious diseases, and occasional epidemics, spurred public health laws, these being almost exclusively the product of state governments. In short, there was plenty for state legislatures and administrators to do during this multi-decade period from the end of Reconstruction to the middle of the next century.

With this significantly augmented role on the part of the state government, the police power was increasingly important as the fulcrum of state authority. As William Novak writes: "The police power increasingly became a more positive public law doctrine that defined modern legislative regulatory power."[27]

PROGRESSIVE LEGISLATION SUSTAINED: THE POLICE POWER AND THE SUPREMES

We often see the rise and fall of Lochner as reaffirming fidelity to a highly deferential approach to reviewing economic regulation, an approach that would come to be called "rational basis" review.[28] However, the reality is that the judicial evaluation of governmental actions that impacted individuals' contract and property rights was meaningful both before and after Lochner.[29] Before Lochner, courts interrogated state regulations, and even though they deferred to legislative judgments and more often than not upheld these laws against constitutional challenges, there was a meaningful modicum of review of the government's exercise of the police power in the late nineteenth century.[30] Because it was deployed most often in state courts, it has long fallen off the radar screen of constitutional scholars, even many trained and tasked to look closely at the history of the period.[31] And after Lochner, notwithstanding the widespread deference accorded to state government's economic regulation,[32] state courts did scrutinize the reasonableness of government regulation to determine whether the police power had been properly exercised.

Munn v. Illinois, described in the previous chapter, illustrates how the Supreme Court saw the police power at the other end of Reconstruction. The Court there emphasizes that the police power has as its central function a mechanism by which the legislature could promote health, safety, and the general welfare in the face of self-regarding, monopolistic business practices. Property, said the Court in Munn,[33] was subject to public control and was embedded in social welfare considerations. This did not mean that the power of control is unlimited, but that for "businesses affected with a public interest," the legislature has an exceptionally wide berth. Chief Justice Waite writes: "We know that this is a power which may be abused; but there is no argument against its existence. For protection against abuses by legislatures the people must resort to the polls, not to the courts."[34] The Court continued to refine its approach to resolving these tensions in later cases, some of which gained prominence at the time, prominence that has persisted as we look to understand this era in our constitutional law.

One such case was Mugler v. Kansas. Peter Mugler was a naturalized citizen who arrived in Kansas in 1872 looking to make his way as a self-supporting new American. In 1877, Mr. Mugler built a brewery, aspiring to make and sell malt liquor. Having no permit to do so, he was arrested and charged with a violation of a Kansas statute which imposed a penalty if he "did unlawfully manufacture, and aid, assist, and abet in the manufacture of vinous, spirituous, malt, fermented, and other intoxicating liquors in violation of the provisions of [this] act."[35] This statute was enacted in order to implement a prohibitionist amendment added to Kansas's constitution in 1880.

Mr. Mugler's challenge came to the Supreme Court in 1887. He complained that these state acts violated his rights under the Fourteenth Amendment. The Court had already considered and rejected, in The License Cases,[36] the argument that these restrictions interfered with the Constitution's assignment exclusively to Congress to regulate interstate commerce. Therefore, the only constitutional objections left available to this defendant was that the state had exceeded its authority under the police power and had violated the privileges or immunities of citizens or had deprived the individual of his life, liberty, or property without due process of law.

In <u>Mugler</u>, Justice John Harlan, writing for the Court, gave voice to one rendering of this regulation. The law, he notes, might be viewed as deliberately singling out the behavior of one individual for opprobrium, an individual who was merely exercising his liberty rights and, in the case of the manufacture of these alcoholic beverages, his rights to use his private property as he wishes.[37] So viewed, he concedes that this approach would be a misuse of the government's power to control private behavior that caused no external harm.[38] However, this misconceives, says Harlan, the nature of the right and the purpose of this regulation.

> [T]he right to manufacture drink for one's personal use is subject to the condition that such manufacture does not endanger or affect the rights of others. If such manufacture does prejudicially affect the rights and interests of the community, it follows from the very premises stated that society has the power to protect itself by legislation against the injurious consequences of that business.[39]

And so this regulation, very much similar to the regulation on grain elevators upheld ten years earlier in <u>Munn</u>, was a perfectly appropriate use of the police power to protect the community from the actions of an individual.

As to who should determine where and how the line is drawn between general welfare and individual liberty, Harlan says "that power is lodged with the legislative branch of the Government. It belongs to that department to exert what are known as the police powers of the State, and to determine, primarily, what measures are appropriate or needful for the protection of the public morals, the public health, or the public safety."[40] Justice Harlan goes further than just rubber-stamping Kansas's judgment, adding the opinion that this restriction on the manufacture of intoxicating liquors is designed to eradicate an "evil," to protect the public health, the public morals, and the public safety, which "may be endangered by the general use of intoxicating drinks" contributing to "idleness, disorder, pauperism, and crime."[41] For Harlan, and presumably the other justices who joined his opinion, the legislature was acting wisely to address a serious social problem.

A critical question in <u>Mugler</u>, as earlier in <u>Munn</u>, was whether the Fourteenth Amendment changes the equation. No, says the Court emphatically. As Howard Gillman notes, "Justice Harlan's statement is not a departure from previous holdings; it is rather, a reassertion of the adjudicative task undertaken by the Supreme Court since <u>Slaughterhouse</u>,[42] and by many state courts before that."[43] This constitutional amendment does not undermine the wide ambit of the police power, that point being a critical element of <u>Mugler</u> and the police power cases considered in the wake of Reconstruction.[44] For, as the Court had said in an earlier case, <u>Barbier v. Connolly</u>,[45] "neither the Amendment, broad and comprehensive as it is, nor any other amendment, was designed to interfere with the power of the State, sometimes termed 'its police power,' to prescribe regulations to promote the health, peace, morals, education, and good order of the people, and to legislate so as to increase the industries of the State, develop its resources, and add to its wealth and prosperity."[46] This last statement proves to be an important one, as the Court from an early stage avoids one possible implication of the Reconstruction amendments, and that is that the font of regulatory authority, at least with respect to guaranteeing the full rights of citizenship (the "privileges or immunities"), was now shifting from the states to the federal government. While difficult issues of federalism persist after these amendments, the Court's declaration that states maintain their police powers and for important purposes ("wealth and prosperity" and the rest) is left undisturbed.

The Court made clear in Mugler, however, that the police power is not unlimited, and those limits are found in constitutional rules and rights established in the Constitution from the beginning of the republic, as in the Bill of Rights (eminent domain is mentioned explicitly) or from the Fourteenth Amendment, especially the protections of due process.[47] This is not a new proposition, but one that echoes the previous decisions of the Court. In Mugler, Justice Harlan notes that the law is ever diligent in ensuring that the enactment and application of the regulation not be arbitrary, thereby raising a concern of discrimination.[48]

The Mugler case illustrates well the Court's imprimatur on the police power's use by the states as a key mechanism of public governance, including in areas where the animate concern was with protecting the common good. By this time in the second-to-last decade of the nineteenth century, it had become well-established that the concept of general welfare undergirding the police power was much broader than that reflected in the *sic utere* principle, one where the government's role is limited to abating individual harm or public harm that could be measured in the way that classic tort law demands.[49] It also illustrates, as will other cases for the remainder of the nineteenth and the first part of the twentieth century, the point that the Fourteenth Amendment did not shake the foundations of the police power and impose a major set of limits, either from equal protection or from procedural due process. A broad interpretation of the police power would persist throughout the post-Reconstruction and Progressive eras, accompanying the expansion of state capacity and the steadily increasing roles of both the state and federal government.[50] At the same time, Mugler reveals that the police power, however difficult to define precisely, is not unlimited and that the main objective of the courts is to discern whether and to what extent a duly enacted law is arbitrary or capricious in a way that warrants invalidation. To be sure, this standard was not invented in this decision, but it was refined over time and, in its refinement, started a bridge of sorts to early twentieth-century decisions, including Lochner, where courts at both the federal and state levels gave police power regulations a more searching judicial review.

The broad scope of the police power was reinforced in a case that would become especially notorious, although not for a long while, Plessy v. Ferguson, decided in 1896.[51] In this case, the Court examined and upheld the operation by the railroad managers of a segregated train. "The power to assign to a particular coach," wrote Justice Brown for the Court, "obviously implies the power to determine to which race the passenger belongs, as well as the power to determine who, under the laws of the particular State, is to be deemed a white and who a colored person."[52] The Court stressed that the police power was not unlimited, and regulations that were mere subterfuges to discriminate against individuals on an arbitrary or unjust basis would be struck down. This statement remains puzzling. It is no clearer a full one hundred and twenty-seven years after this decision how to distinguish the "unjust" discrimination of, say, Chinese launderers in Yick Wo v. Hopkins[53] or other post-Reconstruction cases in which the government was discriminating unconstitutionally. Rather than clarify the standard, what the Court offers instead is a fallacious and fully-discredited argument that Louisiana's train segregation statute is "reasonable" and that any claim by the Black plaintiff that such segregation imposes a "badge of inferiority" it is "not by reason of anything found in the act, but solely because the colored race chooses to put that construction upon it."[54]

Justice Harlan memorably dissented in Plessy. The core insight of his dissent is that the use of the police power to segregate train travel runs squarely against the clear import of the Fourteenth Amendment and its guarantee of the equal protection of the laws. Louisiana simply had no credible reason located in health, welfare, or general welfare for this baldly discriminatory law. The legislature's stated rationale was intentionally discriminatory and so the onus was squarely on the state to describe a reasonable, that is, non-arbitrary, reason for this law, one that could plausibly be grounded in the public's welfare. The unreasonableness inherent in this Louisiana law, Harlan indicates, is found in its intention, in its revealed attitude toward Black citizens, and the manifestation in action of the view that Blacks are inferior to Whites and can constitutionally be subject to unequal treatment. We start, says Harlan, with the equality rights guaranteed to them by the Constitution: "If a white man and a black man choose to occupy the same public conveyance on a public highway, it is their right to do so, and no government, proceeding alone on grounds of race, can prevent it without infringing the personal liberty of each."[55] From there, Justice Harlan examines, and ultimately demolishes, the hypothetical laws that would, if this law were upheld, be *a fortiori* acceptable uses of the police power. He writes

> If a State can prescribe, as a rule of civil conduct, that whites and blacks shall not travel as passengers in the same railroad coach, why may it not so regulate the use of the streets of its cities and towns as to compel white citizens to keep on one side of a street and black citizens to keep on the other? Why may it not, upon like grounds, punish whites and blacks who ride together in streetcars or in open vehicles on a public road or street? Why may it not require sheriffs to assign whites to one side of a courtroom and blacks to the other? And why may it not also prohibit the commingling of the two races in the galleries of legislative halls or in public assemblages convened for the consideration of the political questions of the day? Further, if this statute of Louisiana is consistent with the personal liberty of citizens, why may not the State require the separation in railroad coaches of native and naturalized citizens of the United States, or of Protestants and Roman Catholics?[56]

Having dispatched with the argument that this is a reasonable exercise of the police power, in light of the fact that this act functions as a "badge of servitude" placed on Black railroad passengers,[57] Harlan endeavors to thread the needle of judicial deference, noting that nothing in his opinion should be read as giving judges a roving power to evaluate the wisdom of particular public policies. This is a neglected dictum in Harlan's celebrated dissent, but it is important to put into context the ultimately limited role of judicial review in police power controversies. His warning is worth quoting at length, as it is a coherent summary of the Supreme Court's approach to police power controversies in this critical period:

> A statute may be unreasonable merely because a sound public policy forbade its enactment. But I do not understand that the courts have anything to do with the policy or expediency of legislation. A statute may be valid and yet, upon grounds of public policy, may well be characterized as unreasonable. Mr Sedgwick correctly states the rule when he says that, the legislative intention being clearly ascertained, "the courts have no other duty to perform than to execute the legislative will, without any regard to their views as to the wisdom or justice of the particular enactment." [citation omitted]. There is a dangerous tendency in these latter days to enlarge the functions of the courts by means of judicial interference with the will of the people as expressed by the legislature. Our institutions have the distinguishing characteristic that the three departments of government are coordinate and separate. Each must keep within the limits defined by the Constitution. And the courts best discharge their duty by executing the will of the lawmaking power, constitutionally expressed, leaving the results of legislation to be dealt with by the people through their representatives. Statutes must always have a reasonable construction. Sometimes they are to be construed strictly; sometimes liberally, in order to carry out the legislative will. But however construed, the intent of the legislature is to be respected, if the particular statute in question is valid, although the courts, looking at the public interests, may conceive the statute to be both unreasonable and impolitic. If the power exists to enact a statute, that ends the matter so far as the courts are concerned. The adjudged cases in which statutes have been held to be void because unreasonable are those in which the means employed by the legislature were not at all germane to the end to which the legislature was competent.[58]

With Plessy's prominence as an early case cementing for decades segregation and Jim Crow, Justice Harlan's lone dissent stands out as a powerful declaration of the principle of equality. For the purposes of understanding better the police power, it is also notable for its naming in a most explicit way the fact that the Reconstruction amendments did indeed represent meaningful constraints on the exercise of power at the state level, insofar as they created equal protection and due process limits on government action, limits which were meaningful conditions on the decision of legislatures to impose discriminatory laws and also laws where the connections between means and ends were quite tenuous.

Harlan's dissent is not ultimately in any tension with his opinion for the Court in Mugler. In both cases, Justice Harlan for the Court acknowledged both the broad scope of the police and the imperative of limiting this power. The essential difference was that the state had, in Mugler, a compelling case for a welfarist-based regulation and no evidence that Mr. Mugler had been singled for discriminatory treatment nor a decent argument that the government was acting in ways arbitrary or capricious. By contrast, invidious discrimination was the *sine qua non* of the government's regulation in Plessy. Here the equal protection of laws was necessary to create a baseline limit on the use of the power to disfavor one group. The fabled assertion by the Plessy majority that this discrimination did not attach a badge of inferiority on African Americans was of course risible, but for Justice Harlan it was enough to say that purpose of the law was to discriminate and not to implement an objective that could plausibly be tied to the police power.

Justice Harlan maintains his place as the leading architect on that era's Supreme Court with respect to defining the scope of the police and its limits in yet another important case of the time, and that is Jacobson v. Massachusetts,[59] decided in 1905, at virtually the same moment as Lochner. Jacobson involved a mandatory vaccination requirement enacted by the public health authorities in Cambridge, Massachusetts during the middle of the smallpox pandemic. The plaintiff challenged this requirement, insisting "a compulsory vaccination law is unreasonable, arbitrary and oppressive, and, therefore, hostile to the inherent right of every freeman to care for his own body and health in such way as to him seems best."[60] Writing for the Court, Justice Harlan reiterated the point that it was the responsibility of the federal court to examine whether the exercise of the police was in any way arbitrary or unreasonable. If so, the government's regulation would fail, whether this protection is lodged in a notion of equal protection, due process, or individual liberty. Harlan added that the linchpin of the police power is the promotion of the common good. He notes that "it was the duty of the constituted authorities primarily to keep in view the welfare, comfort and safety of the many, and not permit the interests of the many to be subordinated to the wishes or convenience of the few."[61] In undertaking an analysis of whether this "common good" has been met, the judge should not substitute its judgment for the judgment of the legislature either as to the public health and safety imperative that the regulation is designed to tackle or as to the structural means by which the goal is achieved.[62] In this case, the Court rejected plaintiff's argument that this was not properly delegated to the public health authorities of the state of Massachusetts.

Jacobson is a notable case,[63] especially when we remember that it was decided in the same year as Lochner. The Court accepted what was after all a fairly novel regulation and one that unavoidably intruded on bodily autonomy, stressing the legislature's wide discretion to undertake measures necessary to protect the public health and resisting the argument that an individual's freedom could be sacrificed without any opportunity to show that he specifically should be subject to this compulsion. In its facts and the unequivocal statement of deference and its value, we could see Jacobson as reinforcing the principle that the police power of state governments is vast and the role of the federal courts in interrogating acts under this power quite narrow.

This view is accurate, yet incomplete. We will see as we look at this period that the general welfare ideas underlying the police power that evolved over the nation's first century were quite resilient in the face of libertarian-oriented attacks on energetic state government. Still, skepticism about state legislative policymaking yield important structural reforms. Moreover, courts at the state level were evaluating police power regulations to examine for themselves whether such regulations were arbitrary or unreasonable.

※

The critical developments that we described at the outset of the chapter – anxiety about the interference with property and liberty rights given the broad rendering of the police power and skepticism about legislatures making big and bold regulatory choices – should be considered separately, even though they were mutually reinforcing. We can therefore better understand their character and how they matter for a fulsome understanding of the police power in this era.

PROPERTY RIGHTS AND THE COLLECTIVE WELFARE

Property rights continued to evolve after Reconstruction, and with a valence that bore the imprint of a Republican insistence that certain natural rights, including the rights to private property, were important, if not inalienable. The outcome of the Slaughterhouse Cases was a setback to this effort at strong protection, insofar that it blocked one pathway – privileges or immunities – to the destination of a newly robust protection of economic liberties.[64] However, the idea that property and also liberty of contract were important to protect persisted.[65] Moreover, it underwrote an especially strong view of economic liberties that would blossom into a theory of constitutional scrutiny that would later be labelled laissez faire constitutionalism.

The struggle over the scope of the police power in the shadow of this libertarian view of property rights and liberty of contract was captured well by famed jurist and treatise author, Thomas Cooley. He wrote with his concern with the overbearing actions of state authorities and the underprotection of private property and individual liberty of contract under the US and state constitutions.[66] Cooley's devotion to property and contract rights was not centered in classic natural law thinking and so it would be misleading to see him as motivated by a crude libertarianism.[67] Rather, he created a powerful argument, in what was ultimately a vast amount of judicial and extra-judicial writing, for the critical role of constitutions – and especially state constitutions – in constructing a regime of sound governance and the furthering of the public's welfare. He valued property rights and liberty and worried about legislative excess. And so he "sought constitutional limitations to legislative power because they feared arbitrary and unequal legislation, as well as the identification of legislation with the interests of privileged and powerful capitalists."[68]

What made the struggle over defining appropriate limits on government regulation of property even more vexing was the idea prominent in this era, which was that property rights were yoked to natural rights and natural law.[69] The point is not that property rights were viewed as sacrosanct, but that the protection of the natural right to private property was an important "first principle" and created a presumption that these so-called "vested rights" would be protected against the assertion of state power.[70] Looking at property law through these lens of formalism – or what Duncan Kennedy famously labelled "classical legal thought" – supported a view of property rights as vested, and therefore protected against governmental action, at least where the government was not prepared to pay compensation under its eminent domain responsibilities.[71]

In an important recent book on the original meaning of the Fourteenth Amendment, Randy Barnett and Evan Bernick argue that the privileges or immunities of citizens, and the other rights embedded in the Reconstruction amendments and through statutes and the common law of the time, were grounded squarely in natural rights ideas.[72] The higher law origins of the due process of law – framed in terms from the fourteenth-century British parliament as the "law of the land"[73] – was embraced first by Hamilton and other framers,[74] then by early state and federal courts,[75] and also by the framers of the Reconstruction amendments.[76] In essence, the natural law of due process and private property "impos[ed] a duty on both state and federal judges to make good-faith determinations of whether legislation is calculated to achieve constitutionally proper aims."[77] From this argument comes an originalist argument for an approach to interpreting the police power that is more cautious and ultimately more limiting of state authority and regulatory prerogative than we see in cases of that period and cases in modern times.[78]

Professors Barnett and Bernick capture something important about the mode of reasoning influential on courts in the post-Reconstruction era, as does Barnett writing alone when he argues that the framers had a "presumption of liberty" that impacted eighteenth- and nineteenth-century interpretations of the police power where property and liberty of contract were put into jeopardy.[79] This thesis exaggerates somewhat, however, what was actually happening in adjudication in this critical period, the approximately seven decades between Reconstruction and World War II.

The Supreme Court's commitment to natural rights thinking with respect to property rights and governmental power was equivocal, to say the least. Tellingly, neither <u>Munn</u> nor <u>Mugler</u> reveals a Court on a quest to discover and to enforce the natural right of private property against government under either the national or state constitutions. Rather, the essential thrust of both decisions was to articulate the view that states maintained a significant realm of discretion which economic regulation (<u>Munn</u>) and what was essentially morals legislation with a dose of health rationale (<u>Mugler</u>) was well within the scope of the police power. If there was a presumption of liberty at work in these lodestar cases, it was a presumption rather decisively overcome.

Sometimes the confounding question of where is the best place to look for the source of property rights and the meaning of private property were found in cases that did not involve squarely the matter of government regulation under the police power. One fascinating example is the 1918 decision of <u>International News Service v. Associated Press</u>.[80] There the plaintiff claimed that their rights were being interfered with by a company competing with them for gathering and disseminating news in a timely fashion. They claimed a property right in the news gathering (this distinct from a copyright in the actual publishing of this news, a matter not at issue in this case). The Court dispensed with the defendant's argument this news gathering was property by virtue of the defendant's creative activity by declaring that "the news element – the information respecting current events contained in the literary production – is not the creation of the writer, but is a report of matters that ordinarily are *publici juris*. It is merely the history of the day."[81] Two legal giants of this era, Justices Oliver Wendell Holmes and Louis Brandeis, argued over whether this information was property in their respective concurring and dissenting opinions. For Holmes, the focus on effort and energy, which one might see as derivative of a Lockean conception of property,[82] misses the essential point of property. He writes:

> Property, a creation of law, does not arise from value, although exchangeable – a matter of fact. Many exchangeable values may be destroyed intentionally without compensation. Property depends upon exclusion by law from interference and a person is not excluded from using any combination of words merely because someone has used it before, even if it took labor and genius to make it.[83]

That property, an *in rem* right whose essence is its tangibility and the right to exclude, is classic formalism. Without quarreling with the larger argument that Holmes in his career rejected natural law and formalism,[84] this rejection is not evidenced by his rather formulaic dissent in <u>INS</u>. For Brandeis, too, the right to exclude is the central question that separates out property that can be protected from the fruits of one's labor that enjoys no such status.[85] However, how he gets there is by induction, from a view of property as socially constructed and contingent. He explains

> But the fact that a product of the mind has cost its producer money and labor, and has a value for which others are willing to pay, is not sufficient to ensure to it this legal attribute of property. The general rule of law is that the noblest of human productions – knowledge, truths ascertained, conceptions, and ideas – became, after voluntary communication to others, free as the air to common use. Upon these incorporeal productions the attribute of property is continued after such communication only in certain classes of cases where public policy has seemed to demand it.[86]

Further, Brandeis sees an opening to a legal principle that would see news as a resource which could be commoditized and subject to the classic property rights of exclusion. But, for Brandeis, this is not an appropriate role of the courts, as this is pure public policy. As he writes:

> [W]ith the increasing complexity of society, the public interest tends to become omnipresent, and the problems presented by new demands for justice cease to be simple. Then the creation or recognition by courts of a new private right may work serious injury to the general public unless the boundaries of the right are definitely established and wisely guarded. In order to reconcile the new private right with the public interest, it may be necessary to prescribe limitations and rules for its enjoyment, and also to provide administrative machinery for enforcing the rules. It is largely for this reason that, in the effort to meet the many new demands for justice incident to a rapidly changing civilization, resort to legislation has latterly been had with increasing frequency.[87]

Both jurists reject the argument that news-gathering is property, but in explaining their rejection we can see two different modalities of reasoning about property's content in this second decade of the twentieth century. One is formalistic and the other is pragmatic.[88]

The strong implication of the view associated here with Brandeis (which is not to neglect others whose new thinking was critical to this development) is that property rights are nested in the common good and subject to the intrinsic power, and indeed responsibility, of the government to implement public purposes even where individuals might be compromised in their use of their property.[89] Taken to its extreme, this view creates a force field around the police power and suggests that property rights as such will seldom if ever impede official choice that is made on a reasonable basis.[90] More to the point is the functionalist argument that broad governmental power is necessary to advance economic progress and social welfare. Perhaps the leading voice for this position in the latter part of the period we are focused on here was Brandeis himself. "For Brandeis," Fishkin and Forbath observe, "the nation's industrial and economic orders were fraught with constitutional infirmities that only legislation could remedy."[91]

Progressives who focused on the need for and value in governmental regulation to address problems were not anti-private property. Rather, they were against the misuse of private property, especially by corporations, and were more or less confident in the government's ability to channel the use of private property for socially beneficial aims.[92] In this regard, they were the mirror image of judges and scholars who were not so much wedded to a formalistic conception of private property, one that viewed such property as sacrosanct or even essential to human flourishing as they were quite skeptical about the incentives and capabilities of government to regulate in the public interest with trampling on individual rights. These skeptics were heirs to a tradition reflected in Madison and his expressed concern about factions and about the fragility of individual rights.[93]

These competing ideas came to be reconciled if not in deep theory then at least in police power jurisprudence in this era. This reconciliation is seen most clearly in the way in which the state courts dealt with the use of the police power to regulate individuals' private property rights. In a 1911 case in Missouri, for example, the court considered the constitutionality of a law regulating and controlling signs and billboards.[94] Dissenting from the holding that this was an ordinary safety regulation that met the conditions of the police power under the Missouri constitution, Justice Graves insisted that this law was principally about aesthetics, not public safety, and while the government might have some latitude to enact laws dealing with aesthetic considerations, doing so triggered stricter scrutiny because this law now interfered with the property owner's vested rights.[95] The implication of this dissenting view, which echoes some of the big considerations that would arise in Lochner-era cases of roughly the same period, is that the force of vested property rights grows as the rationale for the exercise of the police power wanes.

In Cleveland Telephone Co. v. City of Cleveland,[96] an Ohio case from 1918, the court considered the question of whether a law fixing rates could be implemented at the local level under the police power. Much of the debate in this opinion involved the question of whether there is some sort of general police power that, with the state's delegation of authority under local government law, widens the scope of governmental discretion.[97] The majority said no, over a vigorous dissent on this exact point.[98] What the court zeroes in on in its holding that this law is an unconstitutional exercise of the police power is the matter of vested rights.[99] The police power should be viewed, the court argues, as distinct from the exercise of a "governmental function."[100] The distinction turns on whether the restrictions are imposed on "personal or property rights of private persons."[101] Decided squarely in the shadow of the laisse faire period constitutionalism, the court declares that, in deciding police power cases, they "have uniformly interfered to restrain the arbitrary and unreasonable exercise of that power to the prejudice of private rights guaranteed by the Court of the State."[102]

It is tempting to see, as some do, the judiciary's approach to the police power as essentially continuous from the earliest Supreme Court decisions – Gibbons, Brown, and Miln, all from the antebellum era, through Munn and Mugler just after Reconstruction and through the beginning of the twentieth century, and through state court cases decided during the Gilded Age and afterward. Yet that narrative sacrifices nuance for a tight theory. On the one hand, the post-Reconstruction era brought us a fundamental shift in our constitutional structure and understanding of equality and citizenship, though it did not, at least as the Supreme Court came to see it, fundamentally reorder the balance between property rights and governmental power. On the other hand, seeing the police power as a continuous thread from the state constitutions' charge to govern with energy to Alger's focus on public rights to the Progressive era's faith in bold governance is to miss some of the tensions revealed both in ideology and in legal decisions of that time. The collective welfare was at the fulcrum of the government's strategy of governing under the police power. And yet this strategy was continuously in tension with evolving and shifting views about the nature and scope of liberty and property. The animating tension between individual property and liberty and the government did not dissolve. Much attention was given through the period from Reconstruction and World War II to how we ought to think about the concept of property affected by a public interest and how we can construct guardrails of various sorts to maintain an equilibrium between governmental intervention and private freedom.

To summarize: We should not imprint onto the thinking of courts and commentators of this era a fading commitment to natural law thinking as the nineteenth century ended and an emergent belief in the new century (which we will unpack in more detail in Chapter 6) in rights as trumps, as essentially countermajoritarian instruments, vigorously enforced by courts to restrain official power.[103] To take just one representative statement of many, Christopher Tiedman, a notorious critic of an expansive police power, begins his treatise by observing simply that courts "cannot nullify and avoid a law, simply because it conflicts with judicial notions of natural right or morality, or abstract justice."

So how then did courts think about the connection between property and the collective welfare? In the years following the end of Reconstruction and preceding the Progressive era, the courts had emphasized the idea of property as having important *jus publici* elements. In 1882, for example, the Supreme established the so-called "public trust doctrine," in Illinois Central Railroad v. Illinois.[104] This significant ruling applied to navigable waters, and could be seen as progeny from the navigable servitude and ancient water law doctrines. This land is held in public trust for all. "The soil under navigable waters," writes Justice Field, "being held by the people of the state in trust for the common use and as a portion of their inherent sovereignty, any act of legislation concerning their use affects the public welfare. It is therefore appropriately within the exercise of the police power of the state."[105] But the opinion has come to be seen as having a considerably more wide-ranging import. Its impact is best understood as another powerful statement of the idea resonant in so many of the public rights cases, that certain property was imprinted with a public obligation and therefore the dominion that a private owner would otherwise have was limited to the extent that the general interest required.[106]

This view is echoed in nineteenth-century decisions that conceptualize the key facets of government regulation as part of a project of protecting so-called public rights, a project that Scheiber summarizes as "robustly pragmatic." Indeed, it is no coincidence that the term "public" preceded "trust," "rights," and "purpose" in distinct constitutional doctrines and these ideas motivated courts to accept governmental authority as not only a matter of discretion, but one of duty. This was not seen as part of a project of effacing liberty and property rights, nor as a project of rescuing a compelling view of public policy through positive law from its roots in natural rights thinking (although this is a common depiction of this time and these strategies). Rather, the case for broad governmental authority under the policy rested on a somewhat more basic, albeit not uncontroversial, idea, and that is that regulating private property was necessary to advance the collective welfare. This was not about undermining property rights, but about constructing such rights around an edifice of common interest and the public good. Struggles over how best to strike this balance between individual liberty and general welfare would naturally continue in ensuing decades, but the rudiments of these ideas were forged during this critical era in which the regulatory power and obligations of state and local governments were taking shape in light of the practical necessities of the time.

THE POLICE POWER AND EMINENT DOMAIN

The *jus publici* notion, in expressing the idea that we are basically all in the same boat together, supported government regulation that limited an owner's prerogatives without necessarily requiring compensation, as eminent domain law would seem to require. Takings law did not exist in any judicially cognizable form until much later in the nineteenth century. Nor did the takings clause apply at all to state regulation until 1897. And it wasn't until 1922, with the Supreme Court's decision in Pennsylvania Coal v. Mahon that there was a serious restriction on government regulation of private property under the police power in the form of a just compensation requirement that emerged from the eminent domain clause of the federal Constitution.

The centrality of the police power in the regulation of private property in this era was, in a sense, a consequence of the Supreme Court's reluctance to turn to the eminent domain power as the main practical option available to state governments who would limit property rights in order to implement the common good. This absence of the takings clause for so long a period – at least up to the Supreme Court's decision in Mahon – is a curious but nonetheless important phenomenon and one that deserves at least some discussion in this account of the police power as the main event in property regulation.

Looking at the issue at a decent amount of relief, eminent domain played a fairly modest role in fights over the use of the government's regulatory power to control the use of private property.[107] One reason hearkens back to the complexity of defining property rights in the decades after the founding period. While commentators and even judges would invoke axioms about the imperative of protecting private property rights, "the society could not easily maintain a legal posture as to property rights entirely free of paradox and contradiction – at least not in an environment of economic growth so tumultuous as that of the United States in the nineteenth century."[108] Moreover, insofar as property rights were viewed in fairly static and even formalistic terms through much of the century, equating regulation of property with the "taking" of property for public use was more pragmatic than the times could easily accommodate. The easier route was the formalistic one. The essential dividing line between a government regulation that would or would not be a taking of private property was whether there was in fact an expropriation or else some sort of physical invasion by the government.[109] Very few of the actions of the government rose to this level, but those that did were considered under the rubric of eminent domain, not the police power.

Key steps in the evolution of the takings versus police power puzzle are found separately in state court decisions during the antebellum period and later decisions by the Supreme Court, especially <u>Munn</u> and <u>Mugler</u>, two cases we have already discussed in the context of the expanding interpretation of the police power. In the state courts, judges wrestled with the question of whether certain governmental interventions destroyed vested rights, whether contract rights, property rights, or both. The 1819 New York case of <u>People v. Platt</u>,[110] illustrates the tensions between government's proper role in abating a nuisance by limiting the owner's right to dam a river, to the detriment of the fish stock, and the owner's vested rights to use his property as he wishes unless the government was prepared to pay compensation.[111] In <u>Platt</u> and other cases from the nineteenth and early twentieth centuries,[112] the courts referred specifically to eminent domain, noting that the government could well pursue its regulatory objectives, but only so long as it was prepared to compensate owners. One important element to keep in mind as one considers these matters of constitutional controversies is that during this era a number of difficult concepts involving property law (e.g., riparian rights, the scope of the navigation servitude, public rights and public trust) were uncertain in content and in application. Courts were therefore juggling issues of private property law with issues of constitutional power. Both concepts were evolving simultaneously. The variations in how different states dealt with these issues in their state courts reveals these complex dynamics.

The turning point in the takings/police power interface came in the famous case of <u>Pennsylvania Coal v. Mahon</u>.[113] Frequently decried and much analyzed,[114] Mahon is the centerpiece of the Court's so-called regulatory takings jurisprudence. It advances for the first time in the Supreme Court the view that a property owner may have an actionable claim for just compensation under the eminent domain clause of the US Constitution even though the federal government does not take title to the property or physically invades it.[115] Eminent domain rules apply, announced Justice Oliver Wendell Holmes for the Court's majority, when a government regulation under the police power reduces to an unacceptable degree the economic value of the property. "One fact for consideration," Holmes writes, "in determining such limits is the extent of the diminution. When it reaches a certain magnitude, in most if not in all cases there must be an exercise of eminent domain and compensation to sustain the act."[116]

As bold and arresting as this proposition was in 1922, it left unanswered many questions for the next hundred years. What amount of diminished value would trigger a legitimate takings claim? Does this mean that all exercises of the police power that have a negative economic effect on a property owner require just compensation?[117] The answer to this question could not possibly be yes, unless a whole bevy of regulations, old and new, including public trust requirements, historic preservation laws, conservation regulations, exaction fees, and so on, would amount to a compensable taking of private property. But if and insofar as there are limits to <u>Mahon</u>'s reach, what are those limits and how does the regulatory takings doctrine square with the police power?

Mahon involved a federal statute, the Kohler Act, a statute that barred coal companies from removing coal when such removal caused subsidence. One company challenged this regulation as a taking that required just compensation, given that the regulation diminished the value of its legitimate property interest. The Court analyzed this regulation and, finding facts that indicated that Mr Mahon had suffered an economic loss by virtue of the government's regulation, held that this loss should be subject to compensation. Holmes's opinion focuses closely on the companies' property rights and the need for their protection by courts. It is therefore tempting to see his analysis as an exercise in formalism, one that bears some family resemblance to Lochner, Adkins, and other "liberty of contract" cases decided in the two decades before Mahon.[118] In this light, we can be puzzled, with others, about how this same Holmes could write a paean to the strong constitutional right of private property and the need of its owners to be properly compensated for their troubles.[119] But Holmes's opinion makes more sense when we see it as truly about the justice's antipathy to wealth redistribution (generally, and here through property restrictions) and his skepticism about the intentions of the legislature in creating these rules.

This does not fully explain the puzzle, however, of why Justice Holmes could reach this striking conclusion, one that would augur a new doctrine of substantial force and once that would create persistent tension between takings and police power doctrines. On the surface of things, this holding threatened to upend the then-state of police power authority under the US Constitution. As Morton Horwitz writes: "As the definition of property was expanded to include not only various uses of land, but also stable market values as well as expectations of future income form property, virtually every governmental activity was rendered capable of being regarded as a taking."[120] After all, health, safety, and welfare regulations commonly upheld under the police power, and with his assent in key opinions of the early twentieth century, have distributive effects. Zoning is a prominent example, but there are also various regulations that are designed to abate nuisances and stop other harms. Legal rules that uphold social interests at the expense of owner prerogatives are redistributive not only in the metaphorical sense that the balance is struck in favor of the public and against the private citizen, but they are redistributive in the real economic sense in that they impose costs on discrete individuals in order to fulfill general welfare objectives.

Justice Brandeis makes this point explicit in his Mahon dissent, although there too he focuses more narrowly on the way in which this federal statute was intended to abate public nuisances.[121] He might have written, though he did not, that by the time of the Mahon decision state and federal courts routinely upheld police power regulations even where they could not be yoked to the classic *sic utere* rationale.[122]

Taking Justice Holmes's analysis on its own terms, there are two essential confounds in this important decision: First, as an effort to curtail legislative excess and to ensure against redistributive measures, the invention of a new element of takings jurisprudence is a rather ham-handed way to accomplish this objective. Second, it is of precious little help in defining the boundaries between what is an ordinary police power regulation, one that does not require any governmental compensation, and what is a regulatory taking. Despite Mahon's centrality in the history of takings law, cited in cases all the way up to contemporary times and therefore part of the essential architecture of eminent domain,[123] it has had a fairly modest impact on other elements of constitutional law in either the federal or state courts that continue to shape the contours of police power regulation. In particular, neither zoning laws nor health and safety regulations have proved especially vulnerable to a takings clause analysis. For example, we will see in the next chapter how the courts in the recent COVID-19 pandemic routinely, and often without any serious energy expended in analysis, rejected takings claims where a business made highly plausible factual arguments that the government's shutdowns caused major economic hardship.

Taking a step away from the doctrinal focus, we can see the 1920s project of establishing a route for establishing a compensation right for regulatory takings under the takings clause as at least clunky, if not ultimately rather ill-fated. One reason was that the state and federal courts were struggling with the instability of property rights notions, a struggle that was embedded in a larger, complex journey from classical modes of legal reasoning toward more modern approaches to understanding the dimensions of private property, to examining issues of government regulation, and understanding whether and how state constitutions limit government. Louis Brandeis was ahead of this curve in adumbrating the social context and empirical bases of property and regulation, but even his prescience in this domain was a product of its time and was not a fully worked theory that commanded consensus among jurists and commentators in this era. Brandeis was a maverick and was viewed by contemporaries as such. Moreover, there is also a realpolitik in all this as well. Regulation and constitutional review went through enormous change as the Supreme Court's membership changed in the New Deal era.[124] At the Supreme Court level, it fell to the Hughes Court to work out what we might call a "political accommodation" that would secure significant governmental prerogative and discretion while also attending to property rights and other aspects of private right, albeit through a more conspicuously process-oriented approach.[125]

As to eminent domain law in particular, its ambiguities and complexities made it difficult to assist the enterprise of configuring the metes and bounds between reasonable and unreasonable government regulation of private property. Viewed generously, it at least set out the terms of the bargain in a way that sought to accommodate private and public interest by, recalling the famous Calabresi and Melamed formulation,[126] by insisting on a liability rule that would enable the government to cost out its regulatory interventions. Good governing is all fine and well, but it comes at a price.

As for determining the scope and shape of the by then well-established police power, the advent and evolution of regulatory takings doctrine meant that the issue of balancing public interest and private right remained in the quagmire. Should the government be able to supplant an individual's private property right in order to protect health, safety, or the common good, and on what terms? Is the ever-present risk of a property owner losing one or more sticks in the property rights bundle merely a condition for living in society? In the period following key Supreme Court cases such as Munn and Mugler, state governments could see the space created by the Court's acknowledgment that the common good did warrant interventions to protect health, safety, and morals. However, such interventions were not then, nor would they ever become, unconditional. The struggle that manifest itself in the Progressive and Populist eras, represented by not only police power controversies, but also eminent domain and due process, was how best to set and enforce those conditions through judicial review.

LEGISLATIVE SKEPTICISM ABORNING

In the book's first two chapters, we noted the ways in which American political culture revealed from the republic's beginning an enormous deference to elected legislatures. This was largely a reflection of our distinct science of politics emerging in the pre-founding period, one cemented by the framers of the US Constitution, and reflected in the idea that state constitutions were documents of limit and sources of the principle that legislative power is plenary. Skepticism about the prominence of the legislature began as early as the Jacksonian era, although deference to legislative judgment persisted.

The period after Reconstruction, however, brought with it a notably greater anxiety about the tendencies of the legislature to act in ways that were seen as undemocratic and overly intrusive into the realm of private freedom. As the Alabama Governor Emmett O'Neal commented in 1913: "We have come to believe that the legislature, like a strong man inflamed by violent passion and dominated by wicked influences, was likely to 'run amuck' trampling down the interests of the just and the unjust alike."[127]

Legislators were increasingly viewed as captured by special interests and dominated by factions external to the legislature.[128] This, of course, was a concern raised famously by James Madison in Federalist No. 10, and some of the "auxiliary precautions" he wrote about included measures to cabin such factionalism.[129] However, the main device he offered – expanding the scope of the republic so as to make a democratically elected legislature harder to control, and also federalism – were less promising as devices to limit excesses in state legislatures. Such legislatures were comparatively smaller, and some were small by any measure. Moreover, the breadth of legislative power meant that interest-group influence would be more impactful on public policy generally. This risk went with the territory, as it were. Madison's original worries therefore were echoed in late nineteenth-century commentary on the state of American constitutionalism.

Concerns that state legislatures were becoming unwieldy, unworkable, and overbearing pushed citizens and officials in states to amend their constitutions (or, in rare instances, to replace these constitutions entirely) in ways that would reduce legislative power. Rather than see the many legislative checks created by state constitutional reforms as destructive of legislative power and as the scaling down of the sphere of politics, it is better to see them as, to use some economic jargon, introducing legislative transaction costs. Legislatures could still engage in active governance, but there would be mechanisms that created burdens, and occasionally barriers, to such actions. In all, legislators would need to forge compromises (often with executive branch officers) and innovate in lawmaking in order to do the people's business.

If we unpack the reasons and rationales for this emerging skepticism, we can see that it does not present itself as primarily an anti-government movement; it does not necessarily undergird the so-called libertarian constitutionalism so commonly associated with the Lochner era and, for some commentators, even the years before that notorious case. Citizens were concerned that legislators were not advancing the people's welfare. They could point to examples of overbearing laws interfering with personal liberty and private property as illustrative. As Edwin Godkin wrote in 1897: "One of the faults most commonly found in the legislatures is the fault of doing too much."[130] At the same time, they could (and did) point to examples of their elected officials not doing enough to reign in rapacious corporations and to redistribute opportunities to those more in need. Indeed, the leading academic accounts of the Progressive and Populist eras focus rightly on the concerns with caste legislation and private regarding legislation.[131] Taking account of those who objected that government did too much and those who objected that they did too little or did what they did incoherently, there was building a robust group of disgruntled citizens, citizens who could capture the attention of those in real or potential positions of power. And so, not surprisingly, the period between the end of Reconstruction and the Second World War was a time of active reform in the wheels of governance, including state constitutions.

Among these reforms were structural mechanisms that were intended to limit the scope of legislative power. These included the imposition of public purpose requirements and of prohibitions on special legislation, balanced budget requirements, and enhancement of the governor's fiscal powers. The development of initiative lawmaking, a manifestation of the view that direct citizen democracy had a role to play in public policymaking, was also illustrative of this legislative skepticism and the need for checks and balances.[132] In addition, there were significant amendments of the US Constitution, including the Seventeenth Amendment (which took the function of electing senators out of the state legislatures and gave it to the people) and the Nineteenth Amendment (women's suffrage), which could be tied, even if indirectly, to concerns about legislative supremacy and its actions in the tenor of the times.

This legislative skepticism led to a fork in the road. Should the courts continue their deferential posture or should they respond to concerns with legislative performance by taking a more skeptical tack? State and federal courts could well have responded to intense concerns with legislative malfeasance by bolstering judicial review of legislative actions. They had the tools to do so through due process especially, and through other measures and mechanisms. Lochner showed one such avenue, as we will discuss next. But note that insofar as skepticism emerged in earlier years, the fact that state courts maintained a largely deferential posture toward police power regulation and also imprinted upon private property doctrines of *jus publici* of various sorts, was strong evidence that the police power of Justice Lemuel Shaw and of less celebrated judges who had approved regulatory interventions to preserve health, safety, morals, and the people's welfare was alive and well. That all said, the Lochner era would test this faith.

LAISSEZ FAIRE CONSTITUTIONALISM AND THE POLICE POWER RENEWED

With the Court's decision in Lochner in 1905 and subsequent decisions in a similar vein,[133] the Court insisted on a much tighter justification for state legislation that infringed on what they described as the liberty of contract. This also pertained to impositions on private property and, while the emergence of a truly robust takings jurisprudence for regulatory takings would await the 1920s, the effect of the Lochner era line of cases was to limit in a significant way the sphere of authority state and local governments exercised in the name of health, safety, and general welfare.

In Lochner v. New York,[134] the Court considered a maximum hours law for bakers in New York. Acknowledging that this law fell under the traditional rubric of the police power, the Court said that this "is a question of which of two powers or rights shall prevail – the power of the State to legislate or the right of the individual to liberty of person and freedom of contract. The mere assertion that the subject relates though but in a remote degree to the public health does not necessarily render the enactment valid."[135] The Court makes two essential claims, each addressing the standard of review of police power legislation: First, "[t]he act must have a more direct relation, as a means to an end, and the end itself must be appropriate and legitimate, before an act can be held to be valid which interferes with the general right of an individual to be free in his person and in his power to contract in relation to his own labor."[136] The first claim reflects a more searching review of the reasonableness of the legislation than was typical in previous cases before the Court, including Jacobson, decided just before Lochner. The second, and even more arresting, claim is that there exists a right to contract that stands against the legislature's efforts to regulate for the public good. Ultimately, the Court dismisses the state's argument that this is a valid health law and, accordingly, holds that this legislation is outside the scope of the police power and, moreover, are "meddlesome interferences with the rights of the individual."[137] Justice Harlan dissented, joined by two other justices, in which he pointed out the many state cases which had upheld public health and safety regulations similar, he suggests, to New York's.[138] Moreover, he detailed the health-related considerations associated with heavy duty employment as a baker. Justice Holmes wrote a celebrated dissent wherein he accused the majority of enacting its own economic theory into constitutional law through a novel reading of the Fourteenth Amendment.[139]

In the standard story, the Court invented substantive due process in this era to protect economic liberties that had long been vulnerable to regulation under the rubric of public interest and general welfare rationales.[140] This rationale, it was said, came out of nowhere, was an indefensible edict – an ipse dixit – that individuals had vested rights against government regulation, and threatened to undermine the basic structure of regulation that enables markets to operate and protected individuals from injury and unfair economic treatment. This was, as Professor Laurence Tribe puts it, "a misguided understanding of what liberty actually required in the industrial age."[141] In this account, Lochner was surprising at the time, deeply mistaken as a decision then, and rightly repudiated two decades later by key New Deal cases which formally overturned the holdings of Lochner and other cases representing similar themes and discredited its essential logic.[142]

This standard story has met resistance by a wide cadre of legal scholars over the past few decades. No one doubts that the Court provided in Lochner and its progeny a more muscular approach to restrictions on property and liberty and was looking with more skepticism at government regulations that had passed muster under older state court cases and Munn and Mugler in the Supreme Court. Revisionist scholars question, however, whether the Court's approach was truly a significant departure from the jurisprudence of an earlier era or was, instead, broadly congruent with the anti-caste philosophy that had long undergirded the courts' view of state legislatures and the expected wisdom of state legislation or the lack thereof.[143] "A consensus is emerging," David Bernstein writes in his provocative book, *Rehabilitating Lochner*, "that the liberty of contract doctrine arose from a combination of hostility to 'class legislation' and a desire to protect natural rights deemed fundamental to the development of American liberty."[144]

One window into the Court's approach in the Lochner era is provided by scholars who see in this era's cases a commitment to laissez faire constitutionalism properly actualized through classical modes of legal thought, and modes that used natural law and natural rights reasoning to reach results and to ground their ratio decidendi.[145] These modes were familiar, having anchored common law adjudication for a significant time, yet in the Lochner era, these methods were mobilized in the service of a new, and in many ways radical, conception of vested rights and the circumscribed role of the government in intervening in the economy and in private choices. The pre-political character of rights and the deontology of constitutional law during the period leading up to the Legal Realism movement helped forge a strong attack on government regulation that threatened private ordering and the neutral market.[146]

For some other scholars looking closer at Lochner and its progeny, the basic approach of the Court majority was, while characteristic of then-*au courant* methods of reasoning, unremarkable. Legal historian Ted White, for example, insists that the formation of a distinct judicial approach to police power, due process, and private rights was neither more nor less than a sensibly wrought "guardian review," one that foregrounded a reasonably searching judicial review by the federal courts (which is White's sole focus) and presumably also by the states. Sometimes the states won, other times they lost; in either event, the Court's focus was on what White calls "boundary pricking," which is to say that they examined the reasons for the state's assertion of power and balanced it against the individual liberty interests.[147] Barry Cushman likewise views the principal Supreme Court decisions in the era demarcated by Lochner and the summative decisions of the New Deal as broadly congruent with relevant precedent, albeit not suggesting that they were correctly decided, but suggesting that the renewal of expansive legislative power in cases such as Nebbia v. New York and Muller v. Oregon was not a radical departure from standard constitutional law. Rather, neither the methods of reasoning nor the interpretation of previous decisions suggested that the Court had taken a radical turn, one steeped solely or even mostly in the commitments to free market libertarianism.

We can bridge in some ways these competing stories by emphasizing the skepticism toward legislatures and legislative regulation that animates these and other decisions in the early decades of the twentieth century. For some scholars, the turn toward greater scrutiny was not a cataclysmic change for conceptions of governmental power and its responsibility to act for the general welfare. Instead, they see Lochner and its progeny as focused on pathologies in the legislative process.[148] The idea here is that the judiciary's approach to the police power has always concentrated on the legislative process and the fundamental fairness of this process, especially from those whose interests could be compromised by interest group influence and self-dealing. Joey Fishkin and William Forbath see this effort as part of an enduring, if unstable, commitment to democracy-as-opportunity, and to an "anti-oligarchic constitution."[149] While themselves skeptical of the motives and techniques of justices in the first two decades of the twentieth century who saw the legislature as a threat to liberty of contract and private property, the basic idea that the courts would interrogate legislation to ensure that it was not arbitrary or in another way unreasonable was well in line with the objective of protecting democracy-of-opportunity. In a similar vein, Howard Gillman sees this skepticism of legislative lawmaking echoing in the Jacksonian democracy and explains Lochner and the epoch of libertarian constitutionalism as an outgrowth of a view steadily growing into the Progressive era that "legislating special privileges for particular groups and classes" stretched beyond what the police power authorized and that the approach that become prominent after the enactment of the Fourteenth Amendment, albeit for a few decades, was one in which the Court "organized its police powers jurisprudence primarily around a distinction between legitimate general welfare legislation and illegitimate factional politics."[150] In this rendering, cases that on first glance look like evidence of a strong commitment to private property and liberty as such are actually best viewed as interrogations into the self-dealing of state legislatures and, relatedly, the inequitable disadvantages on certain individuals and groups meted out by these legislative enactments.[151]

This revisionist argument about Lochner's lack of special novelty is incomplete. This focus supposes that the Court had a rather purposive commitment to redressing flaws in the legislative process and redistributing power to the have-nots., at least as an explanation of the evolution of the police power in the period between the end of Reconstruction and the end of World War II. Much of the debate over the origins and impact of the Lochner era focuses on the question of whether and to what extent the Court developed and implemented a scheme of substantive due process in order to create liberty and property-based constraints on the exercise of power. However, the more fundamental issue for the framing of the police power is how the courts, state and federal, came to view the tactics and strategies that state and local governments pursued in this era to protect health, safety, and welfare. Reading through these Lochner era cases in the Supreme Court, alongside the many less prominent decisions rendered by state judges, an important theme is the overall robustness of the courts' scrutiny of legislative strategy. Was the legislature pursuing a reasonable set of objectives and, even if so, were they using mechanisms that accomplished these ends in ways that were neither arbitrary nor in any other way inconsistent with the general welfare? Lochner-era histories generally focus in on the questions of how solicitous were courts with regard to individual rights, ones mostly unenumerated and, to many, historically underprotected.[152] However, during the two decades demarcating the Lochner era, government at the state and local level developed novel techniques for protecting public welfare (we will consider one of the most important ones in the next subsection of this chapter) and in which the meaning of property and liberty continued to evolve. Moreover, state constitutional changes made more salient the connections between political tactics and societal objectives, objectives realized through evidence-based governmental action. Plucking Lochner from these complex developments risks positing an incomplete, if not distorted picture, of the history of regulation and the ever-evolving police power.

With the end of Lochner and the beginning of the New Deal, the Supreme Court moved sharply away from a skeptical approach to reviewing police power regulations. Summarizing the caselaw of the period between Nebbia and Parrish and the mid-1960s, when modern substantive due process emerged as a means of creating and protecting unenumerated rights against official restriction, liberty of contract quickly faded as a basis for scrutiny and invalidation. Taking its place was a fairly "minimalist, procedural" due process, one in which "due process meant fair process; that was all."[153] The courts largely abandoned the approach of scrutinizing the means-end fit of legislation in order to ensure that the law passes muster under the police power. As we will see in our examination of zoning later in this chapter and in the next, the Court made clear that it was not within the proper role of the courts to scrutinize the wisdom of legislation and, more to the point of the police power, the degree and extent to which a certain regulatory strategy in fact furthered general welfare as it could credibly be measured. The much-heralded Brandeis brief, a shrewd tactic of describing the factual basis and logic of a legislature's approach to regulation in a particular instance, faded not because skillful lawyers could not engage deeply with evidence- and data-driven analysis, but because the courts were no longer interested in taking such a deep dive into the legislature's rationales and regulatory strategies.[154] At bottom, the Supreme Court was largely solicitous of the capability of state and local governments to pursue the people's welfare through a judicious but energetic use of the constitutional police power.

One last point here, not especially profound as an account of Lochnerian jurisprudence, but of consequence for the general argument in this book: Most of the accounts of the Lochner era, whether standard or revisionist or something less well defined, focus like a laser on a handful of Supreme Court cases and do not look closely at what was going in in the state courts. Much more often than not, regulations that were challenged during the Lochner era period were upheld under the police power.[155] This was certainly true of morals regulations, but also true of many regulations of private property and liberty of contract. Indeed, as we discussed earlier with regard to regulatory takings, it was largely from the frustration with the unwillingness of the courts to stop or slow the train of regulations which reduced the value of owners' property that the Court developed an important safety value – regulatory takings. Public health regulations were commonly upheld, especially notable in this era of increasing density and infectious diseases; so too were safety-oriented regulations, a development that was particularly important before tort law would develop doctrines such as enterprise liability and worker's compensation, in order to deal with the uptick of industrially-related injuries.[156] In short, the police power did not wither away during the Lochner period. On the contrary, state legislatures came out of the New Deal period with great powers and with robust capacity and resolve to tackle matters of health, safety, and welfare.

ASSESSING REASONABLENESS IN THIS PERIOD

Out of the progeny of Munn and Mugler in the first years after Reconstruction and, later, in the post-Lochner era, there emerged a better view of the police power and its limits. The standard of reasonableness was invoked in various cases, especially at the state level, and proved to be a moderately formidable restriction on legislative power.[157] This reasonableness standard was hard on its face to separate from an inquiry into the wisdom and means-end fit of legislation; and courts were disinclined, especially as the period of laissez faire constitutionalism passed, to look closely at the reasonableness of legislation. In constitutional review generally, intrusions on so-called economic liberties were subject to rational basis review,[158] a standard that did not really change in the many decades since its emergence as an adjudicatory standard. And while impositions on property rights are not always identical to violations of economic liberties, the courts applied what amounted to the same standard, with one exception which we will touch on here and explore in more detail in the next chapter.

In Chapter 7, we will explore in more depth the courts' myriad approaches to judging reasonableness and improper governmental regulation under the police power in the contemporary US. The discussion there will be more normative than descriptive. Here we want to use judging and assessment in a wholly different sense. The inquiry is not principally into how courts evaluate police power regulations under these standards, except insofar as what one or another court says can illuminate the critical issues. Rather, we want to look at how reasonableness was understood in the key era between Reconstruction and the New Deal as a measure of proper governmental power and the resilience of individual liberty and property interests.

What emerged in the Progressive era and its aftermath was an important new sense about the capacity and ingenuity of government in regulation. As the administrative state emerged as a key mechanism for the exercise of governmental power, attention was drawn to how the government might deploy expertise in the pursuit of good governing. Quite simply, our normative expectations for government performance increased even while concern about how government actually behaved grew. At different junctures, we have seen how structural constitutional reforms were created to limit government power. But this is only part of the story. State constitutional reform and, alongside it, state constitutional adjudication were the fora for the examination of such central questions as: What were the best means of effectuating the salutary aims of government? What were the best structures to ensure that the state and local governments would reach the best balance between safeguarding individual liberties and property rights on the one hand and the "overruling necessity" of government to implement the common good?[159] Novak and other legal historians looking at this period find a nearly unbroken line from distrust of government in implementing new regulatory strategies to the securing of broad and resilient governmental power (with one hiccup in the Lochner era). These broad and dense analyses capture important truths about this period. However, when we look at the treatment of government regulation alongside struggles involving state constitutional architecture and reform, we see that this period was as much about tension as about reflexive confirmation of authority, about how to balance liberty with regulation, and, critically, how law could be designed and used to effectuate a strategy of good governing. This means more than just ensuring that democracy and the rule of law would be observed. It means also that governmental officials would perform well and that regulatory means would reach their desired ends. The principal way in which this would be ensured, as commentators and courts of the time viewed it, is by close attention to reasonableness and rationality in lawmaking.

State and federal courts had long been focused on the question of whether the government's actions were arbitrary or discriminatory. That they less often found arbitrariness in official action than otherwise is not the measure of the jurisprudence

"The Power to Govern Men and Things": The Police Power Evolves

of constitutional review in police power cases. Notably, most of the key cases predated Lochner, and they did not rest on the considerations urged by contemporary scholars such as Tiedeman and Cooley and on the principles that would become prominent after the Court's decision in Lochner and for several years thereafter.

For example, in Lawton v. Steele,[160] decided by the Supreme Court in 1894, the Court considered and held unconstitutional a New York law that instructed law enforcement authorities to confiscate or destroy fishing nets in order to protect the fish. The Court delineated the scope of the limits on the exercise of a police power to impose a general regulation:

> To justify the state in thus interposing its authority in behalf of the public, it must appear first that the interests of the public generally, as distinguished from those of a particular class, require such interference, and second that the means are reasonably necessary for the accomplishment of the purpose, and not unduly oppressive upon individuals. The legislature may not, under the guise of protecting the public interests, arbitrarily interfere with private business or impose unusual and unnecessary restrictions upon lawful occupations; in other words, its determination as to what is a proper exercise of its police powers is not final or conclusive, but is subject to the supervision of the courts.[161]

Concern with protecting against arbitrary imposition of regulation, especially where this disrupts the freedom of individuals to pursue their trade and conduct their business, was conspicuous in key state cases in this period as well. A case from California involved an ordinance that imposed various restrictions on building structures for hospitals for the insane. The plaintiff complained that these ordinances were created after his building, and the substantial investment pertaining to said building, had been completed.

Courts protected against arbitrary regulations in a number of important public health-related decisions in the late nineteenth and early twentieth century, as the government struggled to contain infection diseases through quarantines and other measures. In Jew Ho v. Williamson,[162] the court considered the imposition of a quarantine in turn-of-the-century San Francisco, a quarantine designed to control an outbreak of the bubonic plague. This law had the effect of limiting individual travel and the conduct of business of those of "Chinese race and nationality only."[163] While accepting the power of the local public health authority to impose this regulation, the district court held that this was created in a palpably discriminatory way and so exceeded the scope of the local government under the police power. Moreover, the court illuminated evidence that suggested that this quarantine was likely to be wholly ineffective at controlling the spread of this disease. "[T]he court must hold that this quarantine is not a reasonable regulation to accomplish the purposes sought. It is not in harmony with the declared purpose of the board of health or the board of supervisors."[164]

That reasonableness was thought promising earlier in American legal history as a more muscular standard of review was evidenced in some of the more influential summaries of the police power. In his 1904 treatise, Ernst Freud has an entire section devoted to "the principle of reasonableness."[165] Municipal police regulations "must be reasonable in order to be lawful."[166] The courts, says Freud, were "emphatic in their assertion that they have nothing to do with the wisdom or expediency of legislative measures."[167] Yet still there was a requirement, he argued, a requirement of "moderation and proportionateness of means to ends."[168]

In any event, judicial inquiry into the reasonableness of legislation under the police power in the early decades of the twentieth century was neither recognizable as a precursor to rational basis review as formulated in early Supreme Court cases, nor as a dense interrogation into the efficacy or coherence of the legislature's work product. Remembering Justice Harlan's opinion in Jacobson, the Court's inquiry into what is reasonable, anything more searching than the deferential look the Court gave to the public health agency's policy "would usurp the functions of another branch of government," for "[i]t is no part of the function of a court or a jury to determine which one of two modes was likely to be the most effective for the protection of the public against disease. That was for the legislative department to determine in the light of all the information it had or could obtain."[169]

That the Court's approach was highly deferential did not mean that it would not engage in discussion of the rationale of the government's action. In Muller, for example, the Court departed from Lochner in a fairly explicit way, upholding a law that limited the working hours of women. In a short and otherwise rather perfunctory opinion, Justice Brewer, for an unanimous court, opined at some length about the physical "disadvantage" of women and their "dependen[ce] upon man."[170] It was upon this rationale that the Court distinguished the case from Lochner. And yet the Court's choices about when and how to interrogate a state's reasons for its laws remained unclear, and at times even baffling. In Buchanan v. Warley,[171] a case brought by a White plaintiff challenging a racially restrictive covenant, the Court eschewed relying upon, or even really referring to, an avalanche of arguments made in the form of a "Brandeis brief" against racial mixing, instead insisting, per Lochner, that such covenants restricted the liberty of contract, Q.E.D. Ten years later, in the notorious case of Buck v. Bell,[172] Justice Holmes for the Court reflected upon the reasonableness of a Virginia law which authorized mandatory sterilization. Noting that "three generations are imbeciles are enough,"[173] curiously, Holmes invoked Jacobson as authority for the holding. However, here, unlike in Jacobson, the Court freely interrogated the legislature's purposes and strategy, in order to arrive at the conclusion that the law was unreasonable under the police power.

In the period we are focused on in this chapter, the federal courts grappled with issues of discrimination and arbitrariness, in evaluation the constitutionality of government action. As in the quarantine cases in San Francisco discussed above, the gravamen of the complaint was not with the fact that the government was undertaking to regulating a business affected with a public interest or was limiting property rights, but that it did so in a palpably discriminatory way. When, by contrast, the government was drawing lines between proper and improper conduct in an area in which a property owner on the wrong side of the line would bear a particular burden, the Court made clear, as in <u>Lindsley v. Natural Carbonic Gas. Co.</u>,[174] that "it is only essential that there shall be some rational connection between the fact proved and the ultimate fact presumed, and that the inference of one fact from proof of another shall not be so unreasonable as to be a purely arbitrary mandate."[175]

It would be too pat, therefore, to see the <u>Lochner</u> era's experiment with laissez faire constitutionalism as an abandonment of meaningful judicial review in police power cases. In the next chapter, we will look broadly at the development of the police power, including judicial interpretation, from the mid-century up to the present, and so we will see how the courts approached these issues in broad outline. But it is nonetheless important for the purposes of our evaluation of police power in the critical half-century between Reconstruction's end and the end of World War II to see how the state and federal courts reshaped police power doctrine from a formalistic, natural law-based interrogation into vested rights, and one that began with a studied skepticism about legislative motivation, to an approach that aspired to some degree at least to be a check on legislative malfeasance and arbitrariness and one that, more ambitiously, was concerned with public welfare as a rationale and as an objective of the exercise of the power. As we said at the end of Chapter 2, there emerged in the second century of the republic new ways of exercising police power, including the use of administrative regulation to implement health, safety, and welfare policy. In so doing, the regulation of the police power shifted from standard constitutional review of rights versus power to a more eclectic review structure, one that was found in the internal structure of administrative law and process.

The courts' invocation of the principle that government regulation cannot be arbitrary to pass legal muster would do work in various constitutional law contexts outside the realm of property rights and liberty of contract. While there was little in the constitutional law jurisprudence of the first half of the twentieth century that illustrated a searching review of legislation for arbitrariness or unreasonableness in a more robust sense. However, such approaches would become one of the linchpins of the courts' evolving equal protection doctrine later in the twentieth century and would also factor into the consideration of content and viewpoint neutrality in the consideration of free speech and free exercise controversies. More recently, as we will discuss in Chapter 7, the Court has undertaken to review state and federal laws that, it has been urged, show evidence of animus and should be evaluated under new sorts of equal protection principles, ones that inquire more deeply into legislative and administrative motive.[176] While motivation-centered constitutional review had fallen out of favor, especially after <u>Lochner</u>'s demise, this approach to review made a roaring comeback in key cases involving discrimination against LGBTQ+ individuals and also in recent cases involving executive decisions from the Trump administration.[177]

Beyond constitutional law, the concern about arbitrariness would become critically important in the development of administrative law in the late nineteenth and early twentieth centuries. What would ultimately answer A. W. Dicey and other influential critics of the administrative state (not completely satisfactorily, then or even now, to be sure) is that the courts would maintain guardrails to ensure that administrator were exercising discretion sensibly.[178] They did so by requiring that agency decisions, to use the language codified into the federal Administrative Procedure Act of the 1940s,[179] were neither arbitrary nor capricious.[180] This requirement was likewise central to state administrative law, from truly the beginning of our expanding use of regulatory agencies at the state and federal level and the practice of administrative discretion.[181] We will see later how various bodies of law, especially administrative law and constitutional law, could work together to limit the risks of arbitrary government action and could, more ambitiously, facilitate good governing. For now, we should just see that what came from the end of the Progressive era and by then nearly a century and a half of experience with the police power was both a robust and resilient power to govern, even where private property rights and other freedoms were affected, and also a framework for ensuring that the government did not abuse its power by undertaking actions that were arbitrary or discriminatory.

*

In the Progressive era and deep into the twentieth century, the police power was evolving from, first, an outgrowth of the *sic utere* principle and a means of protecting against public nuisances and other similar public harms and, second, a wider mechanism for protecting the common good through salutary regulation of health, safety, and welfare, to an ever more significant means for implementing more modern forms of regulation to promote the general welfare in an increasingly complex society. To best understand the trajectory of the evolving police power, we should understand both how it became more capacious in its scope, thanks to actual legislative practice and also the imprimatur given by the courts, and also how it morphed from a power exercised mainly through state legislation to one that was a key arrow in the quiver of administrative agencies and municipalities. Perhaps the best policy area available to illuminate these developments is zoning, the topic we turn to next. Emerging in earnest in the second decade of twentieth century, zoning presents an especially tricky set of issues for government policymakers and also for courts, the former involved in constructing new techniques of regulation for a rapidly changing urban environment and the latter struggling to develop appropriate limits on the exercise of this awesome power by state and local governments.

MANAGING PROPERTY THROUGH ZONING

What makes zoning important is not only its ubiquity in modern American urban life, but the fact that the case for zoning power cannot be so easily tied to considerations of health and safety.[182] To be sure, some land use regulations have been yoked to health and safety rationales, thinking of government efforts to reduce blight and the problems of poverty and crime that are associated with certain patterns of property use and residential life.[183] However, the courts have approved zoning laws under the police power without requiring the sort of means-end connection to health and safety that one might have thought were necessary.[184] The approval of zoning reflects a triumph of a particular approach to interpreting the police power, long ago and persisting for decades afterward, and so we should look closely at how these developments came to pass.[185]

Zoning is commonplace now, but it was not always so. Local governments' early efforts beginning in the 1920s to regulate land use by comprehensive zoning regulations were challenged in court by property owners, to no one's surprise, and the courts worked to accommodate these novel regulations within existing police power doctrine. An important early case was Miller v. Board of Public Works of Los Angeles.[186] The California Supreme Court there responded to the argument that this zoning law effaces the traditional constitutional limits on the government's regulatory power, both because there was not a nuisance and therefore the *sic utere* principle didn't apply and because this imposed discrete burdens on particular property owners in order to advance public purposes. Land use regulation under the police power is not limited to abating nuisances, said the court. This form of regulation emerged not as a redundant mechanism for protecting private rights from interference by others, but as a novel means of responding to changing conditions, especially in big urban areas such as Los Angeles. It is understandable and acceptable that the police power would change with it, for

> the police power is not a circumscribed prerogative, but is elastic and, in keeping with the growth of knowledge and the belief in the popular mind of the need for its application, capable of expansion to meet existing conditions of modern like and thereby keep pace with the social, economic, moral, and intellectual evolution of the human race.[187]

This power is not unlimited to be sure, and the court noted that some municipalities have "under the guise of zoning, sought to enact and enforce unreasonable and discriminatory ordinances."[188] The courts' role, therefore, is, as in other police power controversies, to investigate whether these regulations are proper or improper exercises of this regulatory power. Miller is important in clarifying that it is not enough merely to say that this is a zoning regulation, as though this will automatically trigger added scrutiny. The government's role in protecting the *salus populi* having become well established, zoning was viewed by these courts as the kind of practical instrument that government has designed to ensure that owners' use of their private property is consistent with the common good.[189]

The biggest and boldest step in the constitutional law of zoning was the Supreme Court's decision in Ambler Realty Co. v. Village of Euclid,[190] decided just a year after Miller. This decision was both momentous and rather unexpected, given that it was decided by the Supreme Court in the midst of the Lochner era. Moreover, its holding was squarely in favor of local government power, in both its decision to limit significantly a key stick in the bundle of private property rights, and without any compensation, and also the approval of the decision by state governments to permit a general-purpose local government to make this choice.

The property owners in the Euclid case cleverly styled the case as not just about a moderate intrusion on certain property rights as a result of this novel land use regulation, but as an existential threat to individual liberty and, especially, the market economy. "The ordinance," argued the lawyers for the plaintiffs, "constitutes a cloud upon the land, reduces and destroys its value, and has the effect of diverting the normal industrial, commercial and residential development thereof to other and less favorable locations."[191]

One of the lawyers arguing for the town, reflecting upon the Euclid decision nearly three decades after the decision, captures colorfully zoning's logic: "Housekeeping for municipalities is, under zoning, finding an orderliness. Zoning is merely keeping the kitchen stove out of the parlor, the bookcase out of the pantry and the dinner table out of the bedroom. It provides that houses shall be built among houses, apartments in apartment zones, stores in store zones, and industry in zones set aside for industry."[192] Importantly, Euclid's lawyers met the objections to the use of this novel land use regulation head on, not relying solely on the argument that restrictions on private property are typically permitted under a long line of police power precedents, but explaining to the Court what zoning was about, how it was tied to old notions of regulating to proscribe owners' property uses that would harm individuals and members of the general public, and painting a picture that would illustrate how this scheme would help bring order to cities and eliminate the chaos that existed before New York authorities created this new scheme of scientific management.[193]

Euclid was styled by its conservative author as a narrow ruling, and one that he grounded in existing law. And yet the import of Euclid was anything but modest. Most cities eventually adopted some version of zoning regulations, versions which had much in common with one another.[194]

The Euclid decision represents a convergence of a number of developments from the first quarter of the twentieth century that impacts the nature and scope of the modern police power. First, it is a reminder made explicit of the fact that under our constitutional traditions the use of property is subject to the requirements of society and the common welfare. Zoning is a modal example of the need to balance individual property rights with the public good.[195] Second, it pushes past the *sic utere* idea that property regulation is warranted only to abate a nuisance, even if the property owners played no particular role in the conditions that give rise to the decision of the local authorities to create a structure of zoning – indeed, what has become known as "Euclidean zoning."[196] Land use restrictions typical of these zoning arrangements included separation of commercial from residential uses, height restrictions, lot sizes, density rules, setbacks (distance between buildings and property lines), and development rules of various configurations.[197] The idea of *salus populi* as a principle undergirding the police power appears prominently in the arguments made on behalf of the city's zoning policy in the state and ultimately the Supreme Court. It is explored, if a bit more opaquely, in the Court's decision. This decision largely embraces these arguments, even if the precise rationale for its decisions remains somewhat opaque. Third and finally, Euclid represents a commitment to expertise and administrative government in accord with principles of scientific management.[198] Zoning again captures this principle well; and the approval of the municipality's decision reaffirms this movement in regulatory governance.

Zoning law would of course become very prominent for the century (and counting) after the Euclid decision. However, the constitutionality of zoning laws would fade almost entirely from the federal constitutional agenda and mainly from state constitutional law, except in the latter circumstances in which concerns regarding due process in the implementation of certain zoning decisions arose. Viewed through the lens of constitutional adjudication, the Euclid decision nearly completely effaces the security of private property against governmental management of its use through zoning regulations. While the Court might have limited zoning to a narrow *sic utere* rationale, or somewhat more generously limited it to circumstances where the government could show that land use restrictions were necessary to improve health and safety, they did neither of these things, nor did other courts in later cases.

Often neglected in the story of Euclid and the establishment of a fairly safe harbor for federal constitutional purposes around zoning regulations is the jurisprudence of zoning and police power in the state courts in the years following Euclid, especially with regard to non-constitutional principles. One of the more interesting post-Euclid cases was Mansfield & Swett v. Town of W. Orange,[199] a New Jersey case from 1938. The state supreme court began by drawing an interesting, if underdeveloped, distinction between land use planning and zoning. By contrast to the more mechanical method of restricting certain uses through zoning (much of which came to be called Euclidean zoning, after the Supreme Court case), planning "is a term of broader significance. It connotes a systematic development, contrived to promote the common interest in matters that have from the earliest times been considered as embraced within the police power."[200] Moreover, planning is entwined with municipal power and choices made at the local level to manage and control the use of private property. "Planning confined to the common need," wrote the court, "is inherent in the authority to create the municipality itself."[201] But how should this authority be so confined?

In the New Jersey case, the court continues in this vein, describing how the emergence of land use planning in industrializing America pushed open, properly, the boundaries of what were appropriate objects of regulation under the police power. Such power should be concerned not only with public health, public morals, or public safety, but "embraces regulations designed to promote the public convenience or the general prosperity."[202] In so doing, no expectation of compensation was necessary (echoing a key point of the Court in Euclid, and that zoning is not a taking, and so does not fall under the requirements of eminent domain, either public use or just compensation).[203] Nor would planning regulations need to be static and neglecting of "changing conditions" to pass constitutional muster.[204] The only limit is the ordinary one, and that is that the "circumstances and character of the regulation" are neither arbitrary nor unreasonable, the latter being defined by reference to whether the law in fact accomplishes "a legitimate public purpose."[205] Other zoning decisions from the 1930s through the next several decades were largely congruent with the logic and emphasis of this New Jersey case.

Up to now, we have focused on the relentless march of the law toward Euclid and also with state court decisions before and after Euclid, toward upholding zoning under the police power. This development is especially important to see, in that the kind of regulation undertaken through this emerging project of land use planning was truly novel and did push up against the boundaries of what was tied to public health, safety, and morals. Ultimately, it is hard to square Euclid with the traditional police power categories unless we embrace the idea that "general welfare" in fact has meaningful content as a basis for regulation in the service of the common good. The imprimatur the courts put on zoning is an important confirmation of the broad view, manifest most dramatically in the Progressive era, that the police power is about the project of good governing, and that both the state and federal constitutions support that project even as new needs for, and methods of, regulation emerge.

In a strongly critical account of Euclid and the emergence of Euclidean zoning, land use scholar Eric Claeys rightly notes that zoning traces the shift from a classically exclusion based idea of property rights to a governance conception.[206] He writes:

> Euclidean zoning thus transformed the orientation of property rights. It transformed what used to be a negative liberty into a positive entitlement. Once Euclidean zoning had taken over, each zoned lot came with a security – a legal guarantee that neighbors would use their lots consistently with tastes, standards and economic goals set by the control group in the local community.[207]

This is a fairly accurate depiction of not only zoning as it emerges from the Euclid decision, but a transformation conspicuous during and after the Progressive era toward an unsteady, but essential, marriage between owners' bundle of property rights and the public's interest in managing owners' interests in property in order to accomplish public welfare goals. What Claeys misses as a descriptive matter is that this transformation was well underway by the time of Euclid. This so-called negative liberty had long been tied to the necessities of public purpose and the common good. The approval without serious limit of Euclidean zoning no doubt confirmed this emphasis and therefore advanced the transition from vested rights to governance as the best way to think about property rights and their protection in the Progressive era and its aftermath. However, zoning was not a cause of the same. Ultimately, Euclid is best understood as a product of a twentieth-century conception of property rights and regulation rather than a font of these principles and approaches.

There is another important dimension to the rise of zoning in the early part of the twentieth century and the courts' examination of this form of regulation under the constitutions. This concerns the matter of who is doing the regulating. Zoning has been and continues to be almost entirely a matter of municipal law. Sometimes the institution responsible for establishing the basic zoning rules is a general-purpose local government and, where this is so, it is exercising official power under the structure of state law ultimately, with matters becoming more complicated under home rule provisions. Other times the basic decisions are being made by an administrative agency. This was the case in the Town of West Orange case we examined above; and this would become a commonplace in the exercise of zoning power – both in the configuration of the rules and in the implementation of the standards through various zoning boards or whatever they were and are precisely called.

While this fact may seem unremarkable when viewed through our present prism, the question whether the police power could be exercised by an administrative agency on essentially the same terms and conditions as a state legislature was not without consequence. Outside of zoning law, we can find a smattering of state police power cases in which the courts looked askance at legislative delegations of authority. In Thomas v. Smith,[208] a Virginia case from 1930, for example, the court considered whether a revocation of a driver's permit by an administrative official, exercised in accordance with a duly enacted state law, was proper under the police power. Given the "right of a citizen to travel upon the public highways [as] a common right which he has under his right to enjoy life and liberty,"[209] a legislative body can limit this right "by legislative enactment and not by administrative edict."[210]

In upholding zoning laws under the police power, the courts were embracing a new approach to lawmaking, one that was centered on bureaucratic decision-making and administrative discretion. While this embrace was seldom made explicit, we can see the logic of these cases as exemplifying another way of viewing the reality and potential of ambitious public administration in this new era of widespread regulation. This view pushes back against the traditional idea that only the legislature could exercise police power authority because, after all, only the legislature could engage in good governing. Zoning illustrates a distinctly managerial model of the police power.[211] The management happens through a partnership between the legislature and administrative agencies. It is forward-looking, and, in that, it reflects a significant departure from the *sic utere* model of the police power.

The police power has since the beginning of our republic been associated with the legislature and statutory lawmaking. Many statements made this condition explicit, noting that the police power emerged from the idea of plenary legislative power. This was not simply for mechanical reasons, that is, because the legislature is the institution that enacts statutes; it was because the legislature was the institution most connected to the people and most reflective of our constitutional commitment to popular sovereignty.[212] Yet, as the country grew after Reconstruction and into the Gilded Age, the exigencies of the economy meant the regulatory policy was often implemented and occasionally manufactured by sub-state officials and by administrative agencies.[213]

In the context of zoning, which we considered earlier as an illustration of the ubiquitous use of the police power after the Progressive era and into the twentieth century, the typical institutional mechanism for the practice of zoning has been a general-purpose local government, often a charter city operating under its home rule powers, developing the zoning rules under a state enabling act. The implementation of those rules has long been entrusted to boards and bureaus operating under the authority of the local zoning ordinances. These agencies will always be making difficult choices, and the issues of accountability and efficacy have arisen since the advent of comprehensive zoning. Perhaps we can draw a line between the assertion of authority to promulgate the actual zoning regulations and the responsibility to implement these rules. However, this line will be understandably unstable. We can sensibly say that zoning is embedded in state and local schemes of administrative regulation, and is very much an illustration of the police power's evolution from something that pertains solely to legislative lawmaking to mechanisms that involve a confluence of institutions and complex spheres of accountability.

One additional note about the changing role of the police power as it became more embedded in the administrative state. This development also frayed, if not broke entirely, the line connecting police power regulations to the common law. Recall that one of the important themes of the cases, and this is a theme that animates William Novak's framing of nineteenth-century police power, is that the focal point of the state courts' interpretations of the police power, in its purpose and its limits, was the common law, especially as it pertained to evolving ideas of torts and harm and private property.[214] As governments turned more to administrative regulation, they also moved away from reliance on common law understandings of public power, in its nature and in its scope. As Morton Horwitz writes:

> The emergence of industrial society thus meant not only that redistributive motives would inevitably be activated by the reality of an increasingly unequal society. It also meant that the relatively fixed common law categories on which police power doctrines had been erected would fall apart, as any categorical distinction between the health of a worker and the conditions of industrial life became ever more difficult to maintain.[215]

*

In sum, the police power evolved to meet conditions appropriate to a more industrial and economically ambitious era, and the constitutional law involving the police power and its limit likewise evolved to confront these conditions. Accepting that the main restrictions on the exercise of the power would be structural and internal to the legislature was a key part of the jurisprudence of these times. However, the courts would maintain their necessary role in ensuring that the legislature not undertake health and safety regulations for reasons that are arbitrary or discriminatory or else a clear violation of individual rights. Balancing public and private interests would remain the quest of reviewing courts. As Tiedeman would write in his treatise: "Fundamental principles of natural right and justice cannot, in themselves, furnish any legal restrictions upon the governmental exercise of police power. Yet they play an important part in determining the exact scope and extent of the constitutional limitations."[216]

NOTES

1. See generally Stephen Skowronek, *Building a New American State: The Expansion of National Administrative Capacities 1877–1920* (1982); Morton Keller, *The Affairs of State: Public Life in Late Nineteenth Century* (1977); Robert H. Wiebe, *The Search for Order 1877–1920* (1967). For a recent analysis of how this era connected with broader themes of American constitutionalism, see Joseph Fishkin & William E. Forbath, *The Anti-Oligarchic Constitution: Reconstructing the Economic Foundations of American Democracy* (2022), at 138–250.
2. See William J. Novak, "The American Law of Overruling Necessity: The Exceptional Origins of State Police Power," in *States of Exception in American History* 95, 114 (G. Gerstle & J. Isaac eds., 2020).
3. See generally Morton Keller, *The Affairs of State: Public Life in Late Nineteenth Century* (1977); William J. Novak, "Public Economy and the Well-Ordered Market: Law & Economic Regulation in the 19th Century America," 18 *L. & Soc. Inq.* 1 (1993).
4. Susan J. Pearson, "A New Birth of Regulation: The State of the State After the Civil War," 5 *J. Civil War Era* 422 (2015).
5. On Reconstruction generally, see Eric Foner, *Reconstruction* (1988). On Reconstruction and the key legal issues raised, see Masur, *Until Justice Be Done* 303–341 (2021); G. Edward White, *Law in American History Volume II*, at 6–49; Laura F. Edwards, *A Legal History of the Civil War and Reconstruction: A Nation of Rights* (2015).
6. Lochner v. New York, 198 U.S. 45 (1905).
7. 291 U.S. 502 (1934).
8. 300 U.S. 379 (1937).
9. See generally Bruce Ackerman, *We the People: Foundations* 279–34 (1998); Barry Cushman, *Rethinking the New Deal Court: The Structure of a Constitutional Revolution* (1998).
10. See Morton J. Horwitz, *The Transformation of American Law, 1870–1960* (1992).
11. See generally Blake Emerson, *The Public's Law: Origins and Architecture of Progressive Democracy* (2019).
12. See generally Christopher F. Edley, Jr., *Administrative Law: Rethinking Judicial Control of Bureaucracy* (1990).

13. 260 U.S. 393 (1922).
14. See generally J. Willard Hurst, *Law and the Conditions of Freedom in Nineteenth-Century America* 35–41 (1956).
15. See, e.g., Cass R. Sunstein & Adrian Vermeule, *Law & Leviathan: Redeeming the Administrative State* (2020); Adrian Vermeule, *Law's Abnegation* (2016); Philip Hamburger, *Is Administrative Law Unlawful?* (2014); Skowronek, *Building a New American State*.
16. But see David N. Mayer, "The Myth of Laissez-Faire Constitutionalism: Liberty of Contract during the Lochner Era," 36 *Hastings Const. L. Q.* 217 (2009).
17. Ernst Freund, *Legislative Regulation* (Commonwealth Fund, 1932).
18. See Daniel B. Rodriguez & Barry R. Weingast, "Lochner and Lochnerism" (ms. 2023).
19. See Henry S. Haines, *Problems in Railway Regulation* (1911).
20. See John Young, "Interstate Commerce Act of 1887," Center for the Study of Federalism (2006).
21. See generally Tim Wu, "A Brief History of American Telecommunications Regulation," in *Oxford International Encyclopedia of Legal History*, Vol. 5, 95 (2009).
22. See ibid.
23. See generally Hugh R. Slotten, *Radio and Television Regulation: Broadcast Technology in the United States, 1920–60* (2000).
24. See Rodriguez & Weingast, "Lochnerism," at 13.
25. See generally J. Warren Madden, "Origins and Early Years of the National Labor Relations Act," 18 *Hastings L. J.* 571 (1967).
26. On labor violence, see Margaret Levi, et al., "Open Access, Ending the Violence Trap: Labor, Business, Government and the National Labor Relations Act," in *Organizations, Civil Society, and the Roots of Development* (N. Lamoreaux & J. Wallis eds., 2017).
27. William J. Novak, *The People's Welfare*.
28. See generally Thomas B. Nachbar, "The Rationality of Rational Basis Review," 102 *Va. L. Rev.* 1627 (2016).
29. To be sure, the arguments, principally by libertarian legal scholars, for a more robust review of regulation that restricted so-called economic liberties persisted without much interruption well after Lochner. See, e.g., Randy E. Barnett, *Restoring the Lost Constitution: The Presumption of Liberty* (Updated ed. 2013); Dana Berliner, "The Federal Rational Basis Test – Fact and Fiction," 14 *Geo. J. L. & Pub. Pol'y* 373 (2016).
30. The leading treatises of the time summarized these cases. See Thomas J. Cooley, *A Treatise on the Constitutional Limitations Which Rest on the Legislative Power of the States of the American Union* (1871), Christopher Tiedeman, *A Treatise on the Limitations of the Police Power in the United States* (1886), and Ernst Freund, *The Police Power: Public Policy and Constitutional Rights* (1904).
31. Two of the leading analyses of the jurisprudence of this period focus almost exclusively on federal decisions. The focus by Owen Fiss in his Oliver Wendell Holmes Devise book on the period between 1888 and 1910 understandably focuses on Supreme Court decisions involving the police power. Nonetheless, the absence of attention to what was happening with state constitutional law in this critical era leaves us with a misleading picture. See also White, *Law in American History Volume II*, at 379–423 (dense analysis of Court's police power jurisprudence during the Progressive era, while omitting state court cases entirely).
32. A deferential approach exemplified by cases such as United States v. Carolene Products, Inc., 304 U.S. 144 (1938) and Williamson v. Lee Optical, 348 U.S. 483 (1955).

33. Munn, 94 U.S. 113, 124 (1876).
34. Ibid.
35. Ibid., at 656.
36. 46 U.S. 504 (1847).
37. 123 U.S. at 671–72.
38. Ibid., at 659.
39. Ibid., at 660.
40. Ibid., at 661.
41. Ibid., at 662.
42. Referring here to The Slaughterhouse Cases, 83 U.S. 36 (1872).
43. See Howard Gillman, *The Constitution Besieged: The Rise and Demise of Lochner Era Police Powers Jurisprudence* 73 (1993).
44. A somewhat different reading of Mugler than the usual one is given in Randy E. Barnett & Evan D. Bernick, *The Original Meaning of the 14th Amendment: Its Letter & Spirit* 282 (2021) (comparing Harlan's reasoning to Chief Justice Marshall's 'pretext' formulation in McCulloch v. Maryland). "No justice in Mugler," Barnett & Bernick write, "doubted that purported exercises of the police power ... needed to be evaluated for pretext if they deprived people of life, liberty, or property." Ibid. True enough, but there are precious few cases prior to Lochner in which the federal courts found any such pretext. See Nathan S. Chapman & Michael W. McConnell, "Due Process as Separation of Powers," 121 *Yale L. J.* 1672 (2012). Nor is it clear what pretext would exactly mean in this context.
45. 113 U.S. 27 (1885).
46. As Professor Gillman writes, "Harlan's statement is not a departure from previous holdings; it is, rather, a reassertion of the adjudicative task undertake by the Supreme Court since Slaughterhouse, and by many state courts before that"). Gillman, *Constitution Besieged*, at 73. At the same time, this raises the larger question about how impactful was the Court's decision in the Slaughterhouse cases. A full description and analysis of these cases, and others that are central to a comprehensive understanding of Reconstruction era constitutionalism would take us on a tangent. The main lesson for our purposes of these cases is that the Court limited significantly the scope of the Fourteenth Amendment (both equal protection and due process) as a font of civil rights protections, including liberty and property, that might have upended the Court's cases involving the police power. See White, *Law in American History Volume II*, at 32–38 ("[The Court] advanced a minimalist interpretation of the Fourteenth Amendment's Due Process Clause"); ibid., at 37 (minimalist interpretation of privileges or immunities clause). See also Barnett & Bernick, *Original Meaning*, at 176–77.
47. See Barnett & Bernick, *Original Meaning*, at 272–78 ("the idea that legislative power was inherently limited came to be understood as forbidding not only enactments that were not generally applicable or prospective but enactments that were not good-faith efforts to promote constitutionally proper governmental ends"); ibid., at 275 ("[T]he nature of the social compact barred any presumption that the people had consented to be governed by a legislature with arbitrary power").
48. See Mugler, 123 U.S. at 661.
49. This was so, despite Tiedeman, an author of one of the leading treatises on the police, insisting that the *sic utere* principle persisted, and undergirded the police power through the period he reviewed. This view is echoed in Horwitz, *Transformation II*, at 28 ("For judges deciding police power cases in the 1870s, the law of nuisance provided the categories for determining when it was legitimate for the state to regulate on behalf of the health, safety, and morals of its citizens"). However, Novak's depiction of the turn

toward a *salus populi* account of the police power, which goes back at least to Alger in 1851 and arguably before that, is ultimately more compelling. "Police power was basically the crucial site for the expansion of public authority beyond the ancient bounds and jurisdictions of local and municipal self-governance toward a more capacious, centralized and generalized conception of state regulatory and governing power." Novak, "Overruling Necessity," at 103.
50. See Hurst, *Law and Social Order*.
51. 163 U.S. 537.
52. Ibid., at 550.
53. 118 U.S. 356 (1886).
54. 163 U.S. 537.
55. Ibid., at 557 (Harlan J., dissenting).
56. Ibid., at 557–58 (Harlan, J., dissenting).
57. Ibid., at 562.
58. Ibid., at 558–59.
59. 197 U.S. 11 (1905).
60. Ibid., at 26.
61. Ibid., at 29.
62. Ibid., at 28.
63. See Wendy Parmet, "Rediscovering Jacobson in an Era of COVID-19," 100 B. U. L. Rev. Online 117 (2020).
64. See Michael Kent Curtis, *No State Shall Abridge: The Fourteenth Amendment and the Bill of Rights* 175–77 (1986).
65. See Cooley, *Constitutional Limitations*.
66. See ibid.
67. See generally Alan Jones, "Thomas M. Cooley and 'Laissez-Faire Constitutionalism': A Reconsideration" 53 J. Am. Hist. 751 (1967).
68. See ibid., at 755. As to the value he placed on property rights in particular, scholars differ. Says Jones: "Cooley had no special concern for the protection of property rights. He certainly believed in the rights of private property, but he never considered them absolute or even paramount." Ibid., at 760 This inquiry is ultimately less interesting than whether he saw such rights as interfering appreciably with the government's power to protect health, safety, morals, and the general welfare under the police power. Here the best conclusion is that he accepted unequivocally a very broad police power, but conditional on what were essentially due process constraints that would protect against arbitrary and unreasonable action.
69. See Banner, *Natural Law*.
70. See Jennifer Nedelsky, *Private Property and the Limits of American Constitutionalism: The Madisonian Framework and its Legacy* 6 (1989). As Nedelsky summarizes late eighteenth-century framers' thinking, "[P]roperty was not just an abstract symbol. It was a right whose security was essential to the economic and political success of the new republic. If property could not be protected, not only prosperity, but liberty, justice, and the international strength of the nation would ultimately be destroyed."
71. See generally Duncan Kennedy, *The Rise and Fall of Classic Legal Thought* (1975).
72. Barnett & Bernick, *Original Meaning*.
73. Magna Carta, ch. 39 (1215), reprinted in Ralph V. Turner, *Magna Carta Through the Ages* at 231 (2003).
74. Barnett & Bernick, *Original Meaning*, at 267–68 (citing to contemporary statements by Hamilton).

75. See, e.g., Calder v. Bull, 3 U.S. (3 Dall.) 386, 386–87 (1798); North Carolina v. Foy, 5 N.C. (1 Mur.) 58 (1805). See generally Barnett & Bernick, *Original Meaning*, at 270–72.
76. Barnett & Bernick, *Original Meaning*, at 272–76.
77. Ibid., at 262.
78. Ibid., at 289–315 (detailing this argument in a chapter entitled "The Proper Ends of Legislative Power")
79. See generally Randy Barnett, *Restoring the Lost Constitution: The Presumption of Liberty* (2004).
80. 248 U.S. 215 (1918).
81. Ibid., at 234.
82. Ibid., at 246 (Holmes, J., dissenting).
83. Ibid. (Holmes, J., dissenting).
84. Ibid., at 250 (Brandeis, J., dissenting).
85. Ibid. (Brandeis, J., dissenting).
86. Ibid.
87. Ibid., at 262–63.
88. Melvin Urofsky has a different take on the difference, saying that "[b]oth men believed in judicial restraint, but Holmes voiced as he did out of skepticism, not believing in the reforms or, other than as an intellectual matter, in the rights either." By contrast, Brandeis "believed fervently that the people should make policy through their elected representatives … Above all, Brandeis cherished facts, while Holmes hated them." Melvin Urorfsky, *Louis D. Brandeis: A Life* 566 (2009). This is not inconsistent with viewing Holmes as beholden to more essentialist ways of thinking, whether or not yoked to natural law. For an illuminating essay challenging the conventional view that Holmes rejected natural law, see Robert P. George, "Holmes on Natural Law," 48 *Vill. L. Rev.* 1 (2003).
89. See Novak, *People's Welfare*, at 49–50. Novak, in his discussion of the imperative of the "well-ordered society," quotes Chancellor Kent: "Every individual has as much freedom in the acquisition, use, and disposition of his property, as is consistent with good order and reciprocal rights of others."
90. See Melvin I. Urofsky, "State Courts and Protective Legislation during the Progressive Era: A Reevaluation," 72 *J. Amer. Hist.* 63 (1985).
91. Fishkin & Forbath, *Anti-Oligarchic Constitution*, at 195.
92. An exemplar of this theme in the American Progressive era is Herbert Croly, *Progressive Democracy* (1914). See generally William E. Forbath, "The Long Life of Liberal America: Law and State-Building in the U.S. and England," 24 *Law & Hist. Rev.* 179 (2006).
93. See Nedelsky, *Private Property*, at 163.
94. St. Louis Gunning Adv. v. City of St. Louis, 233 Mo. 99 (Mo. 1911).
95. Ibid., at 109 (Graves, J., dissenting).
96. 98 Ohio St. 358 (1918).
97. Ibid., at 361.
98. Ibid., at 387.
99. Ibid.
100. Ibid., at 378.
101. Ibid.
102. Ibid., at 363.
103. In his analysis of property law's transformation in the Progressive Era, Morton Horwitz emphasizes the ways in which vested rights doctrine destabilized property by expanding greatly the category of interests that should and would be considered property. "[S]ince

the vested rights doctrine itself was founded by analogy to the vesting of landed property by way of title, it became increasingly difficult to decide whether other, more abstract and intangible property interests had also been vested." Horwitz, *Transformation II*, at 150. Horwitz proceeds to show how the "collapse of a physicalist definition of property after 1870" was "ultimately the source of [vested rights theory's] undoing." Ibid., at 151–56.

104. 146 U.S. 389 (1892).
105. Ibid., at 459.
106. Ibid., at 461.
107. "It was well recognized that the state or its agents were legally immune from paying compensation for many of the forms of interference with land for a which a private person would unquestionably have been required to pay." Horwitz, *Transformation II*, at 146.
108. Harry Scheiber, "The Road to Munn: Eminent Domain and the Concept of Public Purpose in the State Courts," in *Perspectives in American History, Volume V: Law in American History* 331 (D. Fleming & B. Bailyn eds., 1971).
109. See generally William Treanor, "Original Understanding," at 792 ("In antebellum America, state courts usually required compensation only when the government physically took property or, at most, when governmental actions involved the physical invasion of property"). See also Harry N. Scheiber, "Property Law, Expropriation, and Resource Allocation by Government: The United States, 1789–1910," 33 *J. Econ. Hist.* 232, 236 (1973).
110. 17 Johns. 195 (N.Y. Sup. Ct. 1819).
111. Scheiber, "The Road to Munn," at 337–38.
112. See, e.g., Chicago & Pacific RR v. Francis, 70 Ill. 258 (1973); City of Pekin v. Winkel, 77 Ill. 56 (1875); Rigney v. City of Chicago, 103 Ill. 64 (1882)
113. See Pennsylvania Coal Co. v. Mahon, 260 U.S. 393 (1922).
114. See generally Treanor, "Original Understanding"; Richard A. Epstein, "Takings: Descent and Resurrection," 1987 *Sup. Ct. Rev.* 1, 12 (1987).
115. As the Court said in Murr v. Wisconsin, 582 U.S. – (2017): A"[p]rior to Justice Holmes's exposition in *Pennsylvania Coal Co. v. Mahon*, 260 U. S. 393 (1922), it was generally thought that the Takings Clause reached only a direct appropriation of property, or the functional equivalent of a practical ouster of the owner's possession," like the permanent flooding of property. *Lucas v. South Carolina Coastal Council*, 505 U. S. 1003, 1014 (1992) (citation, brackets, and internal quotation marks omitted); accord, *Horne v. Department of Agriculture*, 576 U. S. ___, ___ (2015) (slip op., at 7); see also *Loretto v. Teleprompter Manhattan CATV Corp.*, 458 U. S. 419, 427 (1982).
116. 260 U.S. at 413.
117. See Treanor, "Original Understanding," at 803 ("[T]he Pennsylvania Coal inquiry into when regulation 'goes too far' is open-ended and unconstrained").
118. See, e.g., Adkins v. Children's Hospital, 261 U.S. 525 (1923); Coppage v. Kansas, 236 U.S. 1 (1915).
119. See, e.g., G. Edward White, *Justice Oliver Wendell Holmes: Law and the Inner Self* 402 (1993).
120. See Horwitz, *Transformation II*, at 15.
121. See Mahon, 260 U.S. at 417 (Brandeis, J., dissenting).
122. See Novak, *People's Welfare*, at 133–38.
123. The Takings Clause reads: "[N]or shall private property be taken for public use, without just compensation." *U.S. Const. Am. V.*

124. See generally Laura Kalman, *FDR's Gambit: The Court Packing Fight and the Rise of Legal Liberalism* (2022); Cushman, *New Deal Court*, at 9–32.
125. Cf. Daniel B. Rodriguez & Barry R. Weingast, "Engineering the Modern Administrative State: Political Accommodation and Legal Strategy in the New Deal Era," 46 *BYU L. Rev.* 147 (2020).
126. See Guido Calabresi & Douglas Melamed, "Property Rules, Liability Rules and Inalienability: One View of the Cathedral," 85 *Harv. L. R.* 1089 (1972).
127. Quoted in Jon C. Teaford, *The Rise of the States: Evolution of American State Government* 13 (2002).
128. See Gillman, *Constitution Besieged*, at 180.
129. The Federalist No. 51.
130. Teaford, *The States*, at 13
131. See Fiskin & Forbath, *The Anti-Oligarchic Constitution*.
132. See generally Thomas Cronin, *Direct Democracy: The Politics of Initiative, Referendum, and Recall* (1989).
133. See, e.g., Adkins v. Children's Hospital, 261 U.S. 525 (1923); Coppage v. Kansas, 236 U.S. 1 (1915).
134. 198 U.S. 45 (1905).
135. Ibid., at 57.
136. Ibid., at 57.
137. Ibid., at 61.
138. Ibid., at 65 (Harlan, J., dissenting).
139. Ibid., at 75 (Holmes, J., dissenting).
140. See generally William E. Leuchtenburg, *The Supreme Court Reborn: Constitutional Revolution in the Age of Roosevelt* (1995); Robert G. McCloskey, "Economic Due Process and the Supreme Court: An Exhumation and Reburial," 1962 *Sup. Ct. Rev.* 34.
141. See Laurence Tribe, *American Constitutional Law* 769 (2nd ed., 1988).
142. See, e.g., Barry Friedman, "The History of the Counter-Majoritarian Difficulty, Part Three: The Lesson of Lochner," 76 *NYU L. Rev.* 1383 (2001).
143. See, e.g., Cushman, *New Deal Court*.
144. See, e.g., David E. Bernstein, *Rehabilitating Lochner: Defending Individual Rights against Progressive Reform* 121 (2011).
145. See ibid., at 120–28.
146. Cass R. Sunstein, "Lochner's Legacy," 67 *L. Rev.* 873 (1987).
147. See White, *Law in American History Volume II*, at 400.
148. See Gillman, *Constitution Besieged*, at 8–18.
149. See Fishkin & Forbath, *Anti-Oligarchic Constitution*.
150. Gillman, *Constitution Besieged*, at 7–8.
151. Lochner-era jurisprudence reflected in what Howard Gillman labels the "anticaste principle." Ibid., at 8.
152. See White, *Law in American History Volume II*, at 379–423.
153. See ibid.
154. Muller v. Oregon, a case in which the Supreme Court upheld a regulation limiting working hours for women, was a hard and somewhat surprising case in the midst of the Lochner era; it would have been a very easy case by the 1940s or 1950s.
155. See, e.g., Victoria Nourse, "A Tale of Two Lochners: The Untold History of Substantive Due Process and the Idea of Fundamental Rights," 97 *Cal. L. Rev.* 751 (2009). For an early account expressing skepticism about Lochner's impact on progressive social

legislation, see Charles Warren, "The Progressiveness of the United States Supreme Court," 13 *Colum. L. Rev.* 294 (1913).
156. See John Fabian Witt, *American Contagion: Epidemics and the Law from Smallpox to Covid 19* (2020).
157. See, e.g., Freund, *The Police Power*.
158. See Williamson v. Lee Optical, 348 U.S. 483 (1955); Carolene Products v. United States, 304 U.S. 144 (1938).
159. See Novak, "Overruling Necessity," at 95–122.
160. 152 U.S. 133 (1894).
161. Ibid., at 137.
162. 123 F. 10 (1900).
163. Ibid., at 15.
164. Ibid., at 23 (emphasis added).
165. See Freund, *The Police Power*, at 57–61.
166. Ibid., at 57.
167. Ibid., at 59.
168. Ibid., at 60.
169. Jacobson v. Massachusetts, 197 U.S. 11 (1905).
170. Muller v. Oregon, 208 U.S. 412 (1908).
171. 245 U.S. 60 (1917).
172. 274 U.S. 200 (1927).
173. Ibid., at 206.
174. 220 U.S. 61 (1911).
175. Ibid., at 82.
176. See A. V. Dicey, *Introduction to the Study of the Law of the Constitution* 107–22 (8th ed., 1915).
177. Romer v. Evans, 517 U.S. 620 (1996).
178. See, e.g., James Landis, *The Administrative Process* (1938).
179. Administrative Procedure Act, §551.
180. Ibid., at §706.
181. See generally Jed Stiglitz, *The Reasoning State* (2022).
182. See generally Sonia A. Hirt, *Zoned in the USA: The Origins and Implications of American Land-use Regulation* (2014).
183. See, e.g., Berman v. Parker, 348 U.S. 26 (1954).
184. See Hirt, *Zoned*; William A. Fischel, *Zoning Rules! The Economics of Land Use Regulation* 27–68 (2015) (describing the structure and administration of zoning laws).
185. For a valuable analysis of early zoning law and conceptions of property, see Nadav Shoked, "The Reinvention of Ownership: The Embrace of Residential Zoning and the Modern Populist Theory of Property," 28 *Yale J. Reg.* 91 (2011).
186. Miller v. Bd. of Public Works of Los Angeles, 195 Cal. 477 (Cal. 1925).
187. Ibid., at 456
188. Ibid., at 450.
189. Miller was not the only word from the states regarding zoning and constitutional authority. The Mississippi supreme court, two years earlier, struck down a zoning regulation as an "arbitrary interference with the individual use of private property by the owner thereof." Fitzhugh v. City of Jackson, 132 Miss. 585 (1923).
190. 272 U.S. 365 (1926).
191. See generally Michael Allan Wolf, *The Zoning of America: Euclid v. Ambler* 50–56 (2008) (detailing lawyers' objections to zoning in Euclid case).

192. James Metzenbaum, "The History of Zoning – A Thumbnail Sketch," 9 W. Rsrv. L. Rev. 36 (1957).
193. See Wolf, *Zoning of America*, at 99.
194. See M. Nolan Gray, *Arbitrary Lines: How Zoning Broke the American City and How to Fix It* 29 (2022) ("The decision in Euclid proved to be decisive … By 1930, thirty-five of the then forty-eight states had adopted some form o zoning-enabling legislation").
195. See generally Stewert Sterk, Eduardo Penalver, & Sara C. Bronin, *Land Use Regulation* 184 (3rd ed., 2020).
196. A concept generally associated with Harold Bartholomew, famous city planner of the early twentieth century.
197. See generally Nicole Steele Garnett, *Ordering the City: Land Use, Policing, and the Restoration of Urban America* (2010).
198. See John Infranca, "Singling Out Single-Family Zoning," 111 Geo. L. J. 659 (2023).
199. 198 A. 225 (N.J. 1938).
200. Ibid., at 228.
201. Ibid., at 229.
202. Ibid., at 231.
203. Ibid.
204. Ibid.
205. Ibid.
206. Eric R. Claeys, "Euclid Lives? The Uneasy Legacy of Progressivism in Zoning," 73 Fordham L. Rev. 731 (2004).
207. Ibid., at 741.
208. Thompson v. Smith, 155 Va. 367 (1930).
209. Ibid., at 377.
210. Ibid.
211. See Shoked, "Ownership," 28 *Yale J. Reg.* at 106.
212. See Gordon S. Wood, *The Creation of the American Republic, 1776–1787* (1998).
213. A good illustration of the Court's grappling with the tension over legislative delegations of authority in this earlier period was the Minnesota Rate Case of 1890. This case, one in a long line of cases involving disputes over the scope and exercise of ratemaking authority by administrative agencies (first in states, later at the federal level), involved a claim that the agency was setting a rate that was unreasonable under the statute. The specific question that came ultimately to the Supreme Court was whether the federal courts could review this agency judgment, made under the aegis of a legislative delegation, to make sure that it complied with the requirements of due process under the Constitution. The Court answered this question with a resounding yes, Justice Blackford writing: "The question of the reasonableness of a rate of charge for transportation by a railroad company, involving as it does the element of reasonableness both as regards the company and as regards the public, is eminently a question for judicial investigation, requiring due process of law for its determination." The Court thus rejected the decision of the Minnesota court to refuse to consider a claim by the railroad under the due process clause. There was a powerful dissent by three justices from this holding, with Justice Bradley writing that "it practically overrul[es] Munn." For these dissenting justices, the "governing principle of those cases was that the regulation and settlement of the fares of railroads and other public accommodations is a legislative prerogative, and not a judicial one." This 1890 case illustrates the difficulty faced by the Court looking to reconcile its broad holding in Munn and Mugler that these businesses could be subject to regulation in the public interest, with due deference given to the legislature's choice about how best to regulate, with the responsibility of ensuring that this discretion could

not be used to ride roughshod on regulated industries' due process rights. What makes the holding less momentous than these earlier cases, and also later cases in which the tension between private property rights and legislative discretion was conspicuous, is that the legislature here had in fact imposed a reasonableness requirement into the statute, and so the question could be viewed more narrowly of whether this requirement could and should be enforced in a state court.

214. See Novak, *People's Welfare*, at 66.
215. See Horwitz, *Transformation II*, at 30.
216. Tiedeman, *Limitations of Police Power*, at 10–11.

4

The Shape of the Police Power in the Modern Era

In the last two chapters, we have taken an intensive and mostly longitudinal look at the evolution of the police power from an authority embedded in state constitutions to a whole power for governments to act in order to further the "people's welfare." Through the long period from the founding through the mid-twenty-first century, legislators and administrators created and implemented regulation to meet the constitutional obligations of active governance. To be sure, they did so in the shadow of shifting conceptions of liberty and private property. A capacious police power survived the turbulence of public skepticism about legislators and legislation, economic crises, and the rise and fall of laissez constitutionalism. How this happened is illuminating, not only in order to better understand the history of the police power, but as a framework for understanding how state and local governments developed approaches to good governance and also how the courts fashioned limits on these strategies through doctrinal innovations.

In thinking about the ways the police power evolved to the present time, it is crucial to consider two developments directly relevant to this topic. These are, respectively, the changing approaches to regulatory governance in the roughly the second half of the twentieth and the first couple of decades of the twenty-first century, and key developments in state constitutional reform, developments that implicate the nature and contents of the regulatory power of state and local governments. Both topics are more capacious than can be comprehensively analyzed in part of one chapter, but some observations are useful to set the table for a robust discussion of the modern police power.

MODERN APPROACHES TO REGULATORY GOVERNANCE

The period after World War II was marked by a faith in American ingenuity and a broad confidence in the government to undertake programs and projects that would enhance the general welfare.[1] Among many examples, the interstate highway system[2] and the creation of the national parks[3] were gargantuan projects, and were not only valuable initiatives in their own right, but they also evidenced, as would also the space program that would begin in earnest in the 1950s,[4] the relentless commitment of the public sector to aspire to great heights of achievement, and to bear the sacrifices and burdens to see achievements happen.[5]

State-level governance was an important part of this omnibus effort. So far as direct programs funding was concerned, states funneled steadily increasing monies into social welfare initiatives, public works, and, especially, education.[6] California's higher education master plan was just one illustration, and an extraordinary one, of a state making a colossal investment to implement a vision of a world-changing program.[7] Other efforts by state governments, sometimes in conjunction with federal projects and sometimes developed on their own initiative, reflected the confidence at the sub-national level in the government's ability and commitment to further public welfare goals, in this period of American expansion and technological progress.

The attention paid at the local level to perceived failures in the overall urban condition was reflected in the continuing efforts at regulating in order to address the externalities that stemmed from an increasingly busy community life. In <u>Kovacs v. Cooper</u>,[8] a rather obscure 1949 case, the Supreme Court upheld a municipal prohibition on "loud and raucous music" against a charge that this curtailed protected expression under the First Amendment. In doing so, they made clear that the "[p]olice power … extends beyond health, morals, and safety … to protect the well-being, and tranquility, of a community."[9] One year later, in <u>Berman v. Parker</u>, the Court upheld against a takings and police power challenge, regulations that were intended to redress the predicament of so-called urban "blight."[10] The impact of <u>Berman</u> on the regulatory power to deal with property use outside the constraints of eminent domain will be discussed in more detail below. For now, it is important merely to note the Court's very broad rendering of the police power's scope in a case decided smack in the middle of the century. Justice Douglas for a unanimous Court declares: "Public safety, public health, morality, peace and quiet, law and order – these are some of the more conspicuous examples of the traditional application of the police power to municipal affairs. Yet they merely illustrate the scope of the power, and do not delimit it."[11]

Growth of state and local regulation was notable as new problems emerged and continuing problems persisted. The increasing urbanization of America generated special pressures to tackle serious public health and safety dilemmas.[12] Simultaneously, the role of the federal government grew massively. The Progressive era, its aftermath, and the New Deal and post-New Deal period illustrated how the federal government addressed through regulation problems that have a nationwide valence. Federal regulation grew in most dimensions and in most domains. The New Deal is especially notable for the creation of myriad new federal agencies, each with substantial jurisdiction over major parts of the economy and social life. With the New Deal, we moved in an era that Sophia Lee calls our "administered constitutionalism."[13] This was a phenomenon of extraordinary consequence, even as the theory of the federal government's role, under ancient paradigms of limited government and enumerated powers, was stress tested by the needs and wants of a population, a population that demanded, and ultimately came to expect, a robust federal presence. Regulatory expansion, in short, happened on both fronts, expansion in state interventions in most facets of social and economic life and also expansion in federal regulation and the national administrative state.

Public faith in regulation was not, however, a linear story from the end of World War II to the present. In the 1980s, with the election of Ronald Reagan, and continuing through the end of the century and into the next, there was an emerging backlash to federal regulation.[14] American politics embraced a wave of anti-regulation sentiment, a sentiment that was captured to some degree in a skepticism on the part of a large segment of the GOP, of political officials in the executive branch, through the administrations of Reagan, Bush I, and even to some extent Clinton and Bush II as well, and of some courts.[15] Fast forward ahead to the most recent decade, there has been an emerging "anti-administrativism" in the federal courts, including the Supreme Court, that can be sourced at least to some extent in a concern about overbearing regulation and the decoupling of regulatory administration from the rule of law.[16] Moreover, the last four decades or so have witnessed a renaissance in attention to the role and important of private property and, we might say, at the risk of exaggerating the point, a property rights revolution.[17] Public interest organizations, primarily libertarian in origin and focus, worked to protect through legal and political strategies private property from what they viewed as overweening government regulation.[18] They had a number of prominent successes, noteworthy in the modern era in which so-called economic liberties were not viewed as fundamental and so strict constitutional scrutiny was not the a prominent part of our tradition of contemporary judicial review.

State and local regulation transitioned in focus as well, as one might expect in a dynamic society and changing political circumstances, and thus the targets of regulation often shifted. In any event, the general trend line in the period from the end of the Second World War through the next thirty odd years was very much in the direction of widening governmental intervention, including in core matters of public health, safety, and morals. With all that, however, the persistence of state and local regulation under the police power has not seriously abated. To take one important area, whose history was detailed in the previous chapter, municipal zoning, land use regulation by local governments has continued without much interference and without serious retrenchment occasioned by judicial scrutiny. To be sure, "zoning is by no means static.... [c]hanged or changing conditions call for changed plans,"[19] as a New York court note in a case from the early 1950s. However, the utility of zoning as a mechanism for regulating the use of private property in order to accomplish what authorities perceived as worthwhile public aims persisted in the second half of the last century and the first part of the new one.

The interesting story of evolving regulatory governance in the long era herein described – basically the last eighty years – involves the evolution of new regulatory techniques, as well as the steadily expanding role of the federal government, including into matters that had historically been left to local discretion (thinking here, for example, of education and housing policy). The sheer breadth of constitutional power of state and local governments to regulate, however, under the police power and other fonts of authority, has remained largely undisturbed. That said, the so-called "rights revolution" did bring meaningful limits on police power regulation; and the internal constraints that stem from the requirements in both constitutional law and administrative law that police regulations not be unreasonable or arbitrary. We will discuss these developments in successive chapters in the next Part of this book. For our purposes here, it is crucial to note that the basic underpinnings of the government's power to regulate under the police power in order to protect public health, safety, morals, and the general welfare were established long ago, as we have seen, and have not been seriously disturbed. The objectives of these powers, however, have evolved as new conditions and needs have arisen; more formally, they have evolved in order to meet circumstances of state constitutions as these documents too have evolved in the last many decades.

STATE CONSTITUTIONAL DEVELOPMENTS

While no new states have been admitted since Hawaii and Alaska in the late 1950s, a number of states have either adopted new constitutions or substantially reformed their constitutions in the period from the mid-1950s to present day.[20] "During the twentieth century," Alan Tarr writes, "formal constitutional change in the states has occurred primarily through constitutional amendment."[21] Moreover, "[m]ost states have amended their constitutions far more frequently during the twentieth century than in previous eras."[22] A number of states undertook meaningful reforms. Some adopted new constitutions, while some adopted particular amendments to implement significant new agendas. In all, just about every state adopted amendments to their constitutions during the second half of the twentieth century and first twenty years of the twenty-first century.[23]

By way of summary, one fairly common element in these reforms was the expansion of the public sphere and the development of new obligations on government.[24] Some of these were framed as so-called "positive rights," a phenomenon we will discuss in more depth in a later chapter. However labelled, these provisions put a greater emphasis on progressive social agendas and, with it, a greater onus on government to undertake initiatives to implement objectives viewed by reformers (sometimes including the people themselves, as where state constitutions were amended through popular initiatives) as critical pieces of the overall vision of governing and public policy within states.[25] It is a commonplace to see twentieth- and twenty-first-century constitutional amendments and changes as part of an agenda of modernization and, for that reason, seemingly mechanical. However, even reforms that were deeply in the weeds on the implementation mechanisms of governing are best viewed as means of rethinking broader policy goals.[26] Other notable constitutional reforms during the twentieth century includes reconfigurations of the overall fiscal systems in states (Hawaii and Colorado's reforms were especially substantial), the overall restructuring of state government (Texas), changes in relations between state and local governments through home rule amendments (Michigan), the expansion of individual rights (New York), major changes in the structure of judicial system (Florida), and creation of new positive rights including natural resource protection and safeguarding the rights of indigenous peoples (Alaska). Moreover, some states adopted entirely new constitutions during the second half of the twentieth century, in response to changes in the state and variegated political pressure.[27]

In writing about the project of state constitutional reform in the modern era, Frank Grad and Robert Williams posit a general view of state constitutional functioning, a view that bears well on the evolution of regulatory power under state constitutions over time: "The least we may demand of our state constitutions is that they interpose no obstacle to the necessary exercise of state powers in response to state residents' real needs and active demands for service."[28] In contemporary constitutional reform, including the substitution of old or new ones, no serious obstacles have been imposed. Rather, and in contrast to a raft of state constitutional reforms in the late nineteenth and early twentieth centuries, at a time of skepticism about legislative power, the shape of constitutional change has been in the direction of improving governmental performance and imposing new obligations emerging from new policy goals.[29] As Jeff Sutton labels it, the project has been one of "[a]mending constitutions to meet changing circumstances."[30]

*

Governance strategies evolved, as one might expect, given changing social and economic conditions. And so state and local governments maintain the same level or type of discretion to regulate that existed in prior eras. In particular, state and federal constitutional law has obviously shifted in important ways over these many decades and especially with the expansion of federal governmental authority and the widening scope of individual rights. The impact of the police power has changed in meaningful ways. Nonetheless, we should recognize, as we summarize these developments, the resilience of the police power. At a core constitutional level, the power of the states to regulate health, safety, morals, and the people's welfare persists in a remarkably strong form. We mentioned in the book's introduction how the police power has faded from view. But it has not faded in relevance and impact as an element in the government's regulatory strategies. This formidable power is at the very center of state constitutionalism. Chapter 4 illuminates some key dimensions of this.

MORALS REGULATION

The roots of the government's interest in, and regulatory power over, morals, go back to the origins of the police power in the states of the United States in the nineteenth century. The essential role and responsibility of the state government to protect the public from immoral activity was well established in early cases involving the police power, and continued as a thread in the nineteenth and into the twentieth centuries. Public morals takes up three long chapters in Ernst Freund's treatise on the police power, and his dense analysis of state cases spans a wide terrain, from games of chance to lotteries to intoxicating liquors to various vices and instances of brutality (including cruelty to animals).[31] No one could doubt that one of the foundational objectives of the police power as it evolved throughout the first and second centuries of the American republic's history was the imperative of protecting society against immoral behavior.

As a categorical matter, the framing of the police power around health, safety, morals, and general welfare has been fairly consistent from the beginning of our republic and in the drafting of the early state constitutions.[32] It has been clear since the founding that morals, if not stated explicitly in the constitutions' text, has been a component of general welfare and the common good. While certain morals regulation has been controversial, historically and currently, it is without dispute that the police power does encompass the power of the state, and, where power is delegated, local government, to legislate to protect public morals.[33] Referring to the nineteenth century in particular, but accurate as a general statement of the scope of the police power through American constitutional history, William Novak writes that "[m]orals police remained one of the matter-of-fact obligations of government in a well-regulated society."[34]

Second, and to some degree in tension with this previous point, police power legislation and regulation in the second half of the twentieth and into the twenty-first century was styled less around the objective of preserving traditional morality and, hearkening back to the early days of American history, eradicating sinful behavior, but was more about preserving social order.[35] This reframing helped support government initiatives that, as in the adult entertainment cases discussed below, helped reduce bad secondary effects of certain behaviors. These have become more often than not the stated rationales for these regulations. In this respect, morals regulation becomes part of the same pattern of police power regulation, in the service of the objection of protecting the public's health, safety, and general welfare. Morals regulation designed to improve the human soul becomes subordinate to the goal of improving the social condition – although we are admittedly eliding here the thoughtful efforts, some based upon sustained religious arguments, and others not, that these two rationales are inextricably linked.

William Novak begins his chapter on public morality in *The People's Welfare* by questioning whether morals regulation is so clearly covered by the police power today, saying "[b]y the standards of late twentieth-century law, the public regulation of morality is increasingly suspect."[36] While the contrast between morals regulation in the twentieth (and presumably twenty-first) century and the nineteenth century is, as Novak describes, significant, it does not follow that morals regulation has fallen out of favor as an element of the state's police power. Indeed, most of the contemporary criminal laws dealing with perceived vices of various forms, not to mention civil laws that impose duties on individuals connected to morals regulation, can be authorized only on the basis that the state has the constitutional power to prohibit certain conduct that the state believes is immoral. The landscape of what regulation is proper and warranted has changed considerably – although entirely in the direction of abandoning efforts to control individual behavior, as the example of laws growing out of the current cultural wars indicates – the constitutional basis of state authority to legislate in this realm has not changed considerably.

At one level, we might see morals regulation as more or less a subspecies of the police power's focus on safety and health. And, indeed, there are illustrative regulations that center the inquiry on the health impacts of certain behavior, and so morality becomes a sort of rhetorical exclamation point, part of what Suzanne Goldberg calls a "composite" basis for regulatory intervention.[37] The famous episode of alcohol prohibition,[38] which arose in several states before the Civil War and, with the temperance movement of the late nineteenth and early twentieth century, in a second state wave prior to the national prohibition through the Eighteenth Amendment, could be seen principally from the perspective of health, not morals.[39] But doing so misses much of the social history of prohibition, as the historical analyses of this episode reveals. In any event, there are simply too many examples of state and local regulations that are focused on acts *contra bonos*, that is, immoral in themselves. A well-ordered society, courts and commentators emphasized, required government regulation of plainly immoral behavior, regardless of any empirical connection to health and safety.[40] As Thomas Cooley summarized the state of the law in his magnum opus on constitutional law in 1905: "Preservation of the public morals is peculiarly subject to legislative supervision."[41]

Morals legislation would come to cover a range of conduct, including consumption of alcohol (whether through absolute prohibition or through regulation), vagrancy, adultery, pornography, obscenity and forms of so-called lewd conduct, prostitution, and gambling.[42] State courts consistently upheld legislative and administrative measures to curtail such conduct, although certainly the trends in regulation evolved in various directions as the legislature worked to gauge the tenor of the times.[43] Some conduct has been persistently viewed by legal edict as immoral, while views on other conduct has evolved, sometimes significantly.

Questions about what sorts of immoral actions should give rise to governmental regulation were persistent throughout the history of our republic, and there was certainly no consensus. John Stuart Mill wrote a famous essay in 1853 laying out what philosophers would come to call the "harm principle," something akin to a *sic utere* idea. This Millian view would cordon off from regulation of immorality as such, on the grounds that efforts by government to promote merely "[one's] own good, either physical or moral, is not a sufficient warrant" for action.[44] Debates over the government's proper role as intervenor in matters of private morals would become pronounced over the course of the next century and a half.[45] Suffice it to say here that the Millian approach did not in any meaningful way affect the jurisprudence of the police power so far as the scope of legitimate governmental regulation was concerned. The courts from the beginning saw the legislature as containing a nearly limitless power to protect the general welfare by any reasonable means. In Thurlow v. Massachusetts,[46] for example, decided four years before Alger, the Supreme Court said: "There may be some doubt whether the general government or each State possesses the prohibitory power, as to persons or property of certain kinds, from coming into the limits of the State. But it must exist somewhere; and it seems to me rather a police power, belonging to the States, and to be exercised in the manner best suited to the tastes and institutions of each."[47] Not content to leave the matter at the total discretion of the state without comment about the basis of the law, Justice Grier wrote in a concurring opinion:

> It is not necessary for the sake of justifying the State legislation now under consideration to array the appalling statistics of misery, pauperism, and crime which have their origin in the use or abuse of ardent spirits. The police power, which is exclusively in the States, is alone competent to the correction of these great evils, and all measures of restraint or prohibition necessary to effect the purpose are within the scope of that authority.[48]

Exactly four decades later, the Supreme Court in Mugler upheld the power of Kansas to regulate alcohol consumption.[49] As we discussed in a previous chapter, Justice Harlan there took the opportunity to opine that the Kansas view was wise and properly designed to help eradicate the scourge of the demon rum.

Early in the next century, the Court went even further in upholding federal regulation of morals, in the context of lotteries. Champion v. Ames[50] was an important case from the early years of the twentieth century in which the Court embraced a very broad interpretation of the Commerce Clause under the US Constitution to authorize Congress's prohibition of shipping lottery tickets. Having established that the interstate movement of lottery tickets is commerce by the measure of Gibbons, Brown, and Miln, the foundational commerce clause cases, Justice Harlan for the Court responded to the question of whether the liberty of individuals to engage in activity legal in their state interposed a restriction on Congressional regulation. He asks rhetorically, "surely it will not be said to be a part of anyone's liberty, as recognized by the supreme law of the land, that he shall be allowed to introduce into commerce among the states an element that will be confessedly injurious to the public morals."[51] Whether the concern with "public morals" emerges from Congress – in which case the four dissenters have a rather good point in decrying the notion tacit in Harlan's opinion that the national government has what is in essence the police power[52] – or emerges from states that prohibit lotteries and therefore have a correlative interest in limiting the importation of lottery tickets remains elusive. And yet the idea that the protection of public morals includes restrictions on gambling is made explicit either way. Likewise, in Marvin v. Trout,[53] decided two years later, the Court made clear that nothing in the US Constitution forbids the state from prohibiting gambling "for the purpose of suppressing the evil in the interest of the public morals and welfare."[54]

In addition to alcohol and gambling, morals laws restricting many aspects of sexual and familial conduct, including fornication, sodomy, prostitution, and polygamy, were common in the nineteenth century, and are fairly common even now. Indeed, there have emerged in the latter part of the last decade ordinances restricting certain kinds of sex toys, restrictions that have largely been upheld under the police power.

For a long time, the courts' acquiescence in morals regulation, combined with the nearly non-existence rights jurisprudence of the time, meant that virtually any morals-related regulation would be upheld, just so long as it was properly enacted and reasonably enforced. Ultimately, there was precious little by way of argument that either federal or state courts found credible in these times that morals legislation stretched the police power too far or that there was an individual liberty interest that would protect individual conduct from regulation on the grounds that the morality of the community was compromised. As individuals' liberty to engage in various conduct, whether or not deemed as immoral, was problematic to John Stuart Mill and to devotees to his harm principle, but not especially to courts.

The revolution in individual rights, which we will consider in more depth in a later chapter, changed this landscape considerably. To take just this one example, consider the legal struggle over abortion laws, occasioned by the Supreme Court's 1973 decision Roe v. Wade.[55] Roe ushered in a nearly four-decade foray by the federal courts into questions involving what state level regulation of abortion was or was not proper. The end of Roe came in 2022, with the Supreme Court's decision in Dobbs v. Jackson Women's Health Organization[56] and, with that, the struggle turned to federal and state law (including state constitutional law). Notably, in the increasingly voluminous commentary on the Dobbs decision, much of it by pro-choice advocates focused on the question "Now what?" there is precious little attention paid to the question of whether and to what extent abortion restrictions post-Dobbs can be enacted under the state police power. Before Roe, that was reasonably well settled. Abortion restrictions, in those states that had enacted them prior to 1973, were styled as protection of public morals (interestingly, even more than they were described as protecting human life). One searches largely in vain for state court decisions in the decades before Roe indicating that this rationale stretched the boundaries of the police power too far. After Dobbs, however, the answer to that question is by no means clear.

The relationship between morals regulations and individual liberty was not a topic explored by the courts in any conspicuous way during the first century and a half of the republic's history. This fact alone is a curious one, given the ambient debate about the proper scope of government in facilitating good conduct and morality. While this large debate frames public opinion and governmental strategy, we need not dwell too much on this mystery. Perhaps the difficulty relevant to constitutional adjudication was the absence of a coherent vocabulary to discuss the nature and scope of individual liberty rights. The kinds of protections that were pushed to the fore of judicial consideration in the first decades of the twentieth century were about a certain kind of liberty, the liberty of contract and the correlative liberty to make a living.[57] These were conjoined with private property rights to make up what came to be described as a form of libertarian constitutionalism that reached its apogee in the Lochner era. But the idea that individuals possessed a general freedom of action – a right to be left alone, as Brandeis and Warren put it in their celebrated article on the right to privacy[58] – derivative from natural rights or from a view of the privileges or immunities of citizenship, a freedom that might trump the government's interest in preserving public morality, was not top of mind to the leading jurists and commentators of the day. The grounding of liberty in a cogent view of autonomy and human flourishing and, likewise, the concern that morals regulation would undermine equality would be a theme that would await the final decades of the twentieth century, in both the scholarly discourse and, ultimately, in the caselaw.

In the past century, leading moral philosophers and many legal scholars have argued extensively over the core question of how much latitude ought government to have in legislating morality and in criminalizing behavior on the grounds that such behavior is immoral.[59] Center stage in the UK during the second half of the twentieth century was the debate between H. L. A. Hart and Lord Devlin over the wisdom of prohibiting homosexual conduct.[60] And prominent philosophers including John Finnis,[61] Ronald Dworkin,[62] Joel Feinberg,[63] George Fletcher,[64] Tony Honore,[65] and Robert George[66] have explored in depth the normative and legal dimensions of morals regulation. While these debates have yielded no consensus on the matter, the strong thrust in much of modern thought is toward skepticism about morals regulation. There had long been vocal critics of particular government regulations of long standing, including critics of the criminalization of relatively minor drug offenses, consensual prostitution, laws prohibiting adultery and bigamy, and intimate matters involving sexual relations including contraception and certain sexual practices. When, for example, the Supreme Court decided Bowers v. Hardwick in 1986,[67] upholding a Georgia anti-sodomy statute, the decision was widely decried as illustrating the overreach by state governments in matters involving morality and intimate sexual conduct.[68] The case became a lightning rod for criticisms of these outdated laws and the lengths to which the Supreme Court, at that time not viewed as especially conservative, would go to defer to these legislative judgments about the morality of individual sexual conduct.[69]

The question of whether the police power authorized morals regulation was, to be sure, a rather abstract one. However, in the practical dimensions of government regulation, laws governing a wealth of activity that could not be easily described as prohibiting actual harm to others – and so came under the rubric of *sic utere* rationales – was commonly subject to state or local criminal law. These included a wide collection of prohibitions, those that would have been familiar to the government and the general public a century earlier, including drug possession and sale, gambling, prostitution, and even some of the old-time "blue" laws involving alcohol sale that had begun at the time of Prohibition.[70]

Lest one conclude that this has been all business as usual, with morals legislation fitting like a glove under the rubric of the police power given the standard construct, we need to examine two descriptive considerations in order to illuminate the state of morals regulation in present day. First, as to regulations of various forms of sexual expression, including adult entertainment, public nudity, prostitution in a public setting, and even some of the regulations dealing with drug dealing and use, those urging that these laws be upheld against challenges under the police power or individual rights protections have often relied not so much on the moral underpinnings of these laws, but on the secondary effects of this conduct. In a number of the more prominent adult entertainment cases, as we will discuss in more depth below, the Supreme Court based its reasoning in favor of government regulation, despite the impact on otherwise protected free expression, on the grounds that these laws were really designed to protect public safety and promote the public's general interest in a safe, orderly community. Not coincidentally, these laws were often drafted with these arguments in mind, so that certain businesses, for instance, were zoned for certain areas, such as a good distance from schools, parks, and churches.

We recognize that modern constitutional law on morals legislation concerning adult entertainment activities is deeply entangled with the evolution of constitutional rights, and especially the First Amendment. These kinds of regulation go back to the beginning of the republic in a fundamental sense, but they have triggered more thorough review as the Supreme Court expanded in the last several decades the protections of the First Amendment and have looked askance of content specific regulations. In a series of cases beginning with <u>Schad v. Mount Ephraim</u> in 1981[71] and continuing through the Court's decision in <u>City of Erie v. Pap's A.M.</u> in 1998,[72] the Court upheld local ordinances that were designed to restrict nudity and adult entertainment. The typical rationale for upholding these laws was that they were not directed toward the content of the behavior, and so were not, strictly speaking, a morals-based regulation at all, but instead were zoning laws that were intended to limit the secondary effects that flowed from these kinds of businesses.[73] As Justice Rehnquist wrote in <u>Renton v. Playtime Theatres</u>, one of these cases, "[t]he ordinance, by its terms, is designed to prevent crime, protect the city's retail trade, maintain property values, and generally protec[t] and preserv[e] the quality of [the city's] neighborhoods, commercial districts, and the quality of urban life," not to suppress the expression of unpopular views.[74] Reducing the issue to "popularity" is a bit of a red herring, after all. The main question is whether front of mind to legislators was the protection of public morals or public safety. To many, the public safety rationale seemed rather dubious, given the long history of nudity bans and the expressed concern with undermining the morals of the citizenry.[75]

Judicial evaluation of adult entertainment regulations has proved tricky in an era in which free expression enjoys preferred protection (a theme we will return to in Chapter 6 in discussing constitutional rights). Let us consider the legal saga in just one state, Pennsylvania, to illuminate these challenges. In 1959, the state high court upheld a ban on sexually explicit dancers fraternizing with the bar's customers, under the general power of the state to regulate establishments that serve alcohol under its police powers.[76] The relevant statute prohibited "lewd, immoral, or improper entertainment" on the premises.[77] As to alcohol control, the court indicated that "[n]o access of state action more plenary than regulation & control of the use & sale of alcoholic beer. The power of prohibition includes the lesser power of regulation."[78] What was somewhat novel was the reference to the greater power of regulating all things involving alcohol with prohibitions relating to the entertainers' behavior viz. the patrons. Is there any limit on what the state could regulate or even prohibit on the salon's premises given that they serve alcohol? The court answered "no" essentially, and upheld this prohibition. The court further upheld this statute as applied to (mostly) nude dancing in a 2002 case, In re Tahiti Bar.[79] By this time, the Supreme Court had decided the adult entertainment cases mentioned above and, in addition, had ruled in 44 Liquormart v. Rhode Island[80] that a ban on advertising the retail price of alcohol was not entitled to a presumption of validity and violated the First Amendment in that it restricted without adequate justification this commercial speech. This decision bolstered the argument that was central to their decision in Tahiti Bar more than four decades earlier, and that is that the fact that this ban was applicable to bars as such was relevant to the constitutional analysis of this content-neutral regulation. As the Pennsylvania court stated: "Although the states may not violate the constitutional rights of their citizens in regulating the alcohol industry, they possess 'ample power' to adopt such measures as they deem reasonable and appropriate to regulate and control the conduct of those who engage in liquor sales and other aspects of the liquor business."[81]

By 2006, however, the US Court of Appeals reversed course. In Conchatta v. Miller,[82] the court acknowledged the consistent findings of the state courts that this law prohibiting "lewd, immoral or improper behavior" was facially constitutional, but objected to its broad scope, noting that what falls under this prohibition has proved "to be a difficult question to answer."[83] That ambiguous scope of the law creates a chilling effect on free speech, especially when considering that it may well apply to entertainment venues in which the serving of alcohol is a rather minor part of the overall enterprise (as, for example, where a theatre showing a play serves booze in the lobby during intermission). This law, therefore, is overbroad, and fails the test for analyzing such police power prohibitions under the First Amendment.[84]

A line running straight through the Supreme Court's adult entertainment cases is that the legislature aspires, according to the courts, to prohibit secondary effects, a rationale that hearkens back to public nuisance and the *sic utere* rationale conspicuous in some of the earlier cases. However, it is difficult to see the history in context in any other way than about prohibiting certain forms of conduct for reasons related to morals. The framework of these lodestar cases does give the courts a two-pronged hook: First it respects the traditional deference to local land use decisions, and so trades on the very deferential approach to land use regulations that is part of traditional post-<u>Euclid</u> legal tradition, without scrutinizing anew the question whether local governments could use its police power to protect the public against immoral conduct; second, it interprets the purpose of the legislation, rightly or wrongly as a factual matter, as prohibiting bad secondary effects, thus bolstering the legislature's argument for why this is a sound use of the police power under even a narrow reading of that power.[85]

As with the adult entertainment cases, clever lawyers could explain these laws as about public safety rather than morals, in that they are intended to reduce bad secondary effects. Some scholars have indeed explained obscenity laws as part of the government's responsibility to abate nuisances.[86] In fact, the Restatement (Second) of Torts includes the legal concept of a moral nuisance, to illustrate this idea.[87] This is more legal strategy focused on the appellate circumstance, a strategy that sensibly accounts for the doctrinal rubric that is easiest to satisfy. However, the better view of the history of these laws is that they are deeply embedded in the government's strategy to protect society's morals. The Court in its principal decisions on this subject has evaded the question of whether a law based entirely on public morals would be acceptable under the police power. (To be sure, this is a question not only for the Supreme Court, but for state courts faced with the same essential challenges.) The bottom line is that the courts come to the same ultimate conclusion. The nearly unquestioned deference given to state and local officials to prohibit conduct that the government authorities believe are noxious illustrates the enduring logic of the police power as a mechanism to ground the government's interventions to protect public morals as part of the general safety or welfare.

In not all circumstances of morals regulation are secondary effects arguments available, however. The government's authority under the police power to restrict private sexual conduct is a complex and important story in its own right. To begin with, it is notable that for nearly the first two full centuries after the adoption of the Constitution and the Bill of Rights, state regulation of morals in matters pertaining to private familial decisions and sexual conduct inside or outside marriage was quite common.[88] Prosecutions under these laws were, to be sure, episodic, but arguments that such laws interfered with constitutionally protected liberty or privacy interests routinely failed, whether brought under the US Constitution or state constitutions. These were seen as matters to be decided through democratic processes and not typically subject to judicial intervention. In the 1960s and into the 70s, the Court decided a number of blockbuster cases, including <u>Griswold v. Connecticut</u>,[89] <u>Eisenstadt v. Baird</u>,[90] and <u>Roe</u>,[91] in which it announced that privacy rights under the penumbra of the Bill of Rights limited certain types of moral regulation. While these laws arose in the context of state laws regulating private conduct and truly intimate matters, they did not immediately portend a narrowing of the state police power so as to limit government's ability to regulate morals.

When the Court decided <u>Bowers</u> in 1986, it was clear that the state regulation of sexual conduct is permitted under the state's police power and was not a violation of an individual's civil liberties. Because the Georgia anti-sodomy law did not on its face distinguish between heterosexual and homosexual activity, <u>Bowers</u> did not raise squarely the question of whether the equal protection provisions of the Fourteenth Amendment was a limit on the particular regulation at issue here. Rather, the plaintiff's unsuccessful legal argument was that these laws were of the same species as those laws governing intimate conduct struck down in the cornerstone cases of the sixties and seventies. Although <u>Bowers</u> is considered a due process case, and so distinctly focused on the scope and reach of the Court's protections of liberty and privacy under the rubric of its modern jurisprudence on this subject, it truly reflects a judgment involving the police power and the room given to state governments to regulate activity that it deems immoral, and so a late twentieth-century stamp of approval on this use of the power.

This approval withered, however, in the years following <u>Bowers</u>. Indeed, much of this withering happened well before the 1980s, as more and more states eliminated these laws dealing with sexual conduct. In the mid-1980s, anti-sodomy laws were rare. Moreover, several state courts had already struck down state prohibitions on such conduct.[92]

In <u>Lawrence v. Texas</u>,[93] the Supreme Court expressly overruled <u>Bowers</u>. In that case, the Court, in an opinion by Justice Kennedy, invalidated a Texas law that singled out certain forms of sexual conduct by homosexual for criminal prohibition. They decided this squarely under the rationale from <u>Griswold</u>, <u>Eisenstadt</u>, and <u>Roe</u>, that is, that this conduct is protected by the liberty and privacy foundations of due process under the Fourteenth Amendment. Justice Kennedy incorporates fully Justice Stevens's statement of the issue in his dissent in <u>Bowers</u>.[94] Stevens had written there: "Individual decisions by married persons, concerning the intimacies of their physical relationship, even when not intended to produce offspring, are a form of 'liberty' protected by the Due Process Clause of the Fourteenth Amendment. Moreover, this protection extends to intimate choices by unmarried as well as married persons."[95]

That this law was targeted specifically toward same-sex individuals was a feature distinguishing this case from <u>Bowers</u>, and also was inapposite from the Court's key liberty decisions, including <u>Planned Parenthood v. Casey</u>.[96] Somewhat curiously, however, Justice Kennedy did not rest the holding on this fact (as would have Justice O'Connor, who concurred separately, arguing this law was a violation of the equal protection of the laws), but instead wrote more broadly about the rationale and impact of this law as interference in private intimate choices.[97] Reliance on this, rather than on equal protection, raises more directly, as Justice Scalia emphasizes in his dissenting opinion, whether there are substantial new limits on morals regulation. "Countless judicial decisions," Scalia writes, "and legislative enactments have relied on the ancient proposition that a governing majority's belief that certain sexual behavior is 'immoral and unacceptable' constitutes a rational basis for regulation."[98] This decision, he goes on, casts doubt on the continuing legality under the Constitution of myriad morals laws.[99] "State laws against bigamy, same-sex marriage, adult incest, prostitution, masturbation, adultery, fornication, bestiality, and obscenity are likewise sustainable only in light of *Bowers*' validation of laws based on moral choices. Every single one of these laws is called into question by today's decision."[100]

Lawrence is a difficult case for understanding the proper scope of the police power in regulating morals. Avoiding the offramp that would have squarely focused on the inequality of this law in its targeting of a class of individuals – homosexuals – for discriminatory treatment means that the Court was wading directly into the question of when the government simply goes too far in regulating sexual conduct. In the end, Justice Scalia was quite right in suggesting that Lawrence raises questions concerning the overall use of the police power by states to regulate morals in other areas, insofar as regulations intrude on private conduct and liberty.[101]

A narrower, and ultimately more plausible, reading of Lawrence is possible, one that does not decree that morals regulation is off limits. The key here is to understand Lawrence as of a piece with Romer v. Evans,[102] decided by the Court in another opinion by Justice Kennedy. Romer involved a Colorado initiative that limited the ability of state and local governments to accord legal protection to LBGTQ individuals, such as prohibitions against discrimination in employment or access to services. The Court struck down this law on equal protection grounds, insisting that it reflected animus toward a traditionally disfavored group and could not be justified under any compelling rationale. "[T]he amendment," writes Kennedy, "imposes a special disability upon those persons alone. Homosexuals are forbidden the safeguards that others enjoy or may seek without constraint."[103] While it is not inconceivable that the government could seek to limit protections from a category of individuals – Justice Scalia in his dissent mentions bans on polygamy; we might also think about denying voting rights to felons – there has to be a legitimate basis for such categorization in order to pass Fourteenth Amendment scrutiny. "A bare ... desire to harm a politically unpopular group cannot constitute a *legitimate* governmental interest."[104]

Read through the lens of Romer, we might view Lawrence, despite Justice Kennedy's equivocations in his opinion, as focused principally on the ways in which Texas was essentially singling out homosexuals for disfavored treatment. So viewed, this law is arbitrary in its enforcement of morals, looking with opprobrium on a class of individuals based upon these sexual orientation, not upon the specific conduct prohibited, conduct which would have been legal had it been engaged in by opposite sex couples. Such a reading lays the foundation for what the Court ultimately did nearly two decades later, in striking down prohibitions against same-sex marriage in Obergefell v. Hodges.[105] On the other hand, this reading limits significantly the import of Lawrence for scrutiny of ordinary morals regulation, regulation that focuses only on the behavior engaged in, without regard to the race, sex, sexual orientation, or any other status of the individual subject to the laws. Could a state, for example, limit any sexual practices between consenting adults? How could such limits be reconciled with Lawrence and Obergefell?

Why is this reading of Lawrence the better one? Ought there to be direct checks and channels, sourced principally in state constitutional law, on government regulation of morals? Morality evolves and we should constantly ask, as members of a democratic society, whether certain forms of regulation have become anachronistic because they assess behavior based upon discredited or at least highly controversial views of morality. Consider the present state of laws governing the use of cannabis. Federal law prohibits any use, possession, manufacture, or sale of cannabis under the Controlled Substances Act.[106] Support for this act has been steadily eroding as public opinion continues in ever-growing numbers to disapprove of criminal prohibition.[107] The vast majority of states provide the cannabis is legal for approved medical use;[108] twenty-three of the fifty states have approved cannabis for recreational use.[109] Leaving aside what the federal government will or will not do to the legal status of cannabis under federal law in the coming years,[110] are there at present acceptable limits on the state's prohibition of cannabis under the police power? This is an important and difficult question. Laws restricting cannabis seem rather arbitrary when considered alongside the use of substances, natural or chemically manufactured, that are not illegal. This has been a frequent criticism of the way in which Congress distinguished drugs in their schedules in the Controlled Substance Act of 1970.[111] In any event, the balance of social harm versus individual liberty is becoming harder to maintain in an era in which the immorality of marijuana is seriously questioned by a growing number of Americans.

Likewise, the government has been given wide latitude to impose restrictions on the conduct of the drug trade. Much of these efforts are part of the strategies of policing, and often are grounded in formal and even informal guidance, rather than through express legislation or administrative regulation. So, in this respect, we might say that they are part of the police power in a more opaque sense. However, there are many instances of real laws on the books that are explained as efforts to protect public safety and general welfare by imposing barriers to and burdens on the conduct of the drug trade, these running in parallel to specific criminal laws those impose manifest costs through the traditional cluster of penalties.

In a similar vein, there are myriad laws criminalizing sex work, these traditionally justified on both morals and secondary effects grounds. The disproportionate impact on women, on people of color, and on members of the trans community illustrate some of the deleterious costs of this continuing effort to make criminal consensual economic relationships involving sex. A recent report of the Yale Global Health Partnership notes, first, that arrests and even prosecutions for violations of ordinances prohibiting sex work persist, even as the public opinion on these matters is evolving and, second, the consequences of these laws are dire. These negative consequences include exacerbating socioeconomic hardship, increased stigma and violence, loss of civil rights as a result of criminal records, and various collateral costs to sex workers' families and their communities.[112]

Why does American law continue to criminalize sex work? It is hard to see such persistence as anything other than the manifestation of moral concern. The age in which all, or even most, of sex work is conducted by so-called prostitutes carrying on their business on street corners and in shady areas of time has largely passed, despite the picture painted in films such as Pretty Woman and, earlier, Taxi Driver. Sex work frequently involves transactions and conduct that is more private than public, including various activities on the internet. And so the "secondary effects" rationale is more elusive than it might have been a half century ago. Rather, one can see the criminalization of sex work as morals regulation that takes sides with Lord Devlin in the famous Hart–Devlin debate of the last century. Despite the efforts in England just after the middle of the last century to draw lines between public and private conduct, and the similar debates in the United States over the course of the many decades to move away from legal strategies that are focused principally on punishing and policing "bad" morals, the widespread criminalization of sex work, a species of the prohibition, through the criminal law of what is seen as deviant sexual behavior, whether or not mostly in the public, continues with rare interruption. Any way you slice it, the police power, traditional and modern, undergirds this problematic morals regulation. That is, without the government's constitutional power to regulate public morals, such regulation would be constitutionally improper as a structural matter, regardless of any relevant liberty interests protected by the Bill of Rights.

Other issues where evolving morals meet traditional governmental regulation are well within what has been called our contemporary culture wars. These include a sudden rise in laws limiting trans individuals access to certain bathrooms,[113] prohibiting gender-neutral bathrooms, and prohibitions on drag shows.[114] With respect to drag shows in particular, at this writing, twenty states have enacted or are hard at work at enacting drag show bans.[115] Although often styled as laws directed toward protecting children safety – one law in Montana, for instance, prohibits not the shows but anyone in drag from reading to children at a public library – these laws typically cut broadly, focusing not on limiting access by age, but eliminating entirely what is seen as an immoral circumstance or activity. Similar efforts are underway in enacting legislation that targets the trans community, including criminalization (typically at the felony level) efforts at so-called gender affirming care.[116] In short order, a number of these bills have become law, and others are being shaped in various ways that advocates believe will survive scrutiny.

Litigation currently rages over these laws. However, they are seldom viewed as invalid on the grounds that the government has wrongly legislated morality under its police power. Concerns, instead, involve what are often more "legalistic" considerations, such as whether the local laws are preempted by state authority or whether they are pretextual efforts to disadvantage certain groups (LBGTQ especially) in order to insist upon a certain view of public morality. How should we assess these matters?

Morals regulation comes up often in the idiosyncratic context of particular states, and their choices to regard certain conduct as immoral. The preceding discussion has emphasized rules and restrictions that are generally seen as emerging from the conservative side of the political spectrum in the contemporary culture wars. However, there are instances of controversial morals legislation that come from the so-called Blue states and communities. For example, cities in California and in some other states have imposed bans that are intended to protect animal welfare. These include prohibitions on the serving of foie gras,[117] coming from the liver of ducks who have often been force-fed in order to yield better-quality food, and also the serving of shark fin soup, because of the ways in which sharks are hunted for their fins.[118] There is not a manifest public health and safety rationale for these laws, at least insofar as humans are concerned. The focus on protecting animal rights has been viewed by state and local legislatures as proper and so these laws have been enacted in response to community public opinion. Where they have been challenged, the usual result is in favor of these laws' legality. Animal welfare laws can raise tricky issues of federal regulatory preemption and also commerce clause constraints where the laws deal with importation or exportation of animal products. But, in the main, governments at the state and local level have been given a wide berth to enact laws that are viewed essentially as taking a strong moral position in favor of animal welfare, even at the cost of consumer choice.

Morals regulation has always been a part of our police power legislation and jurisprudence. The question for our modern era is whether and to what extent it can and should be adapted in light of increasingly contentious struggles over the role of government in protecting against what many argue is licentiousness and attacks on the common good. This is not the place to settle these enduring issues, issues which have long been the subject of debate among not only philosophers who ruminate on matters of what is moral versus immoral conduct, but among those tasked with the responsibility to decide whether and to what extent regulation to safeguard morals, in the *contra bonos* rather than harm-prohibiting sense, is warranted. Nonetheless, what is on offer is an important process suggestion, one broadly congruent with American legal and political history more generally, and the police power in particular. It is that these questions should be addressed and settled in the crucible of democratic debate and, where appropriate, constitutional politics. Just as the contours of the police power are evolving, the subjects of regulatory scrutiny – the very contents of what might be regulated and for what purpose – are likewise evolving. Morals change, and so does the proper role of government in regulating morals. Monitoring and implementing these changes is a critical function of we the people, acting directly and through our elected representatives. And our system of democratic constitutionalism, as a bevy of creative public law scholars teach us, contemplates and even demands dynamic struggle over the defining of the space in which government can and must step in to protect public morals from erosion. There are, to be sure, easy cases in both directions (maybe laws prohibiting blasphemy and adultery are good examples for limiting government intervention). There are harder cases whose difficulty emerges from persistent disagreements about the scope of individual liberty and the collective welfare. Perhaps the hardest cases so far as morals regulation is concerned are those in which individual rights under the constitution are not in any serious way implicated, but yet the question arises of what business government has in intervening with individual choice to live one's life or do one's work in the way they wish. In such cases, one cannot resort to a first-order principle that victimless morals regulation is or is not acceptable to settle this question, as Mill might have wanted, if only because that ship has surely sailed, but ultimately must contend with questions about the proper objectives of governing and the place for individual choice in a free society. These are constitutional liberty questions, to be sure. Yet these are also police power questions. That constitutional debates in litigation and in academic commentary generally focuses on the former and neglects the latter is a casualty of the police power's invisibility. In the case of morals regulations, perhaps more than in any other area, greater visibility to the police power would enrich debate and further the project of reframing law around questions concerning the proper role and function of government in regulating morality.

THE POLICE POWER AND THE URBAN CONDITION

The idea of the well-ordered society plays a consistently large role in the continuing evolution of the police power.[119] After all, order presupposes a decent level of collective security and public health. Securing and maintaining this level is at the heart of the police power, in its origins, its rationale, and its basic logic. Many of the cases involving the police power and its exercise involve the question of whether and on what terms the government may undertake measures to control certain uses of property in order to protect the interest of the government, presumably derivative of the interest of the community the government serves. We discussed in the last chapter the advent and evolution of zoning as a method of ordering urban life through the management of private property and its use, and we saw state courts and finally the Supreme Court giving their blessing to zoning under the police power. However, the issue of how broad is the government's power to regulate the use of land in order to realize objectives in an ever more urban society did not die down because of the Euclid decision from nearly a century ago. Matters concerning zoning and the police power continue to come to courts, as do the related issues of land use regulation and regulatory takings. Taken together, these twin doctrines show the judiciary and the legislature working together, even if unintentionally, to strengthen the authority of the government to address problems of modern urban life through the creative use of the police power.

An important case in this regard is Berman v. Parker,[120] a regulatory takings case discussed earlier. Berman involved a comprehensive plan in the District of Columbia, a plans whose purpose was to deal with slums and sub-standard housing in the area, efforts that they believed would alleviate blight and conditions that contributed to crime and general social disorder. To implement this plan, the city required the razing of many existing houses and other major steps toward redevelopment, requirements that they aimed to implement through eminent domain. To the objection that this strategy did not meet the requirement of taking for a public use, because the land would not be necessarily transferred to the ownership of the district, but would transfer to private developers, the Court deferred to the locality's judgment and accepted that the overall plan had a clear public use. This was, in the end, enough to satisfy the constitutional requirements of eminent domain.

Berman illustrates well the intersection between the police power and eminent domain. The fulcrum of both doctrines is the common good, with the police power expressing this in the *salus populi* idea of general welfare and the proper use of the eminent domain to facilitate a public use. In its relatively short and undertheorized opinion, the Court found that the public use rationale was obvious in this case. But there is more to Berman's logic than meets the eye in this respect. The taking in this case was redistributive in the classic sense; that is, the government was taking individual's property and making it available to other property owners as part of an omnibus scheme of urban renewal. The idea emphasized by the Court in the eighteenth-century case of Calder v. Bull that it is unacceptable for the government to, in essence, rob Peter to pay Paul is nowhere mentioned in Berman. Nor is it prominent in a half century's-worth of cases following Berman, including Hawaii Housing Authority v. Midkiff[121] and Kelo v. City of New London,[122] both instances of policies used to redistribute land from one private owner to another. In all of these cases, the public use requirement is easily satisfied by evidence, largely unquestioned by the courts, that this government action was intended to advance a public purpose.

In Berman and its progeny, the police power and eminent domain work in synergy with one another to further the objectives of advancing the common welfare, even where such advancement requires a wealth transfer. Blight, says Justice Douglas, is a scourge, impacting the District of Columbia community. And it is very much in the public interest to undertake major land use policies, of which eminent domain is one part in a comprehensive strategy, a strategy that can address blight as an urban problem in need of a solution. Hard cases would continue to arise under eminent domain law and also under police power with respect to zoning and its proper scope. However, Berman is important in setting out the broad parameters of a doctrine that establishes a wide terrain of government action concerning individual sacrifice permitted under the constitution in order to accomplish *salus populi* goals.

As the century wore on, and the new century emerged, local governments became deeply invested in regulating land uses and in undertaking efforts to improve urban life. The strategies of doing so intersected in key ways, so that efforts to combat urban blight went along with emerging crime prevention measures (some enduring, others discredited), and with various safety regulations in housing and other circumstances. Such regulations came in various shapes and sizes. However, we can focus on land use regulations as a good window into governmental choice and the shadow cast by the law and practice of the police power.

Consider the controversial emergence of land use regulations designed to protect the character of the community, whether pertaining to aesthetics or the characteristics of residency, or other subjects of restriction. Village of Belle Terre v. Boraas is a well-known case from the early 1970s in which the Supreme Court upheld a municipal regulation under the police power, one that limited dwelling residents to one family.[123] While it was hard to see this regulation as promoting public health or safety, the Court, in an opinion by Justice Douglas, saw this as within the power of the local government to advance the public good, noting that "boarding houses, fraternity houses, and the like present urban problems. More people occupy a given space; more cars rather continuously pass by; more cars are parked; noise travels with crowds."[124] The government could properly seek to ensure for the benefit of the village's citizens "[a] quiet place where yards are wide, people few, and motor vehicles restricted are legitimate guidelines in a land use project addressed to family needs."[125]

The Court saw in Belle Terre an instance of ordinary economic and social legislation, one that had long accepted as constitutionally acceptable. Local governments had an interest on behalf of the public in the number of occupants dwelling in a particular residence. As to the claim that the law targeted certain individuals based upon their status – or, more accurately, their non-status as relatives with one another, the Court rejected this argument, insisting that the legislature can properly draw "[l]ines against the charge of violation of the Equal Protection clause if the law be *'reasonable, not arbitrary,' and bears 'a rational relationship to a [permissible] state objective'*."[126]

The half-century line stretching from Euclid to Belle Terre suggests a fairly straight connection from the law's approval of zoning as a means of promoting the common good in its earliest iterations to a reapproval even after the nation had experienced the Warren Court rights revolution.[127] However, to suggest that this line is an unbroken one would be misleading. The scope of the state and local government's general zoning power has continued to be challenged and the courts regularly confront arguments that certain techniques of land use regulations are unreasonable and counterproductive,[128] leaving to one side the separate question of whether they interfere with individual property rights as defined by contemporary law.[129] The critique of contemporary land use as being unsuitable for its stated purposes has been a persistent one for many years. A year before Belle Terre, for example, noted land use expert Professor Robert Ellickson wrote an important article in which he questioned the modern state of zoning law, suggesting that the rationale for certain techniques, even some widely accepted, were unreasonable and even counterproductive. His argument presaged a steadily growing body of theoretical and empirical scholarship that questions the nexus between zoning and the public welfare as we will consider as part of the police power's future in Chapter 9.

The argument against zoning from the perspective of the general welfare of the community found a receptive ear in a state court one year after Belle Terre, in the New Jersey supreme court's Town of Mount Laurel decision.[130] There the court held unconstitutional a particular zoning regulation enacted under the state's police power, on the grounds that these regulations had deleterious effects on the conditions of low-income individuals (echoing an argument that Ellickson had made two years earlier[131]) in the state. The court insisted that the state government had not been given a free pass of sorts from constitutional scrutiny under the police power as a result of Euclid and its progeny. "It is elementary theory," Justice Hall wrote, "that all police power enactments, no matter at what level of government, must conform to the basic state constitutional requirements of substantive due process and equal protection."[132] This comment echoed the prevailing sentiment of the time, that individual rights as interpreted (often broadly in many state courts and the Supreme Court of this era) could be invoked as brakes on the police power. However, the court said something even more striking with regard to the foundational question of the government's discretion to regulate land use in a certain way under the police power. Such zoning regulations, the court wrote, "must promote public health, safety, and welfare ... [a] zoning enactment which is contrary to the general welfare is invalid."[133] This suggests that even in the absence of a cognizable equal protection claim or a substantive due process claim, the court might invalidate the zoning law as inconsistent with the general welfare. Moreover, general welfare itself is an elastic concept. The court must consider after all "whose general welfare must be served or not ... in the field of land use regulation."[134] The ordeal that has become the Mount Laurel land use situation in New Jersey has been written about widely.[135] Whether the New Jersey supreme court was ultimately unrealistic in its demands for accountability and specific redress is an enduring question and a difficult one. However, the import of the court's reading of the proper exercise of police power in its effort to control the use of land to full public objectives has remained influential. This is so because the court ultimately asked the right question: Is this use of zoning consistent with the government's responsibility to protect the general welfare of the community?

Beyond zoning, the police power has been a source of ample local authority to address myriad problems that are associated with urban disorder. As we discussed in the previous subsection, some of these laws, for example, drug and anti-prostitution laws, have been tied to traditional views of morality. And yet the rationale invoked in many cases in which they have been challenged as constitutionally suspicious has been that this conduct has noxious secondary effects. Without revisiting the issue of whether these laws are really truly about morals or are about curtailing bad effects on the community, an issue that seems impossible to settle given that it rests on complex assessments of legislative purpose among other puzzles, we might hope that at the very least, claims of bad community effects should rest on evidence-based analysis. It is easier to proclaim that society is going to rot without regulatory interventions than it is to do the hard work of measuring the effects of certain behaviors on community welfare and, afterward, measuring the effects of regulatory interventions.

One area of robust local regulation designed to implement public society in urban environments is laws protecting tenants from sub-standard housing. Much of this legislation emerged from litigation challenging what had been too-common landlord behavior. The courts developed various doctrines, such as the implied warranty of habitability, in order to protect tenants.[136] Moreover, responding to persistent racial exclusion in the housing market, state and local governments built upon the federal government's federal housing laws of the late 1960s to develop legislative mechanisms to protect people of color from various practices.[137] One of the most substantial efforts was the development by the Uniform Law Commission in the early 1970s of the Uniform Residential Landlord Tenant, a proposed piece of legislation ultimately adopted by many states.[138] While some of these legal developments can be seen as classically anti-discrimination law, it is important to see the laws as part of a pattern of enhancing public safety and the general welfare, both through minimal standards of acceptable conduct on the part of property owners and through protections against unequal treatment.

The police power can and does supporting governmental efforts to address problems of urban life. These problems typically go beyond blight and so to see the essential police power project as being about, to use an old phrase, urban renewal, is myopic. Improving the urban condition for al its residents means improving the conditions of the least fortunate. Such strategies will inevitably be redistributive. They also focus, sometimes specifically and other times at broad relief, on anti-discrimination. Progress in this domain owes much to the active, creative use of the police power to address deficiencies in the urban condition. Even so, much progress remains to be made.

Once area of public policy in which complex issues continue to surface is zoning. On the question of zoning as a mechanism to improve safety and the general welfare, controversy has steadily grown in recent years.[139] There is a serious debate newly underway about the efficacy and desirability of contemporary land use regulation.[140] This debate has brought together some strange bedfellows. Zoning has occasioned continuous objections from libertarians who point to the heavy-handed use of municipal authority to limit owner choice.[141] Economists, not all of them avowedly conservative, have contributed a large body of scholarship showing the negative welfare effects of the current configuration of zoning in many parts of the country.[142]

In particular, they have connected the affordability crisis and dearth of adequate new housing construction to patterns of zoning law.[143] As a result, we are experiencing a surge in the number of challenges to zoning laws.[144] As always, this litigation grows from the efforts of disgruntled landowners to advance their interests in this traditional venue of conflict. Perhaps more surprisingly, the anti-skepticism movement has had some successes at the legislative level, and advocates of various ideological stripes have adopted the colorful moniker "YIMBY" (Yes in My Backyard) in order to push for legislative and administrative solutions to our contemporary housing crisis (one that is double-barreled, in engaging with issues of affordability as well as the predicament of the unhoused).[145]

In one sense, the current debate is not primarily about the scope of governmental power, but about the best use of this power, that is, the wisdom of certain strategies to implement municipal objectives. However, when skepticism about modern zoning does come to center stage, as we will explore in Chapter 9 in our discussion of the modern police power as a means of redressing America's housing crisis, there are some very creative, if controversial, uses of the police power to impede certain laws, this on the theory that the public's welfare is undermined by the imposition of strict land use laws and therefore its use can, under certain conditions, be a violation of the constitution in that the law is outside the scope of the power.

Urban life is increasingly Americans' life, with now 80 percent living in areas defined by the census as urban.[146] Even if this share stays relatively steady in the future, the steady increases to the US population means that the sheer numbers of individuals living in urban American will increase and, with it, the various problems that accompany density, to say nothing of the serious problems of polarization that is plaguing modern society in the US as elsewhere. The police power is not nearly a panacea, but remains as a key component of the strategies of state and local government to respond to social problems in urban settings and also act preemptively to deal with issues that can simmer to a boil. In this author's home city of Chicago, to take just one example, we are struggling with various upheavals to our urban area – having in our head the idea of a well-ordered society – from property damage occasioned by groups of young people congregating in the "fancier" areas of the city, and with motives that are not at all appealing and temptations that are unattractive. One reaction to these not infrequent episodes is to bring traditional law enforcement resources to bear in order to stop or at least disincentivize this bad behavior. Enforcing the public safety laws on the books is a classic police power strategy after all. However, others in our community are suggesting more imaginative policy actions that go to the root causes of the discontent, or even sheer boredom, faced by these groups (largely made up of young people of color, if this was not obvious to the reader). Such steps could obviate the need for command-and-control law enforcement, while addressing the urban disorder that keeps residents on each. This a complicated issue, but the point is that the police power is both ample and supple; it can provide, in the hands of creative municipal governments, the means of addressing urban problems at their source, without resort to the traditional modalities of criminal law and policing that raises its own set of complications in our fragile polity.

OCCUPATIONAL LICENSING

One important area in which states governments have used the police power as an instrument of consumer protection and control has been in matters of occupational licensing. The licensing of professionals, including in medicine, law, and myriad other settings is nearly entirely a matter of state law. Long ago, state courts rejected claims that state schemes of occupational licensing were improper interferences in the freedom of individuals to practice their trade. Moreover, the federal courts have largely stayed out of these disputes, under its persistent reasoning that such licensing involves economic regulation and is therefore subject to the lowest standard of review.[147] By combination of state and federal caselaw, there has been little room for legal challenges to the contemporary schemes of occupational licensing on the grounds that it exceeds the state's police power.

This is problematic, in that the way in which occupational licensing has unfolded over many decades has been both provincial and protectionist.[148] In the case of medicine, it made it more difficult for many years for individuals to seek public health providers, given how the marketplace was structured to advantage physicians and certain segments of the overall health profession.[149] In the case of law, severe restrictions on legal advice and representation has fueled an access to justice crisis, limiting access to the civil justice system to only those wealthy enough to afford services and savvy enough to know where to look for support.[150]

Occupational licensing illustrates some of key difficulties with the police power as a fulcrum of state specific regulatory authority. To begin with, the reliance on state authority means that the entire system is deeply balkanized.[151] This is troubling in a world in which transactions and human activity often take place across borders. States have different admissions, ethics, and malpractice rules for both lawyers and doctors. The federal government's role is fairly interstitial; and the longstanding efforts to develop and implement coherent model rules so that states could converge on best practices has been a political rollercoaster.[152] Second, the regulatory choices made, including the critical choice of who to license to practice in one or another occupation, are typically made by incumbents.[153] The incentive to pull up the drawbridge on individuals who would enter into the marketplace and potentially take business away from incumbent providers is great. Therefore, we see in the overall structure of regulation rules that seem manifestly in the collective interest of those already in the tent, and not necessarily in the best interests of consumers.[154] Third and relatedly, there is precious little mechanism for citizen input. Occupational licensing decisions are not in the main made in a democratic process. Rules governing lawyers, for example, are forged by state supreme courts and bar authorities to whom courts delegate great power.[155] They are largely cordoned off from the democratic legislature by the tradition of self-regulation, which means as it says that lawyers and judges will be the gatekeepers of the profession. They seldom carry out their work in a way that anyone would responsibility view as transparent. Finally, state courts are quite reticent to get involved in disputes involving occupational licensing. In law, it is these same courts that are doing the regulating, so the conflict of interest – or at least the cultural bias – makes such scrutiny unlikely. Outside of law, courts are understandably reticent to intervene in matters which they have little expertise and in which the wholesale and retail choices are being made by field experts.

Despite the largely hands-off approach to occupational licensing under traditional police power principles, there have been some salutary changes in how the law has responded to difficulties and distress in the areas in which licensing operates. In the medical field, for example, the Covid pandemic accelerated the use of telemedicine and created mechanisms to break down barriers and restrictions in order to get to individuals sensible health measures.[156] In law, there has been some attention paid to state experiments that widen access to legal services by removing protectionist rules and other obstacles. The advent of the so-called Uniform Bar Exam is a promising modern development toward greater access, as is the acceptance by a few (and hopefully growing number of) states to allow lawyers unlicensed in those states to assist with providing necessary legal services after, say, a natural disaster. Moreover, the federal government may well intervene in more ambitious ways, through the targeted use of antitrust laws and, via litigation, through First Amendment claims. There are cases pending involving the latter,[157] and some activity with regard to the former.[158] All of this suggests that the matter of occupational licensing is becoming turbulent in a way that has not been common in the past.

What is important for our discussion in these debates over occupational licensing and its deficits is to explore how explicit is the connection between the status quo and consumer protection. And if and when the state government acts through legislation to reform contemporary practices, it will be within the general framework of the police power, establishing regulations (we can hope) that are in fact serving the public's welfare. Evidence-based efforts by scholars and others to examine more closely the connection between current schemes of occupational licensing and the general welfare of the public are critical to this inquiry. They will help us to develop a strategy of regulation under police power that is truly modern and constructive.

PUBLIC HEALTH REGULATION IN THE COVID-19 ERA

The Covid pandemic from 2020 to 22 brought into the sharp relief questions over how proactive the state and local governments could be in enacting emergency measures under the police power. In this period, states were imposing draconian restrictions on individual and business behavior, including lockdowns distancing requirements, and restrictions on travel. Even as these rules began to recede, litigation over these and emerging restrictions brought to the fore questions of how far the government could go to restrict individual liberty in the time of a pandemic.

We have discussed Jacobson at different junctures, as illustrative of the Court's deferential view of police power regulations, including when public health regulations were at issue. Jacobson followed earlier cases,[159] and presaged later cases, in which the Supreme Court made clear that public health laws were well within the scope of the state government's constitutional authority. This deference to public health measures was echoed in important state cases dealing with public health pandemics. For example, in People v. Adams, a 1992 Illinois case,[160] the court upheld a law requiring individuals convicted of prostitution-related offenses to undergo medical testing for HIV. "Like other measures intended to enhance public health and community well-being," the court wrote, "governmental action designed to control the spread of disease falls within the scope of the State's police power."[161]

Jacobson emerged from some amount of obscurity (outside of public health law circles at least) to become a central source of authority (and also inscrutability) as courts during the recent Covid pandemic worked through difficult questions of the police power's scope.[162]

One of the earliest cases in which Covid shutdown measures were scrutinized under the state and US constitutions was a case out of New Hampshire, Binford v. Sununu.[163] There the Superior Court upheld the governor's executive orders limiting gathering and imposing shelter-in-place regulations, finding that the facts "establish a strong need for immediate intervention" and detailing the statutory and constitutional support for the decision to suspend certain constitutional protections in order to implement emergency measures. The court did not refer in any place to the police power or to Jacobson, but implicit in its opinion was the view that the statute which gave the governor this regulatory authority was consistent with the state constitution. Likewise, in Friends of Danny DeVito v. Wolf,[164] (no, not THAT Danny DeVito), the Pennsylvania supreme court rejected the plaintiff's takings claim, noting that this effort "to protect the lives and health of millions of Pennsylvania citizens undoubtedly constitutes a classic example of the use of the police power to 'protect the lives, health, morals, comfort, and general welfare of the people'."[165]

A 2020 case out of Texas, which ultimately came before the 5th circuit, illustrated an interesting twist on the matter of governmental authority under the police power. In re Abbott involved a Texas restriction on non-essential surgeries, including elective abortions, during the early crisis period of Covid.[166] The court was asked to decide whether such a restriction was consistent with the plaintiff's abortion rights and, as a key threshold matter, whether the governor in the first instance had the authority under the police power to impose this regulation. Judge Duncan for the 5th circuit upheld the restriction, arguing that it was plainly legal under the Court's holding in Jacobson and its progeny. In so doing, he did not suggest that the rule is that constitutional rights "disappear during a public health crisis," but he noted that the Jacobson Court "plainly stated that rights could be reasonably restricted during those times."[167] Having decided that such restrictions were warranted under these circumstances, Judge Duncan resolved the issue of abortion rights by indicating that "nothing in the Supreme Court's abortion cases suggests that abortion rights are somehow exempt from the *Jacobson* framework."[168]

Cases involving Covid shutdowns and other restrictions regularly rejected arguments that such laws were beyond the scope of the police power. Likewise, courts rejected repeatedly arguments that they interfered with property rights (for instance, were takings of private property without just compensation), free speech rights, and due process.[169] They also rejected claims that turned on the government's distinctions between one kind of activity (or business) and other, for the purposes of a health-related restriction.[170] There was some debate, in the legal literature and occasionally in the cases, about whether the courts, state and federal, were supposed to apply something like ordinary judicial review or something extraordinary, given the emergency nature of the decision.[171] This line between ordinary and extraordinary review proved to be of minimal practical impact and, frankly, of less interesting theoretical import than would meet the eye at first glance. After all, neither the Jacobson Court in 1905 nor courts applying the rationale of that decision in the decades following had ever said that there was an emergency exception to judicial review, that the courts should adjure their authority to look closely at the government's purported power to act and at the rights that would be affected, if any, by the exercise of this power. Even under ordinary review, the fundamental question is whether the state constitution permits the government to act in order to protect the public health, safety, and welfare and whether, under all the circumstances properly taken into account, there are individual rights that are at risk from the imposition of these measures.

In our more extended discussion of rights in Chapter 6, we will return to the Covid controversies to see the ways in which the Supreme Court used the First Amendment's protection of religious liberty to overturn particular police power regulations dealing with Covid. This was an important reckoning about public health restrictions and freedom of religion in the United States, as it was carried out in a handful of opinions, each with passionate opinions on both sides of the issue. And yet in none of these cases did the Supreme Court overturn Jacobson; indeed, in no case did the Court seriously interrogate the matter of whether the police power should be viewed more narrowly in light of strong objections to the scope and impact of these highly intrusive public health measures (including shutdowns, gathering restrictions, and vaccine mandates) and claims that the lines being drawn by the government were dubious.

Looking back at this Covid constitutional litigation, it is hard to disentangle the legal reasoning and precedential impact from the profoundly polarized way in which these legal objections were made and these issues resolved. However, it is important to draw out the appropriate legal lessons, for the question of how far the government can go under its public health police power authority is one of present and future relevance. In this light, we can build out from the decided cases, federal and state, and say the following: First, Jacobson survives as the lodestar case for the government's use of public health measures, and even draconian ones, in times of crisis. Second, Jacobson is best understood not as approving a suspension of the Constitution in emergency times, but as a holding that reconciles the matter of official power and constitutional rights (especially due process, which was the most prominent claim in that particular case) under what we might call ordinary constitutional review. Third, and accepting that such review is ordinary, there is nothing static about our constitutional rights jurisprudence. As we will see in Chapter 6, the evolution of constitutional rights in the twelve decades since Jacobson means that the practical import of that holding has been affected in that individuals might meet the legislature's claim of public health exigencies with an assertion that a fundamental right, such as their religious liberty right, has been affected without adequate justification. Fourth, and turning more directly to the practical effects of this Covid episode on public health restrictions, it is hard to predict with any confidence how courts will see the government's proper role in times of emergencies. The polarization of these issues can hardly be overstated; nor can we be confident that this polarization will not seep into judicial decision-making. Certainly the lines between conservative and liberal justices on the US Supreme Court and also on the state courts in which there have been discernible partisan differences can be easily connected to Covid-related public health decisions. Conservatives have been highly skeptical of mandates and the power of the government to issue them, and liberals have been more solicitous of these measures.

Fifth, many of the Covid restriction arguments in litigation had become entangled in debates, often only legal in a tangential sense, over the role of science and scientific expertise. Where the issues were framed around whether a particular mandate made good sense – which is how the conversation in the political process and the media focused upon, understandably – then the court found itself often ahead of its skis. The considerations moved away from Jacobson and the constitutional authority of legislatures, governors, and public health officials to act to contain the virus's effects, toward the question of whether the government's actions were warranted, based upon the reasons given for the decision and the evidence upon which they relied, and the traditional deference given to experts in matters of public health. The tacit assumption of power to evaluate the merits of these public health decisions from other institutions in government was arguably one of the casualties of the Covid public law litigation saga.[172] It would be worrisome if this trend continued in the next major public health crisis or in the enterprise of evaluating episodic public health regulations more generally.

Sixth, and finally, the majority of issues prominent in government responses to public health emergencies do not involve the first-order constitutional considerations that we saw in Jacobson and the few Covid cases we have discussed in this subsection and the religious liberty cases that we will examine in Chapter 6. Rather, public health strategies ordinarily involve regulatory policymaking and detailed implementation strategies undertaken by agencies and administrators. The broad authority is set by statute, of course, and so we can assume that all matters of administrative execution are derivative of statutory authority that is, in turn, compliant with state constitutional authority, including the police power. But the point here is that the devil is usually found in the details. And so the important questions of how best to tackle public health emergencies consistent with the police power are usually to be answered by dense engagement with these matters by those administrators who will deal with these issues as the experts, as the front-line regulators and implementors. Their legal instructions and scope of discretion will generally be constructed by a statutory infrastructure and aided by state (and often also federal) administrative law. The police power considerations will loom fairly far in the background – until, that is, major constitutional controversies of the sort that we saw in the first two years of the Covid pandemic come forth with alacrity and passion.[173]

SUMMARY

We have taken a long tour in this Part of the police power as it evolved from the time of the founding, and he development of the first state constitutions, through the antebellum period, Reconstruction, the Progressive era, and deep into the twenty-first century. In this Chapter, we have seen how some key, persistently controversial issues have been framed around the police power's contents and its purposes. If there is one overarching lesson it is that the police power has proven adaptive to changes in the needs, wants, and conditions in contemporary public policy. (How further adaptive it might be is the subject of Chapter 9.)

Constructing a police power for modern times is not something that can or should happen *tabula rasa*, and this is exactly how it should be. This police power has evolved, as have state constitutions, too. Moreover, and as inevitable, larger legal and political developments have shaped the scope and direction of this power, The police power's evolution has accompanied evolution in strategies and conceptual understandings of regulatory governance. Governance, as we discussed at some length in our discussion of morals regulation, involves not only tactical considerations of how best to regulate, but fundamental questions of whether regulation is warranted. There is no one big answer, of course. In the case of regulation of morals, we might see that the government has gone too far, and risks subordinating individual freedom for dynamic judgments about social morality – something that can be sucked into the vortex of the culture wars. In the case of occupational licensing, the essential problem may be that the government has shied away from tackling a wicked problem with proper regulatory interventions.

In short, deep thinking about the police power invites us to think about more than techniques of governance, but also about the rationales for regulating in a complex modern society.

We should see the police power as resilient and robust as a constitutional power in our states, even if it has eluded attention in contemporary constitutional discourse. It has a logic embedded in *salus populi*, that is, it aims to advance the general welfare, a commitment congruent with the overall objectives of our state constitutions, whether considered individually or collectively. At the same time, questions have arisen in modern times about how exactly it can be used to alleviate various problems, including the compromising of public morals, urban disorder, occupational licensing, and public heath crises. Likewise, we can see ways in which the police power can be misused in the pursuit of addressing these problems (or even in the defining of certain conduct as problematic).

In Part III, we rejoin this discussion by looking at the ways in which the police power might be used more sensibly to tackle wicked problems, and where the stressors are where these problems are adumbrated and regulatory solutions proffered.

The historical exegesis in this Part was important in illuminating the evolution of the police power over our republic's history. In the next Part, we consider further the structure and functions of the police power and also how it is interpreted in circumstances of conflict and controversy.

NOTES

1. Pew Research reports that faith in government in 1958, which was the first year they studied this, was extremely high, with nearly three-quarters of all Americans expressing faith in government, compared to less than 20 percent currently. https://pewrsr.ch/3U1kYkL.
2. See generally Dan McNichol, *The Roads That Built America: The Incredible Story of the U.S. Interstate System* (2006).
3. See generally Dwight F. Rettie, *Our National Park System* (1995).
4. See generally, Douglas Brinkley, *American Moonshot: John F. Kennedy and the Great Space Race* (2020); Tom Wolfe, *The Right Stuff* (1979).
5. Of the big works on the scale of significance of highways, national parks, and space exploration, perhaps the most meaningful modern examples, each illustrating the remarkable magnitude of human ingenuity combined with federal power and investment, would be the creation of the internet and the development important vaccines for infectious diseases, including the COVID-19 vaccine in late 2020. Obviously, and not coincidentally, these were public-private initiatives, not unlike the inventions of the earlier years.
6. See Marvin Lazerson, "The Disappointments of Success: Higher Education after World War II," 559, *Ann. Am. Acad. Pol. Soc, Sci.* 64 (1998).
7. See generally John Aubrey Douglass, *The California Idea and American Higher Education: 1860 to the 1960 Master Plan* (2000).
8. 336 U.S. 77 (1949).
9. Ibid., at 84.
10. 348 U.S., at 35.

11. Ibid. "[W]hen the legislature has spoken, the public interest has been declared in terms well nigh conclusive. In such cases, the legislature, not the judiciary, is the main guardian of the public needs to be served by social legislation."
12. See David Vlahov and Sandro Garcia, "Urbanization, Urbanicity, and Health," 79 *J. Urban Health* 51 (2002).
13. See Sophia Z. Lee, "Our Administered Constitution: Administrative Constitutionalism from the Founding to the Present," 167 *U. Penn. L. Rev.* 1699 (2019).
14. See, e.g., Thomas O. Garrity, "Regulatory Reform in the Reagan Era," 45 *Mich. L. Rev.* 253 (1986).
15. See Sharece Thrower, "Regulatory Delay across Administrations," Research Report, Brookings Center on Regulation and Markets (July 2019); Robert J. Duffy, "Regulatory Oversight in the Clinton Administration," 27 *Presidential Studies Q.* 71 (1990).
16. See generally Gillian E. Metzger, "Foreword–1930's Redux: The Administrative State Under Siege," 131 *Harv. L. Rev.* 1 (2017); Aaron Nielson, "Confessions of an 'Anti-Administrativist,'" 131 *Harv L. Rev. F.* 1 (2017).
17. See generally Bruce Yandle, *Land Rights: The 1990s' Property Rights Rebellion* (1995); Henry M. Jacobs & Kurt Paulsen, "Property Rights: The Neglected Theme of 20th-Century American Planning," 75 *J. Amer. Planning Ass'n* 134 (2009).
18. See Steven M. Teles, *The Rise of the Conservative Legal Movement: The Battle for Control of Law* (2009).
19. Rodgers v. Village of Tarrytown, 96 N.E. 2d 731 (1951).
20. See generally Robert E. Williams & Lawrence Friedman, *The Law of American State Constitutions* 405–41 (2d. 2023) (summarizing state constitutional reform in the twentieth and twenty-first century).
21. G. Alan Tarr, *Understanding State Constitutions* 1390 (1998).
22. Ibid. See also Mila Versteeg & Emily Zackin," "American Constitutional Exceptionalism Revisited," 81 *U. Chi. L. Rev.* 1641, 1644 (2014) ("Americans have participated in extensive and ongoing constitution making at the state level").
23. On the politics of state constitutional reform in the twentieth century, see Tarr, *Understanding State Constitutions*, at 136–72.
24. See Amy Bridges, "Managing the Periphery in the Gilded Age: Writing Constitutions for the Western States," 22 *Studies in Amer. Pol. Devo.* 32 (Spring 2008).
25. See, e.g., Justin R. Long, "Guns, Gays, and Ganja," 69 *Ark. L. Rev.* 453, 453–54 (2016) ("[T]here law reform moments ... have treated state constitutional changes as a tool for advancing their national policy aims"); Justin Long, "State Constitutions as Interactive Expressions of Fundamental Values," 74 *Alb. L. Rev.* 1739 (2010/11).
26. See generally John Dinan, *State Constitutional Politics: Governing by Amendment in the American States* (2018).
27. These states included Florida, South Carolina, Montana, North Dakota, New Hampshire, Louisiana, and Georgia.
28. Frank P. Grad & Robert P. Williams, 2 *State Constitutions for the Twenty-First Century: Drafting State Constiutions, Revisions, and Amendments* 7 (2006).
29. The focus here is specifically on formal change of the document through processes of constitutional amendment or replacement. As Jonathan Marshfield reminds us, however, change can and does happen in various informal ways, as, for example, through judicial decisions. See Jonathan L. Marshfield, "Courts and Informal Constitutional Change in the States," 51 *New Eng. L. Rev.* 453 (2017).
30. Jeffrey S. Sutton, *Who Decides? States as Laboratories of Constitutional Experimentation* 331 (2022).

31. Ernst Freund, *The Police Power: Public Policy and Constitutional Rights* 172–241 (1904).
32. The term "morals" is used frequently in state constitutions, albeit usually in ways undefined.
33. See generally David H. Flaherty, "Law and the Enforcement of Morals in Early America," *Perspectives In American History, Vol. V: Law in American History* 203 (D. Fleming & B. Bailyn eds., 1971).
34. William J. Novak, *The People's Welfare*.
35. See generally James A. Monroe, *Hellfire Nation: The Politics of Sin in American History* (2003).
36. Novak, *People's Welfare*, at 149.
37. Suzanne B. Goldberg, "Morals-Based Justifications for Lawmaking: Before and after Lawrence v. Texas," *Minn. L. Rev.* 1233, 1245 (2004).
38. See generally Daniel Okrent, *Last Call: The Rise and Fall of Prohibition* (2011).
39. See, e.g., Jack S. Blocher, Jr., "Did Prohibition Really Work? Alcohol Prohibition as a Public Health Innovation," 96 *Am. J. Public Health* 233 (February 2006)
40. See Monroe, *Hellfire Nation*.
41. Thomas J. Cooley, *A Treatise on the Constitutional Limitations Which Rest on the Legislative Power of the States of the American Union* 596 (1871).
42. Martin Shapiro, writing in 1961, gives an even longer list: "The following have been uniformly held to show failure to meet the character requirements: perversion, forgery, arson, smuggling, murder, burglary, extortion, narcotics peddling, abandonment, nonsupport of legitimate and illegitimate children, pimping, bribing officials, and obtaining relief on false pretenses. But persons guilty of desertion, divorce (granted on grounds of cruelty), multiple traffic violations, drunk driving, rape, keeping a house of ill fame, indecent exposure, perjury, petty larceny, embezzlement, drunkenness, fighting, multiple minor arrests, giving false information to officials, assault, wife beating, and violation of Sunday laws." Martin Shapiro, "Morals and the Courts: The Reluctant Crusaders" 45 *Minn. L. Rev.* 897, 908 (1961).
43. See John Stuart Mill, *On Liberty* (1859).
44. Ibid., at 63.
45. See Joel Feinberg, *The Moral Limits of the Criminal Law: Offense to Others* (1985).
46. 46 U.S. 504 (1847).
47. Ibid., at 630 (emphasis added). See also Prigg v. Pennsylvania, 41 U.S. (16 Pet.) 539 (1842).
48. 46 U.S. at 632 (Grier, J., concurring).
49. In doing so, recall from Chapter 2 Justice Harlan's own commentary there on the evils of the demon rum.
50. 188 U.S. 321 (1903).
51. Ibid., at 357.
52. See ibid., at 364–65 (Fuller J, dissenting).
53. 199 U.S. 212 (1905).
54. Ibid., at 225.
55. S410 U.S. 113 (1973).
56. 597 U.S. __ (2022).
57. See Roscoe Pound, "Liberty of Contract," 18 *Yale L. J.* 454 (1909).
58. Samuel D. Warren & Louis D. Brandeis, "The Right to Privacy," 4 *Harv. L. Rev.* 193 (1890).
59. See, e.g., Andrew Reath, "Legislating the Moral Law," 28 *Noûs* 435 (Dec. 1994); Jerome E. Bickenbach, "Law and Morality," 8 *L. & Phil* 291 (1989).
60. See Peter Cane, "Taking Law Seriously: Starting Points of the Hart/Devlin Debate," 10 *J. Ethics* 21 (Jan. 2006).
61. See John Finnis, *Natural Law and Natural Rights* (1980). See also John Keown & Robert George eds., *Reason, Morality, and Law: The Philosophy of John Finnis* (2013).

62. See Ronald Dworkin, *Law's Empire* (1988). See also David Lyons, "The Connect between Law and Morality: Comments on Dworkin," 36 *J. Legal Ed.* 485 (Dec. 1986).
63. See Feinberg, *Moral Limits*.
64. See George Fletcher, "Law and Morality: A Kantian Perspective," 87 *Colum. L. Rev.* 533 (1987).
65. See Tony Honore, "The Necessary Connection between Law and Morality," 22 *Oxford J. Leg. Stud.* 489 (Autumn 2002).
66. See Robert George, *Making Men Moral: Civil Liberties and Public Morality* (1995).
67. 478 U.S. 186 (1986).
68. See, e.g., Laurence Tribe, *American Constitutional Law* 1425–29 (2nd ed., 1988); Caroline Wells Ferree, "Bowers v. Hardwick: The Supreme Court Closes the Door on the Right to Privacy and Opens the Door to the Bedroom," 64 *Denv. U. L. Rev.* 599 (1988); Ruth Conkle, "The Second Death of Sexual Privacy," 62 *Ind. L. J.* 215 (1987).
69. Indeed, long before it was officially overruled seventeen years later, Justice Lewis Powell expressed remorse about his decision in that case. See Kenji Yoshino, "Can the Supreme Court Changes Its Mind?" *The New York Times* (December 5, 2002).
70. See generally David Labard & Deborah Henry Heinbach, *Blue Laws: The History, Economics, and Politics of Sunday Closing Laws* (1987). See also <u>McGowan v. Maryland</u>, 366 U.S. 420, 431 (1961) (blue laws "go far back into American history, having been brought to the colonies with a background of English legislating dating to the thirteenth century").
71. 452 U.S. 61 (1981).
72. 520 U.S. 277 (2000).
73. See Young v. American Mini Theatres, Inc., 427 U.S. 50 (1976). See also Barnes v. Glen Theatre, 501 U.S. 560 (1990)
74. Renton v. Playtime Theatres, Inc, 475 U.S. 41, 48 (1996).
75. Indeed, Chief Justice Burger said very much the same in Barnes, writing: "This and other public indecency statutes were designed to protect morals and public order. The traditional police power of the States is defined as the authority to provide for the public health, safety, and morals, and we have upheld such a basis for legislation ... Thus, the public indecency statute furthers a substantial government interest in protecting order and morality." 501 U.S. at 569.
76. In re Tahiti Bar Liquor License Case, 345 Pa. 355 (Pa. 1959).
77. Ibid., at 359.
78. Ibid., at 360
79. Purple Orchid Inc. v. Pennsylvania State Police, 813 A.2d 801 (2002).
80. 517 U.S. 484 (1996).
81. 813 A.2d, at 811.
82. 458 F.3d 258 (2006).
83. Ibid., at 268.
84. Ibid.
85. See generally Robert C. Ellickson, "Controlling Chronic Misconduct in City Spaces: Of Panhandlers, Skid Rows, and Public-Space Zoning," 105 *Yale L. J.* 1165 (1996).
86. See, e.g., Steven T. Catlett, "Enjoining Obscenity as a Public Nuisance and the Prior Restraint Doctrine," 84 *Colum. L. Rev.* 1616 (1984); Doug R. Rendleman, "Civilizing Pornography: The Case for an Exclusive Obscenity Nuisance Statute," 44 *U. Chi. L. Rev.* 509 (1977).
87. See Restatement (2d) Tort, #821 (c)(1).
88. See generally Deborah L. Rhode, *Adultery: Infidelity and the Law* (2016).

89. 381 U.S. 479 (1965).
90. 405 U.S. 438 (1972).
91. 410 U.S. 163 (1973).
92. See, e.g., Jegley v. Picado, 349 Ark. 600, 80 S.W.3d 332 (2002); Gryczan v. State, 283 Mont. 433, 942 P.2d 112 (1997); Campbell v. Sundquist, 926 S.W. 2d 250 (Tenn. App. 1996); Commonwealth v. Wasson, 842 S.W.2d 487 (Ky. 1992).
93. 539 U.S. 558 (2003).
94. "Justice Stevens's analysis, in our view, should have been controlling and should control here." Ibid., at 570. See 478 U.S. at 580 (Stevens, J., dissenting).
95. Ibid., at 574.
96. 505 U.S. 833 (1992).
97. Lawrence, 539 U.S. at 579 (O'Connor, concurring).
98. Ibid., at 589 (Scalia, dissenting).
99. Ibid., at 590.
100. Ibid.
101. In his recent book on substantive due process, James Fleming faces directly the anxiety of Lawrence's basis and limits and argues for a robust substantive due process that would protect intimate conduct of various types and would, without destroying the government's power to protect morals, eliminate a significant amount of regulation of certain types as inconsistent with the Constitution. See James E. Fleming, *Constructing Basic Liberties: A Defense of Substantive Due Process* (2022).
102. 517 U.S. 620 (1996).
103. Ibid.
104. Ibid.
105. 576 U.S. 644 (2015).
106. Controlled Substances Act, P.L. 91–513.
107. "Americans Overwhelmingly Say Marijuana Should Be Legal for Medical or Recreational Use, Ted Van Green," Pew Research Report (11/22/22).
108. Thirty-eight states as of summer 2023. State Medical Cannabis Laws, Nat'l Conference of State Legislatures (updated 6/22/23).
109. "Fact box: U.S. States where Recreational Marijuana is Legal," *Reuters* (6/1/23).
110. "Why National Cannabis Legislation is Still a Decade Away," *Forbes* (6/30/23).
111. See Joseph Hartenian, "Getting Back on Schedule: Fixing the Controlled Substances Act," 12 *Albany Gov't L. Rev.* 199 (2019); Alex Kreit, "Controlled Substances, Uncontrolled Law," 6 *Albany Gov't L. Rev.* 332 (2013).
112. See https://bit.ly/3HX5bMM.
113. "More States Consider Bills Limiting Which Bathroom Trans People Can Use," *PBA* (3/29/23).
114. See "Why Proposed Laws Targeting Drag Shows are Proliferating in America," *The Economist* (2/12/2023).
115. Chamlee, V. (2023). "Anti-drag legislation is sweeping the nation: Here's where each state stands on drag bans." *People* article. https://bit.ly/3vsHlp9.
116. Trans Legislation Tracker (2023). Website. https://translegislation.com/.
117. Gresko, J. and Associated Press (2023). "California foie gras fans are out of luck after ban on the sale of the delicacy avoids a Supreme Court review." *Fortune* article. https://bit.ly/3TPFu7V.
118. Oceana (2011). "California bans the sale of shark fins – Completes West Coast sweep of shark conservation." Press release. https://bit.ly/3TV3zds.

119. On the concept of a well-ordered society more generally, philosophers usually associate this with the writings of John Rawls in his famous book, *A Theory of Justice* (1971). See, e.g., Brian Kogelmann, "Justice, Diversity, and the Well-Ordered Society," 67 *The Philosophical Quarterly* 663 (2017).
120. 348 U.S. 26 (1954).
121. 467 U.S. 229 (1984).
122. 545 U.S. 469 (2005).
123. 416 U.S. 1 (1974).
124. Ibid., at 9.
125. Ibid.
126. 416 U.S. at 8 (quoting Royster Guano Co. v. Virginia, 253 U.S. 412, 415 (1920) and Reed v. Reed, 404 U.S. 71, 76 (1971)).
127. See Geoffrey R. Stone & David A. Strauss, *Democracy and Equality: The Enduring Constitutional Vision of the Warren Court* (2020); Morton J. Horwitz, "The Warren Court And The Pursuit of Justice," 50 *Wash. & Lee. L. Rev.* 5 (1993).
128. See generally Sterk, et al., *Land Use Regulation*, at 136–60.
129. For a consideration of contemporary zoning from a strong property rights perspective, see, e.g., Richard Epstein, "A Conceptual Approach to Zoning: What's Wrong with Euclid," 5 *NYU Env. L. J.* 277 (1996).
130. So. Burl. County NAACP v. Tp. of Mount Laurel, 67 N.J. 151 (NY 1975).
131. See Robert E. Ellickson, "Alternatives to Zoning," 40 *U. Chi. L. Rev.* 681 (1973).
132. Ibid., at 174.
133. Ibid., at 175.
134. Ibid., at 177.
135. See, e.g., Douglas S. Massey, et al., *Climbing Mount Laurel: The Struggle for Affordable Housing and Social Mobility in an American Suburb* (2013); David Kirp, et al., *Our Town: Race, Housing, and the Soul of Suburbia* (1997).
136. The foundational case here was Javins v. First Nat'l Realty, 428 F.2d 1021 (D.C. Cir. 1970).
137. See generally Roger A. Cunningham, "The New Implied and Statutory Warranties of Habitability in Residential Leases: From Contract to Status," 14 *Urban L. Annual* 3 (1979).
138. https://bit.ly/48ggmKS.
139. See, e.g., Robert C. Ellickson, *America's Frozen Neighborhoods: The Abuse of Zoning* (2022); M. Nolan Gray, *Arbitrary Lines: How Zoning Broke the American City and How to Fix It* 29 (2022).
140. www.brookings.edu/articles/the-double-edged-sword-of-upzoning/.
141. See Epstein, "Zoning."
142. See Ellickson, *Frozen Neighborhoods*, at 150–55.
143. Vicki Been, Ingrid Gould Ellen, and Katherine O'Regan. *Supply Skepticism: Housing Supply and Affordability* (New York: NYU Furman Center, 2018). https://bit.ly/4aZOMnN.
144. See generally William A. Fischel, *Zoning Rules! The Economics of Land Use Regulation* 69–128 (2015).
145. We will consider these issues in more depth in Chapter 9.
146. The regular Census provides the relevant data.
147. See Lee Optical (describing rational basis review in the content of occupational licensing.
148. See Aaron Edlin & Rebecca Haw, "Cartels by Another Name: Should Licensed Occupations Face Antitrust Scrutiny?" 162 *U. Pa. L. Rev.* 1093 (2014).

149. Ibid., at 1126–44.
150. See generally Rebecca Sandefur, "Access to What?" *Daedalus* 49–55 (Winter 2019); R. L. Sandefur, "What We Know and Need to Know about the Legal Needs of the Public," 67 *S.C. L. Rev.* 447 (2016).
151. See generally David Engstrom & Daniel B. Rodriguez, "Rethinking Our Bar Federalism" (ms. 2024).
152. See the discussion in Renee Knake Jefferson, *Law Democratized: A Blueprint for Solving the Justice Crisis* 119–46 (2024).
153. See generally Gillian K. Hadfield, *Rules for a Flat World: Why Humans Invented Law and How to Reinvent It for a Complex Global Economy* 219–45 (2017).
154. See Joan Howarth, *Shaping Up the Bar* (2022).
155. See Benjamin H. Barton, *The Lawyer-Judge Bias in the American Legal System* (2011).
156. See Elham Monaghesh & Alireza Hajizadeh, "The Role of Telehealth during COVID-19 Outbreak: A Systematic Review Based on Current Evidence," 20 *BMC Public Health* 1193 (2020).
157. On the Upsolve litigation, currently ongoing, see Nora Freeman Engstrom, "UPL, Upsolve, and the Community Provision of Legal Advice," *SLS Blog* (January 27, 2022). See also Jefferson, *Law Democratized*, at 114–16.
158. See Letter from Maggie Goodlander, Deputy Assistant Attorney General, to North Carolina General Assembly (February 14, 2023) (on file with author).
159. See, e.g., Compagnie Francaise de Navigation a Vapeur v. Louisiana State Board of Health, 186 U.S. 380 (1902) (upholding a ban on the arrival of immigrants into an area in which infectious disease was rampant); Dent v. West Virginia, 129 U.S. 114 (1889) (upholding a law requiring a license to practice medicine).
160. 149 Ill. 2d 331 (1992).
161. Ibid., at 339. A somewhat more problematic instance of the court deferring to state public health police power regulations was City of Legal Rock v. Smith, 204 Ark. 692 (Ark. 1942). Here the Arkansas court upheld a law detaining individuals convicted of prostitution in order that they be inspected for sexually transmissible diseases and, upon discovery of such diseases, quarantined in a hospital or another location without condition or deadline, or any other due process.
162. See generally Wendy E. Parmet, *Constitutional Contagion: Covid, the Courts and Public Health* (2023).
163. No. 217–2020-CV-00152 (N.H. Super. Ct. Mar. 25, 2020) (mem.)
164. 658 Pa. 165 (Penn. 2020).
165. Ibid., at 204 (quoting Manigault v. Springs, 199 U.S. 473, 480) (U.S. 1905).
166. In re Abbott 954 F.3d 772 (5th Cir. 2020).
167. Ibid., at 784 (citations omitted).
168. Ibid., at 785.
169. See Parmet, *Constitutional Contagion*, at 166.
170. See ibid.
171. See Stephen I. Vladeck & Lindsay F. Wiley, "Coronavirus, Civil Liberties, and the Courts: The Case Against 'Suspending' Judicial Review," 133 *Harv. L. Rev. F.* 179 (2020).
172. See Nat'l Fed. Of Indep. Business v. Dep't of Labor, Occupational Safety and Health Administration, 595 U.S. __ 2020).
173. In a recent book on the litigation over Covid and general lessons, public health law expert, Wendy Parmet stresses the ways in which the rule from Jacobson ebbed considerably afterward and that by the time of Covid, there wasn't a strong tradition of deference to public health authorities. See Parmet, *Constitutional Contagion*. This view is hard to

square with the cases, however. There were precious few instances in which legitimate public health measures were struck down by either state courts or the federal courts as exceeding the police power or, for that matter, as violating individual rights. An alternative way to read Prof Parmet's mostly pessimistic rendering of the post-Jacobson landscape is to see her as critical about the courts' failure to articulate and promote a positive rights view of public health. This depiction seems entirely accurate at the federal court level. State courts remain free, however, to enforce whatever positive rights, including public health rights, their respective state constitutions protect.

PART II

Structural Considerations

5

Separating and Distributing Powers and Functions

The police power has long been bound up, as we saw in Part I, with the broad power of the state legislature to govern. Part I's discussion of the police power has taken a somewhat abstract concept – the government's power to protect health, safety, morals, and the general welfare under the state constitution – and looked at how it was operationalized in disputes over more than 200 years of American legal history. In this chapter, we look at some key practical elements of the power, some seemingly timeless and some that have become more prominent in the past several decades and even as recently as the Covid pandemic, a multi-year episode that brought controversies over the exercise of the police power to the fore. This is how the state constitution, relevant legislation, and government practices allocate authority to exercise the police power. At bottom, state constitutional law is clear in caring now only about *what* power is being exercised by government, but *how* it is exercised and by *whom*.

THE SEPARATION OF POWERS IN STATE CONSTITUTIONS: INTERNAL AND EXTERNAL

As we discussed in Chapter 1, the separation of powers were hardwired into the revolutionary-era constitutions. They were often expressed, unlike in the US Constitution, in explicit terms.[1] The decision to preserve a coherent separation of powers was especially notable in light of the fact that the early framers in these documents "tended to exalt legislative power and the expense of the executive and the judiciary."[2] Separation of powers in these early constitutions was intended to meet multiple overlapping needs of these new governments. This constitutional structure provided important limits on what was by any account an extraordinary compass of state legislative power.[3] Even more meaningful were the restrictions imposed on the executive branch, added to reduce the risk of the king's prerogative sneaking in to new constitutional government as a sort of Trojan horse. In addition to regulating governmental action and reducing the potential for the abuse of power, the internal distribution of powers enabled these new states to have a mixed government, and so then able to have the best combination of types of authority, representation, democracy, and wise decision-making.

More than two centuries later, we now see some of these goals as illusory, or at least overly optimistic. How, for example, was bicameralism supposed to help support a mixed government insofar as members of both houses were elected in more or less the same way? How would popularly elected judges help provide a bulwark against runaway majoritarianism, thereby protecting individual rights from government overreach? Constitutional design was shaped around the experiences of colonialism in the eighteenth century and a goal of advancing interests germane to the new states. Events unfolded quickly and conflict, rather than consensus, animated a good amount of the practice of constitutionalism in these critical early years. State constitutions were constructed in thoughtful ways, building upon the new science of politics that was emerging from the republic's founders and principal intellectual architects. Nonetheless, there were limits to how prescient the framers could be. Some structural mechanisms proved problematic, while others endured. However, let us not dwell here on when and how the state constitution makers ultimately came up short in their design for a coherent system of checks and balances, but let us focus instead on how their tactics helped shape a system of mixed government that would help them govern effectively and justly on behalf of their citizens.

There are many examples of how they aspired to do this, but let us take one to discuss in more detail: The creation of the plural executive. State constitutions have long included executive power as "unbundled,"[4] that is, power to be exercised by multiple executive departments, not limited to the governor as the supposed head of the executive branch. This distribution of executive power was designed to cabin executive power, critical in an era in which legislative power was viewed as "plenary" and as essentially superior to power authorized and exercised by other departments in state government. The plural executive, a structure that persists to the present day, notwithstanding changing views on the nature and scope of legislative and administrative power, is emblematic of the sense that constitutional framers had that power should be checked and balanced, even with respect to internal departmental functions.[5]

To be sure, conflicts have arisen frequently over the scope of legislative and executive power in the exercise of certain functions in state governance. The idea of the governor as a superior institution to other executive officials with regard to the exercise of law enforcement has been largely tempered, if not eradicated, by state court decisions that insist that attorneys general, if not other executive officers, have the residuum of executive power assigned to them by either the constitution or statute or both.[6] Viewed in the aggregate, these cases have eroded any notion of an "inherent" executive authority.[7] Governors and other executive officials have only those powers that are delegated to them.[8] Likewise, administrative agencies function under the rubric of assigned constitutional power.[9] Unlike those who would advocate in the federal constitutional context for the view, as did the late Justice

Antonin Scalia for example,[10] that all administrative power is derivative of executive power, in the state constitutional context administrative power is best viewed as a sphere of power that can and often does partake of legislative (read "lawmaking"), executive, and even judicial power.

Recent scholarship by leading state constitutional law scholars have emphasized not only the ubiquity and persistence of state administrative agency power, but also the ways in which such agencies can act in ways that both supplement and check the other branches of state government. Some of the advantages associated with state agencies are, as John Devlin notes, with respect to their independence. "Independent election by the people," he writes, "gives those elected state executive officials far greater autonomy, and far greater control over their departments, than any federal official enjoys."[11] However, as Miriam Sefter notes in her important study of agency independence, part of her larger inquiry into democracy and state political performance under the objectives of state constitutionalism, a combination of factors, including weak norms and strong governors, may stack the deck against agency independence.[12]

So far as the police power is concerned, the principal question is whether one branch and only one branch has the prerogative to exercise this awesome power. As the legislature's power has long been viewed as plenary, the question of whether the legislature has the police power is straightforward (even if the content of this power is not). More intriguing is the question whether other branches have the prerogative to exercise this power. There are three plausible answers, not unrelated, but still fundamentally inconsistent with one another. Ultimately, as will be explained, one is most convincing in light of the best overall view of state constitutional governance.

The first answer is that administrative officers cannot exercise the police power, because such an arrangement would be inconsistent with fundamental principle embedded into every state constitution that the legislature has plenary power and thus cannot delegate this power to another institution within the state government. This does not leave non-legislators without adequate power to govern, but instead embodies the view that state constitutions can and do delegate specific powers to executive, administrative, and judicial officials; moreover, any other powers that are exercised must come from legislative delegations. Just as the US Constitution instructs that the chief executive must take care that the laws be faithfully executed,[13] there is an explicit or implicit charge in every state constitution that officials outside the legislative branch will implement the laws passed by the legislature. This view leaves out any space for the executive to exercise the police power on his or her own initiative.

The implications of this view are substantial. For example, in the case of the COVID-19 pandemic, governors in the spring and summer of 2020 issued executive orders that called for extreme actions (lockdowns, travel restrictions, etc.) to be taken to combat the spread of the coronavirus, and they did so under what they insisted were their police powers. In some instances, the governor was careful to locate this executive authority in statutory delegation and, where so, the argument that this was an unconstitutional exercise of public power was significantly weakened. In other instances, however, the objection was made that the governor lacked any explicit delegation. The implication is that the legislature lacked the constitutional power to circumvent the separation of powers under their state constitution.

A different way to view the matter is to see governmental officials outside the legislature exercising powers under the terms and conditions of legislative delegation. In this respect, the function of the executive or administrative officer is unremarkable and wholly acceptable, the only looming question being whether the statute does in fact give such authority to the officer or agency. This becomes essentially a matter of statutory interpretation. In <u>Wisconsin Legislature v. Evers</u>,[14] for example, decided in the early weeks of the pandemic, the Wisconsin Supreme Court read the governor's emergency powers narrowly, describing how Article IV of the state constitution listed all of the proper bases of executive power, but omitted any mention of a general emergency power, or anything else that would ground the power to impose emergency measures such as he did here.

There is a third alternative, a middle ground of sorts, in the debate over whether the states' separation of powers can accommodate the exercise of the police power by institutions other than the legislature. Under this view, state legislatures can delegate to executive officials and administrative agencies police powers, and so the exercise of such powers is constitutionally legitimate. The fact of legislative delegation and its scope is measured by ordinary techniques of statutory interpretation. Nonetheless, there is an important constitutional limitation to legislative discretion in the form of the nondelegation doctrine. That is, the legislature cannot delegate too much power to non-legislators, for that would run afoul of the separation of powers principle that, as John Locke put it, the legislature cannot delegate the power to make legislators.[15]

In notable contrast with the Supreme Court and the US Constitution, where the nondelegation is basically moribund, a number of state courts have enforced a nondelegation doctrine against certain legislative delegations.[16] In some instances, this power has been essentially a delegated police power, deployed to regulate certain activities in order to protect the general welfare. COVID-19 once again provided an occasion for an important state court decision involving delegated administrative power. In the early days of the pandemic, Governor Whitmer of Michigan invoked the Emergency Powers of the Governor Act of 1945 to impose her emergency orders to shut down businesses in the early part of the pandemic.[17] The statute was a clear instrument of the state police power, providing that when "public safety is imperiled" the "governor may proclaim a state of emergency," then proceeding to lay out some of the requisites for such actions, including, significantly, a requirement that such orders be "reasonable."[18] In a much-watched decision, a closely-divided majority of the Michigan supreme court struck down the statute as unconstitutional "because it purports to delegate to the executive branch the legislative powers of state government – including its plenary police powers."[19]

There is both more and less than meets the eye in this insistent statement of the Michigan supreme court regarding nondelegation and the police power. The decision is remarkable in asserting the police powers are quintessentially legislative powers and, as such, cannot be delegated, even to a coordinate branch of government. It would seem then to follow, *a fortiori*, that no delegation of regulatory power to an administrative agency to protect the public health, safety, and welfare – say, a legislative delegation to a statewide public health agency – would be constitutional. Writing for the court, Justice Markman dispatched the arguments that this delegation could be properly checked through ex ante standards (in the nondelegation doctrine parlance, courts have spoken of the requirement of "intelligible principles")[20] or ex post procedural requirements.[21] In doing so, he distanced this view from other state court nondelegation decisions that have dwelled mostly on process. At the same time, there may be limited impact here because of the incredible breadth of the holding, as well as the exigencies of this pandemic, exigencies which have famously generated unusually vituperative partisan stresses and struggles. Whether this court, or other state courts, will zero in on language in the Michigan decision that declares that police power is a plenary power of the legislature that can only be exercised by this institution remains to be seen.

The three positions are, respectively, administrative officers lack the power under the constitution because they are not the legislature, the state legislature has not delegated this power to agencies under any relevant statute, and, third, the legislature is limited in its choices to delegate under principles derived from the nondelegation doctrine in the state's constitutional law.

So how do we sort out the merits of these different positions on an issue of enormous consequence, to wit, who in the state government may exercise the police power? We should do so by resort to the underlying structure and functions of state constitutionalism, as has been the theme of this book and in accord with the broad framing in the introduction and first chapter.

Let us begin with the separation of powers in state constitutionalism as such. America's "other separation of powers tradition," as Jon Marshfield describes it, looks at state constitutional structures as mechanisms not only, or even primarily, to ensure that majorities will govern and will not be interfered with by factions of the sort that worried James Madison especially, but as means of ensuring that governmental officials could be effectively monitored.[22] "What matters most under the state theory," Marshfield argues, "is that government is separated along lines that allow the public to track and respond to malfeasance."[23] What should be added to this picture of the rationale for state separation of powers in the state tradition is that these mechanisms of governance and of constitutional structure would be in the service of promoting the common good. This preservation requires tempering governmental overreach, and so the careful delineation of structural safeguards and sound administrative procedures[24] and of legal requirements (as the requirement of a public purpose and prohibition on special legislation) helps to ensure that the government is acting for general, not special, interests, while at the same time facilitating the ability of we the people in our respective states to monitor and mobilize governmental action.

Accountability is important with respect to any department of government. And so the instruments of governmental checks hard-wired into state constitutions, along with evolving procedural mechanisms created by statute and reflected in actual administrative practice, function as the composite mechanisms control over governmental behavior. The separation of powers is a coherent mechanism for that, and it is little surprise that it would be adapted from the serious thinking on the part of the framers of the US Constitution on the structure and purpose of state constitutions.[25] These adaptations would continue in the emerging state constitutions of the nineteenth and even twentieth century. Many of the Progressive-era reforms to state constitutions are fulfilling many of the same purposes as separation of powers in the grand sense.

As we move from the general to the more specific, we can see the police power as a power that can be exercised by agencies and departments other than the legislature, and therefore as an important element of governmental purpose and functioning. While the legislative power remains plenary, broad discretion is given to these elected officials to decide how best to protect the common good and which institutions can be called upon to implement wise public policy. That these delegations were seldom mentioned explicitly in the constitutional documents was not inadvertent; rather, these constitutions reflect the understanding that the main choices to be made about whether and to what extent to delegate certain regulatory and administrative powers would best be made by legislatures.[26] They could widen these powers and they could pull them back. They might do so in times of relative calm or in the urgency of a crisis, as in the times of the Covid pandemic.

The nondelegation doctrine fulfills an important function in this regard, and so we should be reluctant to throw out the baby with the bathwater, as has been characteristic of the federal non-delegation doctrine for nearly a century.[27] The insistence upon intelligible principles to guide discretion, especially where the awesome police power is concerned, is important to cabin discretion and limit overreach. In this respect, a sensible nondelegation doctrine helps fulfill the public monitoring function that Marshfield focuses on in his discussion of this "other tradition" of state separation of powers. Also, the requirement that there may be a reasonable basis and strategy for governmental action, something which we will discuss in more detail in a later chapter, is supported by the ability of state courts to regulate legislative action through constitutional constraints.

The advantages of a modulated non-delegation doctrine in the police power context was captured nicely by Chief Justice Bridget McCormack in her dissenting opinion in the Michigan Covid case. At the outset, she recounts the myriad ways in which the state legislature can superintend the processes of administrative regulation. The nondelegation doctrine in its traditional form is focused exclusively upon ex ante instructions. But the reality she introduces into this equation is that much of the worry with respect to rogue administrators becomes managed by ex post devices – of the sort that prominent political scientists have labelled "police patrol" and "fire alarm" oversight.[28] As Justice McCormack notes, neither history[29] nor sensible public policy demand what the majority here (essentially incorporating, as she notes, the views in various concurring opinions by Justice Neil Gorsuch and a few occasional allies), which is a comprehensive set of standards designed to guide administrators and tether discretion to transparent legislative will. "The particular standards in the EPGA," she writes, "are as reasonably precise as the statute's subject matter permits. Given the unpredictability and range of emergencies the Legislature identified in the statute, it is difficult to see how it could have been more specific. Indeed the EPGA contains multiple limitations on the Governor's authority, each limitation requiring more of the Governor 8 when exercising authority."[30]

To summarize, a vigorous separation of powers doctrine in state constitutionalism is consistent with a pragmatic view of the ability of multiple state departments, not limited to the legislature, to implement public policy that protects health, safety, and public welfare. A formalistic conception of state constitutionalism that limits this power to the state legislature is anachronistic as a matter of legal history, as executive officials and administrative agencies have long performed functions under the police powers. More to the point, it does not serve the larger objectives of state separation of powers, objectives that accomplish the twin aims of ensuring that governmental decisions will be made by representative, accountable institutions and can be properly monitored in their exercise while also facilitating the ability of governmental officials and entities to accomplish salutary aims, to engage in which we call good governing.

At the same time, judicial intervention to ensure that our complex mechanisms of government are functioning consistent with the broad goals of the state constitution is not only acceptable, but is essential.[31] Our constitutional architecture and practice give us many avenues for such useful interventions. In previous chapters, we spoke of judicially created and legislative designed mechanisms, including the public purpose requirement, prohibitions on special legislation, debt limits, and various guarantees of equal protection, due process, and reasonableness requirements. The non-delegation doctrine is copasetic with these mechanisms, so long as it is understood as a calibrated tool of sound governance, not a blunderbuss that instantiates a too-skeptical view of public power.

*

So far we have focused on state governmental institutions, be they the legislature, the governor, and state-level administrative agencies. The reality, however, is that the institutions which commonly exercise police powers, especially with regard to the creation and implementation of public safety rules, crime control and public order, and the myriad regulations of the use of private property, are local governments. How should we think about the delegation of power to local governments to protect our public health, safety, and welfare?

THE POLICE POWER AND LOCALISM

That the police power can be exercised only by institutions of the state government, following from the principle of the legislature having plenary power, is largely a shibboleth. The police power has been exercised by other institutions, all under the rubric of legislative authority and, correlatively, under the authority of the state constitution. Prominent among them are municipal governments, those acting in power on behalf of cities, townships, counties, or however else the state sub-divides its power. While police power deployed by local governments is ubiquitous, there are still some complex issues that arise in connection with state/local relations, what Richard Briffault long ago called "localism" (as an analogy to federalism).[32]

This dependence of localism on state choice is true despite a richly textured history of local governance through municipal corporations that pre-date the formation of states and state constitutions.[33] Whatever the practice of public regulation and administration prior to statehood has meant to a fuller understanding of the nuanced and politically salient connection between state and local governments in the US, the framers of our state constitutions, from early days and persistently through the next two centuries, have insisted upon a structural dependence of municipal governments on state choice.

This is not to say that the idea that there is some sort of inherent local authority did not have its moment in the sun.[34] The first great treatise on municipal corporations, authored by Eugene McQuillin, described this view, writing:

> Local self-government of the municipal corporation does not spring from, nor exist by virtue of, written constitutions, nor is it a mere privilege conferred by the central authority ... [I]it is axiomatic that local self-government is not a mere privilege, but a matter of absolute political right, the existence of unlimited authority in the law making body to concentrate all the powers of local government in the state does not exist.[35]

The principal advocate of such a position on the bench was our very own Thomas Cooley. As a justice, he argued for an *imperium in imperio* view of local governments, sourced in preternatural American constitutional history and in natural law. As he wrote in People ex rel LeRoy v. Hurlbut:[36] "The state may mould local institutions according to its view of policy or expediency; but local government is a matter of absolute right, and the state cannot take It away."[37] This view, rather inscrutable in its origins and qualified, as this Cooley quotation indicates ("state may mould"), was put to rest in any event early in the twentieth century and most famously by the Court in Hunter.[38] Hunter involved a constitutional challenge to the actions of two local governments in a municipal annexation proceeding. The Court rejected this claim and, meeting the argument that there is a constitutionally protected status of local governments viz the state, the Court elaborated on the fundamental point that municipalities enjoy no such status, but are beholden to the discretion of the state. As Justice Moody wrote in an unanimous opinion:

> Municipal corporations are political subdivisions of the state, created as convenient agencies for exercising such of the governmental powers of the state as may be entrusted to them.... The number, nature, and duration of the powers conferred upon these corporations and the territory over which they shall be exercised rests in the absolute discretion of the state.... The state, therefore, at its pleasure, may modify or withdraw all such powers, may take without compensation such property, hold it itself, or vest it in other agencies, expand or contract the territorial area, unite the whole or a part of it with another municipality, repeal the charter and destroy the corporation. All this may be done, conditionally or unconditionally, with or without the consent of the citizens, or even against their protest. In all these respects the state is supreme, and its legislative body, conforming its action to the state Constitution, may do as it will, unrestrained by any provision of the Constitution of the United States.[39]

Hunter remains solidly good law, and efforts to resuscitate a sphere of true *imperium in imperio*, with local governments given constitutional status and authority sans legislative or state constitutional delegation, have gone nowhere in the many decades since the Hunter decision.

Just as the Court was settling the question of whether local power could reside in some uber-principle of inherent municipal sovereignty and power, the realpolitik of the situation was pushing hard against efforts to champion local power and autonomy. The principal reason was the disastrous decisions of local governments in issuing railroad bonds.[40] John Dillon devoted a key part of his treatise on local governments to the idea that local government power should be narrowly construed in accord with state authority.[41] "All corporations, public and private, exist and can exist only by virtue of express legislative enactment, creating, or authorizing the creating, of the corporate body ... municipal corporations are created by legislative act."[42] And so, in Dillon's view, "localities had no inherent sovereignty because the sovereign people delegated their entire sovereignty to the states."[43] Not only were states to be viewed as creatures of state governments, but they were creatures on a fairly tight leash![44]

Despite all this, local power did not evaporate in the face of this disposition of the big constitutional question. State constitutions enacted in the nineteenth century (including those, such as California, that were significantly reformed during this same century)[45] went to great lengths to preserve local power.[46] "States began adding provisions to their constitutions that regulated the relationship between the state and municipal governments in the mid-nineteenth century," Jeff Sutton writes, "as the local governments grew frustrated with twin evils: arbitrary, sometimes pretty, oversight of local governments, and negligent, sometimes intentional, neglect of local conditions."[47] Home rule was a structural legal mechanism for ensuring that local governments would have a proper authority for exercising regulatory power without the need to rely upon state legislatures to authorize local power in every instance or to oversee in a micro-managerial sense the performance of local functions.[48]

That municipal governments could enact police power regulations was seldom questioned. To be sure, the content of local ordinances were regularly attacked, and many of the leading police power decisions involved local ordinances, rather than state statutes. But a close look at these decisions through the eighteenth, nineteenth, and twentieth centuries does not reveal a serious argument that local governments should, as institutions exercising the police powers as would state legislatures or administrative agencies, exercise powers that should be viewed more skeptically, and thus more narrowly, than the exercise of power at the state level.[49]

One muddy element in this otherwise rather pristine picture of local governments as police power agents involves the question of whether local governments had or should have more latitude for action, given that they were, after all, closer to the people.[50] Should this be particularly salient in those states whose constitutions contained specific authority for local governments to act, regardless of any separate statutory authority – in what came to be called "imperium in imperio" states?[51]

The basic logic of state constitutionalism in "imperium" states, was that local governments would have plenary authority to act over all matters of local concern. Arguably, a large swath of health, safety, and morals regulation fell under that rubric. Whether and to what extent the inclusion of local affairs language in the home rule provisions of state constitutions was intended to create sovereign authority, that is, the power to act without any state authority to preempt such local actions, remains a difficult historical question.[52] Some courts have read these provisions more narrowly, to maintain what Sho Sato called the "enabling" function of municipal home rule, while some courts have read them more broadly, so as to provide for a "protective" function. The rendering of home rule generally and the sphere of local affairs in particular is of direct relevance to the scope of the police power. After all, to the extent that municipal governments can act with immunity in affairs of local concern, this is quintessentially a delegation of police power to local governments in this area and, by logic, an effacing of the Hunter principle that state governments can direct its "creatures" in the way they wish.

The historical inquiry into the proper scope of municipal power has raised interesting issues of substance to our analysis of the police power and its promise. The latter part of the twentieth century saw the emergence of a strong view of local governance and the fruitful role of municipalities in creating progressive policies.[53] A diverse and growing group of social scientists and legal scholars, including Gerald Frug,[54] David Barron,[55] Saskia Sassen,[56] and Richard Schragger,[57] have described the ways in which more muscular local governance would advance social welfare and why revisiting the question of local power and the constitutional status of municipalities is essential. Though never specifically lodged in arguments about the nature and limits of the police power, a theme culled from these local government advocates was that commitments to democracy, as an attractive normative principle in its own right, or as a component of a sound public sphere, require robust local governance. Further, localism has been defended as a means of advancing substantive constitutional rights. As David Barron writes: "This defense [of localism] proceeds instead from a structural conclusion that substantive constitutional rights sometimes presuppose the existence of a local decision-making process capable of ensuring the protection of those rights."[58]

The case for municipal governments as a fulcrum of the state police power is appealing, for just the reasons sketched, and is illustrative of wider renderings of the values and vitality of local governance. Local governments are necessarily closer to the people than are state governments. Addressing concrete public health and safety issues frequently requires local knowledge.[59] Moreover, the people whose welfare we attend to through the conscientious use of the police power are the people who are found in communities, communities whose shape is ineluctably configured by geographical and legal boundaries.[60] However, we should be careful not to embrace an overly idealized conception of local governments and their functioning. Municipal governments are indeed closer to the people. Yet this is both a virtue and a vice.

The proximity to the people means that they are able to refract more effectively the views of citizens on matters of regulatory governance, and other matters fundamental to the choices made by government officials under the police power. The values of the so-called laboratories of experimentation have long been noted in the context of American federalism. And recent efforts by prominent public law scholars, including Heather Gerken, Cristina Rodriguez, Jessica Bullman-Pozen, and others, have pointed to ways in which sub-national governments can participate in dynamic, collective conversations about policy choices and strategies of implementation.

Encircling these normative and positive debates about the components of decentralized conversation and policy choice is a wider, essential debate about what democracy means in an extended republic. Empowering local governments is a key piece of the puzzle, given their stakes in this debate about democracy and their comparative advantages in accessing and using local knowledge and recognizing citizen wants and needs. This is a larger, denser issue to contemplate and, for the most part, lies beyond the scope of this book. But we raise it to note that unless we can wrestle to the ground the question of whether the constitutional definition of health, safety, and welfare is to be answered at the state or local level, it will become rather difficult to give content to the police power or to assess the performance of state and local institutions in exercising it.

The closeness of local governments to citizen interests can also be a vice. Madison's insight about the role of factions has special resonance in the context of local decision-making, especially as we consider the ways in which "hyper-localism" takes hold in making regulatory choices in many settings.[61] Local decision-makers, often city council members (or the equivalent in zoning and education boards), are pushed and pulled in various directions by insistent local interests. They can become bazaars for the trading of goodies; they can become captured by powerful groups of citizens. The result can be policy that is both short-sighted and, in a broad sense, anti-democratic.

Nadav Shoked has coined the term "the new local" to describe the ways in which sublocal governance operates through mechanisms that are "informal, fluid, task-specific, ad hoc, and geographically indeterminate."[62] It is in the fluidity of these governance mechanisms that questions might arise about the democratic content of local decision-making. Moreover, local policies that generate externalities, as is common, are hard to capture without serious regional or even state-wide assessment and supervision. Even those who would valorize local choice are writing on a slate that includes the practice, long embedded, of state and even national intervention where local choice goes off the rails and where local capacity is limited.[63] it is crucial to say that the best progress in effective regulatory governance requires intentional collaboration among levels and layers of government. General-purpose local governments are one piece of a multifaceted puzzle.

The focus on localism's limits often does, but should not, distract us from focusing on the larger and rather complex point that the most productive route to regulatory success under the rubric of the police power requires collaborative solutions engaging many different levels and layers of government. In a brilliant essay entitled simply "On Participation," Hannah Fenichel Pitkin and Sara Shumer explain that democracy requires a clear-headed appraisal of the myriad dimensions of and venues for participation, thereby cautioning against the romanticization of the local polis or excessive skepticism of that form. They write

> Face-to-face citizen assemblies are indeed essential to democracy, but one single assembly of all is not. Representation, delegation, cooperation, coordination, federation, and other kinds of devolution are entirely compatible with democracy, though they do not constitute and cannot guarantee it .... The point is not to eschew all organization and all differentiated leadership, confining democracy to the local and spontaneous, but to develop those organizational forms and those styles of authority that sustain rather than suppress member initiative and autonomy. From historical examples we know that such forms and styles exist; it has sometimes been done.[64]

This insight can be applied to modern American constitutionalism and commitments to democratic choice. State constitutions, rightly understood and sensibly construed, empower state government to use a constructive mix of institutions at various levels of government in order to attend to the problems that the police power is designed to address. Neither the formal separation of powers nor the expressed and tacit concerns that choices be made democratically stand in the way of this imaginative approach to regulation and governance.

GENERAL WELFARE REQUIREMENTS

One of the more interesting, if poorly understood, elements of state constitutional checks on governmental actions are those that explicitly require that such actions be directed toward the public interest. Progressive-era reforms brought into state constitutions the requirements that legislation have a public purpose.[65] In addition, prohibitions against special legislation were added,[66] as were guarantees of equality, usually framed as equal protection clauses (enacted both before and after the Fourteenth Amendment of the US Constitution).[67] Other doctrines were invented by courts, including the public trust doctrine in the late nineteenth century, a meaningful expectation of "public use" in takings law, certain restrictions on public debt, and, with cases such as Munn and Mugler, a requirement that regulation reveal an acceptable degree to a public purpose. Taking these temporally and structurally disparate provisions as a whole, they represent a view of state governance as motivated by public-regarding, rather than private-regarding, interests. An account of the distribution of the police powers must focus both on *who* is doing the regulating (hence our discussion of other branches of state government, and municipal governments), and also on where they should look in formulating their objectives of promoting public health, safety, morals, and, especially, the general welfare.

Historians of state government and state constitutionalism have highlighted the adoption of public purpose requirements in state constitutions as illustrations of the ways in which citizens in the nineteenth century became unsettled with the choices being made by state legislators and administrators on behalf of private interests and interest groups.[68] Were these requirements that would facilitate a general welfare sense of constitutionalism that goes back to the beginning of the republic, or did the *zeitgeist* of the Progressive and Populist eras push the legislatures and courts toward a truly new of the role of government in a rapidly changing commercial republic? Whether the truth of the matter lies in one direction or another, the key point is that state constitutions were absorbing through these reform efforts and democratic energy a scheme of governance that was intended to connect the police power to a stronger public welfare orientation. That the Supreme Court joined with state courts to further this development is revealing. We would come to see by the *fin de siècle* the imperative of government operating on the people's behalf and with the public interest front of mind. Various permutations of constitutional law tests (thinking of, for example, the rise of the rational basis test in US constitutional law to examine restrictions on so-called economic liberties[69]) made these interventions perhaps less radical than one might have imagined from the discourse and even the express language of, say, a public purpose requirement for legislation. However, there remained something of substance to this insistence on a general welfare orientation to regulation.[70]

A deeper dive is needed, however, to know what was to be, and should be now, the lodestar of the people's welfare. Welfarist accounts of public policy are common,[71] and the aggregation of myriad theories of the public welfare lead us to the vexing conclusion that there is not, nor can we ever truly expect, consensus upon what it means to pursue welfare-enhancing public policy. Debates over the common good have raged from Plato and Aristotle's times, despite the considerations by Bentham and others about utilitarianism as the best grounding for collective interests up to the present. Jodi Short, in her useful inquiry into public interest as a policy framework, has organized various theories into proceduralist, constitutive, and cognitive approaches that have helped shape debates over the public interest, but without pointing to a clear way to discern this interest in democratic processes. Resort in modern times to economic standards, and especially cost-benefit analysis, has gained favor, and indeed is hardwired into many aspects of contemporary regulatory policymaking, especially at the national level.[72] Assessing public policy by resort to cost-benefit principles, while imperfect for reasons many have noted, might nonetheless come the closest to providing a promising perspective at least for examining the demands of government to facilitate the general welfare in regulation under the police power.

More recently, scholars from different points of ideological and methodological orientation have urged attention to general welfare that goes beyond welfarist accounts represented by cost-benefit analysis. In his book on administrative governance, for example, Blake Emerson calls for government to perform a "duty of public care," one requiring government officials "to invest in the welfare of individuals [and] to provide those institutions, services, and protections that are necessary to people's moral and political agency but which they cannot obtain on their own initiative." The reference to "services" and "protections" resonates with a conception, at least a thin one, of the police power has concerned with taking care of the public.

One of the more prominent recent accounts of public welfare that specifically looks to constitutional values is Adrian Vermeule's important defense of what he calls "common good constitutionalism."[73] Explicitly contrasted with what he sees as the Progressive era's focus (what he calls its "sacramental narrative") on individualistic autonomy, common good constitutionalism would read "constitutional provisions to afford public authorities latitude to promote the flourishing of political communities, by promoting the classical triptych of peace, justice, and abundance."[74] He refers specifically to health and safety, and elsewhere describes at length the ways in which this common good constitutionalism obligates public officials to protect public morals.[75] Vermeule's focus is solely on the US Constitution and its tradition, and so the relevance of his view to the police power under state constitutionalism remains elusive. However, this ambitious theory points rather clearly to what he calls a "framework" (presumably then much short of a template) for discerning what is entailed in the common good. The police power, Vermeule notes, "create[es] a loose-fitting garment allowing the exercise of broadly reasonably discretion by government to promote the common good over time."[76] This is, taking into account the larger context of Vermeule's work, especially true of the police power's focus on the protection of public morals against myriad (secular) threats.

A full engagement with Vermeule's theory of common good constitutionalism is beyond the scope of this book. Ditto the various other accounts, some bolder and more worked out than others. But a few general thoughts here, pertinent to our discussion of the police power. First, Vermeule's account finds common ground in many of the cases, and especially the nineteenth-century and early twentieth-century ones (which were discussed in Chapter 3), where the courts aim toward protecting health, safety, and morals even where such powers trample – or as Novak, cited by Vermeule, put it, "destroy[] private right, interest, liberty or property." Common good here could be traded as a phrase for general welfare, and the same essential point would be well illustrated. Common good constitutionalism has doctrinal roots in classic police power cases, those that constructed and advanced the *salus populi* vision of the power. Second, and in some ways in tension with this point, the components of the common good as Vermeule defines it are sourced in what he describes as our country's "classical legal tradition." The resort to old principles and moral commitments to decide modern cases seems anachronistic without a fuller explanation of why we should be beholden to the past. For example, Vermeule has a sidebar note on laws prohibiting blasphemy and laws grounded in the police power, and ruminates about what we have lost with our more modern approaches to free speech protections.[77] Can we really associate laws prohibiting blasphemy or pornography with a convincing modern account of the common good? Vermeule's account has a timeless quality – reviewers have insisted that it is the product of a distinctly sectarian worldview, Roman Catholic, to be exact[78] – that makes it more challenging to defend as a plausible account of the common good. Still and all, there is a through line from an account of the police power as embedded in constitutional objectives and this well-developed theory offered here by one of our leading public law theorists, and this is reason enough to take this account seriously. We can vigorously disagree about whether and to what extent his view of the common good is the best one while seeing the enterprise as broadly congruent with the objective of defining what good governing is about and what it aspires to.

The police power speaks in terms of what the government is able to do. It is a power, after all, and so the legal question must necessarily turn back to how wide a discretion has the government acting under this power. However, we can only understand this matter of discretion and authority when we understand the obligation of government to act in the common good, an obligation that is revealed in our collective discussion about what the public's interest means and legislative demands of government. More succinctly, inquiry into the scope of the power illuminates what the government is authorized to it; and yet a deeper inquiry into the nature of the power helps illuminate what the government *should* do. A full account of the police power must deal with *both* aspects of this – power and performance, discretion and obligation. Any exercise of governmental power to improve health, safety, and welfare must account for the responsibility of the government to act with a public purpose, and in the public interest. These are intersecting principles of state constitutionalism and, perhaps more generally, in the moral authority and government, and we can best see them as structural principles baked into the state police power.

EXPERTISE, DELEGATION, AND THE RULE OF LAW

As we discussed earlier in connection with the use (and misuse) of the nondelegation doctrine to limit administrative power, a persistent concern among commentators and courts at the federal and state level is that the legislature is shirking its lawmaking responsibilities by assigning important tasks and functions to agencies, usually made up of unelected officials and with meagre statutory instructions. This ubiquitous concern has been expressed in both formal and functional ways. Formally, the objection is that the only institution properly authorized to make public policy, whether under the police power or another source, is the legislature. This formalism is made concrete in Article I of the US Constitution, but is also echoed in myriad state constitutions that express a substantially similar distribution of powers, with the legislature assigned the exclusive power of lawmaking. In earlier versions of the nondelegation doctrine, at both the national and state level, it was said by courts that the legislature may not assign its "core functions" to another body,[79] although that rigid rule softened by the time of the New Deal and was displaced by the standard that requires only that adequate intelligible principles be provided.[80] Nonetheless, the formalist objection to delegation has hardly withered away. There remains a drumbeat of scholarly arguments, often drawing upon constitutional history, against delegation on the grounds that it violates the letter and the spirit of the separation of powers.[81]

There is nothing especially new in all this, save for the increasing support within the conservative majority of the Supreme Court and a few state supreme courts. While the use of agencies and administrators to create and enforce regulation has been an omnipresent part of our governmental system from time immemorial, controversy over administrative discretion in the exercise of public power has accompanied its use, going back to the Progressive era, and continuing to the present. For example the legendary Ernst Freund, as Daniel Ernst pointed out in a thoughtful analysis of Freund's effort to bring to the US what he calls an "American Rechstaadt," was concerned about restraining administrative discretion, even while promoting an ambiguous use of the police power to protect health, safety, and the general welfare.[82]

Many scholars from various perspectives, writing about the development of administrative governance in the late nineteenth century, have described why and how administrative bureaucracy emerged as an essential tool for creating and administering this novel new regulatory regime.[83] The story is substantially similar at the state level and, indeed, state bureaucracies emerged even earlier than their federal brethren, as regulation required innovations in governance and institutions which were neither legislatures, named executive entities, or courts, were created to implement policy.

The widespread use of agencies reflected a confidence in the idea and ideal of expertise, or technocratic planning, represented by Max Weber in broad theory[84] and Frederick Winslow Taylor in practice[85] and captured concisely in Mayor LaGuardia's famous statement, "there is no Democratic or Republican way to pave a street."[86] Expertise in administration would become essential to the broadening sphere of regulation, in both states and later in the federal government. The implications of this development for democracy were noticed, and the push toward bureaucratic modalities of policymaking and administration were accompanied by variegated campaigns for such experiments, campaigns reflected in public commentary and in legal advocacy. "Legitimacy," Daniel Carpenter writes, "is the foundation of bureaucratic autonomy in democratic regimes. Only when politicians and broad portions of the twentieth-century American public became convinced that some bureaucracies could provide unique and efficient public services, create new and valuable programs, and claim the allegiance of diverse coalitions of previously skeptical citizens did bureaucratic autonomy emerge."[87]

The rise of administrative bureaucracy persisted well into the twentieth century, and the New Deal was an important focal point for the struggle over the scope and domain of agency governance.[88] In the policy areas that were best suited for the exercise of the police power, regulatory agencies emerged as critical instruments of social policy. This was true at the national level, as the common story reveals, but this was also true at the state and local level.[89] State and national regulation were more often complements than they were substitutes. And it is important to understand the techniques of public power at all levels of government as the state police power reveals a systemic commitment to bureaucratic governance and expertise as a precept of governance.

One feature of administrative delegation largely unique to the states has been the use and utility of special-purpose authorities.[90] These authorities are created by the state legislature to carry out specific functions. They are often funded through own-source revenues and occasionally are constructed in collaboration with regional and local authorities – think here of transportation as an example – in order to function on behalf of the state government.[91] While it is hard to imagine that the framers of nineteenth-century state constitutions expected the police power to be exercised energetically by institutions that were neither the legislature nor general-purpose municipal governments, the reality of modern regulation in the American states is that these special-purpose authorities have become very common, and even essential, to the administration of public policy. To illustrate this phenomenon with some data on special-purpose governments, census data from five years ago indicates that of the approximately 90,000 local governments in the United States, over 50,000 are special-purpose governments. In Illinois, the figure is 6,000 of the 8,900 local governments and in California, there are over 3,300 special districts providing myriad services, including fire protection, sewers, airport, and other transportation, and this is not counting the very large number of independent school districts (nearly 1,000).

In a number of states, the advent of special-purpose governments has transformed enormously both the scape and the techniques of governance. Courts have largely blessed these developments, and various constitutional doctrines (for example, the electoral equality principle)[92] have been adapted to meet the needs of legislatures determined to create these new methods and methods of policy making and implementation. The creation of local administrative bodies to replace for certain discrete purposes the reliance on general-purpose municipal governments has been a notable development of the last century or so as well.[93]

Looking at bureaucratic governance through a wider aperture, concerns about the scope of administrator power have been expressed by critics over many years.[94] The late Theodore Lowi proclaimed in *The End of Liberalism* that the New Deal had "established the principle for all time that in a democracy there can be no effective limit on governmental power."[95] The twin critiques that expertise is too porous to sustain an enduring basis for unelected bureaucrats making policy with little control and, further, that democracy is a superior goal to technocracy have steadily grown in vehemence and in attention. Moreover, with Covid-era restrictions, as discussed in Chapter 4, has come a skepticism toward expertise-based arguments for important limitations on liberty.[96] Some have chalked this up to an anti-science sentiment, pointing especially to vaccine hesitancy.[97] But another way to look at all this is to see this as an example of an eroding faith in expertise as a basis for policy.

There are two stories that are important for our large assessment of the police power generally and for our examination in this chapter of the structural separation and distribution of powers. In a sense, they come in chronological sequence. The rise of expertise as an underpinning of the choice to vest broad authority in bureaucratic institutions has fueled the use of the police power by agencies to implement good policy. After all, the faith in experts and expertise trade on a faith in scientific truth and the ability of governments to find this truth. Ideally, we should agree on what is truly in the service of public health or safety or even general welfare. With such agreement comes less to argue about in making and assessing policy, and so disputes over the content of policy and who decides becomes less freighted with controversy. Without overly romanticizing the sixty or so years from the post-Reconstruction to the end of the Second World War, we can nonetheless view this era as one in which confidence in public health authorities and in local governments regulating the use of land, to take two of the more conspicuous examples of common policy choices, were high, insofar as citizens viewed these as matters which could be solved by experts, preferably by science.

The other story, still very much unfolding, is one of growing skepticism with experts and expertise. With it, there is an erosion in faith in legislatures and courts' ability and willingness to control bureaucracy in its pursuit of public policy. The emergence and persistence of such skepticism is not linear, of course, as this has happened unevenly, and as much more of a punctuated equilibrium than a steady collapse in the faith in expertise. For example, the 1960s brought with it some confidence in health and safety regulation, with the biggest impact being at the federal level, as new regulatory agencies were created in order to implement new welfarist policies.[98] By the end of that decade, we even put a man on the moon, evincing a faith in science and engineering and ability to mobilize resources, vision, and energy to implement a common good. As we moved into the seventies and eighties, skepticism in government grew with Watergate and the Vietnam War fresh in view, and with respect to human well-being at the sub-national level, the concerns about the state of order in our cities and our educational system grew. Concerns with our aging infrastructure also expanded as we came into the new century. Further, we would see in the period after the Great Recession an erosion of trust in expertise in many aspects and elements, without some profound differences noted between national, state, and local institutions.[99] The Covid pandemic has exacerbated this decline of faith; and institutions as consequential as the US President (Trump from 2016–20) and the Supreme Court (from this same period up to the present) have opined on the flaws in unelected bureaucrats – sometimes described as the "deep state" – making public policy with adequate controls.[100]

There is an inextricable, even if sometimes ineluctable, connection between the matter of what power can be exercised under our constitutions and who gets to exercise this power. We have seen in the rise and fall our faith in administrative governance how the "who decides" question gets tangled up in the dispute over whether power can be exercised at all. At the national level, a debate rages on two fronts about the nature and scope of federal agency power. There are serious, if somewhat measured, threats lobbed by the more conservative members of the Supreme Court to resuscitate the nondelegation doctrine to limit Congress's power to delegate governing power to agencies.[101] Meanwhile, this same conservative majority on the Court has constructed the so-called Major Questions Doctrine as a means of reining in administrative power.[102] The idea there is that questions of major social and economic significance should be decided by Congress, not by agencies. This is not the place to take on these normative arguments for a significant change to our constitutional and administrative law. We will note in passing, however, that both of these significant developments in the Supreme Court and other federal courts often rest on undertheorized, if not largely unexamined, premises about the performance of the regulatory bureaucracy, the relationship between Congress and agencies, and the origins of the administrative state.

The legal developments just recounted involve turbulence in federal policy and its implementation mechanisms. However, the currents of policy and public opinion do not easily separate matters into "national" and "state." It is perhaps just a matter of time before some version of the Major Questions Doctrine emerges in state constitutional law to limit significantly the choices that institutions other than legislatures, here including administrative agencies, special-purpose authorities, and maybe even municipal governments, can make in controversial areas of social and economic policy.[103] Whether intended or not, such a move would risk degrading public governance by limiting the objectives and also the strategies of multiple levels and institutions of government in state systems. A more robust set of anti-administrativist legal tactics at the state level would likely hamstring governance instruments, thus effectively limiting the scope of the state police power and making it all around more difficult to govern.

Still, we might come at this conundrum from a different direction. Rather than focusing on the legal consequences of anti-administrativist and anti-regulatory thinking, we might return to the threshold question of how we have arrived at a place where there is so much ambient distrust in the capacity of government institutions to implement the people's will. In an influential paper discussing the matter of trust in government officials, Houston and Harding note that "**trust** refers to a willingness to rely on others to act on our behalf based on the belief that they possess the capacity to make effective decisions and take our interests into account."[104] In the polarized US, government efficacy is often tied to a perception of whether the government is acting in our best interests or, instead, in the best interests of the other guy. This concern with factions was noted by Madison, of course, but what makes it fresh is the increasing rigidity of individual beliefs, a rigidity that can be explained in no small measure by the role of social and other media, population sorting, and other ways in which we have come to form and maintain political opinions in a series of echo chambers. Repairing a broken public and securing a republic that encourages cooperation and empathy, generally and with respect to confidence in government more specifically, is a tall task and one that preoccupies many contemporary big thinkers.

A necessary, even if not sufficient, focal point should be on evaluating government performance, with appropriate evidence and upon measures that agreed upon by otherwise divided social groups. This commitment to evidence-based evaluation of government performance – here including all levels and levers of government – should be equally strong with respect to public health and safety. Without being naïve about the promise of public acceptability and restoring public trust in government, we can say two things decisively: First, the restorative project is absolutely critical to choices made about both the mechanisms of government power (Should we be using agencies more? Less? Is the legislature a more trusted source of regulation? Can we create new institutions that are more likely to garner public trust?) and also about the scope of the power itself. Various legal consequences, not to mention political consequences, emerge from the public's trust or mistrust in government and its regulatory strategies, as we have discussed in this chapter. Second, public trust follows transparency, as well as widely disclosed evidence of success. State and local governments need better press agents! Seriously, the performance of government at the level less conspicuously covered by mainstream media – recalling that we are witnessing the disappearing of a meaningful local press[105] – can only be assessed when it is more widely known. In order to sustain a robust police power, distributed in ways acceptable to our constitutional architecture and objectives, we need to be able to point to evidence of both good and bad governing. That is, if we want to repair the torn fabric of public trust in government.

STRUCTURING POWER, ENABLING GOVERNANCE

State constitutions create the conditions under which state legislatures will work collaboratively with other institutions to implement policy. They are documents that aspire to, and even frequently assume, meaningful institutional collaboration, even while they attend to the risks of excess governmental power and the threat to property and to individual liberty. This commitment to collaboration is essential to realize the aims of good governing. After all, many of the constructive solutions to health and safety issues require coordinated solutions. As we consider specific policy domain later in this book, most issues that are addressed by governmental action under the police power are instances of so-called "wicked problems," those that require imaginative strategies and, at least, inter-institutional coordination. They also require the creative design of institutions. Such design is not inconsistent with, nor is it orthogonal to, the text and structure of our state constitutions and our larger constitutional tradition. On the contrary, the commitment to creative problem-solving and the use of properly constructed institutions that facilitate good governing is deeply and broadly consistent with the best sense of our constitutional system of government. Yet, as we will see in the next chapter, this is not, to borrow from a famous depiction of the US Constitution as a "machine that would go of itself."[106] Fulfilling the promise of a police power that has both integrity to the historical objectives and circumstances that gave it life in the creation (and, where needed, reform) of the relevant state constitution and also is well suited to the needs and wants of a contemporary citizenry requires attention to not only structure but, as is inevitable in our legal order, sensible judicial interpretation. The articulation of a set of principles and doctrines that can ground a successful modern police power is the subject matter of the next chapter.

With respect to matters of institutional design, a few lessons from the previous discussion, here and in the earlier, more historically tinged, chapters. One lesson is that the constitution must aspire in its structure to a balance between majoritarian and counermajoritarian elements. In this respect, we return to our discussion of constitutional strategy in Chapter 2 and also our short discussion of the Constitution's founders early in Chapter 3. We want in our state constitutions a decision-making architecture that will enable it to promote and implement the general welfare. Viewed in a less sanguine way, the constitution must safeguard private interests to a level that reduces the stake of politics, hoping to maintain stability in government and hoping as well to ensure the protection of private liberty and property rights, protection which will be vital to a government that wants to eschew violence and pursue endeavors that will safeguard the common good. In addition, the police power should be seen by well-intentioned governments as a source of authority that she could be exercised in a measured way. We referenced the so-called "presumption of liberty" in an earlier chapter. This captures the important point that the government ought to be duly parsimonious with its use of coercive powers, given the rational fear that citizens might have about government will choose security over liberty, will develop, say, restrictive public health measures even where burdens fall heavily on particular citizens and interfere with their personal goals.

A second lesson is that there is a decent amount of intrastate diversity that should be accounted for in the implementation of certain police power measures. Even in the absence of any notion of inherent local authority, local governments have powers that need not be inert. In Chapter 3, we looked at the advent and role of zoning, quintessentially local powers. Because zoning power is generally focused on local governments, municipal decisions usually drive land use strategy and enable local citizens to, as economist Charles Tiebout asserted several decades ago, sort themselves in order to find a place amenable to their views.[107] Looking at this the opposite way around, it would be good to have local governments promote and implement goals that are relevant only to a certain cohort of folks and do not necessarily aspire to comprehensive treatment or coverage. Ultimately, the police power is a flexible mechanism, one that will enable local governments (general-purpose municipal governments and others), to look at what is the best of goods and services can be made available to respond to the needs and wants of residents.

Finally, democracy and administration entail tradeoffs. We could tie the police power scrupulously to the legislature and to general-purpose local governments, institutions with representatives elected by the people and accountable in ways that classic models of democracy expect. That democratic decision-making is an attractive ideal where the authority of the state is at issue presumably needs no extended defense, either long ago or today. On the other hand, we have learned by experience, political and otherwise, that sophisticated policymaking benefits from institutions who are constructed in order to develop and manifest expertise. Sometimes democracy is rightly sacrificed for more bureaucratic arrangements. The rise of administrative agencies beginning in the nineteenth century and the utility of special-purpose governments for myriad policy tasks indicates that we have committed to such arrangements, even in a system that prides itself for its democratic bona fides. Our system is not either/or, and we can appreciate that social choice requires adaptation and tradeoffs. This is true as much of the police power's use as of any tools of modern governance.

NOTES

1. See, e.g., R.I. Const. art. V. ("The powers of the government shall be distributed into three separate and distinct departments, the legislative, executive, and judicial."). See Jeffrey S. Sutton, *Who Decides? States as Laboratories of Constitutional Experimentation* 193 (2022) ("At the founding, several constitutions separated power implicitly *and* explicitly").

2. William Wiecek, *The Guarantee Clause of the U.S. Constitutions* 21 (1972). See generally Robert E. Williams & Lawrence Friedman, *The Law of American State Constitutions* 267 (2nd ed., 2023).
3. See Williams & Friedman, *American State Constitutions*, at 267–68.
4. See Christopher Berry & Jacob Gersen, "The Unbundled Executive," 75 *U. Chi. L. Rev.* 1385 (2008).
5. See Sutton, *Who Decides?* Chapter 5.
6. See, e.g., Perdue v. Baker, 586 S.E.2d 606 (2003); Matter of Johnson v. Pataki, 91 N.Y.2d 214 (1997).
7. See generally Louis Fisher, "The Unitary Executive and Inherent Executive Power," 12 *J. Con. Law* 569 (2010); William P. Marshall, "Break Up the Presidency? Governors, State Attorneys General, and Lessons from the Divided Executive," 115 *Yale L. J.* 2446 (2006).
8. Likewise, it has eradicated any notion of a so-called "unitary executive" at the state level. On unitary executive theory generally, see Stephen Calabresi & Christopher Yoo, *The Unitary Executive: Presidential Power from Washington to Bush* (2008).
9. See Sutton, *Who Decides?*
10. See Morrison v. Olson, 487 U.S. 654 (1988). See generally Saikrishna Bangalore Prakash, *Imperial from the Beginning: The Constitution of the Original Executive* 63–83 (2015).
11. See John Devlin, "Toward a State Constitutional Analysis of Allocation of Powers: Legislators and Legislative Appointees Performing Administrative Functions," 66 *Temp. L. Rev.* 1205, 1228 n.80 (1993).
12. See, e.g., Miriam Seifter, "Further from the People? The Puzzle of State Administration," 93 *NYU L. Rev.* 107 (2018). See also Miriam Seifter, "Gubernatorial Administration," 131 *Harv. L. Rev.* 483 (2017).
13. U.S. Const. Art. II.
14. 20-cv-00608
15. See John Locke, *Two Treatises of Government* 408–409 (P. Laslett ed., 1963).
16. See Sutton, *Who Decides?* at 193–215.
17. Executive Order 2020–21: Temporary requirement to suspend activities that are not necessary to sustain or protect life. https://bit.ly/3TYSRT8
18. Se Emergency Powers of the Governor Act, 10.31(1)
19. In re Certified Questions, No. 161492, 48 (Oct. 2, 2020).
20. Ibid., at 55.
21. Ibid.
22. Ibid., at 597–98; 608–10.
23. Ibid., at 551.
24. See Sutton, *Who Decides?*
25. See Williams & Friedman, *American State Constitutions*, at 58–73. See also Christian G. Fritz, "Alternative Visions of American Constitutionalism: Popular Sovereignty and the Early American Constitutional Debate," 24 *Hastings Const. L. Q.* 287 (1997).
26. See generally Julian Davis Mortenson & Nicholas Bagley, "Delegation at the Founding," 121 *Colum. L. Rev.* 277 (2021).
27. See Cass R. Sunstein, "Nondelegation Canons," 67 *U. Chi. L. Rev.* 315, 322 (2000) ("the constitutional doctrine has had one good year and 211 bad ones").
28. Mathew D. McCubbins and Thomas Schwartz, "Congressional Oversight Overlooked: Police Patrols Versus Fire Alarms," 28 *Am. J. Pol. Sci.* 165 (1984).
29. "It is armchair history to suggest that the founding generation believed that the constitutional settlement imposed restrictions on the delegation of legislative power or that it empowered the judiciary to police the Legislature's delegations." In re Certified Questions, at 6 n.2.

30. Ibid., at 7–8.
31. Ibid.
32. See generally Richard Briffault, "Our Localism, Part I – The Structure of Local Government Law," 90 *Colum. L. Rev.* 1 (1990).
33. See Hendrik Hartog, *Public Property and Private Power* (1983).
34. See generally Howard Lee McBain, "The Doctrine of an Inherent Right to Local Government," 16 *Colum. L. Rev.* 190 (2016). For a recent defense of the notion of local sovereignty, see Paul R. DeHart & Ronald J. Oakerson, "Are Local Governments Mere Creatures of the States?" 56 *National Affairs* (Spring 2022).
35. Eugene McQuillen, *Municipal Corporations*, I (1928), at 388.
36. 24 Mich. 44 (1871) (Cooley, J., dissenting).
37. Ibid., at 108.
38. For a creative exegesis of localism as a constitutional construct, building upon Cooley's thesis, see David Barron, "The Promise of Cooley's City: Traces of Local Constitutionalism," 147 *U. Penn L. Rev.* 487 (1999).
39. Ibid., at 178–79.
40. See David Schleicher, *In a Bad State* (2023).
41. See 1 John F. Dillon, *The Law of Municipal Corporations* (2nd rev. ed., 1873).
42. Ibid., at 95.
43. Joan C. Williams, "The Constitutional Vulnerability of American Local Governments: The Politics of City Status in American Law," 1986 *Wisc. L. Rev.* 83 (1986).
44. John F. Dillon, *Treatise on the Law of Municipal Corporations*, at 101–102 (1872). On John Dillon's background as a railroad lawyer, a background that likely had influence over his view about local authority, see Williams, "City Status," at 90–100.
45. See generally Harry N. Scheiber, "Race, Radicalism, and Reform: Historical Perspectives on the 1879 California Commission," 17 *Hastings Con. L. Q.* 35 (1989).
46. See Calif. Const. [1879]. See generally Daniel B. Rodriguez, "State Supremacy, Local Sovereignty: Reconstructing State/Local Relations under California Constitution," in *Constitutional Reform in California* (R. Noll & B. Cain eds., 1995).
47. Sutton, *Who Decides?* at 308.
48. See generally Frank J. Goodnow, *Municipal Home Rule: A Study in Administration* (1895).
49. See Chapters 2 and 3.
50. Hartog describes some of the early conflict between the Federalists and the Jeffersonians on this matter, writing "Jeffersonians did not contend that local government could properly be reduced to a powerless agency of legislative authority. They did not mean to deny to city government the power to govern or the power to initiate change. Their concern, rather, was with the location of sovereignty in the legislature and with the capacity of that body to change institutional structures when the popular will mandated change." Hartog, *Public Property*, at 138.
51. See generally Lynn Baker & Daniel B. Rodriguez, "Constitutional Home Rule and Judicial Scrutiny," 86 *Denv. L. Rev.* 1337 (2009).
52. Ibid., at 1367.
53. Dirk Hartog, in his depiction of local power in the context of the Corporation of the City of New York in the eighteenth and nineteenth century, sees this emergence of local authority coming earlier. It was "the city, in its other, more modern aspect of a public government, which became the venturesome agent of public power." Hartog, *Public Property*, at 80.
54. See Gerald E. Frug, "The City as a Legal Concept," 93 *Harv. L. Rev.* 1057 (1983).

55. See Barron, "Promise of Cooley's City."
56. See Saskia Sassen, *The Global City* (1991).
57. See Richard Schragger, *City Power* (2016).
58. Barron, "Promise of Cooley's City," at 603.
59. See, e.g., Lea S. VanderVelde, "Local Knowledge, Legal Knowledge, and Zoning Law," 75 *Iowa L. Rev.* 1057 (1990). The locus classicus of the analysis of why local knowledge is essential in government planning and regulation is Friedrich A. Hayek, "The Use of Knowledge," 35 *Amer. Econ. Rev.* 519 (1945).
60. See Richard Ford, "The Boundaries of Race: Political Geography in Legal Analysis," 107 *Harv. L. Rev.* 1841 (1994).
61. See generally Noah Kazis, "Transportation, Land Use, and the Sources of Hyper-Localism," 106 *Iowa L. Rev.* 2339 (2021).
62. Nadav Shoked, "The New Local," 100 *Va. L. Rev.* 1323, 1335 (2014).
63. See Briffault, "Localism."
64. Hannah Fenichel Pitkin & Sara Shumer, "On Participation," *Democracy* Oct. 1982, at 43.
65. See Williams & Friedman, *State Constitutions*, at 190
66. Ibid., at 199.
67. Ibid.
68. See, e.g., Molly Selvin, "The Public Trust Doctrine in American Law and Economic Policy, 1789–1920," 1980 *Wisc. L. Rev.* 1403 (1980).
69. See, e.g., Lee Optical.
70. This orientation is given modern life through recent efforts by leading legal scholars who draw upon these ideas in forging a "new democracy" (Novak) or "anti-oligarchic" (Fishkin & Forbath) vision of American constitutionalism.
71. See, e.g., Louis Kaplow & Steven Shavell, *Fairness Versus Welfare* (2002); Matthew D. Adler & Chris William Sanchirico, "Inequality and Uncertainty: Theory and Legal Applications," 155 *U. Pa. L. Rev.* 279 (2006).
72. On cost-benefit analysis, see Richard L. Revesz & Michael A. Livermore, *Retaking Rationality: How Cost-Benefit Analysis Can Better Protect the Environment and our Health* (2008); Daniel A. Farber, "Review: Rethinking the Role of Cost-Benefit Analysis," 76 *U. Chi. L. Rev.* 1355 (2009).
73. Adrian Vermeule, *Common Good Constitutionalism* (2022).
74. Ibid., at 36.
75. Ibid.
76. Ibid., at 62.
77. Ibid., at 172–73.
78. Ibid.
79. This older formulation of the nondelegation doctrine is illustrated by J.W. Hampton, Jr. & Co. v. United States, 276 U.S. 394 (1928) and Field v. Clark, 143 U.S. 649 (1892).
80. See A.L.A. Schechter Poultry Corp. v. United States, 295 U.S. 495 (1935); Panama Refining Co. v. Ryan, 293 U.S. 388 (1935).
81. See Cass R. Sunstein, "Nondelegation Canons."
82. Ernst summarizes Freund's struggles, by reference to the emergence of administrative power in Dean Roscoe Pound's influential sociology and law: "The new 'social' or 'sociological' approach had broad implications for law, explored in Pound's brilliant critiques of the constitutional law of the Supreme Court, the construction of 'socialized' juvenile and municipal courts, and the law professor John Welsey Hohfeld's system of jural relations. In Hohfeld's system a common-law rule that created an area of *damnum absque injuria* was no anomaly but a conscious choice of a legal regime, which he called the

jural relation of 'privilege-no right.' Within this realm, which lay between 'plain illegality' and plain 'liberty,' Freund argued, administrators, acting under the police power, could lawfully restrain private acts that were 'legitimate but attended with peril or liable to abuse.' Administrative law was 'the system of legal principles which settle the conflicting claims of executive or administrative authority on the one side, and of individual or private right on the other'." See Daniel Ernst, "Ernst Freund, Felix Frankfurter and the American Rechtsstaat: A Transatlantic Shipwreck, 1894–1932," 23 *Stud. Am. Political Dev.* 171–88 (October 2009). With respect to the reference to Hohfeld, the classic text is Wesley Hohfeld, "Some Fundamental Legal Conceptions as Applied in Legal Reasoning," 23 *Yale L. J.* 16 (1913).

83. See, e.g., Blake Emerson, *The Public's Law: Origins and Architecture of Progressive Democracy* (2019); Joanna L. Grisinger, *The Unwieldy American State: Administrative Politics Since the New Deal* (2012).
84. See Max Weber, *Economy and Society* (1922).
85. See Frederick Winslow Taylor, *The Principles of Scientific Management* (2011).
86. This quotation is widely associated with Mayor Fiorello LaGuardia of New York.
87. Daniel P. Carpenter, *The Forging of Bureaucratic Autonomy: Reputations, Networks, and Policy Innovation in Executive Agencies, 1862–1928* 14 (2001).
88. See, e.g., G. Edward White, *The Constitution and the New Deal* 94–127 (2000); Alan Brinkley, *The End of Reform: New Deal Liberalism in Recession and War* (1995).
89. See Morton Keller, *The Affairs of State: Public Life in Late Nineteenth Century* (1977).
90. See generally Conor Clarke & Henry Hansmann, "Between Public and Private Enterprise: The Role and Structure of Special-Purpose Governments" (Sept. 2022).
91. Jack Georger, "Special Purpose Governments and Special Purpose Frameworks," in *Audits of State and Local Governments: What You Need to Know* (2018).
92. See <u>Ball v. James</u>, 451 U.S. 355 (1981); <u>Salyer Land Co. v. Tulare Lake Basin Water Storage Dist.</u>, 410 U.S. 719 (1973); <u>Kramer v. Union Free Sch. Dist. No. 15</u>, 395 U.S. 621 (1969). See generally Richard Briffault, "Who Rules at Home: One Person/One Vote and Local Governments," 60 *U. Chi. L. Rev.* 339 (1993).
93. See Shoked, "The New Local," describing this phenomenon. See also Nadav Shoked, "Quasi-Cities," 93 *Boston U. L. Rev.* 1971 (2013).
94. In Miriam Seifter's important work on the anti-democratic legislature, for example, the predicament of local agencies exercising broad powers because, so the claim goes, that there are policy experiments has grown and, with it, powerful threats to the democratic structure and purposes of state governance under state constitutions.
95. Theodore Lowi, *The End of Liberalism* xv–xvi (2nd ed., 1979).
96. See Reuel E. Schiller, "Reining in the Administrative State: World War II and the Decline of Expert Administration," in *Total War and the Law: The American Home Front in World War II* 185 (D. Ernst & V. Jew eds., 2002).
97. P. Ball & A. Maxmen, "The Wpic Battle against Coronavirus Misinformation and Conspiracy Theories," *Nature*. (2020).
98. See generally Reuel E. Schiller, "Rulemaking's Promise: Administrative Law and Legal Culture in the 1960s and 1970s," 53 *Admin. L. Rev.* 1139 (2001); Reuel E. Schiller, "Enlarging the Administrative Polity: Administrative Law and the Changing Definition of Pluralism, 1945–1970," 53 *Vand. L. Rev.* 1389 (2000).
99. On the connections between this skepticism and developments in administrative law in the latter part of the twentieth century, see Grisinger, *Unwieldy American State*, at 195–250.

100. See Gillian E. Metzger, "1930s Redux: The Administrative State Under Siege," 131 *Harv. L. Rev.* 1 (2017).
101. See, e.g., <u>Gundy v. United States</u>, 588 U.S. __ (Gorsuch, J., dissenting).
102. See generally Daniel Deacon & Leah Litman, "The New Major Questions Doctrine," 109 *Va. L. Rev.* 1009 (2023); Beau J. Baumann, "Americana Administrative Law," 111 *Geo. L. J.* 465 (2023).
103. See Eric Zoldan, "The Major Questions Doctrine in the States," 101 *Wash. U. L. Rev.* 359 (2023).
104. D. J. Houston & L. H. Harding, "Public Trust in Government Administrators: Explaining Citizen Perceptions of Trustworthiness and Competence," 16 *Public Integrity* 53 (2013).
105. See Martha Minow, *Saving the News: Why the Constitution Calls for Government Action to Preserve Freedom of Speech*, Chapter 1 (2021).
106. James Russell Lowell, *Political Essays*.
107. Charles Tiebout, "A Pure Theory of Local Expenditures," 64 *J. Pol. Econ.* 416 (1956).

6

Constitutional Rights

The focus of this book is on the nature, content, and functions of the state police power. Stripped to its essence, we can think of the police power as the foundation of regulatory authority and public governance in the states of the United States. It is a necessary condition for the government to act in order to protect health, safety, morals, and public welfare. Conceptually, we can understand the state police power as a source of authority distinct from external limits of that power, whether in the form of structural restraints of conditions, such as the separation of powers or individual rights. In the previous chapter, we focused on structural limits, including separation of powers and similar restrictions. In the next chapter, we will discuss internal constraints to the police power's exercise. In this chapter, we discuss what many perhaps associate with the main limits on the state police power, and that is individual rights. This book is not intended as a treatise detailing comprehensively the police power's interpretation in court, and so we will not run through each and every salient constraint in both federal and state constitutional law on the exercise of the power. Rather, we will look at the issue of rights at a higher level of generality in order to better illuminate the nature and substance of the modern police power. We want to look at the way in which rights constrain the police power's exercise so as to better illuminate the underlying logic and function of this power. After all, our preference for a broad or narrow approach to interpreting the police power may well turn on our confidence in the role of rights in regulating the exercise of these powers and, moreover, the willingness of federal and state courts to enforce these rights so as to limit excessive regulations. So we ask this: How does a general assessment of rights fold into our general view about the nature and scope of the state police power?

CONSTITUTIONAL RIGHTS AS TRUMPS

It is an elementary, and essential, point of our American scheme of constitutionalism that the power of government is limited by those rights embodied in the relevant constitution. There may well be other fundamental restrictions – such as, for example, the requirement that the federal government can act only in accordance with its enumerated powers – but rights constraints are the most conspicuous, and also the most contestable, sources of limits on the exercise of power. Alexander Hamilton viewed the inclusion of a bill of rights as unnecessary,[1] given ubiquitous, structural limits of the exercise of governmental power, but ultimately his faith was viewed as overly optimistic. Madison succeeded in convincing his fellow delegates to include a slate of rights as part of our US Constitution.[2] The rest, as the old saying goes, is history, as individual rights have come to be defined, interpreted, and ultimately expanded in the 200-plus years since the adoption of the document.

In their original form, these rights constrained only federal power.[3] They came to constrain state and local power as well, first through the explicit protections wrought by the Reconstruction amendments and, in the next century, by the steady incorporation of (most of) the bill of rights to the states.[4] While there are very few generalizations we can make about the contours of individual rights under the US Constitution, we can say that the courts have never regarded the police power as in any way a source of authority protected from the commands of the Constitution and its prohibition on unconstitutional action. That the police power may not be permitted to trample on an individual's right is at the core of what it means to say that the constitution is fundamental law.

This generalization is of limited practical consequence, however. The question that looms conspicuously in constitutional adjudication is how interventionist or deferential the courts should be in examining governmental actions where constitutional questions are raised. The answer to this question has evolved over more than a century as various approaches to judicial review have evolved. The nineteenth century was reflective of a time where rights-based review looked fairly unfamiliar and deference was the norm. Invalidation of state statutes and acts of Congress were rare. Without saying so explicitly, the federal courts' approach could be captured well by the views of various legal giants of that era, such as Oliver Wendell Holmes, James Bradley Thayer, Benjamin Cardozo, and Learned Hand, diverse thinkers all, but with views that saw the judiciary's role as quite limited to correcting clear judicial error.[5]

Significantly, the Supreme Court intervened in a number of cases in the twenty-plus years that marked the Lochner era. This efflorescence of judicial activism represented a very new approach to assessing and protecting certain individual rights under the US Constitution. In an earlier chapter, we looked closely at the Lochner era and the experience of the Supreme Court in invoking novel, and ultimately unsuccessful, limits on the state police power. Without repeating here the debates over whether and to what extent Lochner era jurisprudence aspired to invent a brand new species of individual rights – economic liberties, protected through some notion of substantive due process – or else was a conventional rendering of what legal historian Ted White has called "boundary picking,"[6] we saw that the federal courts would persist, even after Lochner's demise, in giving a close look to police regulations to ensure that they were not implicating the Constitution's fundamental rights or targeting what the Court would come to call a "suspect class."[7]

As constitutional rights became, in the 1950s and onward through the Warren and even Burger Courts, much more robust and extensive, the scope of the police power was correspondingly narrowed to meet these new judicial ideas of the balance between authority and liberty, between power and rights.[8]

This expansion of rights and contraction of state police power has been revealed in many different contexts. Some of the most profound in their impact has been in regard to the widening scope of equal protection, including but not limited to decisions involving discrimination on the basis of race. Consider the 1985 case of The City of Cleburne v. Cleburne Living Center.[9] There the Court unanimously struck down a zoning regulation, implemented under the normal police power of the local government to restrict certain land uses, on the grounds that this regulation singled out mentally disabled individuals in a way that could only be seen as arbitrary and irrational and, worse yet, reflective of prejudice.[10] Cleburne is especially intriguing in that the Court reached its conclusion without disrupting in any serious way its developed tiers of judicial scrutiny, and the view that the so-called mentally retarded (to use the vernacular of the time) were not members of a suspect class. Cleburne hearkens back to an approach a century earlier in Yick Wo v. Hopkins,[11] which also involved a law that mistreated without a credible rationale a discernible group of individuals without any reasonable basis; and it presaged more contemporary cases in which the Court was concerned about animus and irrational discrimination, a theme we will return to in the next chapter.

The broad interpretations that courts, and especially the Supreme Court, gave to the First Amendment's guarantee of free expression was especially significant in changing the dynamic relationship between the traditionally broad scope of the police power and rights of individuals to communicate freely.[12] While the Supreme Court has never taken an absolutist position on free speech, it has created a scaffold of doctrine in dozens of cases that impose very heavy burdens on government to demonstrate that their police power restrictions are warranted.[13] The police power's scope has changed in important ways as a result of these First Amendment decisions.

No case involving freedom of expression is entirely typical. Laws dealing with communication and expression, either directly or indirectly, are ubiquitous. State and local governments enact criminal laws and underwrite civil justice rules in the tort, property, and contract realm that arguably have an impact on the freedom of expression. Many of these laws are enacted under the police power, and thus are designed to protect the public safety, morals, or general welfare. For much of our constitutional law history, the First Amendment was simply inapplicable to state and local laws. And even after the incorporation of the First Amendment to the states,[14] seldom were state laws struck down as violating the rights of free expression. This was simply not a preoccupation of the Supreme Court in the first century and a half of the nation's existence.

In the years after the Second World War especially, the Supreme Court expanded the free expression guarantee, putting the First Amendment in a "preferred position,"[15] one in which free expression interests would frequently trump police power regulations enacted to protect public safety. In one early case, Terminiello v. Chicago,[16] the Court invalidated local laws that purported to protect against "disturbances of the peace," effectively a police power regulation purporting to protect public safety. Although this regulation was not targeted toward expression as such, the impact of the regulation had the effect of limiting the speaker's free speech rights, and without demonstrable evidence that peace necessitated this rule. Likewise, in Texas v. Johnson,[17] the case in which the Court struck down a law prohibiting flag burning, the Court rejected the "breach of peace" rationale, here because this was seen as more in the nature of a law restricting expression that the government objected to (or, though of the same consequence, individuals would likely object to).[18] In both cases, the Court embraced the fact that difficult expression would cause unrest and unease, and in that sense did not deny that there would be a certain disturbance of the peace, at least in the sense of folks that would likely be riled up in anger. But the Court was clearly drawn to a vision of the First Amendment that privileged expressive conduct over public safety considerations. Laws restricting freedom of expression have been struck down in a variety of contexts, even where the government has acted neutrally and with an expressed interest in protecting public safety and the general welfare.

In no way is this vision an absolute one, however, and so, for example, in Virginia v. Black,[19] the Court upheld a statute prohibiting cross burning where such actions reflect an "intent to intimidate," given that there could well be public safety and general welfare considerations that would outweigh the expressive value of certain speech (or conduct). Nonetheless, the general lesson from these cases is that free speech regulations will always get strict scrutiny and will often be a reliable trump over all but the most carefully considered police power regulations.[20] Indeed, this burst of judicial intervention in favor of free speech rights has been one of the single defining features of modern constitutional adjudication.[21]

In a valuable analysis of the origins of the First Amendment right of free expression, Jud Campbell notes that the primacy of free expression rights was accompanied by an erosion in the priority courts had historically given under the police power to the implementation of the public good through morals regulation.[22] Campbell situates the free expression right in a vision of natural law, a vision that has evolved in a direction in which the Court seems most concerned with minimizing the burden laws impose on free expression and the assurance that the laws are operating neutrally.[23] Whatever the foundational source of free expression in the original understanding, the courts have long accommodated public welfare considerations in considering the constitutionality of regulations that would burden individuals' rights to free speech. Consider, for example, the lengths to which the Court has gone over a long time to protect laws forbidding defamation and also obscenity.[24] As to the latter, the cases discussed in Chapter 4 in which the Court has upheld certain restrictions on the time, place, and manner of adult entertainment also illustrates the courts' willingness to accord some modicum of respect to the underlying public purposes advanced by such regulations. Further, and perhaps more foundationally, the way in which the Court over more than a half century has articulated the values of free expression suggests that it sees this robust protection as safeguarding not only an individual freedom interest – what Professor Martin Redish calls the value of individual self-realization[25] – but also a collective interest in promoting democratic self-government and expressive speech and conduct that enhances the *salus populi*.[26] It would oversimplify matters to say that the Court used to privilege the public good or private freedom and then reversed course. A more synthetic analysis of the caselaw suggests that the Court has long thought the best strategies for protecting the public welfare of free speech lay in the protection of free speech at a level that, rightly or wrongly, it thought would meet the Constitution's objectives of well-ordered liberty.

Such developments have not come without controversy. Conservative justices, beginning most notably with Justice Felix Frankfurter in the early days of free speech jurisprudence, expressed skepticism about the right's preferred position and the Court's activism in this area.[27] These views have been articulated frequently in prominent dissents in free speech cases. Moreover, the sheer breadth of the Court's First Amendment protections has occasioned in the last several years criticism from the political Left as well. Some leading scholars have identified the Court's resolute protections with a sort of "Lochnerization" of free speech doctrine.[28] The idea here is that the insistence on protecting the negative right of individuals to communicate (and also to spend) in a world in which the modalities of expression and opportunities to participate in politics is unevenly distributed is akin to a Lochnerian jurisprudence in which economic inequality is subordinated to individual freedom.

There is much to say about the intriguing argument that freedom of speech doctrine should be criticized largely on the same grounds as Lochner, although to do so requires a deeper dive than we can undertake here into the understandings of what the US Constitution and other constitutions expect the lines to be between public and private conduct and the domains of government and the private sector.[29] For our purposes, it is important to stress just one factor that makes the Lochner/free speech analogy problematic. Whereas the classic critique of Lochner focused on the ways in which interventionist judicial decisions undermined the ability of state and local governments through regulation to level the playing field by implementing regulations that were essentially redistributions of economic power (recall Justice Holmes's criticism that the Court was enacting Herbert Spencer's social statics),[30] the critique of modern free speech doctrine reflected in these claims that it has become Lochnerized generally argues not that ordinary police power regulations should be left in place and expressive freedom thereby curtailed. Instead, the essential argument by those who are complaining about the present libertarian slant of the Court's First Amendment jurisprudence is that the courts should intervene by recreating the First Amendment into a positive right, one that would obligate courts to either insist that legislatures and agencies enact measures that redistribute economic power in a way that facilitates meaningful political freedom and opportunity or create doctrine that has this redistributive effect in and of itself. Lochnerization then becomes synonymous not with Lochner's ill-fated experiment in libertarian constitutional intervention, but with a road not taken. This is a road that views the US and other constitutions as imposing affirmative obligations, as looking to rights in the constitutions that effectively redistribute wealth and power. Constitutional rights become less in the way of trumps and more in the nature of focal points for government obligations that can be satisfied only through edicts directed by courts toward non-judicial governmental entities.

Other constitutional rights have become more recently prominent in battles over the scope and limits of governmental regulation under the police power. Perhaps the most visible contemporary development has been the renewed respect accorded to the Second Amendment. In District of Columbia v. Heller,[31] the Court declared that the Second Amendment guarantees an individual right to keep and bear arms. This decision along with later decisions has limited the ability of state and local governments to restrict the possession of guns under the rationale that there are manifest public safety risks with widespread access to guns.[32] The scope of governmental power to regulate guns is being played out in many cases and will be for years to come, but we knew from Heller and were reminded in New York State Rifle & Pistol Ass'n v. Bruen just recently that the burden faced by the government in showing that a particular regulation is necessary, despite its interference with individuals' right to possess a firearm, is a very high one indeed.[33]

One interesting point of contrast between the Court's extensive jurisprudence under the First Amendment (focusing on speech, but also including its religion clauses) and the Second Amendment is the different lens the Court has, over time, used to view the content and scope of these highly protected individual rights. Free speech and religion doctrine over eighty or so years cannot be easily summarized, but we can say at least that it has been an admixture of dense doctrine, evolving as what scholars might accurately label a sort of constitutional common law,[34] with some attention to policy impacts (as, for example, in the "incitement," obscenity, and natural security cases).[35] By contrast, the focus in the majority opinions has been squarely originalist.[36] From Justice Scalia's seminal opinion in Heller through the Court's 2022 decision in Bruen, the clear talisman for understanding the scope of the Second Amendment right, and also the proper prerogatives of government to limit those rights through legislation, has been the original understanding of the right to keep and bear arms. The Court has waded deeply into this history and we can expect as this body of Second Amendment law continues to evolve, that the focus will remain on the historical origins and original public meaning of the right.

In an interesting research paper prepared for the Brennan Center, legal historian Saul Cornell looks closely at police power cases involving the right to keep and bear arms under the US Constitution and relevant state constitutions, some from the nineteenth century.[37] He finds compelling evidence from some of these key cases, including State v. Reid in 1840,[38] that courts understood the right as an individual right, consistent then with what the Court would say many years later in Heller, but, significantly, they saw it as subject to purposive state police power regulation – hence the holding that the state could properly regulate an individual in their concealing of a gun.[39] Post-Reconstruction constitutions echoed this same view, and Cornell points to the Idaho and Georgia constitutions, the former providing that "[t]he people have the right to bear arms for their security and defense; but the legislature shall regulate the exercise of this right by law" and the latter providing that "[t]he right of the people to keep and bear arms shall not be infringed; but the general assembly shall have power to prescribe by law the manner in which arms may be borne."[40] In this wider historical context, it is a strange position indeed for the current Court to point to the strong protections for private gun ownership without acknowledging that the states were especially diligent about yoking these protections to the imperative of state regulation. Moreover, the nineteenth-century interpretations of the police power gave a wide birth to state regulation. "In short," writes Professor Cornell, "reasonableness has always been a defining feature of the right to carry arms in public under American law."[41]

The jurisprudence of the First and Second Amendments is complex and dynamic. We have focused on just two elements – freedom of speech and the right to keep and bear arms – and have neglected other aspects of these amendments, not to mention other parts of the bill of rights that might stand against the assertions of the police power. Moreover, the treatment of those subjects we have focused on has been incomplete, although hopefully not too cursory. That said, we can reach two conclusions that are germane to the issue of constitutional rights as trumps to state police power regulation. First, and at the risk of sounding banal, the rights described here are viewed by the Supreme Court as in a preferred position. Barring change, we know that interferences with these fundamental rights will be scrutinized strictly. Second, there is and will continue to be concerns that the government will neglect these rights and so, for better or worse, we entrust the solemn duty to courts in exercising judicial review to define and enforce these rights against public action. In order for these (and similar) rights to operate as trumps, it is enough to show that the interference by the government through its police power regulations are trampling upon individual rights without a compelling justification and, further, evidence that the regulations are narrowly tailored and use the least restrictive means of accomplishing the government's purposes. Therefore, even neutral, well-configured regulations are of concern, insofar as they intrude on the rights protected by the Constitution. Lest these principles sound formulaic, we should understand that, taking the history of constitutional adjudication as a whole, there has been a sea change in the last three quarters of a century in how the Court seems individual rights and how it requires these rights to be protected against interference at the hands of government.[42] At the same time, the Court appears to be unmoved by the arguments that the general welfare as we approach the second quarter of the twenty-first century demands more fertile and adaptive regulation to account for the harms of unrestricted speech, especially in an time of changing technology. Likewise its majority is unmoved by largely unregulated gun possession and ownership, in a period of unprecedent gun violence and public fear. Even if the best interpretation of the police power as a broad grant to government to act on behalf of the *salus populi* had stayed more or less the same over the past seventy-five or so years, the practical effect of the police power has undergone a significant change as a result of the rights revolution of this era.

Taken as a whole, federal rights have long been, and continue to be, powerful trumps on the state police power. They ensure that the overall objectives that are intended to be realized through public health, safety, and morals legislation are measured against the impact on individual liberties under the US Constitution and state constitutions. To put this point into a form suitable for a bumper sticker: As rights expand, the police power contracts. But, like any other effort to put dense legal concepts onto a bumper sticker, nuance is sacrificed. When we say that there is a zero-sum tradeoff between the right and the power, we also seem to imagine that the values that undergird the power, in this case the commitment to the ideal of government regulation as furthering the people's welfare, erode in the face of powerful claims of individual freedom and liberty. However, there are alternative ways of thinking about rights as judicially enforceable entitlements, that is, as some things other than trumps.

Returning to the exploration of natural rights and free expression in Jud Campbell's important work, he notes that the framers' understanding of natural rights embedded in a deeply theorized idea of natural law could mean that rights existed alongside public welfare regulation. He writes: "Natural rights thus powerfully shaped the way that the Founders thought about the purposes and structure of government, but they were not legal 'trumps' in the way that we often talk about rights today."[43] Rights-as-trumps, as conventional as this idea is in our modern discourse of constitutional law and politics, needs to be understood as a normative idea, and not as a conceptual requirement of the term's definition. Indeed, a widening group of contemporary constitutional theorists are imagining a certain hollowing out of the traditional Dworkinian notion that rights are essential tools to restrict democracy and that they must operate as trumps.[44] The implications of this movement are intriguing, and while mainly beyond the scope of this chapter, we might say at least that the reimagining of rights might consolidate deep debates about governance strategy and constitutional objectives in a political forum. As Jeremy Waldron has recently noted, consistent with his general critique of judicial review, "[t]o uphold and protect our rights in the future we will need to think about different strategies – a non-judicial politics of rights-protection or at least non-judicial strategies to bolster and complement whatever shreds of judicial respectability are left in this regard."[45] It is perhaps paradoxical that the refashioning of rights as legal protections embedded in a complex understanding of public good, government obligation, and private interest is appealing to theories of constitutional democracy that are seem as novel and progressive, although, as Campbell reminds us, they have deep roots in natural law thinking.

On the other side of the coin, however, there is the idea that we considered in Chapter 1 in our discussion of constitutions and constitutional frameworks. Suppose we can conceive of rights as something other than trumps. If the overarching commitment to the people's welfare through the police power is accompanied by an ambivalence about the need to protect individual liberty and property against government restriction, then we need to imagine, as a bulwark against constitutional failure and as insurance against citizens' rational fear, other auxiliary precautions. Rights have long been part of our vocabulary in measuring security and official discretion. It is hard to see exactly what takes their place if they are seen as intolerable intrusions on the functions of governance.

THE MATTER OF EQUAL PROTECTION AND DUE PROCESS

In adjudicating controversies involving the police power, the courts have long been considered indispensable to ensure that regulations are being administered fairly. The linchpins of this concern with fairness are both external and internal – that is to say, we see doctrine as defining criteria of fairness that can be implemented by courts to ensure that police power regulations are reasonable and fair ab initio. We also see doctrine as developing rules of fairness that can act as trumps, rendering nugatory regulations that fall short of what these rules demand. In the next chapter, we will focus on considerations that are more internal or structural, by which we mean factors that emerge from the definition of the scope of the power itself. Here we say some more about what equal protection and due process brings in by way of external (that is, individual rights) constraints.

That the police power must be exercised consistent with due process rights was made clear by the Court in Jacobson, even though Justice Harlan's opinion was not very solicitous of the plaintiff's argument that he should not be subject to a general vaccine requirement. This claim in 1905 that the plaintiff's principal recourse lies in the political process and not in courts echoed claims brought during the recent Covid pandemic where individuals and businesses insisted that the governor's sheltering orders, insofar as they were not comprehensive, interfered with both due process and equal protection rights. While the courts at both the state and federal levels usually rejected these arguments, they always did acknowledge that police power regulations, no matter how essential to respond to public health emergencies, must be enacted consistently with due process protections and also must be applied consistent with equal protection.

As to equal protection, the standard form of scrutiny that the Court has long given laws that discriminate on the basis of inappropriate criteria apply in full force to

Constitutional Rights

police power regulations. The Court has explicitly disavowed some of its most noxious cases in which equal protection principles were disregarded, including Plessy and Korematsu.[46] The less memorable cases involving the quarantine laws in San Francisco's Chinatown and the razing of homes and other properties in Hawaii, discussed in a previous chapter, are also illustrations of the foundational principle that police power regulations must be equally imposed. That these cases all involve discrimination on the basis of race and ethnicity is no coincidence, of course. The use of regulation to separate and sort individuals and private behavior on the basis of race and ethnicity, in purpose and/or in effect is a long part of our nation's history, and it should go without saying that all such efforts are unworthy of the government in its exercise of these powers.

At the same time, the Court has maintained a controversial fidelity to cases such as Washington v. Davis in which it has demanded evidence of discriminatory purpose to invalidate laws that could be given a neutral reading. Finding clear intent to discriminate is a high burden for complainants and there is precious little reason to believe that the bar is more easily met in disputes involving the police power. Indeed, one could wonder what function this requirement of discriminatory intent fulfills in a world in which equal protection is understood as eradicating the impact of historical discrimination and of leveling the playing field. Such debates come to the surface in present controversies over the use of racial preferences. In its recent affirmative action decisions, SFAA v. Harvard and SFAA v. U. North Carolina,[47] not exactly a police power case, to be sure, as the policy being reviewed was created by universities in order to pursue its own internal goals, the Court read equal protection to impose a nearly impenetrable requirement of neutrality and color-blindness. Where this all might matter for the police power is in the evaluation of state or local laws which also undertake affirmative action in order to, as the government sees it, advance the general welfare. If the Court's recent decisions in the two university cases is any indication, the courts are likely to weigh in on what they may see as the government's policies that discriminate, in the sense that such policies take account of race, even while justified as mechanisms to ultimately eradicate discrimination.

Taken as a whole, equal protection doctrine has boxed in and out certain kinds of objections to police power regulations. It certainly does not seriously restrict the prerogative of state and local governments to draw lines among individuals, businesses, and even key parts of the economy – as we saw in the Covid era and also in a variety of settings in which property-impacting regulations are imposed. Government policymaking would be impossible without the discretion to discriminate and on various grounds, that is, to permit the government to sort and separate individuals and groups on the basic of meaningful, relevant criteria. What it does is focus like a laser on racial discrimination, somewhat less so on gender discrimination, even less on discrimination based on LGBTQ+ status, and maintains certain standards and argument rubrics that will constrict police power regulations in a very concentrated, and (happily) rare, band of cases.

Due process is a tricky concept to apply as an external constraint to police power regulations. First, let's begin with the easy cases. Where the regulation singles out individuals for special mistreatment – say, a requirement that a particular landlord put safety features into her apartment rental, while requiring nothing of the sort for a similar situated landlord – we can readily invoke due process as a brake on governmental action. But this is a far cry from accepting, as the plaintiff maintained in Jacobson, the argument that the government owed a duty to explain why this general vaccine requirement should be applied to this particular defendant. Leaving aside considerations that are more internal (such as claims of unreasonableness or animus, to be discussed in the next chapter), due process does little work in requiring the government to explain why it did not exempt individuals from generally applicable laws. Nor are such claims usually successful when they rest on the argument that the government should not have configured the category of individuals subject to these regulations in one way rather than another. Take for example a strange little Covid case from 2020 where cannabis dispensaries in Massachusetts who were selling their product for recreational use objected to a shutdown order that applied to their dispensaries but not to dispensaries that were selling cannabis for medical use (both under approved state laws) nor to state liquor stores.[48] The Massachusetts court quickly dispensed (pardon the pun!) with the argument that this line-drawing effected a violation of due process and of equal protection. The judge said that this regulation had a rational basis, in that the closure would help dissuade residents of nearby states where recreational marijuana is illegal to come to Massachusetts to purchase marijuana, thereby increasing the risk of Covid spread. This was typical of the run of Covid shutdown cases, given that these executive orders did typically draw distinctions between certain businesses and gatherings which could remain open and others which could not. To be sure, the Court did in three important instances strike down Covid restrictions on certain modalities of religious worship, but we should take from those cases (which were decided by close majorities) that the Court is very solicitous of religious liberty claims under the First Amendment, not that there is emerging a strong impulse to invoke due process to interfere with the government's efforts at line drawing.

Two famous cases in administrative due process illustrate this principle well. In the 1908 case of Londoner v. Denver,[49] the Supreme Court held that a city council decision to impose a certain assessment for property improvements requires an opportunity on the part of an affected landowner to be heard. This was a legislative action, but functioned effectively as an adjudication, a consideration of a valuable claim by resort to facts and relevant laws.[50] Due process was the appropriate tool for imposing this requirement. By contrast, in BiMettalic v. State Board of Equalization,[51] decided seven years later, the Court rejected the due process claim of a property owner who insisted upon a special exemption from an individual tax. "Where a rule of conduct applies to more than a few people," the Court wrote, "it is impracticable that every one should have a direct voice in its adoption. The Constitution does not require all public acts to be done in town meeting or in an assembly of the whole."[52] The BiMettalic situation captures in essence what the typical police power regulation entails, that is, a law applicable to "more than a few people" enacted in order to protect public health, safety, morals, or the general welfare. Objections to this law should be made in the ordinary political process (or, if this is an administrative regulation, in the processes provided in the relevant administrative procedure acts), not in court on the grounds that there is a sort of "due process of lawmaking."[53]

PROPERTY RIGHTS REVISITED

The safeguarding of property rights was a persistent priority from the origin of the first state constitutions and over the course of the following decades, disputes arose in which the courts were obliged to define the scope (and occasionally even the existence) of the property right, before proceeding to the analysis of whether and to what extent government regulation under the police power or another font of authority could take precedence over the owner's interests. As we have already noted, the reasoning in much of the first and into the second century of the republic's history was tethered to classical, and often natural law, ideas, ones that had in mind what were very much essentialist notions of property. Is this a thing that is being managed, regulated, confiscated, etc.? We saw beginning after Reconstruction and into the Progressive era a transformation in the conception of property. Echoing the influential voice of Justice Stephen Field, even in his dissenting opinions (as, for example, in Munn), the courts increasingly saw property as a means of exchange – in other words, for what it could be used for profitably by an owner – and not merely as a thing. This transformation would come to be of great importance in takings jurisprudence, as the court measured the imposition of regulation on the economic value of property, not just on whether title had been transferred to the government. However, this transformation was also relevant, even going back so far as the late nineteenth century, to how courts viewed the nature of property rights and, correlatively, the balance between public and private interest.

Two developments in regard to the reconfiguration of property rights animated this longish period from Reconstruction's end to deep into the twentieth century. One, picking up again on Horwitz's famous description, was that the shift to a market value conception of property meant that "the very conception of property became infinitely expandable."[54] Courts heard creative new claims that owners' investment backed expectations and so "[d]uring this period, American courts came as close as they had ever had to saying that one had a property right to an unchanging world."[55] At the same time, notions of general welfare and the *jus publici* nature of property, described in an earlier chapter, cabined some of this creativity. Many regulations met the bar of public justification under the police power, notwithstanding the clear burden on property rights, in the context of use and exchange. While this change accompanied the shift from private to public law, it is perhaps at least as useful to describe this as a shift from an obsession with property rights to property as a concept intrinsically embedded in objectives of governance and of the common good. Rights do not necessarily dissolve in this governance framework, but it is important to see their contours and contents as defined by the decision-making apparatus and expectations (the latter set by the state constitution, and occasionally the former as well) of democratic governance.

In the twentieth century, debates about the scope and content of property rights continued, as one might expect, given ubiquitous conflicts between owners' interests and the strategies of governments. The idea of property as a bundle of sticks, a hoary concept going back to Blackstone, continued to resonate with courts and commentators, and so rather than the quixotic effort to define property and property rights formally and finally, courts looked in both police power and regulatory takings cases to the nature and magnitude of the imposition on one more sticks in the bundle and, as always, on the government's objectives.

For some period of time beginning in the sixties and continuing for a couple of decades or so, many left-leaning scholars were taken with the notion that, as Charles Reich had explained in 1964, there was emerging a novel conception of new property, one that would encompass a wealth of government created entitlements and services that should become, in their necessity to citizen well-being and human flourishing, protected as property rights in much the same way as tangible, *in rem* rights. This logic bled over to important scholarship calling for constitutional welfare rights.[56] In the main, this effort to identify property rights with the needs of the propertyless would be short-circuited by developments in procedural due process law in the second half of the twentieth century, and especially in the seventies and eighties. To make a very long story short, the Court in Goldberg v. Kelly[57] advanced a strong version of procedural protections applicable to property rights that were far from *in rem*, but were shaped entirely by government-created expectations. And so the welfare beneficiary in Goldberg was given a property right in the continuing stream of benefits such that the government must given him an important measure of procedural protections before it could taken. But just as Goldberg and other cases of that era seemed to move close to the notion that government entitlements represent property that can be protected against interference – perhaps not only in the ending of those rights, but even in the reduction of value – the Supreme Court said that the content of property rights are defined by state law, not by something that is in and of a part of the US Constitution. Moreover, in Matthews v. Eldridge,[58] the Court shifted from a maximalist view of protecting property rights through a bevy of procedural protections to a balancing test, one that would look at the matter of administrative costs and risks of erroneous deprivation (among other factors) to strike the balance between important property rights and government interests.

Where this development left us by the beginning of the 1980s was with the hard question of how best to think about the content of property rights in a world in which states continually shaped and reshaped what property means and the expectations of individuals under the scheme of rights and privileges defined by state law. In an important article in 1981, Frank Michelman, who, perhaps more than anyone else, advanced a highly sophisticated progressive view of property and its protection through constitutional rules,[59] principles, and theories, argued forcefully for a view of property that, contra the Court's decision in Roth and similar cases, derived directly from the Constitution.[60] He would define constitutional property as essentially "political rights," that is, "what one primarily has a right to is the maintenance of the conditions of one's fair and effective participation in the constituted order."[61] These rights would ideally be protected against both eminent domain and also against government action under the police power, as those rights emerge directly from the US Constitution and would thereby restrict any and all interference by state and local authorities, inter alia.

New and creative conceptions of property rights in the half century or so since the progressive efforts at rethinking property and expanding its scope to address wealth inequality have mostly followed a similar script, although this is not to minimize their innovative qualities.

At the same time, largely thanks to the pathbreaking work of Thomas Merrill and Henry Smith,[62] we are seeing the renaissance of the classical notion of property as a "thing," and the view that property's exclusion rights are at the core of understanding both the origins and the functions of private property. It is not clear from this account, however, how property is better (or worse) protected from government interventions under the police power. Property as exclusion can be enormously helpful in defining the parameters of what is or is not property, but it cannot, on its own, blend well the public law governance ideas and strategies under principles of state constitutionalism into the private law underpinnings of property's definition. It is not that there is any inconsistency in the twin projects of defining property rights' boundaries and in defining the boundaries of legitimate government power. It is just that we need more clarity and understanding on the role and function of government in order to assess how centering the right to exclude bears on the constitutional scope of the police power.

Returning to doctrinal matters, we revisit an issue discussed in Chapter 3, and that is the nexus between eminent domain and the police power. A challenge that has not gone away, despite the depiction by scholars that the doctrine is inscrutable and problematic, is how to sort out when it is appropriate to scrutinize government regulation of the use of property solely under the police power or when it is viewed best as potentially a taking of private property and therefore warranting just compensation. Coming on a century after the Court's decision in Mahon, we seem to be no closer to solving the regulatory takings puzzle. This puzzle is problematic not only in leaving us with uncertainty about the proper scope of the government's takings power, but also because we cannot easily articulate a coherent standard that tells us when the government can act to protect the general welfare without facing a significant economic cost (and therefore disincentive) for this choice.

In the famous Penn Central case of 1978,[63] the Court reviewed New York's landmark law, a quintessential instance of the government's general power to regulate land uses. The Court noted that it had long upheld ordinary zoning laws as consistent with the police power.[64] But where, as here, the government's regulation negative affected an individual's use of property in a way that "caused substantial individualized harm,"[65] considering the regulation under the Takings clause is appropriate. Justice Brennan writing for the Court was concerned to replace the wholly ad hoc character of post-Mahon regulatory takings case with workable criteria for evaluation. In Brennan's formulation, the questions to be considered in cases involving economic loss, but short of a government confiscation are (a) the economic impact of the regulation on the property owner, (b) the extent to which the regulation interferes with the owner's reasonable investment-backed expectations, and (c) the character of the government action. Two parts of this Penn Central test are especially illuminating for our understanding of the police power: First, it is not enough that individual property owners suffer a loss, and even a loss of a magnitude different in kind from other individuals affected by this regulation, but these expectations must be "reasonable."[66] Second, the "character" of the government's action becomes relevant. And the historic preservation laws, as with zoning, that purport to "enhance the quality of life by preserving the character and desirable aesthetic features of a city" are acceptable, even acknowledging that they can come at the expense of an individual's right to use their property, one of the proverbial bundles in the stick of ownership.[67]

The focus on the reasons for the government's decision to regulate was critical to a Supreme Court regulatory takings case decided just two years after Penn Central, Agins v. Tiburon.[68] This case, which has largely fallen out of the pantheon of leading modern takings cases, is especially interesting in shaping the framework, at least for that time, within which the police power is examined in light of the takings clause. The key statement is this: "The determination that governmental action constitutes a taking is, in essence, a determination that the public at large, rather than a single owner, must bear the burden of an exercise of state power in the public interest."[69] Bringing to the front and center the question of how to balance private property rights and public values in consideration of the threshold question of whether a taking happened at all was novel and refreshing. This approach was short-lived, however. The Court would ultimately move away from this framework, tacitly at first and explicitly in the new century.

In the forty-plus years since Agins, the Court has bolstered regulatory takings and, with it, has brought more skepticism to the reliance on the police power to ground legal efforts to enhance quality of life. The key case in this modern development is Lucas v. South Carolina Coastal Council.[70] In Lucas, the Court summarized its earlier takings cases, including Penn Central and Agins, insisting that the test is an economic one, focusing on the question whether the regulation "denies an owner economically viable use of his land."[71] What is lost entirely in this is attention to the rationale for the government's regulation and, in particular, the way in which the regulation enhances the general welfare, even while imposing a cost on an individual – something that, upon reflection, is more or less always the case where the police power is exercised, and so too when eminent domain is used to advance a "public use." This theme had been prominent in regulatory takings cases going back to <u>Mahon</u> in 1922.

There have been a plethora of criticisms of <u>Lucas</u> in the years since that case decided.[72] Broadly speaking, commentators stress two essential problems: First, not all advantageous regulations can or ought to be assessed upon an economic basis;[73] and, second, there is little reason to expect that the courts are better at this assessment than are legislators and administrators.[74] These are significant practical concerns, and echo arguments made in Justice Stevens's powerful dissent. Curiously, however, these critiques do not go to the heart of the question raise by <u>Agins</u>: Can certain governmental be evaluated by resort to whether and to what extent there are common benefits, despite the special burden imposed on the individual subject to regulation? If this question sounds familiar, it is because this was pretty much the question asked in the ordinary police power cases throughout the period in which it was viewed through a *salus populi* lens.

By any measure, the operation of contemporary regulatory takings jurisprudence is in serious tension with the use and utility of the police power to regulate private property. All hope is not lost, however, in shaping the police power around the Court's holdings. Let us consider first the impact and next some possible ways through this meandering and maddening tunnel.

What <u>Lucas</u> and its progeny do, among other things, is to shift the focus entirely away from the rationale of the government's action. The "character" of the government's action, as noted in <u>Penn Central</u>,[75] becomes irrelevant to the inquiry. The conventional view is that, in the main, zoning, historic preservation, and even redistributive laws is not disrupted by this refocused analysis. The owner's interest in the ordinary zoning case is real to be sure, but usually the restriction is part of an established plan, a plan which buyers can be expected to know in the first instance. Zoning functions then like a public law version of a running covenant, and the imposition on owner's use, even where meaningful economically, is not an interest that either the federal or state constitution should necessarily protect. The same logic operates in historic preservation, as the Court explained in the <u>Penn Central</u> question described above. In this way of thinking, there is no need for the government to state its rationale for the imposition, save for locating its power in a pertinent statute or regulation.

This neglect is problematic on its own terms. What both the California Supreme Court and the Supreme Court of the US made clear in the <u>Agins</u> litigation is that the government has a burden to explain and justify its promulgation of a regulation that impact property and owner use. This requirement is not divorced from text, as eminent domain clauses typically require a public use (or, as sometimes in state constitutions, a public purpose). And it makes sense from the vantage point of democratic decision-making and transparency in governance.

In addition, the absence of a focus on the government's interest in the regulatory takings context leaves, ironically, given the paean to private property in Lucas and again in Lingle, property rights generally underprotected, at least when measured against other takings contexts. Consider, for example, the Court's 2021 decision in Cedar Point Nursery v. Haddid.[76] There the Court evaluated a California state law that gave, in essence, an easement (a "right to access") over a farm to labor organizers. The Court found this imposition on the owner's exclusion rights a per se taking, saying simply that the government must pay for what it takes.[77] This per se takings holding is distinguished from other scenarios in which takings claims are used. It is different than the imposition on owners' use rights, and thus distinct from the analysis in Penn Central and other lodestar regulatory takings cases. More precisely, it is also distinguishable from instances, as in the famous Pruneyard Shopping Center case,[78] where the owner has generally opened her property to the public and so limits on the owners' right to exclude can be limited without running afoul of the takings clause. None of these lines, however, are helpful either in defining the nature and scope of the property interest. We know that the concern is with the owner's exclusion rights, but why does this emerge as uniquely sacrosanct? Nor do they undertake in any way to assess either the government's objectives under the police power in regulating the use of this private property or to measure the economic loss or other impact on the owner's property rights. Through one lens, Cedar Point Nursery is a big victory for private property owners, as the farmers get to exclude labor organizers and others who otherwise would have the right to come onto their property to further one or another social or political goal. But through another lens, it is just a reminder of how fierce is this conservative Court in protecting the property owners' exclusion rights from even a temporary intrusion, and how blasé it is in protecting owners' prerogatives when it comes to avoiding severe zoning or historic preservation laws or what Professor Molly Brady has called "damagings" or other interferences of consequence on the property owner's ability to use and to profit over her property.[79]

Many decades ago, the distinguished legal scholar Joseph Sax wrote an important article, "Takings and the Police Power,"[80] that aspired to help solve the difficult puzzle of when to distinguish regulatory takings which demanded compensation from intrusions, oft significant, on property rights under the police power. The essential difference, argued Sax, was between the government acting as a guardian of the public interest and the government acting in a way that could be viewed as proprietary, as self-interested in a pecuniary or self-dealing sense.[81] In Sax's account, we would have more trust as a general matter in the government acting in the former way, as we expect when it acts under the police power, than when it acts in the second way, as will be more frequent in the context of regulatory takings. While the Court has never really followed this line of analysis, as Penn Central certainly reveals, this analysis captures a larger truth that could conceivably help in disentangling the vexing pieces of the takings/police power puzzle. We are searching in these property rights cases for either a big truth of the matter – as in early days asking, "is or is there not a property right at issue, such that the government needs to be diligent in providing adequate procedures if not eschewing regulation altogether" – or else measuring the degree of government benefit and individual burden. But these are quixotic adventures, especially when we consider that we are asking these functions of courts, in the context of litigation under the rules of the adversary system we cherish. Efforts to define the inquiry by resort to how the government is deciding whether and to what extent to regulate and to interfere with owners' interests and on what bases it is making these judgments, at least focus the attention at the right places. Here again it is important to recall the good road constructed, although ultimately not taken, in Agins. This case, and likewise Pruneyard – both decided by the Court in exactly the same year –, exemplify a group of justices deeply engaged with the right set of issues about how to assess and to weigh competing interests of owners and of the public. That the current Supreme Court, and many state courts echoing the same themes, has too often collapsed into arid formalisms about property rights' essential purpose in protecting against invasion and, maybe worse yet, a set of incommensurable and chaotic set of variables in a stew made of state positive law, common law, and the exogenous views of justices about what property is and isn't is unfortunate.[82]

We end this discussion of regulatory takings with a comment on two cases decided by the Court in 2005, both of which reflect the precarious nature of judicial intervention to measure the public interest when it comes to the regulation of property rights. Lingle v. Chevron[83] involved a somewhat complicated state statute that aimed to reduce concentration in the retail gas station market. The Court, in an opinion by Justice O'Connor, characterized the emphasis in Agins on whether a regulation "substantially advances" a legitimate government purpose as "free standing," and not suitable to the inquiry relevant to assessing whether a law represented a regulatory taking.[84] O'Connor writes that the "'substantially advances' inquiry reveals nothing about the *magnitude or character of the burden* a particular regulation imposes upon private property rights. Nor does it provide any information about how any regulatory burden is *distributed* among property owners."[85] True enough, but the point of that part of the Agins analysis is not to come to a conclusion, based upon an answer to the question whether the government regulation "substantially advances" a legitimate purpose, that there is no regulatory taking. Rather, it is to help shape the analysis of how to assess the burdens (amount and distribution) of the regulation against the strategy undertaken by the government to realize a stated objective of general welfare. The insistence on a standard that the takings rubric should be fully distinct analytically from the police power rubric is ultimately question begging. These are species of the same genus, that is, an inquiry into whether the government's actions impose such a burden on private property owners' interests that some constitutional matter is implicated – either that the government has gone too far under the police power, or that the government's actions are acceptable but only so long as compensation is paid.

In that same term, Justice O'Connor was on the losing end of a closely divided course in <u>Kelo v. New London</u>.[86] There the Court goes through a set of takings cases that are focused squarely on the question of whether a government regulation is of a "public use" such that eminent domain is a permissible strategy. These public use cases, going back to <u>Berman v. Parker</u>, ask what is essentially the same question in different ways, that is, does the public benefit from the government's imposition on owners' rights? Is this a law that promotes that the general welfare, or merely, as Justice O'Connor fears, simply a law that would replace any "Motel 6 with a Ritz Carlton" or any "farm with a factory"?[87] The answer the Court gives is yes – perhaps not a resounding yes, as the vibe of the Court's opinion, to say nothing of Justice Kennedy's concurring opinion,[88] is that this is a hard case.

These inquiries in those two cases from several years ago are two sides of the same coin. They look closely at the government's revealed interest, in promoting a public purpose at the expense of property rights, and reach opposite judgments about the legitimacy of that strategy. The incoherence of the Court's approach is rather striking. Or perhaps we should be more generous in seeing these cases as illustrative of the intrinsically vexing character of the regulatory takings project on the whole. Either way, it is hard to square current doctrine with a view of the state and local government's regulatory power as aspiring to reconcile private rights with the public good.

To summarize, the focal point of regulatory takings remains, ever since <u>Lucas</u>, on the magnitude of the deprivation – to put it more generally, on the burden imposed on the property owner. The ordinary police power cases, by contrast, continue to be focused on the government's rationale and, of course, any coherent claims that individual rights are being compromised. Neither purports to assess the costs and benefits of regulation. However, the relentless focus on burdens and costs in the takings context, and not in the police power context, leaves these two doctrines as fundamentally incommensurate. As with any analysis of these and related doctrines, this observation comes at a particular moment in time. The Supreme Court will continue to hear regulatory takings cases and commentators will have their say. Likewise, we will be able to see whether and to what degree the federal courts determination to protect property rights through a harm-focused inquiry will seep into police power cases.[89] For now, we might just reflect for a moment, as merely a thought experiment, what might have happened in <u>Mahon</u> had never been decided, and the question of property regulation under the police power was forever decoupled from the evolving – and, again, deeply vexing – character of regulatory takings jurisprudence over a century's time.

THE FORM AND FUNCTION OF STATE CONSTITUTIONAL RIGHTS

In assessing the place and persistence of rights and rights discourse in considerations of the police power, we have been focusing mostly on the contours and impacts of federal constitutional rights, the topic that gets the lion's share of attention in scholarly discussions of the tension between governmental power and individual liberty. But there is another important layer of constraints on the exercise of state police power and that is the body of *state* constitutional rights under *state* constitutions. What role do these rights play in the understanding and implementation of the state police power?

Because all state authority is subject to federal supplanting under the supremacy clause, we might ask why are state constitutional rights necessary? Could not our basic individual freedoms be safeguarded adequately through the bill of rights and the important additions in the Reconstruction amendments?

To give a negative answer to this question, and therefore to make the affirmative case for state constitutional rights as an independent source of limits on public power returns to us to Chapter 1. State constitutions create the foundational objectives and measures of performance of those who would wield power in the name of individual citizens in our states. The structure of governance under a given state constitution reveals these goals, as does the content of rights embodied in the state constitution. Yes, the federal Constitution does create the bedrock for these objectives by the rights it has created. However, a state may confidently supplement these objectives by adding protections to the federal floor. Moreover, they should construct and interpret these unique rights in ways that are best suited to their internal objectives (while also being cognizant about the nature and scope of external constraints). This may happen at the time of the original creation of the state constitution, or later, during periods of constitutional reform or through episodic amendments. The history of state constitutionalism in the United States shows political officers and ordinary citizens deeply engaged in the enterprise of framing state constitutional objectives, creating appropriate implementation mechanisms, and assessing constitutional quality and performance.

It is telling that before the Bill of Rights was made part of the US Constitution in 1789, the early state constitutions were already including rights of their own. "All of our most celebrated constitutional rights," writes Judge Jeff Sutton, "originated in the state constitutions."[90] Moreover, state constitutions have frequently been amended (sometimes by acts of the collective public directly, in those states that provide such a mechanism) to include new constitutional rights. It is impossible to understand state constitutionalism in all its complexity without understanding the instantiation, and sheer ubiquity, of individual rights.

The prevalence and persistence of state constitutional rights has accompanied the growth in state regulatory power. This makes sense, as we think closely about the matter. Expanding state power has revealed distinct threats to individual liberty.

State courts, as we saw in Chapters 2 through 4, intervened occasionally to limit the exercise of state power. And even where they declined to intervene, they took care to remind us that there were in fact rights-based constraints (in that case, due process and equal protection) on the power deployed by state officials. That states had broad power to act does not mean that they have the power to act without constraint. Reference to constitutional rights, including rights embedded in state constitutions, undergirds this important reminder. Rights in both state constitutions and in the US Constitution work in tandem, sometimes redundantly, often complementarily, to keep governmental power within appropriate guardrails.

State constitutional rights are distinct from constitutional rights in the US Constitution in ways worth noting. Political scientist Alan Tarr, who has written widely on state constitutional development, highlights some of the key differences in the language of state constitutional rights in the early constitutions. Often the provisions used the term "ought" rather than "shall," suggesting that these provisions were more hortatory than binding.[91] Another difference, critical to our analysis of the police power, is the emphasis in state constitutions on the community and the general welfare. With respect to the police power in particular, "[s]everal early constitutions even include the police power within their declaration of rights."[92] This more communitarian focus is broadly congruent with the republican character of state constitutionalism in the founding period, noted by Gordon Wood and others and as discussed at greater length in Chapters 1 and 2.

In framing his highly influential analysis of the state police power in its origins and functions, William Novak emphasizes the connection between the emerging state constitutional rights at the time of the framing and the commitment to the general welfare. "Government and society," he writes, with reference to the late eighteenth-century formulation of American constitutionalism, "were not created to protect preexisting private rights, but to further the welfare of the whole people and community."[93] The connecting of individual rights in the state constitutions to general welfare was more complex than a depiction of state constitutionalism as fundamentally Whiggish or Lockean. Certainly some of the rights embodied in the early state constitutions and included in the constitutions adopted throughout the nineteenth century and into the twentieth included what we can see as restraints on government, and so are classically *negative* rights. Madison struggled with Hamilton and Jefferson over whether rights should constrain state-level actors and in the limiting of the Bill of Rights to the national government. The standard story is that he lost that battle. However, this was rather a long and complex struggle, one in which critics of a legislature with unlimited plenary power successfully included declarations of negative rights into the emerging state constitutions. Therefore, we might agree with historian Gary Gestle, that the framers of the early state constitutions derived their view "from a different political principle – one that held the public good in higher esteem than private right,"[94] but still insist that these constitutions regulated governmental power through, among other devices, the inclusion of individual rights.

Early attention by the state constitutional framers to rights was often articulated in the document's design by explicit text. Moreover, often the arguments mustered in favor of it were pitched in a fairly abstract way. For example, constitutional framers would often opine about the value of private property and liberty. However, the precise ways in which these sacred values should restrain the government in its pursuit of the common welfare remained elusive.[95] Once a right was described as part of the fundamental law and its importance was championed, the question remained unanswered of how it might function to constraint governmental power where there emerged a conflict between the will of government and the contents of the right. A key threshold matter, conspicuous in the late eighteenth- and early nineteenth-century debates, was whether and exactly how the courts would intervene through judicial review to measure and resolve conflicts over government prerogative and individual rights embodied in the state constitutions. These debates, early and later, had an unavoidable impact on the character and contours of the police power.

RIGHTS AND JUDICIAL REVIEW

It is one thing to declare the objective of protecting individual liberties within the structure of state constitutions; it is another to provide for the means to enforce these rights through judicial review. Those skeptical that the framers of the early state constitutions saw rights as anything truly distinct from the progressive ambitions to promote the general welfare, as "depende[nt] on the carefully regulated society that government would construct,"[96] have to grapple with the fact that judicial review quickly emerged from the states as a mechanism for reviewing exercises of state power.[97] Judicial review was developed early in our constitutional history by state courts to limit certain excesses in government action, including, in some instances, the tramping on individual rights. Before the Supreme Court decided <u>Marbury v. Madison</u>,[98] it decided <u>Calder v. Bull</u>.[99] While the claims about judicial supremacy in <u>Calder</u> were largely dicta, the Court was unmistakable in its declaration that judicial review accompanied the basic idea of the constitution as fundamental law. Justice Chase wrote:

> There are acts which the federal or state legislature cannot do without exceeding their authority. There are certain vital principles in our free republican governments which will determine and overrule an apparent and flagrant abuse of legislative power, as to authorize manifest injustice by positive law or to take away that security for personal liberty or private property for the protection whereof of the government was established. An act of the legislature (for I cannot call it a law) contrary to the great first principles of the social compact cannot be considered a rightful exercise of legislative authority.[100]

The authority of state courts to review legislative acts to make sure that they were consistent with the state constitution was confirmed in a plethora of early cases, so much so that judicial review under state constitutional law was well established by the time of Marbury.[101]

The emergence of judicial review can best be understood in light of the risks attendant to the awesome authority given to the stage legislature through the police power. Judicial review was a critical check on the exercise of this power, especially necessary given what was emerging in the early nineteenth century (culminating in Barron v. Baltimore[102]) as an unwillingness to rely upon federal constitutional rights to limit state power. It was also important because of a declining faith on Americans' part in the jury as a mechanism to resolve factual and legal issues in connection with constitutional authority.[103] "The country became increasingly comfortable," writes Jeff Sutton, "with empowering judges to resolve constitutional cases and with perceiving them as trustworthy agents of the people."[104] Citizens frequently objected to state legislative decision-making, noting that explicit constitutional procedures were not followed, and that, more seriously, legislators were behaving in ways inconsistent with the common good. Judicial review became a key mechanism for ensuring that the overall objectives of state constitutions were fulfilled. This did not require, for the first several decades at least, any bold effort to expand the contours of the constitutions' rights provisions; it required only that state courts be vigilant in guiding state legislators and other government officials toward a way of good governing that would square the circle of individual liberty and society's general welfare.

Up to now, we have focused on the origins and evolution of judicial review largely as an historical matter. Looked at through more modern eyes, are there reasons to revisit the role and function of judicial review in light of the changing conceptions of the police power? The answer here is a highly qualified "yes." With the understanding of the police power steadily broadened to include the project of what we have been calling good governing, the expectation is that legislatures and agencies will function effectively to create and implement policies that will facilitate health, safety, morals, and the common good. Significantly, there will be meaningful checks on both institutions, the legislature, in the form of some measure of reasonableness review, and agencies, through traditional forms of administrative law. This retains judicial review in exceptional cases, but in a form distinct from what we typically observe as regards evaluation of the content and applicability of individual rights and the compelling interest of state or local officials to administer certain policies.

Another qualification to the general assent in a more circumscribed role of judicial review comes from the imperative that there may be a decent realm for judicial intervention when government officials, motivated as they can be by short-term political considerations, impose serious restrictions on individual liberty or private property with only a tenuous connection to sound public policy. Illustrative of such actions was the decision by the Florida governor during the mid stages of the pandemic to invoke the police power as a rationale for restricting private businesses' choices to require certain mitigation measures, including proof of vaccination, in order to use their services.[105] This followed a strange logic. Mitigation measures were intended to protect public health; the governor's position was that these measures interfered with personal liberty. However, with the sensible legal advice that the liberty claims would clearly fail in the face of the public health emergency, and the historic deference given to public health officials to act in such emergencies, the governor insisted that it was in the interest of public health to forbid private businesses from undertaking public health measures. This was undertaken in the absence of any single source of evidence that public health would be improved by such steps.

Judicial review is an important tool in this context to restrain nonsensical actions that reflect distorted viewed of the police power and of individual liberty. Such review often an instrument of promoting the public good. Rights need not be envisioned solely or even mostly as the means by which the courts protect someone's desire to be left alone, in the misanthropic sense of the phrase. They may well be part of coherent effort to exercise one's freedom in order to promote the common good. Judicial review can function to separate out the rationale for one's invocation of a right, along with the rationale for the government's imposition of a regulation restraining private conduct.

NATURAL RIGHTS

Early conceptions of rights, as many scholars of the founding period have taught us, were associated with natural rights, sourced in pre-political, rather than positive, law.[106] "A natural right is an animal right," Thomas Paine wrote, "and the power to act it, is supposed, either fully or in part, to be mechanically contained within ourselves as individuals."[107] These natural rights sometimes evolved into distinct textual commitments, embodied in the declaration of rights or, as in the US Constitution, in a separate bill of rights. Sometimes these rights remained unenumerated, and so we get the Ninth Amendment of the US Constitution which provides that "the enumeration ... of certain rights, shall not be construed to deny or disparage others retained by the People."[108] And we also get what Anthony Sanders in a recent book has called "baby ninth amendments,"[109] provisions in state constitutions which stand for the existence of unenumerated rights, those viewed mainly as emerging from natural rights.

The natural rights origins of the Bill of Rights in the US Constitution have been a topic of significant debate in the literature on American constitutional history.[110] Moreover, it did emerge in controversies in the nineteenth century over the meaning of privileges or immunities of citizenship or due process under the Fourteenth Amendment.[111] However, it remains largely of historical interest, as the federal courts have shown little attention to the actual discerning of these natural rights and their enforcement in cases in which these rights have been invoked. While it may be that natural rights thinking will have its moment, as an originalist majority on the Supreme Court looks to the natural rights underpinnings of certain protections, such as those found in the first two amendments in the Bill of Rights and also the Constitution's guarantees of privileges and immunities and due process, it is unlikely that natural rights will be distinctly identified by the Court, sourced in the Ninth Amendment, and enforced against governmental action.

By contrast, natural rights thinking persists in state courts, and it is worthwhile to consider how the discovery and enforcement of these rights can be used to limit the actions of state and local governments under the police power. A recent case from Indiana is illustrative of these conflicts. In <u>Members of the Medical Licensing Board of Indiana, et al. v. Planned Parenthood Great Northwest</u>,[112] the Indiana Supreme Court considered constitutional challenges to the newly enacted abortion law, a law that proscribes abortion except in the case of rape, incest, or life or health risk to the mother. This was a law similar to those enacted in several other states, all passed in the wake of the 2022 <u>Dobbs</u> decision by the Supreme Court.[113]

The court considered, and ultimately rejected, the claim that this law interfered with the plaintiffs' liberty rights as contained in Article I, Section I of the Indiana Constitution.[114] Yet, in doing so, the court took great lengths to explain that these protections of inalienable rights of life, liberty, and happiness are "standard in state constitutions" and are "generally understood as constitutionalizing the social contract theory of the English political philosopher John Locke."[115] The police power functions, the court explains, in order to protect "peace, safety, and public good" (the quotation coming directly from Locke), and is the residuum of government power left after ensuring that their freedom not delegated to the government has been safeguarded.[116] The court acknowledges that the document contains a number of specific rights guarantees.[117] However, it sees these rights (hearkening to the original debates about the Bill of Rights among the framers) as just illustrative of the natural rights of every state citizen, rights which can be and often are unenumerated.[118]

The claims expressed by the high court in Indiana are unremarkable as a matter of constitutional history and ideology, at least when viewed at a decent level of generality. That the framers of state constitutions, like the federal constitution, were deeply and broadly influenced by natural rights thinking is well known by scholars, and is an important part of our understanding of the underpinnings of American constitutionalism.[119] What is more notable, and potentially more problematic, is the willingness of the court to develop and implement a jurisprudence of constitutional rights in 2023 that rests on the view that there are Lockean natural rights that infuse contemporary constitutional law. Moreover, in the right case, they can help define the scope of the police power (insofar as they restrict this "general welfare" power to circumstances in which citizens' rights have not been reserved in order to preserve their natural rights to life, liberty, and the pursue of happiness) and can thus do work in limiting the reach of government action. Yet, even the more robust versions of libertarian constitutional theory have been cautious about this view of constitutional rights and the role of the court in locating and enforcing unenumerated provisions.

Is there a place for Lockean natural rights thinking in a modern view of the police power? Mostly no, for the following reasons: First, the expressions of generalized interests in life, liberty, and happiness, while part of the Declaration of Independence's compelling rhetoric, give us, both back then and now, little by way of a discernible constitutional rule or rubric to enforce rights as trumps against government action. Instead, and as the weight of scholarly commentary on both the Declaration and the expressions of the goals of constitutional government has indicated, these expressions of natural rights thinking are helpful in articulating the general ambitions of public welfare and governance. They are hortatory, but no less valuable for that. They can help us better understand, for example, the great objectives of due process in both its original and contemporary valence; it can likewise help frame the enduring inquiry into what we mean when we think of the welfare of We the People, at both the national and state level. But, like the preamble of the US Constitution, the grand articulated goals of, say, promoting the general welfare and securing the blessings of liberty, the content of life, liberty, and the pursuit of happiness cannot do the hard work of defining a sphere of private autonomy and freedom that is unreachable by government regulation. Indeed, if things were otherwise, the development of the police power in the early decades of our republic would have looked much different.

Second, and relatedly, the effort to define the police power by reference to the natural rights of citizens is more than a category error, but risks serious confusion in articulating the fundamental nature of a government power by reference to what natural rights have not been delegated to the government. The Indiana court's opinion in the abortion case is confusing in this respect, positing the relationship between the natural rights of life, liberty, and happiness and the police power. The court proclaims:

> There is symmetry here. While the State worries judicial enforcement of unenumerated rights may overreach, most of the State's police powers are unenumerated too, so there should be equal concern that the State might view its own powers too generously. After all, our Constitution's language in delegating authority to the State for promoting the "peace, safety, and well-being" of Hoosiers is no less capacious than its language guaranteeing Hoosiers' rights to "life, liberty, and the pursuit of happiness." Ind. Const. art. 1, § 1. So, Article 1, Section 1 strikes a balance: it allows the State broad authority to promote the peace, safety, and wellbeing of Hoosiers, but that authority goes no farther than reasonably necessary to advance the police power, and not at the expense of alienating what Hoosiers have commonly understood to be certain fundamental rights.[120]

With this supposed symmetry, the state government will constantly be challenged to show how their regulations under the police power advance the life, liberty, and happiness of its citizens. This becomes simultaneously the rationale for the use of the police power (framed further, in Lockean terms, as peace, safety, and well-being) and also the constraint on this power. The difficulty in deciding when rights function as trumps to power is, of course, a ubiquitous one, and not at all limited to the matter of Lockean natural rights thinking. However, bringing to the fore the enforceability of unenumerated and ill-defined natural rights provides, as here in the abortion case and other matters involving modern culture wars, a tactic made readily available to attack government regulation.

We equivocated above with the term "mostly" preceding "no." Where natural rights thinking can assist in helping us to puzzle through the matter of mediating, even if not solving, the police power/rights conundrum is by better understanding how the articulating of rights against government was the product not of existential dread that the government would crush private initiative and interfere with the citizens' right to be left alone,[121] but, instead, was part of a robust view of the government's obligation to look after the welfare of the community. Part of the end of essential liberty of citizens is the preservation of civil society.[122] This is the standard wisdom of the social compact theory central to Lockean thinking.[123] As the Indiana Supreme Court puts it: "[W]e left the state of nature and entered a civil society, giving up some of our natural rights in exchange for better protection of the remaining natural rights and for the enjoyment of new positive rights."[124] Such thinking, refracted of course through the evolution over 240 years and counting of what is distinctly American in our American constitutional tradition, can help us better understand the scope of governmental power under the police power and also its limits.

And yet ultimately this Lockean natural rights jurisprudence is unhelpful in settling matters involving abortion and other matters where the government's prohibitory power is put alongside rights that are not only unenumerated but are, as the Court majority expressed at great length in its Dobbs decision, profoundly controversial and difficult to administer. This is not the place to investigate in detail whether and to what extent abortion can be limited under the police power, although flagging this issue as an important one for the state courts in the coming years is necessary as there will be frequent litigation involving state constitutions in the post-Dobbs era. Let us say at least that this controversy is not easily solved by resort to natural rights thinking flowing from Lockean social compact theory. If the Supreme Court's mode of reasoning in Dobbs is any bellwether, then state courts are likely to immerse themselves in the now ascendant originalist methodology in order to determine how far state government can and cannot go in restricting abortion rights, and rights that bear on similar bodily autonomy issues (assisted suicide, access to contraception, etc).

THE PUZZLE OF POSITIVE RIGHTS

A marked development in state constitutionalism in the twentieth century, often implemented by direct democracy and enabled by the relative ease of amendment of state constitutions, was creation of new rights that functioned as affirmative obligations on government. These so-called positive rights were distinctive in remarkable ways from what we have long understood as the nature and function of constitution rights under the US Constitution.[125] Whereas these latter rights reflected protections of negative liberties, that is, edicts not to act, so as to violate individual freedom and liberty, positive rights insisted upon government acting to protect the welfare of individuals through access to services and resources.[126] As Emily Zackin writes in her book on positive rights in American state constitutions: "The advocates of protective constitutional provisions consistently argued that, for a certain segment of the population, intrusive government and the risks such government posed to private property and individual liberty were not the most salient or urgent threats to the well-being of every citizen."[127]

The content of these rights differ among the states, but common are rights to educational equity and quality, environmental protection, bail, and housing. The effective protection of these rights required government action in the form of findings that the present provision of these social goods was suboptimal and, in addition, the furnishing of adequate resources – if not by the court itself then indirectly by commands directed toward other state governmental institutions. The history of judicial treatment of positive rights is an interesting topic in its own right, and largely beyond the scope of this book.[128] However, we should say a bit more about how the phenomenon of positive rights, looked at as a whole, implicates our thinking about the police power.

Positive rights present us with a real puzzle. On the one hand, the progressive ideal which has framed the analysis here and elsewhere about the origins and functions of the police power maintains that the responsibility to implement policies that would further the common good, by protecting health, safety, morals, and the general welfare is vested in the legislature, administrative agencies, and other officials with the authority to enact public policy. The state constitution sets out the objectives and the contents of the power, but the responsibility for the implementation of these goals lies outside the four corners of the constitution. What role would positive rights play in this picture other than as a sort of "and we mean business" principle?

On the other hand, we might see positive rights as the *yin* to the police power *yang*; that is, the description of general welfare ambitions in the language of rights encapsulates elements of the public welfare objectives that are incorporated into the wide mission of good governing under the police power. More practically, positive rights give citizens the ability to bring government actors before courts, so as to make sure that they are carrying out their duties under the police power. In this ambitious rendering, the police power is the basis of governmental action, the font of governmental authority; whereas positive rights reflect some of the most central foundations of its obligation. Both are sources of real law; both are judicially enforceable.

A close look at the role and function of the police power suggests that the solution to this puzzle lies somewhere in between these two competing views. The reader might be disappointed in the brute pragmatism of this resolution, but hopefully she will be persuaded that such an accommodation to these competing views reflects a fruitful way of thinking about what is a truly difficult issue, at the level both of history and of tactics.

Positive rights are in and of themselves principally hortatory, at least when measured by the usual yardstick of "How can I get affirmative relief in court?" Seldom have courts used these rights to invalidate governmental actions as inconsistent with the social welfare requirements embedded in the right. "Seldom" does not mean "never," however, and it is principally in the area of educational equity and finance that we see an elaborate and largely sustained effort by state courts to implement a right to educational quality.[129] This has been a highly complex area, and it is hard to measure the overall success of the endeavor without breaking the story in the state-specific stories.[130]

The right to education is rightly viewed as an example – maybe the most compelling example – of a judicially enforceable positive right. However, it relates to the larger solar system of the police power in a more attenuated way. A successful educational system is of course part of a well-functioning society, and so there is an obvious and important connection between educational quality and the general welfare. Nonetheless, the way that state courts have understood, broadly speaking, their charge to enforce the right to education is a responsibility of government to provide educational equity through targeted fiscal strategies. It is not the aspiration to have the best possible schools within a county or a state, however worthy that is as an objective of our state and local government. Rather, the legal construct is one of equity in finance. The overarching goal is to ensure that individuals in district A are being treated in no essential way different than those in district B. Quality differentials, at least as best can be measured by courts, are the problem; and disparities in finance, which will predictably be reflected in test scores and other relatively objective measures, can be examined and adjudicated, with the aim of fixing these disparities through judicial edicts and some supervision of legislative and administrative action.

Policy areas that can be seen as more at the core of the police power, for example, adequate public health, safety from harmful behavior (crime) or substances (drugs), or some general deterioration in the conditions or urban life, are rarely the subject of positive rights. To be sure, some talk eloquently about the right to adequate health care;[131] others will talk about the freedom of movement, enabled only by the provision of various services to aid what is called "instrastate travel."[132] But these have not been translated into positive rights, and so do not really connect coherently to the police power.

Lest we abandon entirely the use and utility of positive rights in our quest to connect rights to the police power, we should think creatively about how the positive rights experiment does help us shape a vision of government as a matrix of institutions that come along with a social obligation. The fact of a police power, and nested in a wide theory of good governing that has permeated this book, suggests that the government has a special obligation under our state constitutional structure to act to promote the "people's welfare." Obligations to govern go beyond the minimalist state and also beyond the *sic utere* idea that government steps in to redress private harm and certain forms of social disorder that make up public law in a narrow sense. The police power is illustrative of these obligations. Likewise, the inclusion of positive rights in state constitutions are emblematic of this same vision of the government as a progressive force for protection of the public interest and facilitator of the social good. We can see positive rights as expressing, at the very least, a symbolic form of this commitment and, critically, a form that is hard-wired into the state constitution, and not merely floating freely as an academic idea. Positive rights, as Zackin reminds us in her important study, were the result of distinct social movements;[133] we saw in the 1960s and 1970s in particular (and even as recently as the past decade with regard to the issue of housing and homelessness) the mobilization of citizens to push for progressive social policy and to use the mechanisms of constitutional change to augur this development. Even with mixed success at the level of judicial intervention the fact of this citizen movement has become an important element of our social change and of the use of constitutional reform to implement such change. Positive rights are a novel mechanism for such change, and can be viewed in partnership with the ancient edifice of the police power as a conventional and vitally important element of ambitious social policy in the service of the common good.

DEFINING AND CONTESTING RIGHTS IN A GOOD GOVERNING FRAMEWORK

Jud Campbell, who we have discussed previously in this chapter in connection with insights about free speech and natural rights thinking, provides a useful way of thinking about the transformation in rights thinking more generally, one that bears on our discussion of rights and the police power. He explains:

> Until the mid-twentieth century, fundamental rights were bimodal. First, courts employed an ostensibly deferential ends-means test to ensure that any legislation restricting natural rights was within the police powers – that is, that the legislature was aiming to promote the public good. These "rights" were not antiregulatory at all, and they did not exclude particular reasons for restricting rights, so long as those reasons were public regarding. Second, courts applied a set of more determinate limits on legislative power that included fundamental common-law rules. In this latter sense, rights were "trumps." Natural rights and common-law rights were thus the twin pillars of American rights jurisprudence.[134] (citations omitted).

In this account, we could glean much from our examination of the proper scope of governance under state constitutions and the US constitution regarding the meaning of individual rights. It oversimplifies this just a bit to say that the rights at issue were subservient to the government's overall interest in protecting and promoting the general welfare. However, this conception of rights explains well the courts' simultaneous regard for private property as a fundamental constitutional value and its willingness to accept ambitious governmental regulation that would limit the discretion owners had over their property's use where such limits were necessary to protect the common welfare. Rights are adapted to the circumstances of constitutional governance rather than the other way around.

But time brought change. Campbell writes:

> The modern notion of constitutional rights, by contrast, reflects a transmogrified synthesis of these earlier ideas. In terms of scope, modern rights privilege certain realms of freedom, like communicative activity, rather than specific, historically defined limits on governmental power or general protection for liberty. Nor do modern rights carry the same implications for governmental authority.... The very idea of rights, then, limits the reasons why the government can restrict them.[135] (citations omitted).

He is examining mostly the free speech protections of the First Amendment to illustrate this point, but the lessons could be applied as well to property rights and other economic liberties. This transmogrification requires the government to tread with much more care when it made a choice that is ultimately redistributive, that is, sacrifices individual dominion over one's property to the public interest. Takings law, for example, makes this caution explicit, imposing a liability rule that ensures that the value of the restriction will be capitalized into the decision to restrict the property owner's rights. In the regular instance of regulation over private property under the police power, however, the mechanism by which the caution is imposed on governmental choice is a strong enforcement of an individual right. We see this also with respect to the Second Amendment. We might have imagined that the "right to keep and bear arms" was part of an overarching goal of maintain public safety. But in the hands of the current Court, it is an individual right that, in Campbell's words, "limits the reasons why the government can restrict them." In so doing, it manages the efface the very rationale for the right.

The transition to this modern view of rights has two major implications for our understanding of the police power. First, the preference for certain individual freedoms means that the government's commitment to public safety, health, and morals will need to be calibrated so that the realm of freedom in these highly protected areas is not too disturbed. In the free speech context, this has important implications, as we have discussed, for morals regulation. Communicative freedom has a privileged place and the government will face a high burden when it restricts such freedom and a nearly impossibly high burden when it does so in any non-neutral way. Gun rights seem also quite privileged and, to the chagrin of a solid majority of Americans, restrictions that are designed to keep us safe and to protect the public from gun violence will be viewed skeptically, with the government carrying a rather high burden in showing that such restrictions are warranted. Second, not only will rights outside of this preferred contexts emerge as trumps restricting government action (leaving here to one side regulatory takings as a somewhat special case), but they will also not be viewed within a framework which otherwise might help us figure out how best to balance governance strategies that are public regarding and motivated by police power's underlying logic and purpose with the concern and interests of individuals who want to be assured that their property and liberty will be protected in a constitutional republic that values freedom and individual choice.

We will see as we turn to further considerations regarding the interpretation of the police power in the next chapter that there are other mechanisms available to courts in navigating these difficult issues and resolving conflicts. What this chapter has illuminated is the way in which the evolving jurisprudence of rights, in both US and state constitutional law interfaces with the police power and the quest for good governing where rights might come into conflict.

NOTES

1. See Federalist No. 84 (A. Hamilton) ("The truth is, after all the declamation we have heard, that the constitution is itself in every rational sense, and to every useful purpose, A BILL OF RIGHTS").
2. Michael P. Zuckert, "Madison's Consistency on the Bill of Rights," *National Affairs*. https://bit.ly/3vtH8lm.
3. See Barron v. City of Baltimore, 32 U.S. 243 (1833).
4. See generally Bryan H. Wildenthal, "The Lost Compromise: Reassessing the Early Understanding in Court and Congress on Incorporation of the Bill of Rights in the Fourteenth Amendment," 61 *Ohio St. L. J.* 1051 (2000). See also Akhil Reed Amar, *The Bill of Rights: Creation and Reconstruction* (1998).
5. See Oliver Wendell Holmes, *The Common Law* (1881); James Bradley Thayer, *The Origin and Scope of the American Doctrine of Constitutional Law* (1893); Benjamin Cardozo, *The Nature of the Judicial Process* (1921); Learned Hand, *The Spirit of Liberty* (1952).
6. See G. Edward White, *Law in American History Volume II: From Reconstruction Through the 1920s* (2016), at 400.
7. "Suspect classes" originates with the Supreme Court's opinion in Carolene Products. See also Marcy Strauss, "Reevaluating Suspect Classifications," 35 *Seattle U. L. Rev.* 135 (2011).
8. See generally White, *Law in American History Volume II*, at 379–423.
9. 473 U.S. 432 (1985).
10. Ibid., at 450.
11. 118 U.S. 356 (1886).
12. See generally Robert Post, "Participatory Democracy and Free Speech," 97 *Va. L. Rev.* 477 (2011).
13. See Janus v. AFSCME, 138 S. Ct. 2448, 2487 (2018) (Kagan, J., dissenting).
14. The free speech clause of the First Amendment was incorporated to the states in Gitlow v. New York, 268 U.S. 652 (1925).
15. See, e.g. Murdock v. Pennsylvania (1943) expressly stated: "freedom of press, freedom of speech, freedom of religion are in a preferred position." https://bit.ly/47wcLYN.

16. 337 U.S. 1 (1949).
17. 491 U.S. 397 (1989).
18. Ibid., at 414.
19. Ibid., at 416.
20. Also illustrative of this strong free speech orientation is the Court's decision in City of Chicago v. Morales, 527 U.S. 41 (1999). Here the Court considered an anti-loitering ordinance, once designed to protect public safety, as the city explained it.
21. See, e.g., Citizens United v. Fed. Election Comm'n, 558 U.S. 310 (2010); Buckley v. Valeo, "424 U.S. 1 (1976).
22. See Jud Campbell, "Natural Rights and the First Amendment," 127 *Yale L. J.* 246 (2017).
23. Ibid., at 268.
24. Ibid., at 277.
25. See Martin H. Redish, "The Value of Free Speech," 130 *U. Penn. L. Rev.* 591 (1982).
26. See Post, "Participatory Democracy"; Toni M. Massaro & Helen Norton, "Free Speech and Democracy: A Primer for Twenty-First Century Reformers," 54 *UC Davis L. Rev.* 1631 (2021); Frederick Schauer, "Free Speech and the Argument from Democracy," 25 *Nomos: Liberal Democracy* 241 (1983).
27. See, e.g., Dennis v. United States, 341 U.S. 494, 525 (1951); (Frankfurter, J., concurring); Minersville Sch. Dist. v. Gobitis, 310 U.S. 586 (1940). See generally Melvin Urofsky, "The Failure of Felix Frankfurter," 26 *U. Rich. L. Rev.* 115 (1991).
28. See Genevieve Lakier, "The First Amendment's Real Lochner Problem," 87 *U. Chi. L. Rev.* 1241 (2020).
29. See, e.g., Minow, *Saving the News*, Chapter 4; Owen Fiss, *The Theory of Free Speech* (1998); Cass R. Sunstein, "Lochner's Legacy," 87 *Colum. L. Rev.* 873 (1987).
30. See Lochner, 198 U.S. at 75 (Holmes J., dissenting).
31. 554 U.S. 570 (2008).
32. See New York State Rifle &Pistol Ass'n, Inc. v. Bruen, 597 U.S. __ (2022); McDonald v. City of Chicago, 561 U.S. 742 (2010); District of Columbia v. Heller, 554 U.S. 570 (2008).
33. 597 U.S. __ (2022).
34. See generally David Strauss, "Foreword: Does the Constitution Mean What it Says?" 129 *Harv. L. Rev.* 1 (2015).
35. See, e.g., Brandenburg v. Ohio, 395 U.S. 444 (1969). See generally Geoffrey R. Stone, "Free Speech and National Security," 84 *Ind. L. J.* 939 (2009).
36. See Reva Siegel, "Dead or Alive: Originalism as Popular Constitutionalism in Heller," 122 *Harv. L. Rev.* 191 (2008). See also Heller, 128 U.S. at 2821 (Scalia, J., dissenting) ("Constitutional rights are enshrined with the scope they were understood to have when the people adopted them, whether or not future legislatures or (yes) even future judges think that scope too broad").
37. See Cornell, S. *The Police Power and the Authority to Regulate Firearms in Early America* (New York: Brennan Center for Justice, 2021), pp. 1–2. https://bit.ly/3TTLnkz.
38. 1 Ala. 612 (1840). Discussed in Cornell, *Firearms*, at 7–8.
39. Cornell, *Firearms*, at 7–9.
40. See Idaho Const. of 1889, art. I, #11. Ga. Const., art. I, #1, para. VIII. See also Fla Const., art. I, #8.
41. Ibid., at 8. See also Jud Campbell, "Natural Rights, Positive Rights, and the Right to Keep and Bear Arms," 32 *L. & Contemp. Probs.* 31 (2020); Saul Cornell & Nathan DeDino, "A Well Regulated Right: The Early American Origins of Gun Control," 73 *Fordham L. Rev.* 487 (2004).

42. See the interesting discussion in Jamal Greene, *How Rights Went Wrong: Why Our Obsession with Rights is Tearing America Apart* 58–90 (2021) (describing the problems with "rightism").
43. See Campbell, "Natural Rights and the First Amendment," at 66.
44. See generally Ronald Dworkin, *Taking Rights Seriously* (1978). See also Dworkin, *Law's Empire*.
45. Jeremy Waldron, "Denouncing Dobbs and Opposing Judicial Review" (ms. May 2022). See also Waldron, "The Core of the Case."
46. Chief Justice Roberts wrote in Trump v. Hawaii: "The dissent's reference to Korematsu ... affords this Court the opportunity to make express what is already obvious: Korematsu was gravely wrong the day it was decided, has been overruled in the court of history, and – to be clear – 'has no place in law under the Constitution'." 138 S. Ct. 2392, 2423 (2018), at 38.
47. 600 U.S. __ (2023).
48. Coronavirus: Medical marijuana dispensaries are called essential in Mass., but recreational pot shops must close under governor's order. MassLive (2020) https://bit.ly/3RT7btQ. A superior court judge upheld this order. https://wbur.fm/3SHopId.
49. 210 U.S. 373 (1908).
50. Cf. Sangamon Valley Television Corp. v. United States, 269 F.2d 221 (D.C. 1959) (noting that due process is required in instances involving "conflicting private claims to a valuable privilege").
51. 239 U.S. 441 (1915).
52. Ibid., at 449.
53. Ibid.
54. Horwitz, *Transformations II*, at 263.
55. Ibid., at 270.
56. See generally William E. Forbath, "Constitutional Welfare Rights: A History, Critique, and Reconstruction," 69 *Fordham L. Rev.* 1821 (2001). See also Cass R. Sunstein, *The Partial Constitution* (1993).
57. 357 U.S. 254 (1970).
58. 424 U.S. 319 (1976).
59. See, e.g., Frank Michelman, "The Pursuit of Constitutional Welfare Rights: One View of Rawls' Theory of Justice," 121 *U. Pa. L. Rev.* 962 (1973); Frank Michelman, "1968 Term – Foreword: On Protecting the Poor Through the Fourteenth Amendment," 83 *Harv. L. Rev.* 7 (1969).
60. Frank Michelman, "Property as a Constitutional Right," 38 *Wash. & Lee L. Rev* 1097 (1981).
61. Ibid., at 1123.
62. See, e.g., Thomas W. Merrill & Henry E. Smith, *The Oxford Introductions to U.S. Law: Property* (2010); Thomas W. Merrill & Henry E. Smith, "The Morality of Property," 48 *Wm. & Mary L. Rev.* 1849 (2007).
63. Penn Central Transportation v. New York City, 438 U.S. 105 (1978).
64. Ibid., at 125: "in instances in which a state tribunal reasonably concluded that 'the health, safety, morals, or general welfare' would be promoted by prohibiting particular contemplated uses of land, this Court has upheld land use regulations that destroyed or adversely affected recognized real property interests" (citing Nectow v. Cambridge, 277 U.S. 188 (1928)).
65. 438 U.S. at 125.
66. Ibid.

67. Ibid., at 129.
68. 447 U.S. 255 (1980).
69. Ibid., at 260.
70. 505 U.S. 1003 (1992).
71. Ibid., at 1010 (citing Agins 447 U.S. at 260).
72. See, e.g., Joseph Sax, "Property Rights and the Economy of Nature: Understanding Lucas v. South Carolina Coastal Council," 45 *Stan. L. Rev.* 1433 (1993).
73. Ibid., at 1453.
74. Ibid., at 1455.
75. Penn Central, 438 U.S. 105.
76. 594 U.S. __ (2021); 1415 S. Ct. 2063.
77. 1415 S. Ct. at 2071 (citing Tahoe-Sierra Preservation Council, Inc v. Tahoe Regional Planning Agency, 535 U.S. 302, 322 (2002)).
78. PruneYard Shopping Center v. Robins, 447 U.S. 74 (1980).
79. See Maureen E. Brady, "The Damaging Clauses," 104 *Va. L. Rev.* 341 (2018).
80. Joseph Sax, "Takings and the Police Power," 74 *Yale L. J.* 36 (1964).
81. Ibid., at 50.
82. See Murr v. Wisconsin, 582 U.S. 383 (2017). See generally Maureen E. Brady, "Penn Central Squared: What the Many Factors of Murr v. Wisconsin Mean for Property Federalism," 106 *U. Pa. L. Rev.* Online (2017).
83. 544 U.S. 528 (2005).
84. Ibid., at 531.
85. Ibid., at 533.
86. 545 U.S. 469 (2005).
87. Kelo, 545 U.S. at 503 (O'Connor, J., dissenting).
88. Ibid., at 490 (Kennedy, J., concurring).
89. See Murr, 137 S. Ct. at 1938.
90. Sutton, *Imperfect Solutions*, at 8. See also Tarr, *Understanding State Constitutions*, at 75–76.
91. See Tarr, *Understanding State Constitutions*, at 77.
92. See ibid., at 78. See, e.g., Pennsylvania Constitution of 1776, Bill of Rights, art. 3; Delaware Constitution of 1776, Declaration of Rights, art. 4.
93. William J. Novak, *The People's Welfare: Law and Regulation in Nineteenth-Century America* 9 (2000).
94. Gestle, *Liberty and Coercion*, at 36.
95. Jud Campbell writes: "[A]ssessing the public good – generally understood as the welfare of the entire society – was almost entirely a legislative task, leaving very little room for judicial involvement." Campbell, "Natural Rights and the First Amendment," at 253. He writes this as a general summary of the view of the framers of the proper role of government. And indeed this view is broadly congruent with the highly deferential approach to the government's assessment of public welfare in its police power functions. However, it still does not paint an adequate picture of how they thought about the relationship between rights and judicial intervention.
96. Gestle, *Liberty and Coercion*, at 37.
97. See Sutton, *Imperfect Solutions*, at 13 ("The first use of the power [of judicial review] occurred in the state courts and arose under the state constitutions"). See generally Saikrishna B. Prakash & John C. Yoo, "The Origins of Judicial Review," 70 *U. Chi. L. Rev.* 887 (2003).
98. 5 U.S. 137 (1803).

99. 3 U.S. 386 (1798).
100. Ibid., at 388.
101. See Sutton, *Who Decides?* at 30.
102. 32 U.S. 243 (1833).
103. See Jack N. Rakove, "The Origins of Judicial Review: A Plea for New Contexts," 49 *Stan. L. Rev.* 1031, 1034–35 (1997).
104. Sutton, *Who Decides?* at 39. See ibid., at 52 ("Once people accept the idea of a hierarchy of laws, it's a small but consequential step to accept that constitutions amount to superior laws").
105. https://bit.ly/3UFUMwy.
106. See generally Barnett, *Restoring the Lost Constitution.*
107. Common Sense [Thomas Paine], Candid and Critical Remarks on Letter 1, Signed Ludlow, Pa. J. & Wkly. Advertiser, June 4, 1777, at 1; see also Thomas Rutherford, *Institutes of Natural Law* 36 (Cambridge, J. Bentham 1754) ("Another division of our rights is into natural and adventitious. Those are called natural rights, which belong to a man ... originally, without the intervention of any human act.").
108. U.S. Const. Ninth Amendment.
109. Anthony Sanders, *Baby Ninth Amendments* (2023).
110. See, e.g., Steven G. Calabresi & Sofia M. Vickery, "On Liberty and the Fourteenth Amendment: The Original Understanding of the Lockean Natural Rights Guarantees," 93 *Tex. L. Rev.* 1299 (2015); Michael W. McConnell, "Natural Rights and the Ninth Amendment: How Does Lockean Legal Theory Assist in Interpretation?" 5 *N.Y. U. L. & Liberty* 1 (2010).
111. See Barnett & Bernick, *Original Meaning.*
112. No. 53C06-2208-PL-1756.
113. Dobbs v. Jackson Women's Health Organization, 597 U.S. 215 (2021).
114. MLB of Indiana, at p. 17.
115. Ibid., at 19–22.
116. The court stresses the following: "Roughly forty state constitutions now contain Lockean Natural Rights Guarantees, and courts in most of those states have concluded the clauses are judicially enforceable." Joseph R. Grodin, Rediscovering the State Constitutional Right to Happiness and Safety, 25 *Hastings Const. L. Q.* 1, 1, 22 (1997). Several state supreme courts have recently analyzed their analogous provisions in addressing claims like the one before us today, and they all concluded those provisions are judicially enforceable. Okla. Call for Reprod. Just., 526 P.3d 1123, 1130 (Okla. 2023); Wrigley v. Romanick, 988 N.W.2d 231, 240 (N.D. 2023); Planned Parenthood Great Nw. v. State, 522 P.3d 1132, 1167–95 (Idaho 2023); Hodes & Nauser, MDs, P.A. v. Schmidt, 440 P.3d 461, 471 (Kan. 2019). We reach the same conclusion based on our review of Section's 1 text, "illuminated by history and by the purpose and structure of our constitution and the case law surrounding it." Price, 622 N.E.2d at 957. MLB of Indiana, at 17.
117. Ibid.
118. Ibid.
119. See Banner, *Natural Law.*
120. MLB of Indiana, at 19.
121. See Warren & Brandeis, "The Right to Privacy, *Harv. L. Rev.* See also Erwin N. Griswold, "The Right to be Let Alone," 53 *Northw. L. Rev.* 216 (1960–61).
122. On ordered liberty, see Palko v. Connecticut, 302 U.S. 319 (1937).
123. See generally Joshua Foa Dienstag, "Between History and Nature: Social Contract Theory in Locke and the Founders," 58 *J. Pol.* 985 (1996).

124. See MLB of Indiana, at 26.
125. See generally Emily Zackin, *Looking for Rights in All the Wrong Places: Why State Constitutions Contain America's Positive Rights* 11 (2013); Helen Hershoff, "Just Words: Common Law and the Enforcement of State Constitutional Social and Economic Rights," 62 *Stan. L. Rev.* 1521 (2010); Helen Hershoff, "Positive Rights and State Constitutions: The Limits of Federal Rationality Review," 112 *Harv. L. Rev.* 1131 (1999).
126. Although not focusing on positive rights specifically, William Novak connects the evolution of the police power in the late nineteenth and twentieth century to the critique of classical liberalism and the emergence of "a new conception of positive liberty – a conception that intersected with simultaneous calls for a more positive law and more positive state." William J. Novak, *New Democracy: The Creation of the Modern American State* 79 (2022). The shift to a more positive liberty conception, a prominent theme in Progressive era ideology had limited impact on American constitutional in this era on the whole, although, as Novak, Scheiber, and others observe, there was a growing recognition of the idea that private property is imprinted with a public purpose.
127. See Zackin, *Looking for Rights*.
128. See Hershoff, "State Constitutions."
129. See generally Sutton, *Who Decides?* at 22–41. See also Goodwin Liu, "Interstate Inequality in Educational Opportunity," 81 *NYU L. Rev.* 2044 (2006); Molly McUsic, "The Use of Education Clauses in School Finance Reform," 28 *Harv. J. on Legis.* 307 (1991).
130. In addition to the sources cited in n. 141, see Goodwin Liu, "Education, Equality, and National Citizenship," 116 *Yale L. J.* 350 (2006).
131. See, e.g., Elizabeth Weeks Leonard, "State Constitutionalism and the Right to Health Care," 12 *U. Penn. J. Con. Law* 1325 (2010).
132. See, e.g., Kathryn E. Wilhelm, "Freedom of Movement at a Standstill? Toward the Establishment of a Fundamental Right to Intrastate Travel," 90 *B. U. L. Rev.* 2461 (2010).
133. Zackin, *Looking for Rights*, at 190.
134. Jud Campbell, "The Emergence of Neutrality," 131 *Yale L. J.* 861 (2022).
135. Ibid., at 945–46.

7

Turning Inside Out

Resolving Conflicts over the Scope of the Police Power

> There is no position which depends on clearer principles, than that every act of a delegated authority, contrary to the tenor of the commission under which it is exercised, is void. No legislative act, therefore, contrary to the Constitution, can be valid.
>
> Federalist No. 78 (A. Hamilton)

In 2020, a group of women in Georgia, organized under the name Reaching our Sisters Everywhere ("ROSE") filed a complaint against the Secretary of State, challenging the constitutionality of the Georgia Lactation Consultant Practice Act. This Act limited strictly the provision of lactation services to providers who had had obtained an appropriate license. These licenses were available only to those who were members of the International Board of Certified Lactation Consultants. This regulation, ROSE argued, prohibited them from providing their services to needy women. They argued that the statute was irrational, lacking in any reasonableness connection to public health, safety, and welfare.

This case came to the Georgia Supreme Court beginning in 2020, and was finally decided in 2023. If it were considered under the rubric of Supreme Court of the US precedent, it would surely have failed. Alleging a due process or equal protection claim that this exercise of the police power was unjustified by any plausible public health rationale would have failed under a web of decisions, arguably going back to Munn and Mugler in the nineteenth century, running up through Nebbia v. New York,[1] an important New Deal era case that illustrates the Court's retreat from Lochner era jurisprudence, and, most definitely, by the Supreme Court's decision in Williamson v. Lee Optical in 1955.[2] In that case, a unanimous Court upheld a regulation that limited, for reasons not at all apparent from the legislative record or statutory text, the provision of certain eyeglass services to registered optometrists and ophthalmologists. As in the Georgia case Raffensberger v. Jackson,[3] the plaintiffs in Lee Optical attacked this law as lacking any reasonable basis and as reflecting an arbitrary distinction among service providers. The Court, in an opinion by Justice Douglas, made relatively quick work with this argument, insisting that, even if the law was stupid, "it is for the legislature, not the courts, to balance the advantages and disadvantages of the new requirement."[4] While the statute is not immune from review in any formal sense, Justice Douglas made clear that the standard of review in these matters of economic regulation is highly deferential. He wrote: "[T]he law need not be in every respect logically consistent with its aims to be constitutional. It is enough that there is an evil at hand for correction, and that it might be thought that the particular legislative measure was a rational way to correct it."[5] Douglas makes a rather half-hearted effort to deal with the forceful argument that the statute was palpably ineffective at curing a problem that, in and of itself, elided description, and then concludes that "[t]he prohibition of the Equal Protection Clause goes no further than the invidious discrimination. We cannot say that that point has been reached here."[6]

Lee Optical illustrated the "apogee of deference," as historian Ted White describes it.[7] It was reinforced in later cases and, indeed, remains rock solid as a precedent. It is cited regularly by the Court in instances in which occupational licensing and other economic liberty litigation is brought in federal court. And where justices dissented in important substantive due process claims involving individual liberties and privacy, including Griswold, Roe, and Casey, Lee Optical is notable again as an illustration of why Lochner's reasoning fails and why the only question, says Justice Rehnquist in his Roe dissent, is whether the law being challenged bears "a rational relation to a valid state objective."[8]

The Georgia court in Raffensberger was unmoved by the thread of Supreme Court decisions since the Court retreated in the New Deal from its close interrogation of economic liberty-impacting regulations. Whereas these cases reflected a "nearly toothless deferential posture the Court has assumed where stated regulated business and industrial conditions,"[9] the supreme court of Georgia's approach was anything but. The language of the due process clause of the Georgia Constitution was essentially identical to that in the Fifth Amendment of the US Constitution. And yet Georgia has "'long recognized' that this provision 'entitled Georgians to pursue a lawful occupation of their choosing free from unreasonable government interference'."[10] This understanding of due process (and, the court noted in an important footnote, also equal protection under its constitution) has been unbroken from the beginning of its constitutional law, through constitutional reform, and up to the present day.

The question begged by this broad account of what due process and equal protection ensures by way of occupational freedom is what deference is owed to the judgment of the legislature that certain regulations are proper under the police power. The key statement of the Georgia court is this: "[U]nless an act restricting the ordinary occupations of life can be said to bear some reasonable relation to one or more of these general objects of the police power, it is repugnant to constitutional guarantees and void."[11] The discrimination that matters in occupational restrictions (and presumably any other regulation that draws line between individuals able to engage in certain business activities on certain conditions) is not necessarily "invidious discrimination along the lines of modern equal protection analysis."[12] Rather, the courts should be concerned with "the imposition of arbitrary (i.e., not reasonably necessary) burdens on the ability to pursue a lawful occupation."[13] Thus the court in one fell swoop distances itself from any conceivable kind of rational basis review, review which would eschew any consideration of the means-end fit or the evidentiary basis of this regulation and also makes clear that the state will need to provide some reasonable justification (which they equate here with non-arbitrary) for this particular regulatory strategy.[14]

In one sense, Raffensberger's approach hearkens back to Lochner. In another sense, the court conjures a standard of review that is internalist and purposive. It is internalist in that it looks to the rationale and method of regulation – what Hamilton calls the inquiry into the "commission under which it is exercised" – to determine its constitutionality. It is purposive in its further inquiry into whether the statute's means are tied adequately to its ends. Unlike in Lochner, the court in Raffensberger does not dwell excessively on the applicable liberty interest. Presumably the only liberty interest at stake here is the right to pursue an occupation or else the right to furnish services to individuals in need. These feel like manufactured liberty interests, even if we subscribe to some decent amount of freedom of action. Instead, the question at the center is whether this law makes the regulation makes any good sense, in light of the government's stated aim of promoting public health and safety. The court concludes that there is insufficient evidence that this law is "reasonably necessary to advance a specific health, safety, or welfare concern."[15]

*

This detailed consideration of a recent state case illustrates the issues we explore in more depth in this chapter, drawing upon some of the more historical dimensions of constitutional review in Part I and the more conceptual and doctrinal discussion in the previous chapter on the role of rights review in police power cases. Rights claims will continue to loom large, in both the federal and state context, in disputes over the government's police power regulations. Yet, as we discussed in the previous chapter, this will mostly be true of rights claims brought under those enumerated rights that have long enjoyed a preferred position. Relatedly, the protections will be most salient for individuals who are part of a suspect class, therefore raising the antennae of courts worried about equality under the law. By contrast, judicial review of regulations that impact individuals' property and liberty rights, and that are not focused on whether adequate procedures have been given under the Due Process clause or whether the actions are a regulatory taking, have been minimal, at least since the retreat from economic liberties review in the period of Lochner and, albeit unsteadily, in the first half of the century

What are the limits that grow out of the police power itself, that is, separate from constitutional rights as trumps? Constitutional law is not unfamiliar with internal constraints. For example, the question of whether Congress can exercise certain powers under the rubric of the Commerce Clause is an interrogation into the meaning of this power-granting provision. The puzzle is even more puzzling, to be sure, in the state constitutional context, because here we embrace the principle that state constitutions are documents of limit and so the legislature is viewed as having plenary power. However, this power must be defined, and its outer boundaries established. Plenary power is not the power to act without any constraints. The focus in this chapter is on the configuration of these constraints growing out of the police power itself. To put the point in a homely way: Rights are part of the perspective of we the people looking for outside limits on government; structure looks from an internal vantage point outward.

REASONABLENESS

A plethora of police power cases stretching back to the early nineteenth century and continuing through Raffensberger and other cases involving governmental regulations of various shapes and sizes under the police power use the term "reasonableness," standing alone under the spotlight or connected to other words nearby, to describe what is necessary to uphold a state law under the constitution. However we might critique "reasonableness" as a criteria too opaque for meaningful judicial review, the prominence of reasonableness in constitutional review is understandable. Under a vastly diverse range of theoretical views about the proper role of government and scope of government action, some deeply philosophical, others more pragmatic, we nearly always come back to the question: Has the government acted in a way that we regard as reasonable?[16]

That said, resort to the generic and ultimately inscrutable notion of reasonableness standing alone is ultimately a fool's errand. There is little content to this standard other than that imputed by other considerations and elements, as we will investigate more fully below.[17] Viewed practically, reasonableness might be little more than a residual category, something that captures in an omnibus rhetorical way the notion that laws ought not be stupid; they ought to be based upon a sensible and even sufficiently rigorous analysis of the problem to be solved and the ways in which this law will tackle this problem. Unreasonableness in this account is little more than a trope, invoked as a synonym for a bad law. That this is a problematic basis for judicial intervention under our constitutions is revealed in a vast body of constitutional scholarship, perhaps most cogently by James Bradley Thayer in his exhortation that courts review legislative acts for only clear error. Thayer writes: "[T]he constitution often admits of different interpretations; that there is often a range of choice and judgment; that in such cases the constitution does not impose upon the legislature any one specific opinion, but leaves open this range of choice; and that whatever choice is rational is constitutional."[18] But even judges willing to intervene in proper cases to either narrow the scope of ill-configured legislation or, in extreme instances, to invalidate these laws as exceeding the bounds of what the government ought to able to do under its police powers have found the residuum of unreasonableness to be part of a robust test.

But there is a deeper concern than just with opacity and fear of over- or underinclusive review. Reasonableness as an account decoupled from other, sharper standards of sorting out proper from improper legislative action can easily slide into a judicial assessment of the merits of a particular law. Investigating the rationale of a law and the connection between its ends and means – akin to what the Court has long used in strict scrutiny review of legislation in fundamental rights cases – inevitably substitutes legislative for judicial judgment. This is a feature, not a bug, of such review. Gerald Gunther's fabled comment that strict scrutiny is strict in theory but fatal in fact is best understood as revealing not only the consequence of such interventionist review, but the purpose behind such scrutiny.[19] And this purpose could and should be implemented by an informed cynicism of the reason for the law ("Is the state interest compelling?" "Is this the least restrictive means?"), the strategy ("Is this law narrowly tailored"), and a consideration of alternatives. The thumb, in such strict scrutiny review, is squarely on the scale in favor of protecting individual rights against governmental overreach. By contrast, the police power has long accepted a wide ambit of governmental power and also an acceptance that the government knows best how to effectively govern. Intervening to determine whether the government's approach is or is not reasonable risks collapsing what is essentially strict scrutiny review into a shapeless, but ambiently utilitarian, approach to reviewing the form and strategy of legislation.

This is not to say that judges have not proffered approaches to judicial review that aim to assist in the inquiry as to whether the government has exercised its wide regulatory discretion to impede upon individuals' liberty. Even where this liberty cannot be sourced in any particular state or federal constitutional provision, the Court has undertaken, albeit in a somewhat piecemeal fashion, the task of interrogating laws that interfere with privacy and intimate relations. For example, in his famous dissent in Poe v. Ullman, Justice Harlan looks skeptically at the anti-contraception law enacted by the state legislature, insisting that "[t]hough the State has argued the constitutional permissibility of the moral judgment underlying this statute, neither its brief, nor its argument, nor anything in any of the opinions of its highest court in these or other cases even remotely suggests a justification for the obnoxiously intrusive means it has chosen to effectuate that policy."[20] Moreover, it is the "utter novelty" of this law that warrants his skepticism and ultimately, he argues, dooms this law as in excess of the police power and in violation of the substantive due process rights of liberty.[21]

Although not embracing the substantive due process formulation, Justice David Souter's concurring opinion in the 1997 assisted-suicide case Washington v. Glucksburg[22] also illustrates one approach to evaluating legislative reasonableness.

He says there that "[i]t is only when the legislation's justifying principle, critically valued, is so far from being commensurate with the individual interest as to be arbitrarily or pointlessly applied that the statute must give way."[23] Stripped to its essence, this flips the script on the traditional deference accorded to legislation except when it interferes with fundamental rights. It asks, instead, is this legislation arbitrary? Pointless? The burden is on the legislature to justify its policy, not only the rights-holder to show how a policy about which the court stands agnostic is in conflict with their liberty (or other substantive) rights.

Harlan in Poe and Souter in Glucksburg attract inordinate attention by scholars who would urge on courts a more searching review, more latitude to call out truly dumb laws for opprobrium and possible invalidation. Nonetheless, the spotlight on these and similar opinions is at least interesting for a focus on a road not travelled. Certainly there has not been any meaningful review of economic regulations under federal constitutional law in many decades. And the treatment of preferred constitutional rights, as we discussed in the previous chapter, has long followed the architecture of tiered review. And so we can ultimately be less alarmist (if we fear more muscular scrutiny) or less hopeful (if we welcome it) about the courts embrace of so-called reasonableness review, the kind of review illustrated by the Georgia case that began this chapter. For in the lion's share of the cases, including contemporary ones, what the courts look to is not an open-ended consideration of statutory reasonableness, but other factors that raise doubts about whether the police power was truly being used for good governing, for furthering objectives central to state constitutional purpose.

ARBITRARINESS

In Raffenberger, the Georgia high court used "reasonably necessary" as a syllogism for "arbitrary." The main apparent concern here was that the state enacted a law that drew a line between acceptable and unacceptable conduct – or, more precisely here, acceptable versus unacceptable providers of services – that could not be justified as anything other than arbitrary. For example, if the principal concern here was with competency and public safety, they might have established comprehensive quality control guidelines, perhaps with a test. Putative plaintiffs might still quarrel with the heavy-handedness of such quality control. They might challenge the law alleging that such laws were too strict in design, effectively keeping well-intentioned folks locked out of providing important services. But notice that this is a different kind of objection, in that it does not claim that the legislature is acting arbitrarily, but just that it is acting unreasonably, if based upon some assessment of whether such (to them) severe limitations are justified. After all, if the court must interrogate each standard-setting regulation, they are interfering deeply with the legislature's policymaking discretion. However, the court does concern itself with claims that the drawing of lines through police power regulations is utterly senseless, and therefore arbitrary.

Turning Inside Out: Resolving Police Power Conflicts 243

The law's concern with arbitrariness is ubiquitous. Even a minimal examination of the basis of a state law might require the lawmakers to explain why they drew lines that included some and excluded others from the law's reach, whether by way of protection or of prohibition. This explanation might come in the form of a "whereas" clause, as are typical in both old and modern legislative acts; it might come in the form of legislative history; or it might require some judicial creativity in assessing legislative purpose. Interrogating legislation to determine whether or not it is arbitrary has been a common, if somewhat episodic, element of constitutional review in both federal and state courts for generations. For example, the <u>Cleburne Living Center</u> case,[24] which we described briefly in a previous chapter, is a relatively contemporary instance of the Court invalidating a law that did not, as it viewed it, infringe on fundamental rights or impact a suspect (or even a quasi-suspect) class. Rather, it was the sheer arbitrariness of the law's impact that warranted invalidation. "[T]his record does not clarify how," wrote Justice White for the Court, "the characteristics of the intended occupants of the Featherston home rationally justify denying to those occupants what would be permitted to groups occupying the same site for different purposes."[25] This arbitrariness gave rise to an uncontested belief that the permit requirement in Cleburne rests only "on an irrational prejudice against the mentally retarded, including those who would occupy the Featherston facility and who would live under the closely supervised and highly regulated conditions expressly provided for by state and federal law."[26]

Arbitrariness as a rubric for review can be sensibly deployed in a range of cases. However, it carries with it some risks of uncertainty. When used in the administrative law context, for example, the basic thrust of arbitrariness review is procedural, that is, it smokes out real reasons for the government acting, reasons that can be evaluated on the basis of a record of some sort to make sure that there are, at the very least, not capricious, nor are they rationally indefensible when measured by what the statute does or does not require.

This approach has been described in modern federal administrative law as "hard look review."[27] Efforts to go beyond proceduralist review, to something more searching in the sense that it assesses the overall merits of the agency's decision is not unprecedented. Colin Diver long ago called this strategy "synoptic review,"[28] and Martin Shapiro has commented informatively on the tendency of the federal courts in the latter decades of the twentieth century to look at the overall reasonableness of agency performance, this at the risk of substituting the courts' judgment for the judgment of Congress.[29] Still, this approach has been heavily criticized as beyond the scope of what courts should do in reviewing agency action.[30] In any event, it is important to understand that administrative law review is not free-floating; its standards are forged through the deep analysis of the agency's enabling law. Review that is trans-statutory (itself an awkward locution given the nature of administrative governance) is mainly directed to ensuring that the agency is providing reasons adequate to warrant the use of the awesome power of the government, use outside the four corners of the structure of Articles I–III of the Constitution.[31]

Bringing the subject back to constitutional review of police power regulations, we see the same essential logic at work here. Even without the principle of legislative supremacy, we can expect that the legislature has a wide lane of discretion to choose its preferred regulatory ends and means. With it, the tilt is toward a more limited judicial role in assessing the legislature's regulatory choices. Constitutional review must necessarily assess what is or is not merely arbitrary by resort to what obligations the constitution imposes on legislative or administrative action. And so we are back squarely to the question of how much demand the text, structure, and (especially) purpose of the police power imposes on the government to act rationally and non-arbitrarily.

Arbitrariness review absorbs the assumption that random decisions by government are intrinsically unacceptable. But this view may not be so clear in all cases. Suppose that the government enacts a law that forgives student loan debt up to an amount of $25,000 per person, regardless of the amount of individual debt. This is a policy intended to address hardship, but of course it does so only in a partial way. Some former students carry $250,000 worth of debt, and so this relief is relatively modest. Some carry $25,000, but have sufficient wealth that the burden was consequential. And all this is not to mention, as we hear today in arguments over student loan forgiveness, that the line is drawn between individuals with student debt and others who did not take out student loans, for whatever reason, but still face crushing debt. Suffice it to say that there are many dimensions upon which such a law makes arbitrary distinctions. This does not necessarily mean that the law is stupid or that partial help is unwarranted, but that there is not a rationale that can meet any strict standard of assessing "why x but not y?" Police power regulations of this type are common; indeed, they are especially common in a world in which states can enact laws for what we have called *salus populi* reasons, and not merely as a matter of *sic utere*. The general welfare has not been understood to mean that individuals are equal beneficiaries of equal sufferers from legislative or administrative acts.

Arbitrariness review is a conventional part of our constitutional review toolkit, especially so far as state constitutional review of police power regulations are concerned. But it carries its pitfalls. It can be overinclusive, as where legislatures drawn lines for what are entirely pragmatic reasons. It can also be underinclusive in that laws that are neither arbitrary nor targeted on particular individuals or groups for discernible reasons might raise constitutional concerns not addressable by "arbitrariness" review. Nonetheless, courts have persisted in their inquiries into the arbitrariness of legislative action under the police power.

ANIMUS

Concern with laws that draw lines in ways that reveal "invidious discrimination" or what the Court in United States Dep't of Agriculture v. Moreno memorably called "a bare ... desire to harm a politically unpopular group,"[32] has been longstanding.

We can see as far back as Yick Wo the Court's concern with baseless discrimination and animus in legislation.[33] Justice Harlan's famous dissent in Plessy,[34] which we discussed in Chapter 3, illustrates well the dismay with laws that convey to those denied protection or facing burdens a badge of inferiority. What the past few decades have revealed is a greater skepticism of legislative action that reveals animus in just this way described.

Even so, animus has seldom been used in an ungrounded way, but rather has been packaged usually with strict scrutiny of laws that impose burdens on members of protected classes under classic equal protection doctrine.[35] Evidence of animus is used to support a claim of invidious discrimination, not to define what is in fact invidious. In more modern parlance, animus is what fuels efforts to subordinate members of disfavored groups, to enact laws and regulations that segregate, sort, and ultimately humiliate individuals on the basis of what are typically immutable characteristics that are anathema to those in power.[36] The law sensibly (even if inadequately) imposes constitutional barriers, flowing from both the US Constitution and state constitutions, to such acts of subordination.[37]

A more recent phenomenon, still emerging and so understandably more difficult to frame as a distinct element of modern constitutional law, is the resort to animus as the main basis for invalidation of legislation under either the equal protection, due process clauses, or both. We have already discussed two of the exemplar cases of this modern development, Romer v. Evans and Lawrence v. Texas. Another example of this use of animus in this way is the Court's 2018 decision in Masterpiece Cakeshop v. Colorado.[38] In that case, the Court considered a constitutional challenge under the Free Exercise clause to a decision of the Colorado Civil Rights Commission objecting to the bakery owners refusal to make a cake for a same-sex wedding couple. Accepting that the Commission may have been acting consistent with Colorado's anti-discrimination laws, but scrupulously avoiding taking the step of invalidating those laws as violative of the First Amendment, Justice Kennedy rests his opinion for the Court ruling in favor of the bakery on his view that Commission acted with unacceptable animus in their evaluation of their claim. "The Civil Rights Commission's treatment of his case," Kennedy writes, "has some elements of a clear and impermissible hostility toward the sincere religious beliefs that motivated his objection."[39] It is hard to excavate from Justice Kennedy's opinion a clear through line from earlier cases such as Romer and Lawrence, and so the exact role played by animus in this inquiry into unacceptable discrimination under the First Amendment remains somewhat inscrutable. In any event, Masterpiece Cakeshop must be understood in the special context of the Court's religious liberty jurisprudence and the focus on government neutrality in matters religious, this a *sine qua non* for the evaluation of constitutional claims under this clause of the First Amendment.[40] However, the broader point – that government decisions evincing animus raise red flags – is illustrated in this recent opinion, here by the author of Romer and Lawrence.

Sticking for now with the development of animus as a strong constitutional principle in Supreme Court jurisprudence, it is important to highlight three cautionary notes: First, the conundrum of assessing legislative purpose and motivation does not evaporate even as courts focus studied attention on the reasons for discriminatory laws. In evaluating skeptically the Court's rationale for invalidating the Colorado civil rights commission's decision in Masterpiece Cake Shop, Leslie Kendrick and Micah Schwartzman summarize the cluster of familiar and deeply-theorized arguments against the judicial assessment of motivation and intent in legislative (and, as here, administrative) decision-making.[41] These arguments range from the ontological claim that intent does not exist in ways that are tractable for judicial decision-making and, further, even if it did, we could not draw conclusions from the aggregated intent of multiple decision-makers, to the epistemic objection that "[c]ourts may not be able to know with any reliability what reasons motivated a particular action or decision."[42] Perhaps most vexing, for the purposes of assessing whether animus can do the work of separating and sorting constitutional illegitimate from legitimate bases, is the objection that a law can be justifiable under the conventional standards of constitutional evaluation, even if ill-motivated. As Kendrick and Schwartzman note, "[w]hether an action is permissible, or allowed, turns on whether that action is justified, not on whether the officials who carried it out believed it was justified … [W]hat matters is whether there are sufficient reasons for an action and not whether officials were motivated by those reasons."[43]

Second, these arguments against animus-based reasoning have been articulated by justices in other opinions. In his dissents in Romer and Lawrence, Justice Scalia exclaimed that unacceptable animus is extremely difficult to define, despite our intuition that it permeates certain legislative decisions. In Romer in particular, Scalia explains that one of the difficulties with relying on animus as a basis of constitutionally relevant opprobrium is that it does not acknowledge that there are kinds of animus that we permit legislatures to express, and that we indeed want them to do so. Scalia mentions the example of polygamy and shows unequivocally that Congress's animus, undoubtedly reflecting public opinion of then and now, was directed at the state of Utah, which had refused to outlaw polygamy in the state. As a result, Utah's application for admission to the union was long postponed until they were willing to formally renounce plural marriage. Animus toward individuals whose conduct has disqualified them from government benefits is common, whether we are considering felon disenfranchisement, sexual predator registries, or other such laws. How do we distinguish between acceptable and unacceptable animus in assessing laws? This inquiry, of course, parallels the difficulties we have already considered in connection with the evolution of morals regulation under the police power.

From a big picture perspective, animus can be seen as motivating most of the kinds of morals legislation we discussed in Chapter 7. We criminalize, for example, gambling and prostitution principally because of the animus we hold against these activities. More precisely, we have animus toward individuals who engage in these activities. While we might climb off that moralizing precipice saying (silently) something like "love the sinner, but hate the sin," the essential point remains: It is our antipathy toward certain activities that motivates our decision to proscribe one act while permitting another.

More recently, the Court has expressed some unease about the use of animus as a criterion for constitutional review. In the case of Trump v. Hawaii,[44] for example, the Court heard the objection that the ban on immigration of individuals from certain Muslim majority countries was the product of the Trump administration's antipathy toward these groups, rather than a legitimate concern with national security. Over Justice Sotomayor's impassioned dissent in which she argued that this evidence of animus ought to be relevant to the Court's analysis of the constitutional claim,[45] the Court declined to consider evidence of animus and prejudice in evaluating the legality of a ban on immigration of individuals from certain Muslim countries. "[T]he issue before us," writes Chief Justice Roberts for the Court, "is not whether to denounce the statements. It is instead the significance of those statements in reviewing a Presidential directive, neutral on its face, addressing a matter within the core of executive responsibility."[46]

Despite some of these criticisms, animus can furnish a critical part of the inquiry of government strategy under the police power. Returning to the overarching objective that motivates this book's normative argument, commitment to good governing under the state constitution surely requires that the government treat individuals in its charge fairly and without prejudice. Animus directed at a group based upon any characteristics, but certainly those characteristics that are immutable and not the product of behavior or conduct that we have a vested interest in restricting in order to reduce public harm, should never be a reason for imposing a regulation or denying a public benefit. In reality, however, we know that animus is ubiquitous. Indeed, it may well be on the rise in our polarized politics. We further know that personal animus can and does aggregate itself into a collective force that influences politics and generates legislation. And it may behoove federal and state courts on whose shoulders the responsibility rests to resolve conflicts over the scope of the police power to investigate laws for evidence of animus in both their origins and their implementation. Even if animus does not ultimately furnish the essential basis for invaliding the law, it can illuminate the legislature's purpose and objective, potentially relevant considerations in both constitutional and statutory interpretation contexts.

To make this discussion somewhat less abstract, it is important to see the troubling rise in efforts at the state and occasionally local levels to translate animus toward disfavored groups into state laws. We can think here especially of the plethora of anti-LGBTQ+ and, more particularly, anti-trans bills that have emerged at the state level.[47] These bills may or may not raise issues under the US Constitution. Despite watershed decisions such as Romer, Lawrence, Obergefell v. Hodges,[48] United States v. Windsor,[49] and Bostock v. Clayton County,[50] the jury is still out on the lengths to which the current Court is likely to go to protect LGBTQ+ rights against interference. Now and in the next several years, it is likely that the main battleground for the fight over such rights will be in state courts adjudicating state constitutional claims.[51] In these fights, the consideration of animus may well become important. More than in the past, courts should be prepared to look at the expressions in public of legislators and executive officials to put some contextual reality into legislative acts and regulations that can often by styled as neutral and acts of equality rather than revelations of base discrimination and prejudice. To be sure, advancing evidence of animus does not mean that these cases will decide themselves. Looking fairly at the other side of the coin, advocates of various anti-trans bills have simultaneously revealed ignorance and an absence of empathy while at the same time advancing arguments that what they are really concerned about is the welfare of families, of enabling families to make choices without the interference of outside actors (such as health professionals) and guarding against decisions by minors that can have permanent consequences. These are difficult issues, bound up seemingly inextricably with the modern culture wars, and, like other such difficult issues, they are likely to end up before judges in litigation. But the narrow but important part here is that a full evaluation of the legality of these controversial actions under the modern police power, a power that has long given wide deference to public authorities acting in the name of public health, safety, and morals, should consider the ways in which prejudice and animus have factored into choices about how best to advance the public welfare and how to assess the rights of free individuals to pursue their own choices, especially in the most profoundly intimate matters.[52]

SELF-DEALING

A foundational principle undergirding the police power is that the legislature, through the use of its awesome plenary power, will act responsibly to further the public interest. This principle goes back to the origins of state constitutions, persists through early court decisions involving the power, and has also been hard-wired in state constitutions through such devices as the public purpose requirement and the prohibition against special legislation. In light of this principle, courts are occasionally receptive to claims that the legislature is acting for private-regarding, rather than public-regarding reasons. Under this logic, where there is critical evidence that regulatory initiatives reveal what Cass Sunstein famously called "naked preferences,"[53] actions taken under the police power should be struck down. The fundamental idea is that there is a baseline of proper governmental action under the relevant constitutional commands, a baseline that emphasizes that whatever the legislative output, the consideration of policy should be carried out with public-regarding aims in minds, not their own self-interest.

The notion of a self-dealing legislature is a complicated one, however.[54] Legislators are appropriately response to constituent demands, as part of their democratic commitments. These demands are manifest in unequal ways, and this has always been the case. The structure of the legislative process reveals many elements, both features and bugs, that will push legislation in directions that meet the needs and wants of interest groups. Clinging to a positive view of the legislature as eliding these elements and always putting the public interest first is naïve. Similarly unrealistic is a rigid normative commitment to a faction-free legislature. Therefore, courts will always be faced with the difficult challenge of sorting between laws that are adequately public-regarding – good enough for government work, we might say – and those that reveal considerations that are so tangibly private-regarding that the requirements embedded in the police power are not met.[55]

Courts have faced this ubiquitous challenge in the US constitutional law context. Lacking an explicit public purpose requirement or special legislation prohibition, courts have looked episodically at the propriety of legislation under the doctrines of equal protection and due process. Cases are infrequent in which the Supreme Court has invalidated a piece of legislation on the grounds that a plausible public purpose is lacking. That said, there are cases, even some landmark ones, where the gravamen of the problem is that the legislature, Congress or in the states, has configured processes that are rather manifestly private-regarding.

Perhaps the best examples are found in the Court's election law jurisprudence. In these areas, thinking of the Court's reapportionment jurisprudence beginning with Baker v. Carr [56] and also race-relevant cases such as Gomillion v. Lightfoot,[57] the Court has acted where the justices have been skeptical of the underlying reasons for certain electoral structures. In Gomillion, even a pillar of judicial restraint as was Justice Frankfurter notes that this "was not an ordinary geographic redistricting measure, even within familiar abuses of gerrymandering."[58] "If these allegations, upon a trial, remained uncontradicted or unqualified, the conclusion would be irresistible, tantamount for all practical purposes to a mathematical demonstration, that the legislation is solely concerned with segregating white and colored voters by fencing Negro citizens out of town so as to deprive them of their pre-existing municipal vote."[59] Calls for intervention have been persistent in the scholarly literature for many years. Richard Pildes and Sam Issacharoff have written about the risks of partisan lockups in the political process and the prospect of fruitful judicial intervention;[60] other scholars have looked at various legislative and electoral rules and have opined that there are available doctrinal structures to temper these power instantiating policies.[61] Indeed, one of our most important normative paradigms in all of constitutional law – John Hart Ely's democracy-reinforcing theory of judicial review[62] – is concerned at an elemental level with self-dealing (among other tangible political process problems).

In the state constitutional law context, we have available not only the same supply of doctrinal hooks to attach skepticism about legislative self-dealing, both from federal constitutional rules including due process and equal protection, but also state constitutional rules, which are least as capacious in design and function for these purposes. Moreover, we have the logic of the police power itself. In other words, state courts can look at the police power under their own constitutions and, consistent with decades of precedent that have adverted to "reasonableness" as a basis of serious scrutiny, interrogate state laws to determine whether they reveal nakedly private interest and therefore do not honestly attend to the public's interest in health, safety, morals, or furthering of the general welfare. Such scrutiny, to be sure, may to eradicate the mechanisms of self-interest that underlie the legislature's behavior. Concerns have been raised, especially by scholars working within the traditions of public choice theory, that legislatures are essentially transmission belts for interest group influences.[63] Nonetheless, judicial review, insofar as courts pay attention to the avowed public purpose of the legislation, can at the very least raise the costs to the legislature in making and implementing policy that smacks of self-dealing.[64]

INTERPRETIVE CANONS, PRESUMPTIONS, AND OTHER SHORTCUTS

Our history of judicial review in the American context reveals myriad uses of interpretive canons to assist courts with resolving what might otherwise be difficult disputes. (We will leave here to one side the true meaning of "difficult," noting just that this may be difficult in the interpretive or political sense.) The canon of constitutional avoidance is a classic example of such a principle used to avoid deciding on constitutional grounds where other bases are available.[65] In addition, the various clear statement rules emerge to put the onus on the legislature to express their intentions to accomplish an objective that might otherwise be legally suspect. Taken together, these canons and presumptions are "shortcuts" in the sense that they enable courts to reach results without the strong arm of constitutional invalidation.

We can see these mechanisms functioning in the context of the police power. For example, state courts have looked closely at whether and to what extent the state legislature has authorized other governmental entities, be they general-purpose municipal governments, special-purpose agencies, or ordinary administrative agencies to exercise police powers. In doing so, courts have relied on some of the familiar (at least to them) interpretive canons, for example, Dillon's rule, named after the author of the famous treatise noted earlier, in order to settle the question of what the legislature has or has not done. Even more important as an example of this practice has been the presumption described in many state judicial opinions of the nineteenth century in favor of securing liberty and private property. In Forbes' Case,[66] a New York case from 1860, the court considered whether a certain criminal vagrancy statute should be upheld under the police power, noting that such statutes "are constitutional, but should be construed strictly, and executed carefully in favor of the liberty of the citizen."[67] In a Massachusetts case from 1846, Commonwealth v. Tewksbury,[68] the court upheld a law forbidding the taking away of sand and gravel from the owner's own beach, on public safety grounds, but observed that the police power is "a high power, to be exercised with the strictest circumspection, and with the utmost sacred regard to the right of private property and only in cases amounting to an obvious public exigency."[69] These observations need not be read as equivocations by courts on the fundamental question of whether the power enables the government to act, but they do function as guides of a certain sort to legislatures in enacting such statutes and to later courts in construing the scope of the power in close cases.

Another venue in which interpretative guidance is potentially promising is in the determination of the statute's purpose. Is the government using the police power to actually facilitate public health, safety, and general welfare? In the preceding subparts of this chapter, we have looked at this question from the standpoint of constitutional adjudication. But there is another way to come at this question, and that is to interrogate the statute's context, its objectives, and its mechanisms in an effort to reveal as best as possible the overall statutory purpose. In the heyday of the so-called Legal Process era (roughly from the 1950s through the early 1980s),[70] purposive statutory interpretation was viewed as an entirely proper, for some the most compelling, approach to discerning statutory meaning in difficult cases.[71] As Henry Hart and Albert Sacks expressed it, the court should look at the legislature as "a group of reasonable persons pursuing reasonable aims reasonably" and should do their best to look at statutory purpose in order to give a reading of the statute "that the words can bear."[72] While purposive statutory interpretation has lost much of its luster, as the modern courts have embraced textualism as the most credible theory of interpretation, its use in discerning the connection between the underlying objectives of the police power under a state constitutional tradition and the purposes of the statute can be especially helpful.

THE POLICE POWER AND ADMINISTRATIVE LAW

The discussion thus far has centered upon constitutional review of state or local legislative action. Interrogations about the "reasonableness" of legislation under the police power, unpacked as we have above, are intended to determine the ultimate question of whether this power has been exercised consistent with the state constitution. However, there is another body of law that will often be brought to bear in the consideration by courts of whether the power has been misused. This is state administrative law. It will provide the principles, rules, and standards for the courts to consider when evaluating the exercise of the power by institutions other than the state legislature, including local governments and state and local administrative agencies.[73]

Without going into depth about the components of state administrative law (which will differ from state to state in any event), we can make some general observations about the rule and function of administrative law in police power controversies. First, considerations of reasonableness are omnipresent in administrative law.[74] Courts at both the federal and state level have always looked at the reasoning process of agency officials to determine whether the agency decision passes muster. This phrase "substantive review" is often used in the administrative law context to distinguish the enterprise from "procedural review," the latter focusing on the question of whether the agency has complied with required procedures and the former capturing the general inquiry into whether the agency provided adequate reasons for the actions taken. Thus, whatever concerns we have about close interrogations by courts into the reasonableness of legislative action, some of which we surfaced and summarized in the first subsection of this chapter, we should regard reasonableness review as by and large business as usual in the administrative law context.

Second, we should ask: Are there guidelines in doing this review in the administrative law context that are especially well-suited to disputes involving the police power? One guideline, an important consideration in administrative law is that agencies should be required by courts to reveal transparently the evidentiary basis of their actions and, where evidence is introduced by others in the rulemaking or adjudicatory process, the agency should reveal why they rejected some evidence and considered others.[75] As part of its responsibility to undertake hard look review of administrative rulemaking, they should make sure they have reasoned well from premise to conclusion and they should to the extent possible base their decisions on the best available science, especially where the matters involve public health and safety, where there are truly facts and scientific elements to the decisions reached by the relevant agencies. The closer the agency's choices come to evidence-based considerations – which will be often, but not always, in the police power context – the more the agency's reasoning process should be tethered to the facts.

At the same time, the courts in undertaking their administrative law responsibilities should give agencies an appropriate space for discretion, this in order to acknowledge the important place and prominence of expertise in administrative decision-making. We discussed expertise as an important element in the evolution of the police power generally (Chapters 2 and 3) and in the steady acceptance of the legislature's decision to delegate to agencies police power functions in order to get the best advantage of expert decision-making (Chapter 5). Administrative law that defers in appropriate ways to the judgment of agencies is key to the overall functioning of a regime in which choices about health, safety, and even in some cases morality. The essential idea is that decisions are made by those who have expertise and can balance the demands of democracy with the imperative of good governing in ways that are as objective as possible and, where not possible, reflect reasonable disagreement.[76]

Another way to think about the role of administrative law as a partial substitute for more searching constitutional review of regulations under the police power. After all, one way to maintain a commitment to a light-touch judicial review while also interrogating the basis for the particular policy choice is to look at administrative regulations to ensure that they are well-reasoned, non-arbitrary, and procedurally fair, standards which are familiar parts of mainstream administrative law, whether in the state or federal governments. As we saw in our discussion of rights and judicial review in Chapter 6, such interventions maintain legislative power after all, since the focal point is on the agency, not the legislature. If we worry that vigorous constitutional review is a too-blunt tool for addressing goals of sound public policy and fair regulatory decision-making, administrative law, by contrast, can provide greater nuance and flexibility, with fewer costs to democracy.

In reconfiguring the focus from constitutional law to the administrative law, the issue moves away from the big issue of "Does the legislature have the power to do X or Y?" to "Has the agency/municipality acted properly in exercising power that we can accept without further interrogation that the legislature has delegated to the relevant administrator?" Administrative law provides the government with a softer landing. Second, courts have more flexibility in using administrative law doctrines in the ways that are typical in both federal and state contexts. So, for example, the court might find that the agency has, in enacting a public health regulation, acted in an arbitrary, and therefore illegal, way. This gives the agency an opportunity to revisit their regulatory choice and to do so without running a legislative enactment gauntlet. Or maybe the court orders that the regulation not apply to a particular individual or entity (perhaps for reasons having to do with arbitrariness or other bases) but leaves the regulation otherwise intact. Still yet, the court might impose certain procedural requirements, presumably sourced in administrative law doctrine or relevant statutory procedures, requirements which regulate how the agency can exercise their delegated police power, without fundamentally challenging the fact that they have this power. As one final example, consider a judicial decisions that holds that the agency has erroneously interpreted the statute and in a way that renders the agency's judgment ultra vires. This strategy, again, draws a distinction between the authority of the agency to act under the police power and the propriety of the way the agency acted. These (and other) doctrines are part of the classic toolkit of courts in administrative law. Insofar as they are geared fundamentally to ensuring that an agency has acted in ways consistent with sound and fair administration, there is built-in flexibility in how the court goes about its evaluation.

*

As explained in the introduction, this book endeavors to focus on the origins, the shape, and the functions of the police power. The question of how best to interpret the police power in matters of dispute is a part of this inquiry, although it is not the central point. The reasons for its relatively cabined place in an analysis that covers a wide amount of terrain both temporally and conceptually is two-fold: First, whether the government has exceeded its authority under the police power, either because it has violated someone's constitutional or (considering federal supremacy) statutory rights entails a close look at the particular legal architecture, including both text and doctrine. Not only are there many potential rights objections that stem from federal law, but there is the brute fact that we have fifty distinct states, with their own constitutions and bodies of law. So, anything more than a 10,000 feet look at interpretive issues here is unrealistic, especially in a book that doesn't aspire to be a treatise. Second, at the risk of sounding overly grandiose, the issues of interpretation, hopefully raised in a clear way in this and the preceding chapter, can be resolved best by a more coherent understanding of the overall purpose of the police power. Courts will decide concrete cases in accordance with their favored rules and techniques of interpretation. And law professors, including this one, will reserve the right to criticize or applaud these decisions for how well they fit with our own favored approaches. However, we are remiss if we do not properly situate this awesome and often misunderstood power in a framework, even an incomplete and evolving one, that helps answer the question, put colloquially: "What is the police power about anyway?"

That all said, this chapter concludes with some normative views about the basic parameters of the interpretive approach to the police power, taking account especially of the myriad state court cases in which state supreme courts have aimed to give shape and content to the overall structure and scope of this power.

TWO CHEERS FOR MODERATE SCRUTINY

The great police power treatise writers of the late nineteenth and early twentieth centuries, along with distinguished scholars who tackled the big question of what the police power means and how it should best be construed, were in general agreement on three big principles: First, the police power was broad in its scope and had been and should be read as accepting government regulation that advanced public health, safety, morals, and the overall welfare of the community (which is not to say, as we have already discussed, that everyone agreed on what this "welfare" entailed); second, this power should be scrutinized by courts with an appropriate appreciation for the prominent role and value of private property and individual liberty, crucial parts of the constitutional firmament in which the police power functioned; and, lastly, the disputes over the scope of the police power would be justiciable, in both the federal and state courts; moreover, so far as the state courts were concerned, having the responsibility to interpret their own constitutions, it would principally fall upon their shoulders to look at the government's exercise of this power to determine whether it was reasonable.

With the hindsight of more than a century, during which police power disputes continue to arise, the same basic principles animate the interpretation of the police power. We can characterize the courts' approaches, viewed holistically, as revealing a sort of moderate scrutiny. While no effort has been made to truly count all the police power cases decided in two centuries' time or any subset, a decently informed observer would notice that state and local governments prevail in the vast majority of cases where the exercise of the police power is contested; and when they lose, it is usually because the power runs up against a constitutional right that trumps the legislature or agency's action. Still, the argument has always been available that the agency has acted in ways arbitrary, or unreasonable in some other sense. The Indiana case which began this chapter is an exemplar of the state courts' insistence that the government present decently rigorous arguments for why they encroached on individual liberty or property rights in order to implement a policy. It is jarring to an audience whose familiarity with the constitutional caselaw involving economic liberties is mainly limited to federal constitutional cases, cases which, since the end of the <u>Lochner</u> era and the Court's momentous decision in <u>Lee Optical</u> in the early 1950s, have almost never struck down an economic regulation on the grounds that such a regulation was patently unreasonableness. By contrast, state constitutional law occasionally does march to the beat of another drummer.

Looking at the recent Covid-related cases, it is noteworthy how frequently lawyers on behalf of individuals and businesses framed their arguments against certain measures, such as shutdowns and gathering limits, as basically "this restriction makes no sense and dumb laws should not be allowed to stand." Few Covid regulations were struck down on this basis. On the other hand, state courts did not reject these arguments out of hand. The extent of scrutiny suggested that there remained room in state constitutional jurisprudence for a decent examination of these public health regulations. Tellingly, the Supreme Court in <u>Jacobson</u> was explicit in saying that individuals could challenge police power regulations under the US or relevant state constitution, and they could do so under a theory of equal protection or due process that, in essence, made out a strong claim that the legislature's approach here made no good sense.

All of this is to say that the courts' approach to interpreting the police power has been less than strict, but, on the whole, tougher than what we find in the run of US constitutional law cases in which a rational basis standard has been used. If rational basis is minimal-level scrutiny, and strict scrutiny has been, as Gunther wrote, generally "fatal in fact," state judicial review under the police power is somewhere in between. Some might label it "rational basis with a bite;" or "rational basis plus,"[77] but ultimately the label matters less than the overall gestalt of the approach.

This moderate scrutiny has much to recommend it. It does open the door somewhat to plausible arguments that the legislature has acted in untrustworthy ways. The focus, as we have discussed above, on animus and self-dealing reveals such skepticism, and a moderate scrutiny of state legislative and administrative decisions can, in the right hands, smoke out government decisions that are noxious and inappropriate, when judged by reference to the values of our state constitution. When combined with arbitrariness review, which has more or less always been around, standing ready to strike down a state or even federal law (as in <u>Yick Wo</u>, and a century later in <u>Cleburne</u>) that reveals that our treasured legislatures sometimes act irrationally and, where they do, judicial review is an important line of defense.

Moreover, review by state courts that goes beyond rational basis enables courts to focus on protecting private property and liberty of contract in a more meaningful way than the federal courts have done since Lochner's end and since the Court in Lee Optical swept away in a breathtakingly shallow opinion by Justice Douglas any credible argument that an interference with so-called economic liberties is more or less nonjusticiable. Federal and state courts have been haunted by the ghost of Lochner. Even now, Lochner and Lochnerization is a convenient pejorative phrase, something to be hauled out where the judge or commentator is annoyed by the depth of judicial intervention (or, in the case of the so-called Lochnerization of the First Amendment, the absence of intervention that would provide what in their view is some appropriate redistribution of economic and political power).[78] State courts need not be haunted by Lochner, however. For one thing, they never really got the memo that economic liberties and private property rights are at the mercy of the legislature. There are a number of important, but largely neglected by legal scholars, state court cases that have protected economic liberties against interference. We could quibble and quarrel about the wisdom of particular state decisions to be sure, but the larger point to be made here is that the effort to protect liberty and property and, in a more measured sense, to balance these liberties with the imperative of enacting and implementing policies to advance the overall welfare of the relevant citizenry even at the price of some liberty or property interests has not withered away in the state constitutional context. It will not do to say that "Lochner is alive and well" and, as such, such a claim would be rather facile. But what has persisted is the effort by state courts to look at the myriad rights and values wired into their state constitutions and, in that process, to interpret responsibly the police power to ensure that the government is pursuing the public's good and is governing well.

Why only two cheers? Putting Lochner's ghost and also the tortured history of rational basis review in US constitutional law to one side, there have been good reasons for the courts being very judicious when they examine closely the structure and purposes of legislation in order to determine whether the government's approach has been reasonable. Legislatures enact statutes in a very complicated way, with a wealth of pressures and incentives, not to mention formal and informal rules. While we can envision, when we think about American politics and democracy in the most noblest sense, a kind of "due process of lawmaking."[79] But when we bring the rubber of this standard to the road, it is challenging, to say the least, for courts to do the necessary interrogations to determine whether a police power statute was enacted for the "right" or the "wrong" reasons. We can be more optimistic about evaluations that are focused on means and ends, but even that raises the specter of Monday morning quarterbacking. Especially interventionist approaches risk stifling legislative innovation and do not account for either the ingenuity of legislatures and agencies in developing strategies that might seem opaque to an outside reader or also the complexity of legislation in its enactment and implementation phases.

In addition, the effort to examine the reasonableness of legislation, which is formulated as an inquiry into the legislative product irrespective of its tangible impact on a right that the courts would protect under its constitution can become rather aimless. It gives the state court a role perhaps more akin to the French constitutional court than a court that decides cases and controversies. Scrutiny of the government's power independent of this scrutiny of rights is necessary as a matter of constitutional logic, and yet it should be cautiously used.

At the end of the day, the state courts have an important, indeed vital, role to play in interpreting the police power and in resolving disputes over questions of whether the government has gone too far. This is true as an historical matter. It is likewise compelling as a matter of state constitutional theory. Courts have an obligation to ensure that the police power is being properly viewed. This is especially important in the state context in which the legislature has the plenary power of governing, and so where an unregulated legislature poses risks for democracy and, as we considered in Chapter 1, the stability of our constitutional regime.

NOTES

1. 291 U.S. 502 (1934).
2. 348 U.S. 483 (1955).
3. S23A0017; S23X0018 (Decided May 31, 2023). [Citations are to unofficial report of decision.]
4. 348 U.S. at 489.
5. Ibid.
6. Ibid., at 489. See also Ferguson v. Skrupa, 372 U.S. 726 (1963).
7. See White, *Law in American History Volume III* 552(2006).
8. Roe v. Wade, 410 U.S. 113, 143 (Rehnquist, J., dissenting).
9. White, *Law in American History Volume III*, at 557.
10. Raffensberger, at 12 (quoting from Jackson v. Raffensberger, 309 Ga. 736 (2020), a decision from the court at an earlier stage in this litigation).
11. Raffensberger, at 15.
12. Raffensberger, at 16.
13. Ibid.
14. Notably, the Raffensberger court denied the government an off-ramp, in that it rejected the argument that the plaintiffs here could continue their work as lactation peers and counselors "because such work is not a clinical service." Raffensberger, at 17. Instead, the court viewed the plaintiff's activities as squarely inconsistent with the statute and therefore as suffering a clear interference with their ability to conduct their occupation as lactation service providers in Georgia.
15. Ibid., at 21. The court invokes earlier Georgia decisions that strike down laws which seem to have only a tenuous connection to public safety (and, in the process, seemingly ignoring that these laws may be grounded in general welfare considerations, even if not tangibly furthering of public safety or health).
16. See, e.g., Brandon L. Garrett, "Constitutional Reasonableness," 102 *Minn. L. Rev.* 61 (2017). "Even criticisms of the application of the rational basis test largely ignore the import and breadth of its demands, perhaps because the argument against rationality starts at such a considerable rhetorical disadvantage." Thomas B. Nachbar, "The Rationality of Rational Basis Review," 102 *Va. L. Rev.* 1631 (2016).

17. Thomas Nachbar summarizes the essential objection to rationality review (synonymous with reasonableness review, for our purposes): "Rationality review is highly problematic as a constitutional matter. There is no textual basis in the Constitution to justify reviewing legislation for its rationality. Indeed, the test is counter-textual (as implementing the Due Process Clause) in as much as it examines the product rather than the process of lawmaking. But even if rationality is itself a good thing, rationality review is a potentially limitless and unprincipled usurpation of legislative authority by the judiciary. Even taking general substantive judicial review as a given, there is nothing about the means-ends rationality that pervades rationality review that is inherent in the U.S. constitutional order." Nachbar, "Rational Basis Review." See also Nathan S. Chapman & Michael W. McConnell, "Due Process as Separation of Powers," 121 *Yale L. J.* 1801 (2012).
18. James Bradley Thayer, "The Origin and Scope of the American Doctrine of Constitutional Law," 7 *Harv. L. Rev.* 129, 144 (1893).
19. See Gerald Gunther, "The Supreme Court 1971 Term, Foreword: In Search of the New Equal Protection," 86 *Harv. L. Rev.* 1 (1972).
20. Poe v. Ullman, 367 U.S. 497 (1961).
21. Ibid., at 545.
22. 521 U.S. 702 (1997).
23. Ibid., at 710.
24. Cleburne, 473 U.S. 432 (1985).
25. Ibid., at 444.
26. Ibid.
27. Jim Rossi, "Redeeming Judicial Review: The Hard Look Doctrine and Federal Regulatory Efforts to Restructure the Electric Utility Industry," 1994 *Wisc. L. Rev.* 763 (1994).
28. See Colin Diver, "Policymaking Paradigms in Administrative Law," 95 *Harv. L. Rev.* 393 (1981).
29. See Martin Shapiro, *W–o Guards the Guardians? Judicial Control of Administration* (1988).
30. See, e.g., Thomas McGarity, "Some Thoughts on 'Deossifying' the Rulemaking Process," 41 *Duke L. J.* 1385 (1992).
31. See, e.g., Lisa Bressman, "Beyond Accountability: Arbitrariness and Legitimacy in the Administrative State," 78 *NYU L. Rev.* 461 (2003).
32. 413 U.S. 528, 534 (1973).
33. See also Palmore v. Sidoti, 466 U.S. 429 (1984). "The Constitution cannot control such prejudice, but neither can it tolerate it."
34. See Plessy.
35. See, e.g., Sidoti.
36. See Derrick Bell, *And We Are Not Saved: The Elusive Quest for Racial Justice* 167 (1987); J. M. Balkin, "The Constitution of Status," 106 *Yale L. J.* 2313, 2358 (1997); Ruth Colker, "Anti-Subordination Above All: Sex, Race, and Equal Protection," 61 *NYU L. Rev.* 1003, 1058 (1986).
37. See Jack M. Balkin & Reva B. Siegel, "The American Civil Rights Tradition: Anticlassification or Antisubordination?" 58 *U. Miami L. Rev.* 9, 10 (2003).
38. 584 U.S. __ (2018); 138 S. Ct. 1719.
39. Ibid., at 1737.
40. On the concept of neutrality in free exercise of religion jurisprudence, see generally John Witte, Jr., et al., *Religion and the American Constitutional Experiment* 170–205 (5th ed., 2022).
41. Leslie Kendrick & Micah Schwartzman, "The Etiquette of Animus," 133 *Harv. L. Rev.* 132 (2019).

42. Ibid., at 165. See also John Hart Ely, "Legislative and Administrative Motivation in Constitutional Law," 79 *Yale L. J.* 1205, 1212–17 (1970); Larry G. Simon, "Racially Prejudiced Governmental Actions: A Motivation Theory of the Constitutional Ban Against Racial Discrimination," 15 *San Diego L. Rev.* 1041, 1097–107 (1978).
43. Ibid., at 151. See also Richard H. Fallon, Jr., "Constitutionally Forbidden Legislative Intent," 130 *Harv. L. Rev.* 523, 563–69 (2016).
44. See Trump v. Hawaii, 585 U.S. __ (2018).
45. See ibid., at 27(Sotomayor, dissenting).
46. Ibid., at 29.
47. "G.O.P. State Lawmakers Push a Growing Wave of Anti-transgender Bills," *New York Times*. https://nyti.ms/41X4qMO.
48. 576 U.S. 644 (2015).
49. 570 U.S. 744 (2013).
50. 590 U.S. __ (2020).
51. "Challenging Anti-trans Legislation under State Constitutions," *Brennan Center*. https://bit.ly/3S1OXq2.
52. "Anti-trans Laws Face Legal Roadblocks in Several States," *PBS*. https://to.pbs.org/47zodzZ.
53. Cass R. Sunstein, "Naked Preferences and the Constitution," 84 *Colum. L. Rev.* 1689 (1984).
54. See, e.g., Jonathan Macey; "Promoting Public-Regarding Legislation through Statutory Interpretation: An Interest Group Model," 86 *Colum. L. Rev.* 223 (1986).
55. See ibid., at et seq.
56. 369 U.S. 186 (1962).
57. 364 U.S. 339 (1960).
58. Ibid., at 341.
59. Ibid., at 337.
60. Samuel Issacharoff & Richard H. Pildes, "Politics as Markets: Partisan Lockups of the Democratic Process," 50 *Stan. L. Rev.* 643 (1998).
61. See, e.g., Miriam Seifter, "Countermajoritarian Legislatures," 121 *Colum. L. Rev.* 1734, 1777–94 (2021).
62. See John Hart Ely, *Democracy and Distrust* (1980).
63. See generally William M. Landes & Richard A. Posner, "The Independent Judiciary in an Interest Group Perspective," 29 *J. L. & Econ.* 875 (1975).
64. See Macey, "Public-Regarding Legislation," at 260–67.
65. See Eric S. Fish, "Constitutional Avoidance as Interpretation and as Remedy," 114 *Mich. L. Rev.* 1275 (2016).
66. In re Forbes, 19 How. Pr. 457 (N.Y. Sup. Ct. 1860).
67. Ibid.
68. 11 Metc. (Mass.) 55 (1846).
69. Ibid., at 65.
70. See generally William Eskridge & Philip Frickey, "The Making of the 'Legal Process'," 107 *Harv. L. Rev.* 2031 (1994).
71. See generally Aharon Barak, *Purposive Interpretation in Law* (2005); Philip P. Frickey, "Structuring Purposive Interpretation in Law: An American Perspective," 80 *Aus. L. J.* 849 (2006).
72. Henry Hart & Albert Sacks, *Legal Process: Basic Problems in the Making and Application of Law* (W. Eskridge & P. Frickey eds., 1994).
73. See Jeffrey S. Sutton, *Who Decides? States as Laboratories of Constitutional Experimentation* 183–234 (2022).

74. See generally David Zaring, "Rule by Reasonableness," 63 *Admin. L. Rev.* 525 (2011). The matter of "reasonableness" as an integral standard of administrative law has been a serious flashpoint in current debates about Israeli public law reform. See Amichai Cohen & Yuval Shany, "The End of 'Reasonable' Governance in Israel?" Lawfare (February 21, 2023).
75. A classic article on hard look review in administrative law is Merrick Garland, "Deregulation and Judicial Review," 98 *Harv. L. Rev.* 505 (1986).
76. See Yohan Dotan, "Deference and Disagreement in Administrative Law," 71 *Admin. L. Rev.* 761 (2019). See also Jeremy Waldron, *Law and Disagreement* (1999).
77. See Thomas B. Nachbar, "Rational Basis 'Plus'," 32 *Const. Comm.* 449 (2017).
78. See Genevieve Lakier, "The First Amendment's Real Lochner Problem," 87 *U. Chi. L. Rev.* 1241 (2020).
79. See Hans A. Linde, "Due Process of Lawmaking," 55 *Neb. L. Rev.* 197 (1976).

8

The Police Power and Federalism

In this chapter, we consider more carefully how the states' broad police powers are nested in an American constitutional system in which a good deal of discretion is maintained by the federal government to decide whether and to what extent to displace state with federal policy. Whether consistent or not with late eighteenth and early nineteenth-century understandings of federalism, there has been a relentless expansion of federal regulatory power, especially since the New Deal and the period demarked by the sixties and early seventies, a period occasionally labelled the Second Reconstruction.[1] This emerges out of a clear sense that the national government expanded its power and, in key respects, supplanted state and local power in areas of social and economic policy. Despite the emergence of some meaningful limits on federal power under the Constitution, especially in the years since the Court decided United States v. Lopez,[2] United States v. Morrison,[3] and New York v. United States,[4] we can see the police power adapting to the twentieth-century expansion in national power and prerogative.

That said, the police power remains significant, notwithstanding the great expansion of national authority. While the national government has expanded the scope of its power and into areas that historically had not been practically subject to federal intervention, the national government still leaves the lion's share of decisions to regulate private property, protect public health, ensure citizen safety, and further public welfare through state and local regulation to state and local governments. We could debate whether and to what extent the Constitution permits the national government to displace state and local authority in areas traditionally decentralized, but most of this debate would be purely academic. As a practical matter, the state police power matters greatly and is in no real danger of being eradicated by the federal government through design or direction.

The focus of this chapter is not on constitutional federalism per se, but on the impact of expanding federal power on the exercise of the states' police power. The relationship between national and state regulatory power has been a thread through this book, but it has not been its principal topic. Nor is it now. Our main objective is not to situate the police power in a positive and normative account of constitutional federalism, as interesting and valuable that such an analysis would be. Rather, we are interested in the impact of federal authority and, more broadly, federalism in principle and in practice, on the functions of the police power in the modern administrative state. To summarize: We can see that the greater use of federal authority to regulate the use of private property and business conduct, consequences of contemporary administrative regulation has imposed appreciably more burdens on individuals and businesses. What are the practical consequences, if any, for the state police power of these added burdens? In short, what are the consequences of an expanding federal role?

FEDERAL POWER EXPANDS, STATE POLICE POWER ENDURES

The expansion of the federal government's role in regulating private and business conduct is a story frequently told and, when viewed through a practical lens, is explained as part of a necessary intervention into the actions and activities of individuals, business leaders, and governments. State regulation proved incapable of meeting the demands of an increasingly complex economy. Moreover, the demands of equal citizenship imposed by profound changes to our constitutional order after the Civil War led to a more robust and active federal government.

The feds expanded involvement can be measured in the first instance by major national legislation, including the Interstate Commerce Act, the Sherman Antitrust Act, the Food & Drug Safety Act, and the Federal Trade Commission Act, to mention just these notable Progressive-era statutes.[5] Congress stepped in to address issues that could conceivably have been tackled by the states through their ample regulatory powers, but were not being attended to adequately, at least as viewed by public opinion and ultimately by Congress and the executive branch. As well, innovative legislative action characterized the New Deal period, as President Roosevelt and Democratic allies in Congress constructed a novel national apparatus for the implementation of vigorous national regulatory policy, especially with regard to the economy and the workplace.[6] Here, blockbuster statutes such as the Securities & Exchange Acts, the Federal Communications Act, and the National Labor Relations Act loom large in this regulatory history.

In addition to expanding national authority, a principal innovation during this half-century period running from soon after Reconstruction through the so-called Second New Deal was the development of what Stephen Skowronek calls the "expansion of national administrative capacities" and the creation of the modern administrative state.[7] In the early years of late nineteenth-century and early twentieth-century federal regulation, it was unclear exactly what were to be the right mix of institutions and implementation mechanisms to undertake national goals. On the one hand, for example, the Interstate Commerce Act created a powerful multi-member bureau, the Interstate Commerce Commission, to carry out its functions in transportation ratemaking.[8] On the other hand, at essentially the same time, Congress enacted important new antitrust legislation, leaving to federal law enforcement and the federal courts the principal responsibility to define what conduct is impermissible and to ferret out and punish wrongdoers.[9]

As we approached the New Deal, however, Congress had become more purposive in its creation and use of administrative agencies to carry out its regulatory objectives. These agencies were given important authority to set general public policy, authority ratified by the Supreme Court in important pre-New Deal and New Deal era decisions. Moreover, Congress had, albeit less decisively, accorded to agencies the power to create rules of binding effect, a power codified in the Administrative Procedure Act of 1946.[10] Looking ahead from this era, agencies created in the 1960s and 1970s were especially ambitious in using this rulemaking power. With these choices, administrative agencies emerged as the fulcrum of national regulatory power, a position that would become further entrenched in the decades following the New Deal.

As the need grew in our nation in the second half of the twentieth century to build a much greater administrative capacity, the federal government undertook many more initiatives. They did so largely with the blessing of the courts, albeit with some turbulence in the third decade of the twentieth century when a skeptical Supreme Court endeavored to put some limits on federal authority.[11] Though not entirely an invention of the Progressive era, the national government's role certainly expanded as we moved steadily toward the *fin de siècle* in the late 1800s.[12] Important social and economic issues that had been left largely to state governments to deal with or, in some cases, to the market in that they were essentially unregulated, came to the fore of national legislators and critical pieces of federal legislation was enacted by Congress. After a period of some quietude and resistance, not coincidentally during periods in which the Republican Party was largely ascendant in Congress, the White House, and the federal courts, the New Deal period brought forth a wealth of new, ambitious legislation.[13] Congress and the administrative agencies created during this fertile period for public policy were intervening in economic and social life in myriad ways. They were defining a new vision of national power. The courts for the most part gave its imprimatur to these developments.[14] This vision carried through the rest of the twentieth century and also into this century.

The main shifts in federalism and the breadth of state power came about through two developments, neither of which can be traced to changing views about the police power per se. One was incorporation, that is, the application of virtually all of the Bill of Rights to the states.[15] This was a development of the Supreme Court in second half of the twentieth century. The other was the use of federal authority under the commerce clause (and, to a much lesser degree, section 5 of the Fourteenth Amendment).[16] These reflected monumental changes in the fact and rationale of the authority exercised by the national government and, likewise, the immunity of the state government from federal control. However, these changes did not fundamentally undermine the state's power to protect health, safety, and welfare, save for the critical condition that state power must do go beyond its domain by discriminating against out-of-state interests (thus violating the dormant commerce clause or the privileges and immunities of citizenship) or creating unwarranted externalities. Within its rightful domain, states could (and did) continue to wield its police powers.

The incorporation of the bill of rights affected the scope of the police power, however, insofar as it created new limits on state authority in the form of constitutional rights, a topic that we discussed at length in Chapter 6. The rather sensible view that official action would be subject to constitutional limits, whether this action came by way of the federal government or state and local governments, was propounded by Madison and other framers; however, this view was rendered nugatory by the Supreme Court a half century after the Constitution was adopted, in the case of Barron v. Baltimore.[17] Barron held that the bill of rights would not be applicable to state and local governments. Without specifically overrunning Barron, the Warren and Burger Courts, beginning in the 1950s, held in a series of key cases that various rights contained in the first eight amendments were part of a scheme of ordered liberty and should, especially given the enactment of the Reconstruction amendments, be incorporated via the Due Process clause of the Constitution.[18] The incorporation of these rights obviously impacted the operation of the police power, in that it created meaningful limits on the use of this regulatory authority. We saw in an earlier chapter how these constitutional rights, especially those in the First and Second Amendments, emerged to create significant limits on the police power.

The expansion of the commerce clause began especially during the New Deal era, when the Court decided a number of major cases upholding legislative authority to regulate segments of the economy at the national level.[19] Especially with its decisions in in the 1960s upholding the Civil Rights Act under the commerce clause,[20] the Court created an architecture of national power that has proved durable. In a related vein, the consistent use of the so-called dormant commerce clause to limit state action viewed as protectionist and discriminatory put brakes on state laws that aspired to further discrete state purposes. In a number of these dormant commerce clause cases, the stated reason given for the state's law was public health and safety. The task undertaken by the federal courts was to consider whether the law, however persuasive was the argument that it was about health, safety, or the general welfare of the community, effected a constitutionally unacceptable burden on interstate commerce.

There is a message tacit in these cases decided under the commerce clause, in its two iterations, direct and dormant, and that is that the strength of the case for a state law intended to protect the interests of state citizens must give way to the overall welfare of the nation. This message is an old one, of course, and as we saw in Chapter 2, the Court has been resolute in its commerce clause jurisprudence, beginning with Gibbons v. Ogden, to make clear that the police power standing on its own gives no special warrant to the state in disrupting the free flow of commerce. There are often two welfares at stake, that of the community whose law is enacted on their behalf and that of the common community of American citizens. So, while the general idea remains intact that the state's regulatory power is left undisturbed by a widened national regulatory presence, the constitutional rule that lies at the background of these evolving conditions is that the interests of a common national economy will reliably trump the specific interests of states no matter how sound is the police power rationale for enacting certain safety, health, and morals measures.

This triumph of federal constitutional authority has been nonetheless tempered somewhat by doctrinal developments over the last three decades or so. First in <u>United States v. Lopez</u>,[21] and next in <u>United States v. Morrison</u>, the Court read the commerce clause as requiring a greater connection to the imperative of national authority – at the very least, Congressional findings that the situation required national intervention.[22] These notable commerce clause decisions was accompanied by a renewed attention on the part of the Rehnquist Court to separation of powers constraints on legislative and executive action, and there were a handful of significant cases that imposed what amounted to procedural limits on the strategies Congress could use in implementing policy.[23] In a somewhat similar vein, the Court created a novel "anti-commandeering" doctrine that forbade the federal government from relying on state institutions to carry out national goals.[24] To complete the picture during this key period of the 1980s to roughly the end of the century, the Court created a canon of statutory interpretation – named after its decision in <u>Gregory v. Ashcroft</u> – that imposed a higher burden on Congress when it enacts legislation that displaces state power.[25] Through these judicial decisions, augmented by administrative decisions within the executive branch, federalism became more robust, even though the fundamental expansion in national authority has not eroded.

Beyond the doctrinal edifice of the commerce clause claim the national welfare will always trump state interests and preferences, we can ruminate about whether there is a larger claim at work here, that is, that the national interest is the relevant focal point in assessing considerations of general welfare that are tied to the police power. One way to think about the police power's advancement of the *salus populi* is that it must be ever attentive to the national welfare. As chaotic is the present state of dormant commerce clause jurisprudence; as we were reminded in the last Supreme Court term when a very decided court decided <u>National Pork Producers Council v. Ross</u>,[26] at its core is the idea that state parochial interests cannot impede a national marketplace, a marketplace being in the public interest as the framers thought central in the creation of a federal commerce power in Article I and in the enactment of the US Constitution more generally. The energy in this bold claim about national interest driving state decision-making should be tempered, however, by the reminder crucial to the overall argument of this book, and that is that the state police power is embedded in understandings of the role and function of state constitutions. To make the larger, and rather ambitious, point that state constitutions are principally constructed in design and interpretation as servants to a larger national interest requires much more analysis than embedded in either two centuries plus worth of Supreme Court caselaw on constitutional federalism or in the scholarly exegeses on the place of state constitutionalism in our American republic. Moreover, this claim would be, in any event, in serious tension with how the framers understood the idea of reserved powers under the Tenth Amendment, and also how both federal and state courts viewed the best interpretations of the police power's scope under the *salus populi* rationale.

One last observation regarding the resilience of state regulatory power in light of the Court's many federalism decisions. After some quiet with regard to national/state disputes at the constitutional level, the Roberts Court has developed some doctrinal innovations that have the effect, if not the design, of cabining national power, principally at the administrative agency level.[27] The direction of at least a plurality of the current Court (and perhaps even a majority, although it is too soon to tell this with certainty) is "anti-administrativist,"[28] in that these more conservative justices are quite skeptical about the vast power exercised by federal administrative agencies. A few justices have called for a resuscitated non-delegation doctrine to limit agency power;[29] the Court is on the verge of overruling its 1984 decision in Chevron v. NRDC,[30] a decision that ushered in an era of significant judicial deference to administrative agencies' statutory interpretations;[31] and, perhaps most notably, the Court has invented a so-called Major Questions Doctrine, which essentially requires that matters of economic and social significance shall be resolved by statute, not by administrative regulation.[32]

Taken as a whole, these decisions restrict the tactics of the federal government in their claims of authority, even if they do not weaken national authority in a formal sense. In other words, these anti-administrative decisions are not about federalism as such, but they can lead to the same end, which is that the national government's discretion to make policy in the matter that it believes best suited to sound implementation is limited. At the same time, we should not overstate the significance of these developments from the vantage point of the national scope of regulatory power. The space of national power, having been greatly expanded in the Progressive era, the New Deal, the Great Society, and in eras in between and afterward, is broad and resilient.

IS THERE A NATIONAL POLICE POWER AND DOES IT MATTER TO THE STATE POLICE POWER?

A key question is whether the broad national power that exists under the Constitution comes at the expense of the state police power. This question can hardly be answered in the abstract, for the matter must be illuminated by resort to specific controversies that involve the overlap of federal power on state authority as traditionally measured. This question was a focal point, or at least was made so because of Justice David

Souter's dissenting opinion in United States v. Morrison, a 2000 case in which the Supreme Court invalidated the Violence Against Women Act as outside the scope of Congress's commerce power. Justice Souter argued that this holding was outside the realm of previous Court precedents involving the commerce clause in that it presupposed that once an issue was one that had long been handled at the state regulatory level, it was not for the federal government to wade in through its commerce authority. "The premise," Souter writes,

> that the enumeration of powers implies that other powers are withheld is sound; the conclusion that some particular categories of subject matter are therefore presumptively beyond the reach of the commerce power is, however, a non sequitur.... To the contrary, we have always recognized that while the federal commerce power may overlap the reserved state police power, in such cases federal authority is supreme.[33]

At the heart of the case, both the majority and dissenters agree, is whether this act falls under the established definition of commerce.[34] The very expansive definition of commerce, one that denies, somewhat strangely to be sure, a discernible line between commercial and non-commercial activity and likewise denies an interpretation that would limit the scope of the federal power to economic activities, has supported broad Congressional power. This was reaffirmed by Wickard v. Filburn[35] in the New Deal and again in Gonzales v. Raich,[36] a case decided contemporaneously with Morrison. But this power is not without judicial limits, as the Court made clear in both Morrison and Lopez. Two lessons relevant to our discussion can be drawn from these modern spate of cases, even accounting for the vigorous disagreements reflected in the dissenting opinions in each case: First, no justice has gone so far as to argue that the national government has a general police power. Despite Chief Justice Rehnquist's characterization of Souter and his allies position as suggesting such a power, a careful reading of the dissenting opinion here, and also in Lopez and Raich, is that the key question if whether the traditional scope of the police power over various local matters, including basic elements of criminal law and domestic activity, means that the federal government must stay out of these issues as a categorical matter. It is ultimately a fruitless and even odd disagreement between the majority and dissenting opinions. After all, Chief Justice Marshall made rather clear in Gibbons and the other early commerce clause cases we discussed in Chapter 2 that the state's police power authority was indeed part of the reserved powers of the states, and did not belong with the federal government, but, at the same time, this power could not interfere with commerce. This fundamental principle of constitutional review remains good law, even as the Court has and presumably will continue to struggle with the question of how best to limit the scope of what commerce means.

Second, and related to the first point, is that there can surely be instances of simultaneous regulation by the federal and state governments of various activities related to public health, safety, and morals. Yes, the Court draws a line in Morrison that rules out criminal law relating to violence against women as defined in this historic act. However, it does not rule out in any way, shape, or form, federal criminal law in toto. The criminal law books are filled with conduct that is punishable by the states and also the federal government under statutes. Drug laws are an obvious illustration of this, but there are many other examples as well. Interestingly, federal laws that criminalize certain activities on the grounds that such activities are immoral – rather than, say, that they impede the free flow of economic commerce – have been long upheld as constitutionally acceptable under the commerce clause. And so while the Court insists that "[t]he Constitution ... withhold[s] from Congress a plenary police power,"[37] the scope of national power in areas that have traditionally been the primary province of state regulation is strong and, and even after Lopez and Morrison, largely intact.

While this is not principally a point that emerges from the Court's federalism decisions, it is worthwhile mentioning, as it gives shape to a "no" answer to the question asked in the title of this chapter's subsection, and that is that the functioning of the state police power is not seriously affected by the ubiquitous national power to regulate many of the same subjects through the criminal law and other forms of law as would the states. Preemption of state regulatory authority is not without meaning; however, it is seldom the case that the national government displaces state authority because the feds have decided to step in. There have been very few areas of social life and public policy where the position of either Congress or the courts have been that the states may not meddle through its use of the police power on the grounds that these areas have become exclusively federal. This is true even through periods in which there has been very strong support for national interventions and a corresponding skepticism about the states' capacity and willingness to address the problems at issue. Moreover, it is more typical that the national government has actively encouraged states to exercise authority under its police power, and whatever other added authority given by Congress, to advance health and safety objectives. The 1960s and 1970s were an important time in which such encouragements took place, as the federal government got itself more involved in urban policy[38] and other areas that had largely been the province of the states.[39] Health care policy was another area in which Congress pushed states to undertake initiatives,[40] this illustrated well by the provisions of the Affordable Care Act that incentivize states to participate in insurance exchanges.[41] In the area of environmental law, federal statutes and administrative regulations have set up structures to encourage states to innovate, even while insisting that minimum national standards be enforced. And even in the area of antidiscrimination law, an area whose history illustrates the critical role of federal intervention given the states' quiescence or, as with Jim Crow, even worse, state and local governments will frequently enact protections for subordinated communities that go beyond the federal baseline. To be sure, these episodes are not principally about the police power *qua* police power, yet they are good illustrations of the general point, and that is that expanding federal power has not supplanted state authority under the police power.

Looking at the national regulatory landscape broadly, national and state governments have worked, and continue to work, in partnership with one another in many key policy areas.[42] The national government must find its authority to undertake the federal functions of this partnership in the US Constitution, although two centuries' worth of caselaw on constitutional federalism has given the feds a fairly wide berth in exercising authority under Article I. This national authority exists often alongside the police power of the states and so it is in the confluence of these two powers that these two levels of government interact in ways that a commentator on federalism once described as a system of marble cake federalism.[43]

There are precious few instances in which the courts have been asked to settle a dispute over the federal government's effort to displace the state police power through national legislation. The modal controversy involving federal regulation implicates not the question whether the state has properly acted, but whether the national government may regulate at all under its enumerated powers.[44] Preemption presents what we can credibly label a federalism issue, but, in reality, preemption is a statutory interpretation issue.[45] We consider whether and to what extent the federal government's actions can be properly read as supplanting actions of the state or, more generally, keeping states out of the domain altogether, as in controversies over so-called "field preemption."[46] Finally, an issue that has become prominent over the last thirty or so years, that of anti-commandeering, concerns the limits on Congress's ability to conscript state or local officials into national policy.[47] This does not implicate the scope and content of the police power of state government in any important way.

At bottom, any assertion by the national government that it has a police power analogous to the police power in the American states is belied by both our American constitutional history and by the logic of American constitutionalism. As to the former, recall the basic idea that the federal government is one of enumerated powers, as this is beyond the scope of this book and is covered amply in the large historiography on the formation of the US Constitution. Within these limits, the only conceivable source of a national police power would be the "necessary and proper" clause invoked as a police power of sorts to accompany the federal government's broad power to regulate interstate commerce. But the connection here is an especially weak one, as even a broad rendering of that clause, plausible after <u>McCulloch v. Maryland</u> and supported by myriad scholars over the long expanse of American constitutional history, assumes that the powers referred to in that sweeping clause can only be, as Chief John Roberts wrote in the Affordable Care Act case, <u>NFIB v. Sebelius</u>,[48] "exercises of authority derivative of, and in service to, a granted power."[49] This is not necessarily an idle debate, as prominent constitutional scholars have argued that the reference to general welfare in the Constitution's preamble might be a source of such power. Nonetheless, the conceptual and historical architecture of our American constitutional order has never embraced the idea that there is a national police power, and neither the text nor the history sustains such an idea.[50]

To this point, we have been dwelling in the comfort of big constitutional theory. We might ask the same question from a more practical vantage point. Does the expansion of federal authority carry along with it at least an implication that states should be more circumscribed in the use of the police power to carry out objectives that, in modern times, can be realized more effectively by national policymaking? It is a commonplace in the literature on regulation and government to point out that solving society's wicked problems requires an active central government, one that will account for externalities and lassitude on the part of state governments. The federal government, in these accounts, is needed to save the day in the face of the inadequacies of state and local government. While the empirical and theoretical bases of a reasonably active national role are compelling, it is naïve to see the national and state governments as substitutes rather than complements. What these arguments for a reliably muscular national government, perhaps something akin to a federal police power, do not support is a limit on the states' ability to protect health, safety, and general welfare through a capacious police power. The expanding national role has not accompanied an erosion of state authority, either as a normative matter or as a practical matter. As to the latter in particular, it must be said that the state and local government's role in creating and implementing regulations in the areas of health, safety, and morals has not seriously abated since the 1930s; if anything, it has grown by most measures.

Much of the preceding discussion has been framed in the negative. That is, we have insisted that the evolution of national regulatory has now disrupted the legal and practical underpinnings of state regulatory initiative. However, we should still press on the point of whether our expanding national government has generated new perspectives on federalism that has implications for how the police power functions. This is where we turn to next.

DYNAMIC FEDERALISM MEANS A DYNAMIC POLICE POWER

Traditional federalism debates have been mired in disagreements about what are the states' separate spheres. Under what conditions can the states as sovereign exercisers of legal power without risking federal intervention? Resort to categories and factors to support the placement of lines separating federal from state concerns has proved difficult, despite occasional forays by the Court into that kind of analysis in resolving disputes. In recent years, a large number of public law scholars looking anew at federalism have helped reorient the conversation from this "separate spheres" analysis to a deeply pragmatic and avowedly political perspective on federalism.[51] All of this diverse research and analysis points to a picture of a dynamic federalism, one that escapes from the relentless question of "Who's in charge?" and pursues instead the more practical question of "How should the many relevant institutions of American governance work together to carry out important objectives and, further, how should we deal with constitutional conflict?"

Yale Dean Heather Gerken has called for a robust federalism which protects the power of sub-national governments as a means of poking and provoking national political institutions and officials into making more socially just decisions.[52] The power of the servant is the power to dissent, to exercise, as she puts it, "'voice' in an exceedingly muscular form."[53] These dissenters, acting within the authorized governance frameworks of the state and local governments, can stir up trouble and engage in conflict, as well as collaboration and conflict on behalf of dissenting minorities. "States and local officials administering federal law," Gerken writes, "can edit the law they lack the power to authorize precisely because they are inside the system, not outside of it." So, for example, the decision by San Francisco mayor Gavin Newsom in 2004 to issue marriage licenses to same-sex couples, despite any reasonable basis in existing state constitutional law for this decision, had the beneficial effect of engaging the national debate in a constructive way. But what of the fact that this political move by the mayor was beaten back by the California Supreme Court? Says Gerken: "While local resistance surely has its costs, minority rule at the local level generates a dynamic form of contestation, the democratic churn necessary for an ossified national system to change."[54] What federalism all the way down aspires to do is to help the project of building good national policy.[55] This is true not only of the functions of state governments to implement federal law, but also in the circumstances in which state governments are enacting state law. So, this is a really remarkable twist: Even purely state law should be seen as a means of advancing national interests. As her Yale colleague, Abbe Gluck, puts it succinctly: "Congress has asked the states to enact their own state laws, create new state institutions, and pass new state administrative regulations – in other words, to exercise their sovereign powers in service of the national statutory project."[56] To summarize, federalism creates the space for democratic contestation by citizens exercising voice at the sub-national level and in ways that national authorities are obliged to respect and this will counteract the power of majorities to use federal institutions to dampen dissent and disable minorities. Loyal opposition by sub-national governments enables minorities to speak truth to power. Taken as a complete story of what federalism purports to accomplish, it does help explain a hard puzzle: Why ought state and local governments flourish, notwithstanding the post New Deal reconfiguration of national/state relations and the necessary augmentation of federal power?

The larger point that this and other related literature supports is the idea that American federalism is not about boundary drawing and the quest for separate spheres of regulatory prerogative, but is about creating mechanisms consistent with the ambitions of American constitutionalism to facilitate a dynamic, interactive, and interinstitutional process by which dynamic American politics can be explored and improved and the project of good governing refined and implemented.

Health and education policy are excellent examples of this dynamic federalism in operation. States maintain principal control over some key aspects of the health system, such as occupational licensing and the determination of whether quarantines or cordon sanitaire restrictions are necessary. Other aspects, including matters of data privacy, insurance under the ACA, the development of vaccines and prophylactics to assist with major, cross-border infectious disease emergencies, as well as other elements of health care delivery that demand efficiencies of scale, will involve active federal intervention. The system could not effectively run without the engagement and collaboration of the national government and the governments of the states.[57] Education policy, likewise, involves issues that benefit from federal engagement short of displacement of local control. Not only are there dynamic policy issues at work that implicate national interests and values, but they are also considerations of constitutional rights, of both teachers and students, that mean that state and local choices are made in the shadow of national law.[58]

Paeans to intergovernmental collaboration are perhaps the easiest part of this inquiry into dynamic federalism as a description and an aspiration. Who could be against cooperative federalism? More difficult is the question of how to resolve serious conflict. States will frequently disagree with one another, especially in area of hyper-partisanship. And state views will conflict on occasion with the views of the national government. The dual challenge is to ameliorate the conditions of conflict and create rules that can resolve conflict when it happens, but in a way that preserves both goodwill and policy innovation. The default might be, unavoidably, a respect for the federal government's supremacy in matters that rightly implicate national concerns and, likewise, a respect for state autonomy where there is no basis for federal control or interference. But what about the myriad situations that fall between these two extremes?

To understand the way out of conflict we need to understand the source and reasons for this conflict. At one abstract level, we can see that conflict usually stems from disagreement about policy, rather than disagreement about federalism. Citizens often behave as policy entrepreneurs, seeking sustenance from that level of government that supports their preferences. But we need still to take the lens out a bit to see whether this conflicts maps onto institutional instabilities. The most plausible model available about how institutions – and here we are talking about the two primary levels of government, states and the federal government – is that sketched by James Madison and Alexander Hamilton in the Federalist and refined in more complex ways in the centuries since. Madison made the important point in the Federalist No. 10 that individuals and public officials will pursue their own ambitions and therefore "ambition must counteract ambition." Yet it was Hamilton who dug deeper into the question of how to think about the competition that would likely arise between layers and levels of government. In Federalist No. 28, he reminded us that "power is almost always the rival of power." Indeed, the national and state governments are frequently rivals, as are state and local governments. They compete for the loyalties of, and the benefits of, citizens. They use electoral structures and political institutions, including, for example, political parties to mobilize support, to secure acquiescence, and, where necessary, to divide and conquer. Yet it is crucial to see this opportunism on the part of state and local governments not as institutional self-dealing or as some conspiracy to undermine electoral accountability, but as tactics to effectuate the will of the people, whose preferences and objectives are realized through the actions of these units. Conflict can be navigated at the policy level. But it must also be navigated at the institutional level.

Further, this relationship can be viewed as one between principals and agents, with the citizens being the principals. They will have an admixture of policy preferences. A critical mass of citizens care about, say, a clean environment, the financial well-being of their family, access to education, reliable health care, equality of opportunity, and national security. Others will have a different mix and priority of preferences. Some of these goals are best realized through national policy – national security, for example – others through local policy (say, land use), and, for the rest, the relevant group of citizens may well be agnostic about which level of government implements their preferences. Knowing that different policy goals align with different institutional capacities and tactics, rational individuals are likely to want governing institutions to be made up of multiple principals, that is, of a mix of institutions, all working in a synthetic system. The basic point is that citizens will want – and let us go a step further and say *ought* to want – a system in place that is most likely to successfully aggregate these preferences and, in the case of those in the minority, ensure that their rights are protected against majority expropriation and oppression.

This principal-agent formulation has implications for federalism in a couple relevant senses: First, on occasion, citizens will be indifferent about states' rights and local autonomy. Sure, they may have ideological preferences on the matter, but history suggests that these ideological preferences will give way to their policy preferences. This is illustrated in all its glory by the infamous Tea Party protest sign which read "keep the government's hands off my Medicare." Second, citizens will want their units of government to maintain sufficient authority and flexibility so as to carry out their will when they are tasked thusly. For the citizens, we can think about their strategies as a sort of political arbitrage. That is, citizens will use their knowledge about their own preferences, including their discount rates, and also knowledge about the governmental institutions which are in a position to facilitate or undermine these interests. Sub-national governments are engaging in a similar process of political arbitrage. And they do so not only as automatic aggregators of constituent preferences, but as institutional actors with their own interests. In making their decisions, they will often cooperate with the central government, and occasionally with other states or local governments in the horizontal context. Other times, however, their strategies will bring them into conflict with central authorities. And it is here when they are truly caught between two masters – the central government on the one hand and their citizen principals on the other. This dilemma is intrinsic in a federalist system, as our framers well understood.

Despite the risk of conflict and confrontation, these institutions of governance need and want the flexibility to act on behalf of their citizens and to maintain the discretion and the power to pursue objectives without unnecessary interference. Sub-national governments can be the conduit for the pursuit of discrete and general interests by citizens. As such, citizens have a strong interest in ensuring both a plurality of such governments and a reasonable assurance that they have appropriate authority and techniques to manage conflict. Furthermore, these subnational governments want and need legal protections in order to protect their prerogatives as institutions of governance. As Professor Ernest Young says about states: "The emphasis on the institutional interests of state governments is critical because virtually all the important benefits of federalism stem from the existence of the states as self-governing entities. States cannot function as checks on the power of the central government, or as laboratories of experimental regulation, if they lack the institutional ability to govern themselves in meaningful ways."[59]

This idea of political arbitrage is a particularly resonant theme with regard to local governments, and this because of the intriguing fact that local governments can be formed in a more customized way, by contrast to the states, which exist in the form established at the time of their admission to the union and, under the Constitution, cannot be changed at the will of the federal government or the citizens writ large. Charles Tiebout pointed out many years ago that the size of local governments reflect the interests of citizens reflected in their choice to exit and enter and to create a geographically defined polity that advances their interests.

That citizens want the flexibility to implement their goals through the right kind of institutional mechanisms may explain the steadily growing use of special-purpose governments. Like municipalities, special-purpose governments are creatures of the state; but, unlike municipalities, they are truly customized creatures. They are more like a robot than like Frankenstein's monster, the latter of which resembles a human being of sorts, and the former need not be human in any discernible way, shape, or form. More to the point, the special-purpose governments enable states to circumvent the limits of local governments and to accomplish goals that might otherwise be frustrated by localities. Local citizens can and will often look toward quasi-governmental institutions, such as common interest developments, in order to create mechanisms for implementing their preferences and, more radically, to retreat from the public sphere. These sorts of customized institutions threaten to upend or at least problematize the traditional conception of localism by giving citizens the opportunity to create a governance strategy that is more carefully tailored to their specific policy interests and concerns.

While these institutions are not immune from governmental action or influence, they are intriguing devices to drive decision-making from the government to smaller institutions over which local citizens have comparatively greater control.

Note that a comprehensive theory of localism, and perhaps even of federalism, requires attention to these structures, and also to how they connect to the police power.

Still to consider, even if just briefly here, is how best to negotiate matters of constitutional conflict. Both federalism and localism provide the frameworks within which these issues are negotiated, both in the political process and courts. For those who might be called "new process federalists," the focus on political processes requires some additional attention on the dynamics of relations among governments and, also, on what motivates public officials and, further, how they take these motivations into the venue of discrete institutions of governance. Jessica Bulman-Pozen and Dean Gerken shrewdly capture the point that federalism can capture this interinstitutional struggle. Here I quote:

> Federalism divides power and offers a structure for substantive views to compete. It does not specify what the recipients of divided power should use it for, nor does it equate particular views with one level of government or the other. Claims that political actors undermine federalism by marshaling arguments for state power in an opportunistic way and treating federalism as a convenient arrangement through which to pursue policy agendas indict our Founders as well as contemporary politicians. More deeply, such claims overlook the significance of federalism in establishing loci of political conflict, whether this conflict is driven by state institutional interests, partisanship, or something else.[60]

Policymaking need not be a zero-sum game. However, even though collaboration may be the modal choice, governments will want to protect their discretion to engage in political arbitrage. Moreover, conflict will happen. That is in the nature of politics, where there is heterogeneity in policy preferences and the intensity of such preferences. Therefore, there will be instances in which the interests at stake mean that the assertion of local power will provide benefits captured at, say, the local level and, by such capturing, unavailable to officials at other levels of government. To think about this in more theoretical terms, some local officials may be relentless budget maximizers; others may be good Burkeans.[61] The view that these governance institutions pursue their own objectives, pursuits which come into conflict with other levels of government, accommodates the myriad incentives and motivations that emerge from citizen preferences, however forged and articulated.

The police power functions in a dynamic environment in which our various political and legal institutions act and react with one another in order to safeguard their interests and realize their objectives. This need not be a Hobbesian war of all, ratcheted up from the individual to the institutional level. It may be overlain with a scrupulous commitment to collaboration and the means and mechanisms to sustain this collaboration. The principal point of this discussion, however, is that an assessment of federalism that captures the dynamic between the state and local governments exercising vigorous authority under the police power can become enmeshed in some vexing inter-governmental struggles; likewise, the competition for impact and influence between state and national governments can have a similar valence. As to matters of good governing and its facilitation, we should remember Ronald Reagan's statement about the former Soviet Union: Trust, but verify.

CONSTITUTIONALISM AS A THEY, NOT AN IT

The state police power, as we have discussed throughout the book, is nested in our schemes of state constitutionalism. It is from those constitutions that the power is derived; and the overall purpose and function of the police power is to implement objectives that are instantiated in these state constitutions, principally the promotion of the general welfare and complementary goals, including the protection of health, safety, and public morals. Moreover, the structural limits on the exercise of this power are found in the implicit instruction that the government act in a fashion neither arbitrary nor with animus, and overall with a public purpose. These have been fashioned in our analysis as state constitutional objectives. However, it would be incomplete to dwell on state constitutionalism without describing further how our state constitutionalism is embedded in our American constitutional framework and mission. Constitutions are, after all, the fundamental law of states that are part of a nation of United States.

Short of painting a complete and coherent picture of state constitutions as part of the project of American constitutionalism, an ambition beyond the scope of this book, two general observations are relevant to this particular project. First, the state constitutions are fashioned as instruments of particular state objectives and while there are common elements across the fifty states – elements whose commonality permit us to speak about state constitutionalism as a coherent concept – it is important to acknowledge and understand the particularities that might ground a particular approach to regulatory power and to private rights (among other aspects of that state's constitution). Constitutions are thus a "they" in their diversity and their functions. To be sure, they are tied together by the fact that there is a US Constitution that will provide a general framework of governance and of rights within which these separate state constitutions function. This is made clear only in the brute fact of supremacy as established in the US Constitution, but also in Article IV's requirement that the United States "guarantee to every State in this Union a Republican form of government."[62] Through this important provision, however erratically enforced as a matter of constitutional doctrine, the US Constitution makes clear that it has a stake not only in the results of state political and legal processes, but in the nature of the process itself. This principle, more than any other, ties together state constitutions in a common bond, one that directs them to organize their lawmaking and law-implementing institutions to facilitate the goals that benefit republican governance. This is not to say that the US Constitution expresses a particular view about the content and scope of the police power, but that it does express to states a commitment to safeguard republican governance and the goals that such a system of governance entails.

Second, it is important to see American constitutionalism as safeguarding, through structure and practice, overarching goals of a polity that is represented by both national governments and by their own state and local governments. This idea is communicated by specific constitutional principles and doctrines, including federalism and also the post-incorporation, post-Reconstruction conception of ordered liberty emerging from our constitutional rights we enjoy as free citizens, regardless of our location. Up to now, we have focused especially on the way that the police serves the goal of state constitutional project. We need not miss in such a focus, however, the deep and broad ways in which the state constitutions work constructively to facilitate omnibus goals of the American constitutional object. To make this more concrete, think of the idea of regulation designed to protect public health. Health of citizens is a broad goal, one by any measure central to the well-being of free citizens and from which most other goals and obligations arise. Political officials and commentators have gone further in saying that health is a human right, a positive right that should be protected by governments at all levels. But we need not go that far to make at least the point that the pursuit of public health, though embedded in the state police power and the state government's obligation under this power to protect public health. Addressing the predicament of violence crime can also be understood as raising not only local goals, but national objectives. How can We the People benefit as citizens of our extended republic if we fear for our safety in our communities? There are many other examples we could conjure up to illustrate the idea that the state police power facilitates goals that span state borders, and, viewed more broadly, that the state constitutions are not only charters of fundamental law within the confines of the state, but are embedded in a more general constitutional rubric. Although conversations about constitutional theory and constitutional law often neglect to give due to state constitutions, we can recognize as we reflect more deeply on the matter that constitutions are a "they" that make up what is ultimately a common discourse, a national agenda, and a set of evolving objectives in whose service the many powers vested in national, state, and local governments remain.

American constitutionalism is a they not an it in that we fulfill our constitutional ideals by creating and improving mechanisms by which governmental institutions at all levels perform the essential functions of protecting public health, safety, and morals, and advancing the common good. The allocation of responsibility – how and to whom – is a complex and contestable matter of dynamic politics and ultimately of democracy. But the core principle is that we are all in this together and, further, that our fifty-one constitutions work in synergy, to enable the right institutions to protect our interests and goals. This is a principle of American constitutionalism that transcends one location or a narrow, one-size-fits-all conception of the general welfare. Moreover, this idea of a dynamic American constitutionalism, one that pedigrees the US Constitution as the fulcrum of our collective national constitutional objectives, while also acknowledging that the prerogatives of states to exercise reserved powers is reflected in our ideas of American federalism. Ultimately, therefore, constitutional federalism has a deep stake in the successful use of the police power in the American states.

NOTES

1. See generally Gary Donaldson, *The Second Reconstruction: A History of the Modern Civil Rights Movement* (1999); James M. McPherson, "The Dimensions of Change: The First and Second Reconstructions," 2 *The Wilson Q.* 135 (1978).
2. 514 U.S. 549 (1995).
3. 529 U.S. 598 (2000).
4. 505 U.S. 644 (1992).
5. See Skowronek, *Building a New American State*; Joanna Grisinger, "The (Long) Administrative Century: Progressive Models of Governance," in *The Progressive's Century: Political Reform, Constitutional Government, and the Modern Administrative State* (S. Skowronek et al. eds., 2016).
6. See generally, Daniel Ernst, *Tocqueville's Nightmare: The Administrative State Emerges in America, 1900–1940* (2014); Marver Bernstein, *Regulating Business by Independent Commission* (1955).
7. In addition to Skowronek, *Building a New American State*, see Joanna L. Grisinger, *The Unwieldy American State: Administrative Politics Since the New Deal* (2012).
8. See generally Paul Stephen Dempsey, "The Rise and Fall of the Interstate Commerce Commission: The Tortous Path from Regulation to Deregulation of America's Infrastructure," 95 *Marq. L. Rev.* 1151 (2012).
9. See generally Herbert Hovenkamp, *Opening of American Law: Neoclassical Legal Thought, 1870–1970* 206–19 (2014).
10. P.L. 79–404. On the origins of the APA, see McNollgast et al., "The Political Origins of the Administrative Procedure Act," 15 *J. L. Econ. & Org.* 180 (1999).
11. See generally Barry Cushman, *Rethinking the New Deal Court: The Structure of a Constitutional Revolution* 156–76 (1998).
12. See William J. Novak, "The American Law of Overruling Necessity: The Exceptional Origins of State Police Power," in *States of Exception in American History* 111–15 (G. Gerstle & J. Isaac eds., 2020).
13. See Ernst, *Tocqueville's Nightmare*.
14. See G. Edward White, *Law in American History Volume II: From Reconstruction through the 1920s* 37 (2016).
15. See G. Edward White, *Law in American History Volume III* (2019).
16. See generally Mark Tushnet, *The Hughes Court: From Progressivism to Pluralism, 1930 to 1941* 161 (2022).
17. 32 U.S. 243 (1833).
18. See, e.g., McDonald v. City of Chicago, Ill., 561 U.S. 742 (2010); Mapp v. Ohio, 367 U.S. 643 (1961); Everson v. Board of Ed. of Ewing Twsp., 330 U.S. 1 (1947).
19. See Tushnet, *The Hughes Court*, at 272–306.
20. See Heart of Atlanta Motel v. United States, 379 U.S. 241 (1964); Katzenbach v. McClung, 379 U.S. 294 (1964).
21. 514 U.S. 549 (1995).

22. 529 U.S. 598 (2000).
23. See Bowsher v. Synar, 478 U.S. 714 (1986); INS v. Chadha, 462 U.S. 919 (1983).
24. See Printz v. United States, 521 U.S. 898 (1997); New York v. United States, 505 U.S. 144 (1992).
25. Gregory v. Ashcroft, 501 U.S. 452 (1991).
26. 598 U.S. 356 (2023).
27. See, e.g., Biden v. Nebraska, 600 U.S. __ (2023); West Virginia v. EPA, 597 U.S. 597 (2022); Alabama Ass'n of Realtors v. Dep't of Health & Human Services, 594 U.S. __ (2021).
28. See Metzger, "1930s Redux."
29. See Gundy v. United States, 588 U.S. __ (2019).
30. 467 U.S. 837 (1984).
31. See generally Thomas Merrill, *The Chevron Doctrine: Its Rise and Fall, and the Future of the Administrative State* (2022).
32. See ibid.
33. 528 U.S. at 639 (2000).
34. See ibid., at 628 (Souter, J., dissenting).
35. 317 U.S. 111 (1942).
36. 545 U.S. 1 (2005).
37. See Morrison, 528 U.S. at 618.
38. See, e.g., Charles S. Bullock III, "Cooperative Federalism and Fair Housing Enforcement," 99 *Social Sci. Q.* 728 (2018); Daniel Elazar, "Urbanism and Federalism: Twin Revolutions of the Modern Era," 5 *Publius* 15 (Spring 1975).
39. See, e.g., Erin Ryan, "Federalism and the Tug of War Within: Seeking Checks and Balances in the Interjurisdictional Era," 66 *Md. L. Rev.* 503 (2007); Harry N. Scheiber, "American Federalism and the Diffusion of Power: Historical and Contemporary Perspectives," 9 *U. Tol. L. Rev.* 619 (1978).
40. Abbe R. Gluck & Nicole Huberfeld, "What is Federalism in Health Care For?" 70 *Stan. L. Rev.* 1689 (2018); Abbe R. Gluck, "Intrastatutory Federalism and Statutory Interpretation: State Implementation of Federal Law in Health Reform and Beyond," 121 *Yale L. J.* 534, 539–40 (2011).
41. NFIB v. Sebelius, 567 U.S. 519 (2012).
42. See generally Heather K. Gerken, "Federalism and Nationalism: Time for a Détente?" 59 *St. Louis U. L. J.* 997 (2015).
43. https://bit.ly/42J1X8X.
44. See McCulloch v. Maryland, 17 U.S. 316 (1819).
45. See William Buzee, *Preemption Choice: The Theory, Law, and Reality of Federalism's Core Question* (2008).
46. See, e.g., Gade v. Nat'l Solid Wastes Mgmt. Ass'n, 505 U.S. 88 (1992); Rice v. Santa Fe Elevator Corp., 331 U.S. 218 (1947).
47. Printz v. United States, 521 U.S. 898 (1997); New York v. United States, 505 U.S. 144 (1992).
48. 567 U.S. 519 (2012).
49. Ibid., at 560.
50. More recently, University of Michigan law professor, Richard Primus, has insisted that Congress cannot be limited to enumerated powers of the Constitution. While he does not conclude from this argument that the national government has a police power, one key implication of his view is that the powers of the Congress are not delineated in any meaningful way in that document and so actions that promote the general welfare

are perfectly consistent with the Constitution so long as not restricted by rights protections. See Richard Primus, "The Limits of Enumeration," 124 *Yale L. J.* 576 (2014). See also Richard Primus & Roderick M. Hills, Jr., "The Suspect Spheres, Not Enumerated Powers: A Guide for Leaving the Lamppost," 119 *Mich. L. Rev.* 1431 (2021).
51. See, e.g., Robert Schapiro, *Polyphonic Federalism* (2009); Neil S. Siegel & Robert D. Cooter, "Collective Action Federalism: A General Theory of Article I, Section 8," *Stan. L. Rev.* 115 (2010); Ernest Young, "Federalism as a Constitutional Principle," 83 *U. Cinc. L. Rev.* 1057 (2015).
52. Heather K. Gerken, "Foreword: Federalism all the Way Down," 124 *Harv. L. Rev.* 4 (2010).
53. Ibid., at 14.
54. Ibid., at 47.
55. Ibid., at 47–48.
56. See Abbe R. Gluck, "Our [National] Federalism," 123 *Yale L. J.* 1996 (2014).
57. See ibid., at 2004.
58. See ibid., at 2016.
59. See Young, "Constitutional Principle," at 1066.
60. Jessica Bullman-Pozen, "From Sovereignty and Process to Administration and Politics: The Afterlife of American Federalism," 123 *Yale L. J.* 1920 (2014).
61. See generally Richard Bourke, *Empire and Revolution: The Political Life of Edmund Burke* (2015).
62. U.S. Const. Art. IV.

PART III

The Police Power's Promise

9

Spheres of Regulatory Governance

[An examination] will reveal the police power not as a fixed quantity, but as the expression of social, economic and political conditions. As long as these conditions vary, the police power must continue to be elastic, i.e., capable of development.

Freund, *The Police Power*

Good governing has been used in two senses throughout this book. One sense, reflected largely in the historical exegesis and description of present legal practice in Part I, is that state and local governments have long had, and continue to have, a very wide berth to enact and implement laws that aspire to promote the common good and the public's welfare. Limits on this capacious authority come from various constitutional constraints, including rights sourced in both state constitutions and also the US Constitution. As we explored earlier, these limits are also found in the important, dynamic, yet often neglected, commitment to government action that is neither arbitrary nor discriminatory − what can be captured in the overarching requirement that government actions not be unacceptably unreasonable, arbitrary, the product of animus, or the result of self-dealing. State and local governments are asked to navigate these tensions between governing in the name of the people's welfare and ensuring that property and liberty are adequately protected. The evolving story of the police power in our nearly quarter of a millennium's worth of experience in the American states is that governments aspire to do their best to reconcile these conflicts and pursue meaningfully progressive governance; and where they fail, courts will sometimes intervene, with the larger aim of keeping this balance intact.

Health and safety are enduring elements of police power's objectives; morals, too, albeit in ways that have evolved as we rethink the role of the State in legislating and regulating individual and social morality. If the police power has an essence, it is the key source of government's authority and obligation to promote the general welfare and, under the rubric of state constitutionalism, to help secure the objectives that are intended to be fulfilled by official action on behalf of the people in our respective constitutional republics.

In the final Part of this book, we turn to what are conspicuously normative matters. The basic claim is that to the extent that state constitutions vest massive, if measured, power in state and local institutions to regulate for the common good, we should expect of our legislators and administrators good governing. These expectations stem directly from our ambitious state constitutional project. This is not the usual way we think of constitutional objectives, as constitutional theory in the United States typically focuses on the negative rights aspects of constitutionalism, that is to say on the ways that it constrains governmental power and thereby protects our well-ordered liberty. Moreover, attention among scholars has focused nearly exclusively on the US Constitution. What this misses is the important, and, yes, progressive, sense in which constitutions, including state constitutions, set out ambitions and aspirations for good governing, and it also sets up the mechanisms for realizing these key objectives. As Professors Fishkin and Forbath summarize the objectives of emergent constitutionalism as traction in ambitious regulation developed in the Gilded Age and afterward: "[I]n institutional terms, this vision of the democracy of opportunity came to stand for the primacy of legislation and administrative state-building in meeting the challenges of modern government."[1] The responsibilities that We the People, with the capitalized letters pertinent to the national context and we the people in lower case referring to our common aspirations as state residents, impose on our elected representatives and others who act in the name of federal, state, and local governments are embedded in our constitutional frameworks and in their fundamental principles. Good governing as a general constitutional principle is manifest most importantly in the state's police power.

What the concept means in operational terms will be contestable and ever-evolving; further, the objectives and practices should emerge from conversations that are sustained by participation in our democratic traditions (including new traditions we invent). The contours of these practices will emerge organically and, we might even say, best from the bottom up, not from the top down. Broadly speaking, we want governing that is successful and aspirational, is democratic in a thick sense of that term, and is well designed to implement the public good. The framers of the US Constitution understood this when they spoke in the Constitution's preamble of the promoting the general welfare (among other ambitious goals). And the framers of state constitutions have consistently understood the obligations of subnational officials, be they elected or appointed, to advance the common interest and good of their citizens through diligent protection of the health, safety, and welfare of those within their charge and responsibility.

In this penultimate chapter, we focus on some concrete policy areas that are within the project of governing at the state and local level, and are so precisely because of the evolution of the police power as a constitutionally sourced authority, rooted in not only discretion but *obligation* – for government to act, to decide, and to perform functions. This description of some policy areas is necessarily incomplete; and so the reader should not view this as, by any measure, a comprehensive list of policy areas for state and local governments to tackle. Rather, it is a description that focuses on some of the more difficult and pressing issues – super wicked problems, as that phrase has been defined[2] – that contemporary governments face in this century. Moreover, this is not intended as a polemic in favor of one or another particular governmental policy or strategy. The main point is to advocate for a more creative and ambitious use of the police power to tackle these issues in meaningful, constructive ways. To put a finer point on it, the police power is fundamentally about good governing, and good governing aspires to a resolute focus by well-intentioned, competent, collaborative, adequately resourced public officials on the major issues of our times.

REGULATING EXTERNALITIES: NEW *SIC UTERE* PRINCIPLES

In our deep dive into the jurisprudence of the police power in Chapters 2 and 3, we saw how the state courts were moving steadily away from the *sic utere* rationale for governmental intervention under the police power and toward a view that William Novak persuasively describes as *salus populi*, that is, focused on promoting the common good, not merely addressing harm.[3] That all said, the courts still look to *sic utere* to nest a particular vision of the police power as a mechanism by which the government can look after individual safety and health needs and interpose themselves between what would otherwise be threats to citizen welfare. The police power, then and now, provides a source of authority of government to redress wrongdoing and harm. We saw as one key example of this the use of the police power to abate nuisances, be they private or public.[4] This continues to be a broad power as the concept of nuisance has evolved. We also discussed this in connection with the government's persistent role in addressing the so-called secondary effects of certain conduct, be it adult entertainment, prostitution, drug dealing, or other social vices. Here we might imagine a set of new and improved *sic utere* principles that can undergird one important aspect of the police power.

One novel *sic utere* principle for a robust modern police power is that the notion of harm should not be limited to demonstrably tangible harms that are past-focused, that is, that have already occurred and can be measured as if in a court dealing with the determination of damages.[5] The harms that the government might aspire to deal with may be prospective,[6] and perhaps even speculative.[7] So, for example, redressing potential harm from environmental damage, as in the puzzle of human contributions to climate change, can often be prospective in nature, but nonetheless fits into models of harm.[8] Police power laws dealing with threats to public health – think of strategies to deal with the harms that befall individuals who are unhoused – can be similarly prospective, yet also based upon the *sic utere* paradigm that the government should address harm.

This is not primarily a point about the metaphysics of conduct, that is, an acknowledgment that harm that occurs later can still be regarded as harm and therefore we should prepare by suitable regulations. Rather, this is a point about pragmatic public policy. We should be looking at threats to the public welfare that unfold more slowly or uncertainly. Climate change is in many senses a slow moving trainwreck (although, as we are witnessing, perhaps not as slow as we had expected and hoped). The temptation to wait until serious, concrete harms occur should be tempered by our ability to tackle future harms through present actions. We can see the advantages of proactive measures to deal with prospective harms, as such decision-making may succeed in more efficaciously solving wicked problems whose main impact has yet to come. In a related vein, threats that might emerge because of new technologies which we do not yet fully understand, such as deep learning in artificial intelligence, may be addressable more effectively if we have some coherent, evidence-based solutions to potential problems.[9] The classic notion of *sic utere* sits uneasily with these kinds of harms, given that they are unavoidably speculative and with damage that cannot be easily assessed. Hence the need for new *sic utere* principles and sensible, well-informed police power regulations to help confront them.

A second *sic utere* principle is that the damage that is being suffered, whether prospectively or retrospectively, need not be associated with identifiable individuals. Here we want to draw a distinction between the traditional modality of tort law, both conceptually and practically, as the classic *sic utere* mechanism to recognize and redress harm, and the police power under novel *sic utere* principles. Stripped to its essence, tort law relies on our ability to assign duties between individuals and those who would suffer damage from the conduct of a putative tortfeasor.[10] Such duties are important in our ability to assign blame and responsibility; and given the rather uncontroversial duty that individuals owe to their fellow beings to not engage in tortious behavior, it is typically not difficult to ascribe duties in ways that tort law can accommodate. This will be more difficult, however, if we see the conduct as creating risks to the community that are not so easily associated with specific individuals or groups. Take, for example, the sticky problem of nuclear proliferation. This is damaging conduct, associated with particular behaviors and individuals we can point to.[11] However, few would suggest that such conduct is tortious, in the sense that modern tort law suggests. (It could be prohibited or regulated, to be sure, but notice that such efforts will likely go into the *salus populi* box). Such a view, however, may well illustrate the comparatively greater suitability of regulation under the police power to tackle certain issues where duty is elusive versus tort law, law which is quintessentially private law.

Likewise, causation imposes challenges to tort law regulating certain behaviors.[12] The recent Covid pandemic illustrates a conundrum with assigning blame. We could fathom that individuals who are Covid positive and therefore transmitters of the virus should not be exposing individuals to the virus where this could be effectively avoided. However, individuals contract the virus in places and contexts in which it will be nearly impossible to determine who caused this result. The difficulty in establishing causation has easily defeated most liability lawsuits during Covid, limiting recoveries to those narrow contexts in which courts have been willing to ascribe blame to individuals or businesses solely on the grounds that they have acted with gross negligence or utter indifference (such that they have found blame even where causation cannot be established with meaningful certainty).[13] Even worker's compensation has proved to be a difficult framework for Covid recovery, such that a number of states changed their laws, at least temporarily, to flip the presumption of causation so that individuals could claim credibly that their disease was contracted in the workplace.[14] All of this is to say that tort law has to go through fairly elaborate contortions to get to a place where individuals can recover under the familiar principles of tort law.

The police power need not be tied to these traditional tort law principles. Police regulations may be viewed from one vantage point as the public law analogue to tort law. But we can see that, even where regulation is being used for *sic utere* reasons, police power regulation has a special capacity to account for harm-causing behavior by limiting such behavior. Using the Covid example again, the government might create a scaffold of regulations that oblige businesses to take certain precautions or oblige individuals to report their infectiousness status in order to reduce the likelihood of harm. We can imagine, too, a regime of compensation for such harms, paralleling what we see in the context of other mass injury events, such as 9/11, but this entails regulatory measures that will likely look beyond the police power to certain fiscal strategies.[15] Or the right strategy might be an admixture of regulation and public subsidy. In short, the police power can underwrite a theory of governmental power that aspires to tackle harms that are societally diffuse and not absorbed into traditional ideas of corrective justice and discrete harms.

Steps to address, for example, systemic racism in law enforcement or in zoning or in the provision of public health – to take three examples of profound social problems – are not susceptible to ordinary attribution to particular individuals, either with respect to victims or perpetrators. We know that that systemic racism causes major harm; and we further know that the burdens of this racism fall on the shoulders of communities of color. Without detailing specific policy innovations that might tackle racism in these contexts, it is worth reiterating that such efforts push against the classic model of *sic utere* in the sense of redressing wrongs that can be identified with particular individuals. Such strategies, therefore, rest on a reconfiguration of this classic model (along, of course, with connecting reform in this vein to a *salus populi* conception).

These are just principles, and the devil, of course, lies in the details. The burden of elaborating more exactly how certain police powers might trade on these novel *sic utere* principles is greater in its need for precision than this book can bear. The basic essential takeaway point is that there remains in the progressive account of the police power room for a enduring connection between the *sic utere* ideal that has long grounded legal obligation to redress harm that results from private activity – think of various forms of noxious discrimination, for example – and an ambitious, creative police power.

One additional point bears mentioning in the context of our discussion of addressing harm. The government's responsibility to address harmful activity comes with it an expectation that it will do so in a way that is balanced and accords with ideas that account responsibly for benefits as well as costs. One traditional view of regulation's domain emphasizes what has been labelled The Precautionary Principle.[16] This principle obliges government to regulate certain harms whenever there is a plausible risk. To the extent that the risk is especially serious, regulation is required even in the face uncertainty, both about the likelihood of harm and the efficacy of government regulation to redress this harm.

The efficacy of this principle is controversial, however. As Cass Sunstein has stated: "The weak versions of the Precautionary Principle state a truism – uncontroversial in principle and necessary in practice only to combat public confusion or the self-interested claims of private groups demanding unambiguous evidence of harm, which no rational society requires."[17] In its stronger iteration, this principle can block innovation and progress. The dilemma for governments is how to implement public health and safety regulations under the police power that ensure a decent assurance of safety without imposing burdens that can reduce innovation and plainly impose high costs that are out of proportion to the goals sought and, indeed, may well be counterproductive. For example, many measures undertaken during the Covid pandemic, including the decisions at the local level to close down schools, have raised hard issues involving the precautionary principle and the attendant dilemma in regulating. In a somewhat similar vein, efforts to regulate certain technologies, as we will discuss below, implicate the precautionary principle, especially insofar as we worry about the potential risks associated with rapidly evolving technology rather than its current use. There is no obvious solution to this dilemma, but developing principles for good governing under the police power should be cognizant of and deliberate about the precautionary principle in regulation, especially with respect to novel problems and technologies.

WHO ARE THE PEOPLE IN THE "PEOPLE'S" WELFARE?

The *salus populi* idea has played a fundamental role in the development and refinement of the police power. Where this idea has special punch is with respect to the goal that typically comes at the end of the conventional rendering of the police power, that is the part described variously as the people's welfare, the public interest, the common good, and the general welfare (among other variations on this same theme).

Yet, who exactly are the people in the configuration of the people's welfare? Although not addressed in detail in our exegesis on the evolution of the police power in the first three chapters, it would be impossible to give a coherent account of regulatory strategy and purpose during American history without accounting for issues of subordination and inequality,[18] particularly around race and gender.[19] Such matters affect how we think about regulation and regulatory choices over American history and also how we think about the overall concept of the general welfare of the community. First and most obviously, the choices that we were made by government and on behalf of the citizenry in the democratic processes of state legislatures in our nation's first century and deeply into the next were made nearly exclusively by White men.[20] Access to the channels of political and legal power were incredibly slow for the out groups (people of color, women, immigrants, the disabled, the poor), even after the enactment of the Reconstruction amendments.[21] Voting rights were scant, and all the evidence points unmistakably to a series of policymaking decisions through the post-framing, Jacksonian, antebellum,[22] Reconstruction, Progressive and Populist eras that were not meaningfully inclusive, palpably neglectful of the views and interests of out groups, and in many years positively discriminatory. Legal redress was thin, and even later was episodic.[23] As Novak puts it, "despite the aspirations or pretensions to national equality voiced in formal political documents … early American states and localities were in the constant habit of using their local police powers to pass discriminatory laws differentiating their populations along nearly every conceivable social status."[24]

These developments were manifest in political activity – acts and omissions – and also in legal decisions that remain in the pages of federal and state reports. Plessy was a lowlight to be sure, but other cases, especially The Civil Rights Cases of the 1870s,[25] helped write a script of exclusion and subordination.[26] States were well within their constitutional powers to act in more inclusive ways, but the evidence does not suggest that, taken as a whole, states were particularly progressive on matters of race and gender, to take just two of the most important objects of discriminatory actions.

If one wanted to add some positive elements to this dire story of inequality, one could point to some of the important Progressive era reforms that empowered the rural poor and small businesses, including businesses who were serving individuals otherwise excluded and disadvantaged. The Granger movement, for example, the focal point of the Supreme Court's decision in Munn, reflected the political activity of small farmers to gain some measure of equality against monopolistic agriculture.[27] Later, the rise of regulation at the state and federal level to combat unfair trade practices (the Federal Trade Commission being emblematic as a creation designed to tackles these problems) and to address unsafe food and drugs had, if indirectly, a leveling effect on inequality's impacts. Certainly the Reconstruction era, with constitutional amendment and legislation brought through the "second founding" a new structure of citizenship, at least formally.[28] But this "whataboutism" ultimately cannot address coherently or comprehensively the predicament of subordinated groups during, especially, the first century of the republic's history and hence the first century of the police power's existence.

So what do we make of the *salus populi* by this reference point in light of this troubling history? We should be realistic about what the people's welfare meant and did not mean during a big amount of our history. The people's welfare was focused, alas, on the welfare of individuals who counted.[29] This problem, to the extent it was addressed at all, was dealt with mainly through social movements and structural reforms. Naturally, the Nineteenth Amendment's enfranchisement of women was a critical development in the movement toward political power and, with it, a *salus populi* that covered men and women alike.[30] Slow structural process in voting rights for minorities was crucial and so the Voting Rights Act of 1965 was a watershed (even if an incomplete one). Other structural reforms, through legislative, judicial decisions, and administrative action, helped broaden the scope of the people whose welfare was the focus of government action.

To make this point more explicitly normative, we should always be contemplating in our evaluation of the modern police power and its potential for facilitating good governing the breadth and dimension of inclusion (as well as empathy) in the configuration of governance institutions and the assessment of progress. It is hard to see from the evidence that the police power *qua* police power did much work in advancing equality objectives. Legislatures showed little empathy and vision and, where they did, these efforts were at best episodic. Courts seldom helped matters. In looking forward to the ways in which the police power can provide a fulcrum for the exercise of meaningful regulatory power in order to realize the objectives of good governing under state constitutional objectives, we should think about becoming more ambitious in our goals. The common good, should be constructs of meaningful generative potential. That is to say, we ought to measure how effective is government regulation in advancing public welfare and moving toward the common good in part by how inclusive these choices and choice processes are. Even more ambitious would be recognizing that the redressing of deeply embedded systems and schemes of inequality is a coherent and critical component of the modern police power's objectives. This has not been so to any appreciable degree in our history, but there are no clear reasons why it should not be so today.

The reasons to think about the police power as a vehicle of redress and even rehabilitation are at least two fold. First, and perhaps foremost, such an objective aligns with what is simply the right thing to do as a society. Repairing a broken fabric of citizenship made broken by choices our ancestors made and did not make is a component part of what the nation owes by way of its fundamental ideals. And while we can and will disagree about the best tactics of repair, we should be manifestly committed to this ideal. The US Constitution in its preamble speaks of forming "a more perfect Union." This ideal undergirds the philosophy of state constitutionalism as well, with perfection being an aspiration reached through the decisions made by government on behalf of the people, certainly including the use of the governments' formidable regulatory powers. Second, speaking to the interests and needs of a diverse policy, not omitting our expanding group of stakeholders, we have said helps attend to a concern raised in this book's first chapter, and that is assuaging the fear of those in the minority that their rights will not be trampled upon by a system that privileges majoritarian decision-making. Successful constitutions, as we described, are ones that reduce the stakes of politics. Finding a balance between majoritarian and countermajoritarian interests, and sustaining this through what is largely a self-enforcing equilibrium, is critical to maintaining constitutional stability.

In sum, scrupulous attention to who is included in the "people" whose welfare is being advanced is an important objective of the police power, insofar as this power is tethered to the larger objectives of American constitutionalism, to protect order and to form a more perfect union.

※

In the remainder of this chapter, we look at some specific policy areas that a robust view of the police power will tackle. Whereas the extended discussion of the police power's policy domain in Part I's chapters was largely historical and focused on how courts have interpreted the police power over our two plus centuries of American constitutional law, the focus here is avowedly normative; we can look at the potential of the police power to ameliorate harms and advance societal welfare. And we should be concrete in doing so.

HOUSING ACCESS AND AFFORDABILITY

The jurisprudence of the police power points to an enormously ample authority, as we have discussed in earlier chapters, vested in state and local governments to regulate the use of land. Although Euclid was decided nearly a century ago,[31] the main message of that case, that the government can establish a comprehensive zoning plan to which residential and commercial property owners must comply, remains largely accurate as a description of modern zoning and the police power. At the same time, state and federal courts have frequently described the authorities that government has under the police power as changing in response to new conditions. This is a key point to consider. What could be a proper exercise of the police power at one point in time could be unreasonable at another in time depending upon changed circumstances.

What was long viewed as the progressive underpinnings of zoning as a strategy to fulfill public regarding objectives of land use in the face of more narrow economic self-interest of private property owners has come under scrutiny as evidence reveals some of the deleterious effects of exclusionary zoning. Some of the more baleful land use regulations are those requiring minimum lot sizes, height restrictions, prohibitions on multiple detached units on a lot (affecting so-called "accessory dwelling units" also sometimes called "granny flats"), and restrictions on developing housing on previously open land. Each of these zoning strategies, as leading economists and land use experts have written, effectively limit the building of more housing, especially housing suitable to folks with more limited means. Zoning power has been occasionally abused,[32] and the general welfare of existing and, especially, potential, community members has been on the whole compromised.[33]

There is an irony in all this, in that the basic strategy of zoning was defended in Euclid and afterward as a quintessential example of the responsible use of the government regulation under the police power to implement public interest objectives, to trade off private property owner's interest in developing their property however they want for a commitment to wider goals. Now it is in the structuring of these putatively public-spirited laws that we see the police power's goals being undermined in the operation of contemporary land use strategy. We briefly describe the predicament and next describe how the police power can be used to help alleviate it.

To frame this discussion, let us consider some of the contemporary debate over the zoning strategies that the government has long used to maintain a certain form of order in their communities. While these strategies are not uniform, there has been a heavy reliance on the strategies mentioned above. In addition to this menu of typically available restrictions, zoning authorities often impose residency limits in multi-family housing, such as apartment buildings. Finally, there remain a handful of municipalities that have adopted residential rent control as an instrument of social equity. When viewed in combination, these land use restrictions have come under criticism for their impact on the availability of affordable housing.

Zoning restrictions present a key source of the problem. First, the existence of restrictions on building dense housing and on smaller lots – what Ellickson calls colorfully the "zoning straightjacket" – predictably limits building options and housing supply.[34] Furthermore, even measured steps to alleviate these severe restrictions carry their own problems, as a recent *Harvard Law Review* note summarizes it: "[W]here zoning laws do permit the construction of higher-density housing, density-reducing regulations – such as height restrictions, minimum lot size requirements, prohibitions on accessory dwelling units (ADUs), or setback requirements – impair affordability by forcing each unit to bear a greater share of the cost of land."[35]

In a blunt assessment of the claims made by modern defenders of restrictive land use regulations, David Schleicher summarizes the critique:

> [L]and use regulations in rich regions from 1980 to 2020 prevented housing growth to match growing housing demand, limiting access to hot job markets. The result is a loss of economic output of staggering proportions, as workers have been unable to move to higher-paying jobs. Further, in the presence of high demand, excessive land use regulations result in high housing costs, causing huge rent burdens, homelessness, and economic inequality through capital appreciation for homeowners.[36]

It is well worth considering whether and to what extent current land use regulations that are intended to promote the general welfare of the community can have the opposite effect. As we discussed in Chapter 4, one of the intriguing dimensions of the

New Jersey court's decision in the Mount Laurel affordable housing lawsuit is the close consideration of whether the implementation of longstanding forms of land-use policy might have as an unintended consequence the reduction in affordable housing.[37] And, if so, whether and what extent, as the court considered in that case, the objective of zoning under the rubric of the police power was being undermined.

The social movements generated by affordable housing advocates, and also the longer-lived efforts by property rights advocates, have made these issues much more prominent in the public's eye and on the government's agenda.[38] The so-called "YIMBY" movement has evolved in parallel with the steadily more powerful post-Kelo property rights movement.[39] Both are important fulcra of legal advocacy and democratic power. (It has made, too, for some rather strange political bedfellows, but that's beside the point here.) In any case, the challenge for policymakers considering reforms that might enhance housing, ranging from basic shelter for the presently unhoused to home ownership at a reasonable cost, and everything in between, is to consider carefully the connection between contemporary zoning regulations and these housing matters.

Two conclusions regarding the police power follow from this critique of modern land use decisions. First, there is a steadily growing case for states intervening to limit local land use authority.[40] This reflects a step away from where zoning has been situated for the nearly 100 years since the Euclid decision. The state is well within its power under its constitutional authority to rein in local prerogatives and local zoning rules. Doing so does not necessarily mangle the idea that local governments have delegated police power to protect the health, safety, and welfare of the citizenry. Responsible land use laws can still be seen as manifestations of just this authority. However, the broad legal authority of local governments to create and enforce land use laws is not inconsistent with the use of state-level authority to preempt local laws or, where warranted in extreme situations, to wrest back control of local land use policies so that the fundamental choices are, going forward, exercised at the state level.[41]

The second conclusion, one more radical than the first, is to look closely at local laws to see whether they meet the tests of the police power. Are they being created and imposed in a reasonable way?[42] The argument that they have not been reasonable grows out of the claim, based upon empirical evidence, that the land use laws are actually undermining the general welfare. As the modern critique reflects, the operative basis for these restrictive land use laws is protectionist, a NIMBY sensibility that sacrifices the interests of individuals seeking affordable housing. In a court of law, this argument would be a hefty lift. Suffice it to say, however, that the underlying logic of the police power points courts to a consideration of whether judges might ask whether certain regulations are inconsistent in objective and in strategy – in other words, do they sacrifice the public's welfare for the interest of incumbent local interests? In this regard, the police power, somewhat incongruously, can be used to limit the exercise of certain instances of local governmental power.

We should approach the question of modern zoning law and the police power with a dose of reality, however. Let us separate two imagined states of the world. Even supposing that the accumulated evidence suggests that the use of various zoning measures (height limits, residency caps, setbacks, etc.) is counterproductive in that it reduces the supply of available, affordable housing, it would be a bold step indeed to hold such measures unconstitutional on the grounds that they undermine public welfare. The historic commitment of courts to permit to the legislature the choice of how best to deal with the regulation of land through zoning, a commitment that is century old, is a big impediment to a constitutional rule that would in fact stand in the way of legislative discretion. The property owners' rights to do what they wish with their land, forever appealing as a libertarian shibboleth, is not going to do the work of restricting state or municipal zoning power in the absence of a compelling argument that the overall structure and strategy of zoning is rotten root and branch. Zoning's modern critics are hard at work making these arguments, but one can remain skeptical that this robust scholarship will translate into a profoundly novel legal principle. Two other possibilities seem more promising: First, the decisions of municipal and (especially) state authorities to reign in certain traditional zoning strategies and to reconfigure in moderately ambitious modern, evidence-based ways can become more common, as the YIMBY movement steadily increases its influence and, moreover, bedfellows from the Right and Left ends of the political spectrum, to say nothing of moderates, become less strange and more common. A revolt in the zoning area is not unimaginable, but it is vastly more likely to come from political decision-makers, at various levels of government, than by activist judges. Second, zoning can become eroded as a sort of death by a thousand cuts. Governance institutions responsible for land use choices include administrators and local boards, the latter either elected or appointed by officials who are themselves elected. Such boards can become captured by groups of common interests, including landowners and social movement activists concerned with zoning's impact on affordability and access. Where zoning decision-making is owned by these local (or even hyper-local) institutions), the effect of certain decisions will undergo meaningful change, this without disturbing the overall constitutional power of government to zone.

We also face an enormous crisis of homelessness.[43] The predicament of the unhoused are not solely the result of zoning decisions. Rather, the epidemic of unhoused Americans is the result of intersecting factors, including the erosion of state and local safety nets, including mental health services, the high cost of housing stemming from various reasons, the erosion of purchasing power as a result of inflation and the absence of a living wage, the miasma of veterans' benefit administration, and other factors that lead individuals to the streets. And on these streets individuals, disproportionately people of color and other victims of social discrimination and economic subordination, suffer in various ways.[44] The wicked problem of the unhoused is complicated in both its origins and in its promising strategies. No effort, even a preliminary one, is undertaken here to offer any novel solutions to this problem. However, we can see at the very least that the ample scope and breadth of the police power creates many pathways to addressing the unhoused epidemic. To be clear, a comprehensive strategy would entail laws not necessarily directed toward the unhoused individuals themselves. Indeed, it may well be that some of the regulations typically used in this context, such as anti-vagrancy, anti-peddling, prohibitions on sleeping in public spaces, etc., are ill-suited to the problems being addressed and should be considered on both compassion and efficacy grounds. Some steps that would address how individuals are rendered safe from both the natural elements and from individuals they encounter, both private persons and law enforcement, are surely advisable. So too are laws that would address the often dire public health issues that plague the unhoused. The police power is governance power and an obligation to good governing means an obligation to help the least unfortunate, those on our safety ladder's bottom rungs. This is where we found America's unhoused, and this ought to be a focal point for government action under the rubric of the awesome police power.

The call for the creative use of the police power to deal with housing availability and affordability is borne of an ambitious and opportunistic vision of the government's role and responsibility as regulator. However, we conclude this section on a cautionary note, one that raises concerns with a strategy that has emerged in the last couple or so decades as at least a rhetorical mechanism to anchor a more ambitious strategy of improving on both affordable housing and on the predicament of the unhoused. This is the creation of a so-called constitutional right to housing.[45]

Insofar as the larger theme of this book is that the police power should be yoked to state constitutional objectives, it is worth looking closely at the demands for constitutional reform that would create a positive right to housing in state constitutions. As tempting as this development would be, there are reasons to believe that in the end, its deficits will likely outweigh its advantages. First, the shape of the right is intrinsically opaque. It is one thing to say that the unhoused should have a right to housing that would generate responsibility, fiscally and logistically, to furnish adequate shelter to individuals. This poses some substantial practical challenges, but we could at least wrap our heads around the concept that every needy individual should be able to access a roof over their head and four walls to provide basic security. It is another thing entirely to view the right to housing as something that would propel government to undertake choices that would create the conditions for anyone to live in housing that they can afford and that, furthermore, meets their needs and even wants. Advocates for a constitutional right to housing are often opaque on this question. Such decisions would involve much more than the eradication of various land use restrictions of the sort described above; it would entail the infusion of enormous sums of money to ensure that individuals would have housing. Would this mean that landlords would be especially subsidized to ensure an adequate supply of affordable housing? Would it mean that the government itself would purchase real estate sufficient to take care of individuals in need? Would there be a subsidy that would go to individuals to use, as they would, say, food stamps, but only on housing? These are difficult policy questions; and even if they are not impossible to answer, it would seem that a positive constitutional right that does not undertake to address these puzzles but simply declare that there is a housing right, declared by government and ready to be invoked by individuals is highly problematic.

The creative use of the police power to address the relationship between inadequate housing and public safety, health, and welfare is different than yoking this power to a constitutional right to housing. As we explored in our discussion of positive rights in Chapter 6, there are challenges with constructing rights that can be used not principally as trumps but as entitlements, with all that this implies for the relationship to citizens and the government. There are positive rights that are more workable in modern public law and life and others that are much more complicated. The right of housing is of the latter category, and so should be viewed with caution, if not skepticism.

TRANSPORTATION AND CITIZEN SAFETY

American transportation policy has long been built around the paradigm that we are a country on the move. Many policies, national, state, and local, can be understood as promoting, freedom of transport and, as a result of aggregate citizen preferences, automobiles. Such choices have caused impacts to the environment, as is well known.[46] Addressing vehicle pollution through federal, state, and even local regulation has been a prominent objective for more than a half century, and such efforts have made a noticeable difference, as those of us of a certain generation can attest personally and as the scientific facts demonstrate.[47] Choices to favor the automobile have also affected the configuration of urban life, as Jane Jacobs and others have famously described.[48] What has been less conspicuous in the discussion of transportation policies and the favoring of auto transit has been the impact on public safety.

In a recent article on pedestrian safety, Gregory Shill notes in reference to the data from recent years that "[d]eaths of people on foot struck by motor vehicles surged more than 46 percent during that decade, outpacing the increase in all other traffic fatalities by nine to one. There are no signs of improvement this decade."[49] Moreover, these deaths are unequally distributed by race, with Black Americans having a risk of being killed as a pedestrian two-thirds higher than White Americans. The reasons for this overlap, but include the design of city streets, decreasing obedience to traffic regulations, and, as Shill points out, the growing size of the modern automobile. There are steps that the federal regulatory agency tasked with addressing issues of vehicle safety and design could address through attention to the last aspect of the program. The second problem, driver neglect of current rules, can be addressed by more vigorous law enforcement (and perhaps other constructive efforts at improving law-following more generally, not to mention compassion for the risks imposed on mankind). The first problem, however, can be addressed if at all by sensible police power regulations. In a comprehensive 2021 study entitled "Dangerous by Design," two interest groups involved in municipal planning and street safety, Smart America and the National Complete Streets Coalition, explored at a granular level the matter of pedestrian safety and proposed various design strategies to alleviate these dangers.[50] Few of these common-sense ideas have been implemented, much less those that require a deeper understanding of street engineering.

Viewed overall, local regulation has neglected to an appreciable extent the impact of auto-friendly policies on citizen safety. Particularly vulnerable have been disabled individuals and also cyclists. Impacts cannot be measured solely by injuries and deaths, although this is obviously the most salient measure of consequence. Impacts include choices made by individuals not to walk in areas where their safety could be at risk, and individuals not to ride their bicycles but instead to utilize other modes of transportation, including automobiles, even though this is not their preferred choice and, moreover, this choice has potentially negative consequences on society.

There is a compelling argument, for the reasons we have reviewed elsewhere in this book, that the government has a special obligation to look out for the safety and welfare of citizens in physical spaces and areas which we know to be in harm's way. Extraordinary progress could certainly be made by a scrupulous, data-driven look at the transportation policy and public safety. This could yield various solutions, none of which need to be detailed here but are described and amplified in a burgeoning literature on transportation policy and public safety.[51] Effective strategies for this wicked problem requires collaboration across all levels of government. Certainly local governments have a unique place in all this, given their power and responsibility to make good choices for the structure of the cityscape.

The police power is ideally situated to provide a source of authority to improve individual safety on the roads. There are some challenges inherent in coherent strategies, however, given that the situations involve an admixture of three considerations – the driver, the individual on the road, and the condition of the road itself. To use the police power effectively, local and state authorities must examine closely all three elements and see how best to confront these synergies. Here we see the challenge and ultimately the opportunity that is presented by a reading of the police power that focuses on changing conditions and the need to update what is truly good governing for modern circumstances and the need to address our most wicked problems.

GUNS

In 2021, there were over 48,000 deaths by guns in the United States, a number that had grown by 10,000 since just 2018.[52] The rate has increased steadily in the last 25 years.[53] Moreover, the correlation between the stringency of gun laws in a state and the death rate from guns is very strong. The death rate per 100,00 is highest (between

26 and 34) in Wyoming, Alabama, New Mexico, Louisiana, and Mississippi (from fifth highest to highest) and are lowest (between 3.4 and 5.6) in Rhode Island, New York, New Jersey Hawaii, and Massachusetts. The data is unmistakable: The states with the most lax gun control laws have the highest rates of gun death (which include both homicides and suicides).[54]

The regulation of firearms has been a complex matter of societal disagreement and political struggle for decades. Even while damage wrought by individuals using firearms continues to grow, we have been largely stymied in our efforts at meaningful progress. Our predicament has taken on an added layer of complexity, and a major one, by the Supreme Court's holdings in the last fifteen years that there is a judicially cognizable individual right to keep and bear arms.[55] It would be too simple to say that the Court's gun rights jurisprudence is the reason for the paucity of state and local gun control. We cannot be certain whether is the constitutional law or the state and local politics, or both, that has limited legal efforts. But there is no doubt that the police power's capacity for dealing with the problems of modern gun violence are limited in both practical and legal ways.

This is not the place for a comprehensive discussion of Second Amendment jurisprudence. However, there are a few important lessons to draw from the raging legal, political, and social debate over firearm ownership. We should begin with a set of facts concerning the remarkable daylight between the Supreme Court's view about the constitutional limits on certain gun regulations and the public opinion relevant to state and local choices.

Public opinion on gun control matters has fluctuated somewhat over the years in which it has been measured. And different research organizations have come up with different results, sometimes meaningfully different. However, one reputable polling company, Gallup, has data indicating that the percentage of Americans supporting strong gun control measures has been over 50 percent consistently for the past ten years, while the number of Americans who would keep them as it is has been less than 40 percent and when combined with the number who would make them less stringent, hasn't exceeded the "more stringent" group since October of 2014.[56] Pew's data likewise shows that supporters of stricter gun laws have consistently (for the past six years) exceeded the combined total of "need stronger" and "fine the way it is" groups.[57] The plethora and publicity of mass shooting events has not moved the needle massively, but there has been an uptick in support for more stringent laws and law enforcement in the last couple of years.

By contrast, the Supreme Court has been moving in the opposite direction. The Bruen decision has also strengthened the right of private ownership of firearms and will surely impact, in ways still to be seen, the legal ability of state and local governments to impose meaningful limits on gun ownership. One website ("The Trace") specifically devoted to covering issues pertaining to gun violence and regulation has detailed the various responses in the states and local governments to the Court's 2022 decision.[58] This is, to be sure, a very much evolving situation with many lawsuits pending. We can saw confidently, however, that in this post-Heller era in which the right to carry firearms has been declared to be an individual right, our governments at all levels are limited in important respects from imposing gun control under its police powers, given the protections of the Second Amendment as viewed, albeit controversially, by the modern Supreme Court.

What the Court's declarations in Bruen and earlier cases tell us about the narrow path to acceptable gun control is that the governments aspiring to impose stricter controls must develop not only plausible evidence-based arguments for their policy choices, but need to connect these arguments in a coherent originalist framework, that is, a view that explains how a particular policy is consistent with the original public meaning of the Second Amendment. This burden, while high, need not be insurmountable.[59] Advocates for stronger gun control will need to investigate the history of not only gun ownership in the founding era, but also the history of the police power. That has gone largely neglected in gun litigation, and without prejudging exactly what this history will reveal, it seems at least a promising vehicle for considering on the Court's own terms, how the original public meaning of the Second Amendment was affected by conceptions of regulation, and not merely prerogative and liberty. In any event, the ultimate focus of the government's argument should be on the longstanding responsibility of the government to protect the public safety and welfare of the community. Traditional arguments that sought to locate the Second Amendment right to keep and bear arms in a well-functioning militia are unavailing after Heller. Also unavailing are arguments that are conspicuously non-originalist, in that they rest on a view that is basically this: Such a view, as the Court majority explained in Bruen, conflates a mechanical of original intent with the Court's methodology of choice, original public meaning. Whether persuasive or not, a solid majority of the Court holds that the original understanding of the Second Amendment is that the government would carry a very heavy burden of showing that a gun regulation meets a compelling state interest and is narrowly tailored to the need identified.

Even the most vigorous proponents on the Supreme Court for the protection of gun rights under the Second Amendment have acknowledged that this right is not absolute and that government has some latitude to impose appropriate gun control measures. The police power comes into this frame to the extent that the government can invoke a rationale for why a certain strategy of regulation is very likely to improve public safety and enhance welfare. Some regulations can be expected to fare well under the requirement that a strong safety rationale be demonstrated, and others less well. Nonetheless, there remains, even after Heller, McDonald, and Bruen, a role for the police power to play in the configuration of the constitutional law of gun regulation in this third decade of the twenty-first century and beyond. To believe that the headwinds of a significant rights constraint on government power undoubtedly limits the domain of the police power. But it does not render the police power nugatory; and it ought not to deflect entirely our attention to the police power as an important legal construct of relevance when we consider the nature and scope of the government's regulatory power to protect health, safety, and the common good.

As to specific regulatory tactics, a recent Rand study indicates that the three most effective strategies for reducing gun deaths, homicide and suicide included, would be the following: Restrict the way in which individuals store guns and ammunition in their homes, restrict who can carry a concealed weapon, and restrict circumstances in which individuals can use deadly force in self-defense outside of their own homes.[60] It would seem that only the second of these strategies implicates the Second Amendment under current precedent. There are other policy steps, some considerably more controversial and legally risky, and so a politically sensible approach under the police power would focus on those strategies that are likely to yield the highest payoff with the lowest risk and cost. This satisficing strategy would save lives, although it does kick down the road somewhat the can of more comprehensive gun control measures, including handgun bans, blanket prohibitions on certain individuals from possessing certain or any firearms, and the banning of entire categories of weapons. Given the combined state of current law and of politics, an incrementalist strategy may be the most plausible and efficacious under all the relevant legal and political circumstances.

ENVIRONMENTAL PROTECTION

As the environmental movement has moved from infancy to maturity in the more than half century after its origins in modern American politics, we have seen arise a series of social movements mobilizing energies and efforts to address these myriad environmental problems.[61] Some of these movements build on the classic playbook of mobilizing political and legal institutions, along with committed citizens, to address continuing environmental problems, such as air and water pollution. Others have focused on comparatively new environmental problems, including climate change. Finally, with the burgeoning environmental justice movement, we are reminded of the impact of significant harms through carcinogens and other toxic substances to citizens in local communities, be they urban or rural, and that the results have had disproportionate impacts on poor people and on citizens of color.[62] This is the predicament of environmental racism, a condition that has festered alongside the general threats to the environment through pollution in its various forms and also the misuse or overuse of substances that can cause impacts on living conditions and on the long-term welfare of our planet.

A large and growing literature has focused on the synergies available through national and state collaboration.[63] Top-down command-and-control regulation now seems somewhat quite anachronistic, and even naïve, given what we have learned about the efficacy of more multi-institutional strategies.[64] Moreover, literature in the so-called "new governance" tradition has illuminated the value and virtues of public/private initiatives, thus interrogating in sensible ways the entire idea of traditional government regulation as the sole, or even the best, mechanism for addressing environmental problems.[65] It is important to see this emerging call for more imaginative techniques of regulation as stemming not only from capable, interested academics advocating novel strategies, but from the advances in science that has made data-driven, evidence-based approaches more promising. Building bridges between strategies that are conceptually promising and practically possible must be the highest priority, and here is where science, in its various forms, and deep institutional analysis (attentive, too, to local knowledge) make and keep a productive and activist marriage.

What remains less conspicuous in the literature and commentary on environmental protection is the particular role of local governance in tackling environmental problems. To be sure, environmental threats are almost quintessentially cross-border in their effects; the very idea of pollution as externalities, thus implicating collective action dilemmas, suggests that seldom will a geographically defined local government have the tools to tackle these complex problems effectively. But ultimately these familiar ideas which undergird more centralized strategies prove too much. Local governance can and does play an important, and indeed even vital, role in assembling strategies and structures to tackle particular environmental threats.[66] Moreover, as the vexing ordeal of environmental racism illustrates, addressing the often second-order consequences that flow from certain private conduct and governmental responses is essential, and in that domain local governments and democratic local institutions have a comparative advantage.

The experience of the residents of Flint, Michigan during the water contamination disaster of 2014–16 illustrates this dynamic phenomenon.[67] State public officials had made the dangerous decision, without meaningful input, to shift the community's water supply from Lake Huron to the Flint River, the consequences of which for public health were catastrophic. The responses at the regulatory repair level were substantial, and the evidence collected suggested that rapid work had solved the worst of the dangerous conditions. Moreover, state legislation and even a federal statute was enacted in the hopes of ensuring that another crisis of this type and magnitude would not recur. However, the fallout with respect to public trust and local democracy still persists years later. A Politico report in 2020 analyzed the paradox: As the title indicates, "Flint Has Clean Water Now. Why Won't People Drink It?"[68] The answers lie in the political history of the city and the context and conditions within which this crisis unfolded and in which steps were taken or not taken to address public discontent. As one citizen put it: "There would not have been a water crisis if we had democracy in the city."[69] The road out of Flint's persistent problems – a political trust crisis emerging from an environmental crisis – requires engagement and problem-solving at the local level. Michigan can neither enact laws to solve it nor in any meaningful way drive progress beyond its evidence-based public health interventions. Less dramatic versions of this conundrum play out in environmental issues of local salience throughout the country.

Designed in its very origins as a source of authority to protect the health and welfare of citizens, the police power is well suited to tackling important environmental problems. However, where matters can hit legal snags is when the challenge presented to government is whether and to what extent local governments can address directly some of these serious problems without acting under the aegis of particular state or even federal legislation. Can and should municipal governments take a broad view of its role under the police power to address environmental problems that are having special impacts on local citizens? Yes indeed, and we should see the police power as a warrant for robust local initiative and as a promising font of innovation in safeguarding the welfare of the community. Others have written powerfully about the promise of an effective environmental localism.[70] What is required in order to facilitate strategies that promote sound environmental protection strategies at the local level is an acknowledgment that the police power is a source of constitutional authority well suited to local governance and strategic action.

Another practical road sometimes taken in tackling wicked environmental problems can be sustained by a robust view of the police power as an engine of good governing and that is the development of special-purpose governments. Many states – California is an especially prominent example – have constructed special-purpose governments to address issues that have proved intractable to ordinary general-purpose governments, be they municipal or state-wide. While the challenges raised by such governmental structures from the perspective of democracy and efficacy have been noted by many who have focused on this important phenomenon, the development of this model of governing has given us more imaginative institutional solutions to issues of health and safety protection. In particular, they have enabled the use of novel fiscal strategies and methods of circumventing difficult political obstacles in order to further public interest goals. These advances in good governing are undergirded by a vision of the police power that, as noted in an earlier chapter, sees the state constitution as facilitative of innovative institutions and regulatory strategies. Environmental protection and transportation externalities, as described above, are especially well suited to some of these more innovative techniques. Sometimes new wine calls for new bottles.

INFRASTRUCTURE AND WEALTH INEQUALITY

The multifaceted impact of wealth inequality has been noted by a growing chorus of commentators and social scientists.[71] The issue is enormously complex and the already far-flung analysis in this and the preceding chapter is hardly the place to delve deeply into the causes and consequences of this expanding inequality. However, let us first acknowledge that this is a serious social problem, and that our American constitutional scheme can accommodate, given the will to act, steps and strategies to deal with various aspects of this wealth inequality, short of a reconstruction of our system of capitalism and of the elemental commitments of our republic to individual liberty and property. In recent years, a number of prominent legal scholars, including professors Fishkin and Forbath, whose important contributions to constitutional theory have been discussed elsewhere in this book, have spoken about our constitution as the fundamental means to protect a vision of democracy-as-opportunity.[72] In his recent exegesis of the project of state-building and democracy in the period from the Progressive era to the New Deal, William Novak gives as one example of "the progressive pursuit of a social democratic state" the imperative of addressing wealth inequality through constitutional means.[73] Not surprisingly, the vast majority of this literature focuses on the capacity and obligation of the federal government acting under the rubric of the US Constitution, using whatever traditional or novel techniques are available to the lawmakers, the judges, and to We the People, to redress these inequalities. Implicit in this is that neither state nor local governments can, should, or will engage in the project of redistribution or in any forms of redress of inequality.

We should not take this is a given. We can see through the twin lenses of our history and normative political theory how state constitutions have supported ambitious social policy, even including regulation that has had discernible and intentional redistributive effects. Indeed, the fact that state constitutions, by contrast to their federal counterpart, address fiscal policy in often quite specific ways indicates that the designers of these constitutions knew and indeed expected that state and local officials would be making policy through regulatory choices that would have redistributive effects. To be sure, such decisions are traditionally made through the tax system, and so it is tempting to say that this entire subject is properly considered under the taxing power, however configured in state constitutions. And yet this is truly a difference without a difference. The prerogatives and obligations of state and local governments to address public welfare through the police power can and should include matters entailing fiscal choices that have effects on relative wealth and thus on equality. The government could act in heavy-handed or in light-handed ways, and we can reasonably disagree on overall strategy or particular tactics. It is enough to say here that the ever-evolving police power undergirds governmental decisions to address in meaningful ways wealth inequality at a statewide or even local level. It is inevitable, of course, that there will be legal challenges to redistributive strategies, insofar as some choices may implicate the freedom of individuals to use their own private property and other resources. This does not mean that the government is not acting under its police power but merely that, as we have discussed throughout this book, that there are limits to the exercise of that power and that the resolution of this controversies will usually require judicial intervention, as has always been the case. The essential point is that the police power is a mechanism available, fully consistent with its origins, its evolution, and its adaption to modern conditions and circumstances, to government to address issues of wealth inequality. The question then is less one of proper authority, but of political will.

There is also the particular infrastructure decision-making that affects wealth inequality, as scholars have identified,[74] and as our current Secretary of Transportation, Pete Buttetieg, has said, further to this point, "there is racism physically built into some of our highways."[75] Infrastructure-related regulations under the police power can aspire at promoting the general welfare through attention to wealth inequality. The challenge faced by public policymakers is to make scrupulous use of evidence, and create transparent opportunities for the furnishing of evidence in the processes of regulatory decision-making, that focuses not only on the dense engineering and fiscal considerations undergirding chooses about building roads, bridges, dams, and other elements of our physical infrastructure, but also the relationship between the building choices made and note made and the impact on patterns of racial and wealth inequality. These are, to be sure, often federal issues, given the federal government's outsized role in American infrastructure. Still, there are a stream of infrastructure investments and projects, sometimes in collaboration with federal officials and sometimes solely decided within the state (think, for example, of building projects at K-12 schools and at public colleges and universities), that are connected to the state police power and the discretion given to promote public safety and the general welfare. It is especially in this domain that questions of wealth inequality could and should be raised.

Another way to think about the connection between infrastructure choice and wealth inequality is through decisions that enhance the access of all members of the public to public goods. Here we might think about open parks and civic spaces. Looking at the government's role in addressing wealth inequality by redistributing resources is important to be sure, but it is also narrowing; it is narrowing in that it supposes that this is the only cogent solution to addressing inequality and poverty is more building. Leaving aside here the profound controversy over whether the government should pull more levers to do exactly that, we can see ways in which regulation can address wealth inequality by reducing the consequences of such inequality for participating in democratic life. Many aspects of our civic culture, along with essential goods and services, including access to good public education, are subject to elements of a market economy, and individuals are therefore subject to the prices assigned to such services. This predicament is deeply embedded and has features that create walls and gates around poorer citizens. The police power can address some of these conditions by taking certain elements of our culture and community and providing access. Responsible limitations on private owner's right to exclude in order to enable access to beaches and open spaces is a step in that direction; so too are conditions that local governments might impose on private entertainment firms that would use public lands, with appropriate permits, to charge fees for access to a concern or a sporting event. Even something as prosaic as requiring a certain allocation of space to individuals of limited means to cultural and educational events would, in enhancing access, not make poorer local citizens wealthier, but would reduce the impacts of being less wealthy, a means of redressing one consequence of wealth inequality. Other creative solutions we can leave to other fruitful conversations among citizens and policymakers, but the essential point is simply that the objectives of good governing under the police power might include decisions that address wealth inequality in concrete ways, even if that power cannot or will not bear the weight of more radical responses to the conditions of poverty and of subordination in its various forms. Our state constitutional tradition, noting both the broad, enduring ideals of promoting social welfare and also the manifestation of some these ideas through the establishment of positive rights, and the police power itself, can well sustain these concrete means of tackling in some small, but meaningful ways, the wicked problem of wealth inequality.

REIMAGINING PUBLIC SAFETY

While the strategies of safety regulations have evolved in significant ways over the history of our republic, the basic notion that public safety is a core part of the police power has always been prominent. Indeed, as we touched upon in both the Introduction and in Chapter 2, the police power's origins lie in a concern with the basic security of the citizenry. The power, after all, refers explicitly to policing. It is worthwhile, then, to reflect upon how the central ideas of governance and public security have evolved – what does public safety truly mean and what are the best policing strategies for realizing the aims of safety and security? While these questions are enduring ones, the answers have become more creative in recent years.

Barry Friedman has written an ambitious and important recent article that tackles the question of what modern public safety means in a provocative way and, more to the point, in a way that helps us understand better what the police power is becoming in this modern era.[76] Friedman contrasts the classic protection function associated with public safety regulation, one that concentrates on the government's duty to protect individuals from threats to their well-being and to their property rights, with a new idea of safety as the protection of multiple dimensions of social harm.[77] "Just as the notion of the protection function," Friedman writes, "itself will evolve ... so too will the understanding of what safety encompasses."[78] Public safety requisites will include harms that emerge from the status and situation of vulnerable individuals, such as the unhoused or the mentally ill. These harms may not be caused by identifiable others in the traditional *sic utere* sense, but they are nonetheless harms that have palpable effects and can be redressed through government interventions.

Contemporary legal doctrine has been reticent to impose affirmative government obligations on government to redress harms that result from situations that the government did not "cause," in the formal sense of the term. DeShaney v. Winnebago County, a 1989 Supreme Court case in which the Court rejected the argument that the government faced liability for its failure to intervene in a social services situation in which a young child was tragically injured, has been held up as an exemplar case for the difficulties in existing doctrine which separates government's legal and moral obligation in order to keep important notions of state action and state responsibility in certain lanes.[79] Independent of the question of whether DeShaney is correctly or incorrectly decided, there is a wider inquiry in the background of this debate, and that is whether the government has certain public safety responsibilities, and correlative powers, to address circumstances of harm that arise from complex social settings such as that faced by the boy in that case.

The fundamental issue, as Friedman frames this, is how we ought best to think about public safety in modern America. Safety is not just about the direct harm-causing behavior, be it real or potential; it is also about the situations that vulnerable citizens face by being where they are in the community. The mechanical way to think about this is to juxtapose benefits they have not received with harm that the private individuals or governmental officials have caused. Thus described, the conversation usually turns to whether and to what extent the government should be obliged to furnish benefits to those in need. This is a worthwhile question, to be sure, whose answer requires a complex set of assessments, theoretical and practical, philosophical and economic. However, a reframing of this question would look at what are rather clear threats to public safety by the absence of certain conditions that the government could address with regulation. Friedman sees this as implicating a constitutional imperative, one that is cognizable in both political and legal settings. And so he says that "What constitutionalizing accomplishes is to fulfill dialogue – or maybe just a power struggle – that goes to courts into the game of demanding that government do better."[80] Even if we stop short, at least until further consideration, of viewing this as an affirmative government obligation, as a positive right, we can still see the police power as a mechanism for promoting public safety as public safety is reimagined.

Supposing that we come to a common understanding that the government has positive obligations to furnish us with safety, in situations like the young boy in DeShaney faced and those in similar predicaments, we might still be stuck on the question of what safety means. Friedman's account boldly lists what he views as the essential elements of safety and security, those including basic subsistence, housing, health and well-being, and opportunity. These are, naturally, in addition to the obligations long viewed as central to the government's role, that is, the protection of the citizenry from harm to their person or property. That is, as Bentham wrote, "the paramount object" of government,[81] an object that was in fact encoded in many of the early state constitutions, such as Virginia's, which says that "government is, or ought to be, instituted for the common benefit, protection and security of the people."[82] What Friedman's effort at reframing the answer to the question "what is public safety" accomplishes, whether or not his particular set of objectives are compelling (much less achievable) is the critical agenda of making more modern, and thus much more relevant, the notion of public safety that underlies the police power's mission. The point, as he says, "is simply that there are many things that threaten us in similar ways, and with the same ultimate effects, as physical violence." Insofar as we credit these various threats as actual impositions on the public's safety, we should likewise rethink the present contents of our constitutional objectives and, with it, rethink the fundamental purposes of the police power.

Beyond reimagining public safety, modern approaches to the police power must account for the imperative of addressing crime through sensible prohibitions, fairly applied and oriented toward deterring and punishing violations of the social order – in short, the police power is at the heart of a rational scheme of criminal law. As we revisit and perhaps rethink the foundations of criminal law, we will inevitably rethink the core mechanisms for the implementation of this law through regulation, and usually prohibition, and that includes the police power.

Insofar as the police power authorizes ex ante regulation, we generally conceive of the implementation of this regulation as entailing other considerations, so essentially involving matters of strategy and tactics rather than the scope of power. This distinction proves too much, however. In thinking about the public safety objectives of the regulation, we ought to think about how our policies will be implemented.

Bringing this closer to the ground, there is vigorous debate about the proper role and functions of policing in the contemporary United States. Many advocate for new models of law enforcement; others insist that the basic models work, so long as there are adequate supports; and still others would defund the police. This is an active debate (often among activists) in which one big challenge is to keep it under more light than heat. Within the wide space for disagreement about what, if any, change is needed, we might still be able to converge on some general matters, matters that are at least shaded, if not directly shaped, by our modern police power.

Without digging too deeply into the component parts of this continuing conversation about police tactics, one interesting feature in some of the current thinking is that more attention is focused on mechanisms of law enforcement that necessarily will involve more ambitious use of technology and also public-private partnerships that challenge the traditional models of policing that rely mainly on human agency and the one-two punch of defining the rules of the road, setting the range of penalties, and tasking police officers to find criminals and hopefully stop crime. One prediction from early 2023 about "what's next" in modern policing is the rise of so-called "precision policing." Claiming that such policing "is rapidly becoming the foundational model that modern policing strategies are build around ... [t]he key to implementing precision policing tactics is the availability of real-time intelligence on in-progress situations. This is a fundamentally technology-driven strategy."[83] Precision policing has garnered adherents from major police forces and from various commentators who see it as an efficient and efficaciousness method of managing big data and harnessing new technologies to the complex issues involved in surveillance, apprehension, and even crime prediction.[84] Such models (part of what has often been labelled, if somewhat opaquely, the "new policing") have encountered heavy criticism from commentators who have pointed at ways that it departs from socio-legal research that has emphasized the benefits of community policing and human scale engagement in order to address the causes of crime, and not only its episodes.[85] Debates thus joined, the question that lurks in the background is how we ought best to think about the constitutional power of state and local governments in creating the right mechanisms of law enforcement to promote public safety. Must the regulators ultimately choose sides in this difficult debate? And, if so, what, in addition to evidence and careful empirical analysis, ought governments use to make educated assessments of what are truly the best strategies to protect citizen safety?

PUBLIC HEALTH AND PANDEMIC LESSONS

We have considered at different junctures the connection between the police power and public health, a matter that goes back to the very beginning of the republic. After all, it was as early as Gibbons v. Ogden, when Chief Justice Marshall used the example of a quarantine for public health purposes, as an exemplar of the government's broad police power.[86] Public health would be mentioned again by the Court in these early cases, and there would, too, be occasions for the courts to look specifically at state public health measures, as in Jacobson in 1905, and the roots of the police power as a strong source of authority for safeguard the health of our citizens. In short, public health has always been a foundational instance, indeed perhaps the modal case, for state and local governments to have awesome power to act, robustly and rapidly. Moreover, public health regulation has lent itself to the sort of administrative regulation that, as we have discussed, has transitioned in some degree the police power to something that can only be exercised by elected legislatures to something that is part and parcel of our administrative state.

With the recent pandemic, we have learned new lessons. These lessons are illuminating as we consider legal strategies and the puzzles of dispute resolution in litigation when the next major public health emergency emerges. One lesson is that individual rights, and especially religious liberty, are viewed by the current Supreme Court as important constraints on the exercise of the government's police power. The warning that public health emergencies do not mean that constitutional rights are suspended, an obvious truth, drives a good chunk of the Court's thinking in the recent cases concerning religious liberty and the First Amendment. Chief Justices say in the Roman Diocese case that "even in a pandemic, the Constitution cannot be put away and forgotten."[87] And Justice Gorsuch, says, even more colorfully, "Even if the Constitution has taken a holiday during this pandemic, it cannot become a sabbatical."[88] Until the Court's decisions of 2020 and 2021, the Court had almost never waded into controversies over the use of regulation to combat novel viruses and other threats to public health and the impact on religious liberty. It was not as though there were never religious or other civil liberty objections raised to certain measures. State and federal courts had given rather short shrift to First Amendment arguments against mandatory vaccines for children enrolling in public schools. Nor, looking beyond religious liberty, had courts shown much sympathy to civil liberties claims brought against public health measures during the height of the HIV/AIDs crisis in the US during the 1980s. But these COVID cases have suggested that there is a new sensitivity to these kinds of liberty claims. Moreover, there is an impatience, often close to the surface in the opinions of conservative judges at both the federal and state level, with state and local officials undertaking what they see as intrusive public health measures to address these long-lasting public health emergencies. While it is hard to have a discussion of these legal issues without bringing in the polarized politics of the COVID period, we can say at least that the pandemic has shifted somewhat the structure of the police power jurisprudence in the direction of a somewhat greater solicitude to civil liberties claims, especially pertaining to religious liberty.

A second lesson from the pandemic, and a hopefully less polarizing one, is that the efforts of state and local governments to create and enforce public health measures has revealed some of the most difficult and vexing matters of American federalism. What Justice Brandeis celebrated as the value of the laboratories of experimentation through regulatory innovations can be seen in light of COVID strategies as an often confounding series of truly experimental strategies, undertaken without consistent national administrative guidance and often with strong evidence of path dependence. To take one obvious example, the initial spate of sheltering orders in March and April of 2020 were nearly identical to one another, despite the variegated needs and conditions of states and local governments. This is understandable, as our governments were scrambling under unimaginably stressful conditions, with the rapidly expanding (and evolving) coronavirus and the imperative to act immediately and decisively. However, this cookie-cutter approach became less obviously sensible as time passed and as governments presumably gathered more fine-grained information and local knowledge. What we saw in the pandemic was that the police power as a necessary constitutional power for action gave little if no practical guidance to government officials in how best to protect the public health, nor did it in any way incentivize these officials to work collaboratively across borders to implement strategies that would be more comprehensive in effect and benefit from more collective wisdom.

Perhaps this was the role of the federal government, as the consolidating, if not, strictly speaking, centralizing, force in this vital national effort. And yet this illustrates a third lesson from the pandemic, and that a consequence of the absence of a national police power is that the federal government has a limited menu of regulatory options to confront the pandemic's impact. Within these limits, to be sure, are a significant number of important interventions, including financial support and creative mechanisms for facilitating collaboration across the states. Moreover, within the federal government are key agencies, such as the FDA and the CDC, whose role in combating a health emergency are vital. Still, decisions to limit freedom of movement and behavior, such as business shutdowns, certain mitigation measures including social distancing and masking, and mandatory vaccinations, are largely within the purview of the states and decisions made by state (and local governments) under the police power. Public health emergencies do put in sharp relief the respective roles of national and state governments under our constitutional systems of government, while also reminding us that coherent strategies to tackle problems that cross borders and impose burdens on citizens across the nation require collaboration and purposive collective action.

GOVERNANCE AND CONTROL: SHALL WE WORRY?

Michel Foucault long ago warned us about the risk of authoritarianism immanent in the use of the police to control behavior deemed anti-social. He connected this to a general theory of social power, noting that the "[p]olice power must bear over everything …. It is the dust of events, actions, behavior, opinions – everything that happens; the police are concerned with those things of every moment."[89]

The connection between the police power, in its origins and its underlying logic, and the maintenance of social order through appropriate use of the criminal law is a critical piece of the puzzle. Indeed, as we saw earlier in our discussion of the work of some leading scholars on the police power, including Markus Dubber and Christopher Tomlins, the police power comes into early American law through a deeply embedded notion of regulatory power as a means of social control. The all-encompassing quality of police power regulations – and the attendant work of actual policing – is a fearsome mechanism by which public authorities monitor citizen behavior, remove bad elements, and exercise supervisory control. As Vattel described it, government under the police power acts a "teacher and a wise father."

The analysis throughout this book paints a picture of the police power that ameliorates some of the more totalizing elements of this power, and shows how governments, including the courts in adjudication, viewed the police power as a coherent mechanism for protecting the people's welfare. Thus a mechanism would look after individuals' interest in having their liberty and property rights protected while also looking to further objectives of health and safety, objectives in which all citizens have a stake. At first glance, this conception seems rather benign. Who, after all, could be against good governing? However, the implications of a robust police power for regulatory policy can be vast; they can be creative in addressing wicked problems, as have considered in this chapter; and they can even be transformative, insofar as they rehabilitate an old, but still pertinent, view of state constitutions as embodiments of the people's will and objectives while supercharging the police power to frame and help implement these objectives through progressive legislation and administrative regulation. That all said, the police power is not all-encompassing; it is not all of the legal architecture of governance. It is connected in largely themes of American constitutionalism and legal culture, the content of which we have considered in uneven detail throughout this book.

This is not to say that the authoritarian use of the police power is unimaginable. We are experiencing in the current United States the reshaping and deploying of familiar mechanisms and institutions to do damage in our democracy. There is no intrinsic reason why the police power could be dragooned into these anti-democratic strategies. And so there is a broader sense of the police power that animates the concerns raised especially by Dubber in his extensive, thoughtful writings about the police power. This is one that ties the police power to the power of policing, and through the journey from Italy through British common law and natural concepts and finally into American regulatory policy, brings forth a template for more overarching control. This is the police power feared by Foucault. It is, as styled in this account, fearsome, in that it can authorize an overbearing state that, through its *polizia*, through its attention to managing the household, be totalizing, if not totalitarian, in its function.

What is the best response to this ominous concern? First, we should emphasize that the authoritarian account is flatly inconsistent with the vision painted in this book. So far as governments would redeploy the police power to authoritarian or even totalitarian ends, let them articulate their own vision of the police power. Skeptics about the police power and its provenance as a supposedly lawless source of authority to manage our collective "household" do not do so, but instead merely illuminate risks. Second, there are institutional and legal guardrails in the form of democratic legislatures and courts to protect against these risks. Third and finally, the embedding of the police power in theories and traditions of constitutional governance creates a special kind of safeguard.

Still and all, what do we do with the fact that the police power is framed around policing as a strategy for regulating behavior and managing conduct? The answers to these difficult questions, here incomplete, lie in the ways in which we develop checks and channels for government's exercise of its powers. Where Dubber and others are right to remind us of the risks attendant to a capacious police power is in the context is in two important contexts: First, in matters of morals regulation, where the risk is that the government will be pushed toward interfering with individual liberty and private choice (including in intimate matters) in the name of maintaining some version of the well-ordered community and Judaeo-Christian ethics, and will do so under their police power. This is a real risk, in our present era where the desire among Right-wing conservatives to "own the libs" and to fight the culture wars through establishing ever more directive, and even cruel, policies is animate. The police power will inevitably be used to control conduct – it is a regulatory tool, after all – but government ought not to draw from its historic mission of protecting public morals through regulatory intervention authority to engage in perfectionist agendas, ones that sacrifice liberty and also endanger the public's safety and health (mental and physical). A second fear is that the reliance on the criminal law to implement police power objectives fuels government actions that are worrisome on two levels, at the level of law enforcement, given our worry about contemporary policing and the progress still to be made in rooting out racist and other sinister practices in our police departments, and at the level of penalties. Violating a police power regulation may well come with consequences that range from incarceration to probation and the attendant limits on liberty to financial penalties and other collateral consequences. These results may well be warranted, and we entrust our elected representatives to make these difficult choices. But the ambient worry – our own priors may guide us to whether we find this an objection or merely a concern – is that the police power is used as a mechanism of interfering more actively in private conduct and behavior through the heavy hand of the criminal law. This is not the place to explore in any meaningful depth the matter of alternative penalties and punishments. It is enough to say only that the police power can and should be thought of principally as a means of governing in the direction of general welfare and the well-being of the community; it need not be a fulcrum of a society focused on instantiating opprobrium through the criminal law and meting out punishment that is focused more on suffering than on the commonweal's repair.

As to the matter of crime and criminal justice in particular, we should think about the sources and impact of crime in a responsibly empirical way in order to ground legal solutions and strategies. It is difficult, but yet imperative, to separate the contagious fear of crime in the community from the facts of the matter.[90] Insofar as the police power aspires to reasonable regulation, albeit with proper deference to governmental decision-making, it will be important that public officials undertake strategies that deal with actual crime, not just perceptions, occasionally hyperbolic, of a lawless society. Moreover, it is imperative that government actions involving both criminalization of conduct and the processes of enforcement, from arrest to sentencing, be implemented in a non-discriminatory way. This is, in and of itself, a wicked problem. Our criminal justice system is infused with structural discrimination, persistent and ubiquitous, and with squalid consequences for a society, viewed nationally or locally, that aspires toward fairness and equality.[91] Attention to crime and punishment requires an agile and constructive use of the police power, yet this use must be consistently attentive to the discriminatory underpinnings of our criminal justice system. Taking account of this predicament requires focus on all aspects of the system, beginning with how crime is defined to how the police behave to how the system operates after arraignment and throughout the trial and sentencing problem.

From one vantage point, we might be tempted to say that the concern with anti-discrimination is built into the process through constitutional rights protections, especially the Fourth through Eighth Amendments of the US Constitution. However important are these rights, that cannot fulfill the ultimate objectives of fair criminal justice, including reasonable police behavior, without looking with equal energy at how government sources and operationalizes the police power they have to carry out their responsibilities of combating crime and imposing proper punishment. Finally, a modern police power should look with fresh eyes on alternatives to the traditional mechanisms of punishment, mechanisms which rely on incarceration, civil fines, and various other punitive measures which are often lumped in as the "collateral consequences" of conviction.[92] The difficulties with traditional models are myriad, and they include concerns with discrimination, as noted above, but there are also structural considerations, for example, the over-reliance on plea bargaining and economic incentives for private prisons, that permeate the system across the board. It is worth considering, in our effort to think creatively about a well-suited police power for today's wicked problems, how we might think about the present modalities of punishment.[93] The question we ask that is tied directly to choices about the police power is this: How do present or alternative modalities of punishment for criminal offenses effectively promote public safety and general welfare? Are there less onerous means of accomplishing the same goals and, if so, might the police power's commitment to balancing individual liberty with general community goals counsel a greater use of these less onerous means?

*

This discussion, as noted above, does not purport to survey the wide range of policy areas that state and local governments confront. Nor is it intended to rank order the problems by a measure of seriousness. Rather, the aim is to draw upon the analysis of the police power in previous chapters to illuminate the contexts in which governments can and maybe should act under the rubric of their state constitutions and relevant legal authority (thinking, for instance, of the home rule power of cities) to address significant social and economic problems and to respond to emergencies. Much of the discussion of the police power in the literature has been historical; moreover, the focal point has been the nineteenth and early twentieth century, when the police power was taking shape and the scope of national and sub-national authority was being scrutinized by courts and contested in the policy arena. To go back to the very beginning of this book's introduction, the police power has largely faded as a subject of serious scrutiny by constitutional scholars. In this neglect, we have failed to consider the dynamic and relevant role of this extraordinary power, a power that enables and even obliges government to govern, and to do so on behalf of the general welfare of the public.

NOTES

1. Joseph Fishkin & William E. Forbath, *The Anti-Oligarchic Constitution: Reconstructing the Economic Foundations of American Democracy* 140 (2022).
2. See Richard J. Lazarus, "Super Wicked Problems and Climate Change: Restricting the Present to Liberate the Future," 94 *Cornell L. Rev.* 1153 (2009).
3. See William J. Novak, *The People's Welfare*.

4. Ibid.
5. See generally Ariel Porat & Alex Stein, "Liability for Future Harm," in *Perspectives on Causation* (Richard S. Goldberg ed., 2010).
6. See Maureen K. Ohlhauson, "The Procrustean Problem with Prescriptive Regulation," 23 *Commlaw Conspectus* 1 (2014).
7. See, e.g., Lynn A. Stout, "Uncertainty, Dangerous Optimism, and Speculation: An Inquiry into Some Limits of Democratic Governance," 97 *Cornell L. Rev.* 1177 (2012).
8. See the section on loss and damage in the US Framework Convention on Climate Change Report, https://bit.ly/3vHswyO. See also OECD Project on Losses and Damages from Climate Change. www.oecd.org/environment/cc/losses-and-damages/.
9. On the "pacing problem," see Adam Thierer, "The Pacing Problem and the Future of Technology Regulation," Mercatus Center Report, (8/8/18).
10. On the concept of duty in tort law, see Keith N. Hylton, "Duty in Tort Law: An Economic Approach," 75 *Fordham L. R.* 1501 (2006).
11. "Nuclear Disarmament: A Public Health Imperative," *Physicians for Social Responsibility.* https://bit.ly/3HiaB4j/.
12. On causation in tort law, see generally Dan Dobbs et al., *The Law of Torts* $33 (2nd ed); *Restatement (Second) of Torts* $13 (1963).
13. See Daniel Hemel & Daniel B. Rodriguez, "A Public Health Framework of COVID-19 Business Liability," 7 *J. L. & Biosc.* 1 (2020).
14. See generally Nate Holdren, *Injury Impoverished: Workplace Accidents, Capitalism, and Law in the Progressive Era* (2020); John Fabian Witt, *The Accidental Republic: Crippled Workingmen, Destitute Widows, and the Remaking of American Law* (2006).
15. Jill R. Horwitz, Albert De Diego Carreras, & Daneil B. Rodriguez, "COVID-19 and Tort Law's Limits: A Proposal for Tort Replacement" (ms. 2023).
16. See T. O'Riordan & J. Cameron, eds. *Interpreting the Precautionary Principle* (2013).
17. See Cass Sunstein, *The Laws of Fear* 88 (2005).
18. On matters of subordination in employer-laborer relations, see generally Christopher L. Tomlins, *Law, Labor, and Ideology in the Early American Republic* (1993).
19. See Alexander Polikoff & Elizabeth Lasser, *A Brief History of the Subordination of African Americans in the U.S.: Of Handcuffs and Bootstraps* (2020); Roy L. Brooks, *The Racial Glass Ceiling: Subordination in American Law & Culture* (2017).
20. See, e.g., Sophia Moreau, "Discrimination and Subordination," in *Oxford Studies in Political Philosophy*, Vol. 5 (D. Sobel ed., 2019).
21. See, e.g., Lucinda M. Finley, "Sex-Blind, Separate But Equal, or Anti-Subordination? The Uneasy Legacy of Plessy v. Ferguson for Sex and Gender Discrimination," 12 *Ga. St. U. L. Rev.* 1089 (2012).
22. See William J. Novak, *New Democracy*.
23. See Novak, *New Democracy*, at 50 (describing Virginia and South Carolina efforts to exclude under its police power Black population).
24. Ibid., at 37.
25. 109 U.S. 3 (1883). On The Civil Rights Cases, see White, *Law in American History Volume II*, at 38–49.
26. See, e.g., Marianne L. Engelman Lado, "A Question of Justice: African-American Legal Perspectives on the 1883 Civil Rights Cases," 70 *Chi-Kent L. Rev.* 1123 (1995).
27. "Change in the Countryside: The Granger Movement and the Rural Community," *Stony Brook Undergraduate History Journal.* https://bit.ly/3tRMg2i.
28. See generally Eric Foner, *The Second Founding: How the Civil War and Reconstruction Remade the Constitution* (2019); David P. Currie, "The Reconstruction Congress," 75 *U. Chi. L. Rev.* 383 (2008).

29. See Novak, *New Democracy*, at 41 ("particularities of religion, class, gender, ethnicity, and race found their way into the very foundation of the police power regime").
30. See generally Reva Siegel, "She the People: The Nineteenth Amendment, Sex Equality, Federalism, and the Family," 115 *Harv. L. Rev.* 945 (2002).
31. *Village of Euclid v. Ambler Realty Co.*, 272 U.S. 365 (1926).
32. See Ellickson, *Frozen Neighborhoods*.
33. See generally Joshua Braver & Ilya Somin, "The Constitutional Case Against Exclusionary Zoning" https://papers.ssrn.com/sol3/papers.cfm?abstract_id=4728312.
34. Robert C. Ellickson, "The Zoning Straitjacket: The Freezing of American Neighborhoods of Single-Family Houses," 96 *Ind. L. J.* 395 (2021).
35. See Note, "Addressing Challenges to Affordable Housing in Land Use Law: Recognizing Affordable Housing as a Right," 135 *Harv. L. Rev.* 1104 (2022).
36. David Schleicher, "Exclusionary Zoning's Confused Defenders," 2021 *Wisc. L. Rev.* 1315 (2021).
37. See <u>Southern Burlington County N.A.A.C.P. v. Township of Mount Laurel</u>, 67 *N. J.* 151 (1975).
38. A good journalistic account of this movement in California is Conor Dougherty, *Golden Gates: Fighting for Housing in America* (2020).
39. See generally Ilya Somin, *The Grasping Hand: Kelo v. City of New London and the Limits of Eminent Domain* (2015).
40. See, e.g., John Infranca, "The New State Zoning: Land Use Preemption amid a Housing Crisis," 60 *B. C. L. Rev.* 823, 828, 836–39 (2019); See Nestor M. Davidson, "Localist Administrative Law," 126 *Yale L. J.* 564, 618 (2017).
41. See, e.g., Sara C. Bronin, "The Quiet Revolution Revived: Sustainable Design, Land Use Regulation, and the States," 93 *Minn. L. Rev.* 231, 233 (2008); John Infranca, "The New State Zoning," at 879–81.
42. See Braver & Somin, "Against Exclusionary Zoning."
43. See German Lopez, "Homeless in America," *The New York Times* (July 15, 2022). See also "The Spike in Homelessness in US Cities Isn't Slowing Down," *Bloomberg.* https://bloom.bg/3SfAYya.
44. "Homelessness as a Public Health Law Issue: Selected Resources," CDC. https://bit.ly/41WPGoa.
45. Lisa T. Alexander, "Occupying the Constitutional Right to Housing," 94 *Neb. L. Rev.* 245 (2015).
46. See, e.g., Ian D. Williams & Michael Blyth, "Autogeddon or Autoheaven: Environmental and Social Effects of the Automotive Industry from Launch to Present," 858 *Science of the Total Envir.* 59987 (February 2023).
47. For a comprehensive review of these accomplishments, see https://bit.ly/48n3OkV.
48. See generally Jane Jacobs, *Cities and the Wealth of Nations* (1984); *The Economy of Cities* (1969).
49. See Gregory H. Shill, "Regulating the Pedestrian Safety Crisis," 97 *NYU. L. Rev.* Online 194 (2022).
50. https://smartgrowthamerica.org/dangerous-by-design/
51. Ibid.
52. "Guns," *NSC Injury Facts.* https://bit.ly/3vBo3Om.
53. "What the data says about gun deaths in the US," *Pew Research Center.* https://pewrsr.ch/4aSO8sd.
54. "Gun Ownership in America," *Rand.* www.rand.org/research/gun-policy/gun-ownership.html.
55. See <u>District of Columbia v. Heller</u>, 554 U.S. 570 (2008).

56. See Pew Research data, https://pewrsr.ch/4aSO8sd.
57. See ibid.
58. "Tracking the Effects of the Supreme Court's Gun Ruling," *The Trace*. https://bit.ly/3RWT6LR.
59. See generally Joseph Blocher & Darrell A. H. Miller, "What Is Gun Control? Direct Burdens, Incidental Burdens, and the Boundaries of the Second Amendment," 83 *U. Chi. L. Rev.* 295 (2016); "State Firearm Laws After *Bruen*," *Rand*. www.rand.org/pubs/perspectives/PEA243-1.html.
60. "Firearm Use and Storage Restrictions Associated with Reduction in Firearm Deaths," *Rand*. www.rand.org/news/press/2020/06/15.html.
61. See generally Richard Lazarus, *The Making of Environmental Law* (2004).
62. See, e.g., Luke W. Cole & Sheila R. Foster, *From the Ground Up: Environmental Racism and the Rise of the Environmental Justice Movement* 16 (2001); Jedediah Purdy, "The Long Environmental Justice Movement," 44 *Ecology L. Q.* 809 (2018).
63. See Erin Ryan, "Federalism and the Tug of War Within: Seeking Checks and Balances in the Interjurisdictional Era," 66 *Md. L. Rev.* 503 (2007).
64. See Robert L. Fishman, "Cooperative Federalism and Natural Resources Law," 14 *NYU Env. L. J.* 179 (2005).
65. For a survey, see Jeremy Richardson, "New Governance or Old Governance? A Policy Style Perspective," in *Oxford Handbook on Governance* 311 (David Levi-Faur ed., 2012).
66. See Daniel B. Rodriguez, "The Role of Legal Innovation in Ecosystem Management and Local Innovation," 24 *Ecology L. Q.* 745 (1999).
67. "Declaring a Water Crisis over Isn't the End of the Ordeal," *The Conversation*. https://bit.ly/48zBP2o.
68. "Flint Has Clean Water Now. Why Won't People Drink It?" *Politico*. https://politi.co/48wz568.
69. Ibid., at 15.
70. See also Rodriguez, "Ecosystem Management."
71. See generally Matthew Desmond, *Poverty, by America* (2023).
72. Joseph Fishkin & William E. Forbath, *The Anti-Oligarchic Constitution*.
73. See Novak, *New Democracy*, at 88.
74. "How Infrastructure Has Historically Promoted Inequality," *PBS*. https://to.pbs.org/3tKQ4CD. See Samuel Jones, et al., "Methodological Framework and Feasibility Study to Assess Social Equity Impacts of the Built Environment," 146 *J. Const. Eng. Mgt.* (2020).
75. https://bit.ly/42EVUCo.
76. Barry Friedman, "What is Public Safety," 102 *B. U. L. Rev.* 725 (2022).
77. Ibid., at 730. See, e.g., Federalist No. 10.
78. Friedman, "Public Safety," at 745.
79. See, e.g., Steven J. Heyman, "The First Duty of Government: Protection, Liberty and the Fourteenth Amendment," 41 *Duke L. J.* 507 (1991).
80. Friedman, "Public Safety," at 755.
81. Jeremy Bentham, *Bentham's Theory of Legislation* 124 (Charles Milner Atkinson ed., trans., 1914) (1802).
82. Va. Declaration of Rights, ch. 1.
83. See Sahil Merchant, "Key Law Enforcement Trends to Watch in 2023," *Fusus Blog*, January 3, 2023.
84. Precision Policing: A Strategy for the Challenges of 21st Century Law Enforcement. Manhattan Institute. https://bit.ly/3HjZ2Kc.

85. See, e.g., Jeffrey Fagan, "Race and the New Policing," in *Reforming Criminal Justice, Vol. 2: Policing* 83 (Erik Luna, ed., 2017).
86. See Gibbons, 220 U.S. at 15.
87. Roman Catholic Diocese of Brooklyn v. Cuomo, 592 U.S. 14, 19 (2020).
88. South Bay Pentecostal v. Newsom, 570 U.S. __ (2020) (J. Gorsuch).
89. See Michel Foucault, *Discipline and Punish: The Birth of the Prison* 213 (1975). See also Novak, *People's Welfare*, at 148.
90. See Jonathan Simon, *Governing through Crime: How the War on Crime Transformed American Democracy and Created a Culture of Fear* (2009).
91. See, e.g., James Foreman, *From the War on Poverty to the War on Crime: The Making of Mass Incarceration in America* (2017).
92. See, e.g., Michael Pinard, "Collateral Consequences of Criminal Convictions: Confronting Issues of Race and Dignity," 85 *NYU L. Rev.* 457 (2010).
93. See generally Michelle Alexander, *The New Jim Crow: Mass Incarceration in an Age of Colorblindness* (2012).

10

Techniques of Regulatory Intervention

New Legal Tools to Solve Wicked Problems

Our depiction of governmental action under the police power has to this point in the book followed a fairly conventional script. We have viewed the strategies of good governing as mainly involving regulation, and have supposed that by regulation we mean the typical forms of command-and-control governance, constructed through some measure of public law, usually criminal law. Civil redress plays a role, but note that the basic mechanisms of civil justice come in the form of what we regard as private law, with courts working to resolve controversies by adjudicating claims through the civil justice system. While command-and-control prohibition through the criminal law is indeed the model example of governmental action under the police power, a richer account of good governing should look at the variegated techniques of available public action in order to determine how we the people in the contemporary American world should implement strategies of effective governance. In this chapter, we explore some of these techniques, some viewed as types of regulation and others as alternatives to regulation. To be sure, not all of these strategies are necessarily implemented under the rubric of the police power (e.g., some economic incentives, tax policy under the constitutional taxing power). They are nonetheless relevant to our general inquiry, in that they illustrate the interface between traditional uses of the police power and alternatives that might accomplish the objectives of constitutional governance at least as effectively, if not more.

CLASSIC REGULATION

Models of regulation have developed largely around descriptions of market failures, aiming to get to the question of when government should intervene and for what purpose.[1] Debate rages over whether something should properly be labeled a market failure and, even if so, whether and to what extent regulation is the answer. It would seem from the ample literature that the debates over whether regulation is needed go through various waves. In the 1970s and 1980s, so-called public choice theory was a conspicuous part of the discussion of regulation.[2] Scholars steeped in neoclassical economics applied insights and evidence from the private sector, where regulation in some form was long seen as an antidote for pathologies in business behavior and the market, to the public sector and to government agencies. Cleverly turning the subject of public interest regulation on its head, it brought to the table the subject of political failures, problems that would be expected to beset government's efforts to regulate in the public interest.[3] Depending upon how hard the critique hit, the case for regulation was at least tempered and, in other instances, the brief against undertaking regulation in a particular area was made on the basis of the public choice critique.

Other theories of regulation have emerged over the same period of time, and scholars continue to look closely at both the theories that underlie the government's regulatory strategy, generally and in some targeted subject matters, and also evidence that could shed light on whether and in what circumstances regulation would work effectively. That these theories and critiques have had some meaningful impact upon public policy is illuminated by many episodes in past decades. One of the most notable was the erosion of airline price regulation in the late twentieth century, on the evidence mustered by Alfred Kahn and other critics of traditional forms of regulation.[4] Theories which are ultimately skeptical about regulation have been met with theories that have pointed more optimistically to regulatory experiments that have yielded benefits, and of the scale and scope that government promised when these new programs were created. Perhaps two of the most notable success stories are, first, the regulations, here dating from the early years of the twentieth century, dealing with unsafe food. With the work of federal and state authorities, under the rubric of national, state, and even local level governments, we have significantly alleviated the problem of inadequate food safety and have saved lives and helped industry gain the confidence of a public historically skeptical of sustenance made available by anonymous businesses; and, second, the safety of air and train transport. Without minimizing notable accidents, especially with respect to commercial train travel in recent years, these two modes of transportation are remarkably safe and consistently so, due in great measure to the oversight work of the relevant federal agencies, working with state and local authorities, to ensure safety. In the last year, 835 million (unadjusted) passengers were carried on US airlines, and 658 million in 2021. And yet there has not been a fatal air crash on an American commercial airline since 2009.

The debate over how to regulate is, in an important sense, more meaningful as a practical matter than the debate about whether to regulate. After all, most segments of the economy, most scenarios that Americans encounter, both within and outside their homes, are subject to regulation in some form. A quick look around the house, any house, makes this clear. Given the ubiquity of regulation, the ship has largely sailed on the matter of whether some regulation in some form is necessary. Questions remain especially pertinent, however, concerning how we should go about regulating. Taking account of the kinds of situations that we deal with in connection with the police power, many of which have been discussed in the previous chapter and elsewhere in this book, the usual mechanism of regulation is what has been labelled command-and-control.[5] The most prosaic way to describe what goes on is to say that the government establishes a rule of conduct, one that is either prohibitory or mandatory (or some combination of both) and empowers the proper authorities to carry out the purpose of this regulation by identifying miscreants and imposing the appropriate penalties.

Vast swaths of regulation follow this model. We have discussed zoning at many junctures of this book, and zoning is a good example of the use of command-and-control regulation. So, too, are the plethora of health and safety regulations that we associate with federal and state agencies of different shapes and sizes. Indeed, this form of regulation is generally the most common technique available on the typical regulatory shelf. The paradigmatic example is the criminal law, of course, law which establishes a line between proper and improper conduct and establishes prohibitions that are enforced by the power of law and command obedience with mechanisms designed to assure that these commands are met. The signal advantage of this classic form of regulation is its certainty, its ease of implementation, as the subjects of regulation and the instruments of law enforcement both know (it is assumed) what behavior is allowed and what is prohibited. The signal disadvantage is its inflexibility. In this inflexibility, it eliminates any incentives to behave even better than the command instructs. This is a particular problem where there is ascending value to more conduct above the prohibition line, such as in the case of air or water pollution. Less pollution is better, but the command-and-control regulation gives no incentive to pollute any less than the minimally permissible amount.

Beyond command-and-control regulation, there are regulatory approaches that have greater flexibility and are occasionally used to enhance policy goals. Disclosure regulation is a common alternative to regulation by edicts that insists on a particular level of activity. The way in which states typically regulate campaign financing, California's Fair Political Practices Commission being a pioneer in this development, is usually through disclosure regulation. This is especially valuable, as in the campaign context, when command-and-control runs into potential constitutional objections.

Various incentive-based regulatory techniques have been advocated, in the environmental context and elsewhere.[6] These include various forms of taxes, fees, subsidies, and myriad regulatory techniques that are distinct in that they are structured around incentives, rather than edicts. A more modern approach to the police power sees economic incentives as important components in an organic strategy to tackling wicked problems and in addressing obstacles to other modalities of regulation. We should be both ambitious in the use of such alternative mechanisms, but also cognizant of the limits of the standard economic models which undergird such approaches.

The critiques of incentive-based regulation are voluminous.[7] Many stem from skepticism about the underlying economic model. But one of the earliest and valuable critiques came from well within the economic literature, and that was a paper by economist Wallace Oates and his colleagues.[8] Oates noted that many of the principal benefits associated with decentralized, incentive-based regulation could be gained from sensitivity at the command-and-control level to matters of efficiency and efficacy. In a nutshell, the problem is not with the nature of edicts and centralized commands – in our case, "centralized" might be at the state or even the local level – but with the approach that these ultimate decision-makers take to configuring the regulatory system.

The reality of the matter is that incentive-based regulation is still in its adolescence, as a well-studied mechanism for wicked problem-solving outside of the pollution context.[9] We clearly need more attention paid to how such models of regulation – what are sometimes called "new governance" models – can help us solve some of the key problems described in Chapter 8, such as housing, infrastructure, etc. Moreover, it is not apparent how incentives-based models can be used to address so-called morals issues, recalling that the improvement of public morals remains one component part of what we see as an objective of the police power.

A somewhat close cousin to all these alternatives are performance-based regulations, ones that set a standard (so, in that sense is a "command"), but leaves discretion and flexibility to a regulated entity to develop whatever action steps will meet the standard (and so lacks the element of "control").[10] Finally, scholars, and especially Jon Hansen and Kyle Logue, have written about the strategic use of tort law, through the device of enterprise liability, to handle social problems that are not easily susceptible to various forms of ex ante regulation.[11]

TAXING

The consideration of taxation as a device more effective than regulation at implementing public policy objectives begins with the difficult and enduring threshold question of whether and to what extent taxation is suited to this purpose. The most important scholarly contribution to the question of how taxes might be used to affect behavior, and not simply to raise revenue for the functioning of society, is that by British economist Arthur Cecil Pigou a century ago.[12] Pigou developed the idea of Pigouvian taxes, that is, taxes designed to reduce negative externalities.[13] The objective of these taxes is to force consumers or businesses to internalize the costs of their activities through the use of tax policy as a pricing mechanism. In the Pigovian model, this strategy will be more effective than standard forms of regulation, principally because the setting of the tax (set to the marginal cost and marginal benefit of the activity) does not require the full body of information demanded by command-and-control regulation. Nor is this pricing mechanism subject to the same rent-seeking behavior of individuals competing over a menu of regulation.

Pigovian taxes, as explained in modern economic theory by William Baumol and refined in more contemporary work,[14] will potentially function as an effective tool of implementing good public policy. They will leverage the economic incentives of the economy's participants to reduce bad things and then to enhance public health, safety, and general welfare.[15] To be sure, some of the value of Pigovian taxes rests on assumptions about economic conditions – for example, the assumption that the marginal costs individuals face are essentially equivalent across regulatory regimes[16] – and also about the reliability of governmental institutions to make these decisions accurately through calibrated tax expenditures. Like other policymaking devices based upon mainstream economic theory, the practicability rests on the conditions in the real world, not on the chalkboard.

Some work in the modern law and economics tradition has broadened the claim about the role of Pivogian taxes to look at tax policy more generally. Kaplow and Shavell, for example, write that what they call "corrective taxes" can function as effectively as regulatory mandates.[17] Even if they are just equally as good, the political costs of regulatory decision-making may tilt the scale in favor of sound tax policy as a means of furthering health and safety.[18]

Let us leave to one side the standard critique of neo-classical economics that underlies the consideration of taxes as a substitute for regulation. For this critique, whatever its shape and salience, may also be levied at regulatory decision-making in various configurations. Classic command-and-control regulation imagines that sensible use of penalties and punishment will affect behavior in an optimal way, and so the assumption of rationality is baked in these models in much the same way as with taxation as a means of affecting public policy. A different critique is that tax policy is less effective as a general governance strategy because it is hard to set the prices of activity where they need to be to reach an equilibrium, one in which safety and public health is safeguarded. The general welfare objectives of governance are also hard to realize when the option is imposing a tax on certain activities.[19] Some businesses will be readily willing and able to absorb this tax; others will pass on this tax to consumers of the goods and services provided; and still others will absorb tax at even a high level in order to pursue certain objectives. Moreover, an interesting critique by David Weisbach and Jacob Nussim emphasizes that the basic economic conditions mean that it does not much matter whether the regulation is formed through taxation or through edicts or another scheme.[20] What matters is the institutional matrix within which these decisions are made. As they write:

> If the underlying policy is held constant, there are no effects of putting a program into or taking a program out of the tax system even if doing so hurts or enhances traditional notions of tax policy. Welfare is the same regardless of whether the program is formally part of the tax system or is located somewhere else in the government.[21]

Ultimately, comparison is hard because we need more clarity on what we are aspiring to do through taxation or regulation.

We have been focusing on the capacity of traditional regulation and now also taxation, as a mechanism for furthering the ultimate goals embedded in the police power, that is, to protect public health, safety, morals, and the general welfare. While we generally do not think of regulation as a means of wealth redistribution, we often think of taxation as fulfilling this purpose. This raises a question that we should at least touch on in this large discussion of the police power, even if the contours and implications of the debate lie beyond the scope of the book, and that is whether we might think of competing regulatory techniques as fulfilling an objective of redistributing wealth and redressing inequity and, further, how does this objective relate to the underlying purposes of the police power?[22]

To begin with, we might view redistribution here as not a per se goal of the police power, but as a means of effectuating the more central goal of promoting public health and safety. We can stipulate that there is meaningful differential impact of certain behavior on poorer individuals. Certain strategies under the police power might well – let us say more forcefully should – account for these differences. For example, the government could develop public health strategies that are targeted toward the poor. Drawing from our recent Covid pandemic experience, consider mitigation rules that are focused on places in which more economically disadvantaged employees are housed (for example, the back part of restaurants, by contrast to customer areas or in factories where large numbers of blue-collar workers, possibly with areas of sub-standard ventilation, are engaged). Regulation in this setting might address public health issues concretely, and in doing so effectuate what is in essence a redistribution of economic goods from a comparatively wealthier employer to her less well-heeled employees.

We consider this strategy in the context of a discussion of taxation because one of the essential dilemmas is whether the goal of redressing wealth inequality that has tangible effects on public health (or safety) is best met through regulation tailored toward economic disadvantage or else through taxation. With the latter, we can impose generally applicable regulations – and thereby avoid claims that the lines drawn through regulation are arbitrary or otherwise unreasonable – but attend to economic disadvantage through the tax system. To be sure, the choice may not be an either/or one; we could tackle wealth inequality through regulation and also through taxation. However, an overall commitment to good governing under constitutional ideas should be conscious of which sorts of regulatory strategies are best designed to effectuate these goals. Insofar as wealth redistribution is a purposive outcome of tailored regulatory strategy, we should carefully consider whether relying on a system that in its design and structure, that is, the taxation system, is or is not truly the best way to accomplish these goals.

TAKINGS, REVISITED

At various junctures in this book, we have considered the legal doctrine of regulatory takings. This doctrine emerges out of a concern that a capacious approach to interpreting the police power might swallow up private property rights. Without any demand for compensation, governments would favor regulations that pursued positive governmental ends at the expense of property owners, what are often the "little guy" in the controversy about regulation and its scope. Here let us broaden our inquiry to consider takings more generally.

Certainly the government can restrict through regulation the use of one's private real estate. The protections we described in previous chapters are framed through the picture of private property as a social good and as an essential duty of government, meaning that property should be regulated in order to promote the general social good. This gives a picture that is incomplete, or maybe even distorted. Regulations which impact discrete individuals in their use and self-regulation of their property risk building up social capital and salutary accomplishments on the backs of individuals and therefore inequitably. Moreover, government action to pursue a social good rests on an assumption, largely uninterrogated thus far in this book's discussion of the police power as a means of protecting the people's welfare, that the government is acting in benign ways and is adequately internalizing the costs of its actions. The requirement that the government pay for a taking of private property, whether this taking happens through confiscation, unacceptable "physical invasion," or value-reducing regulation, would help keep government under proper checks. It introduces what Calabresi and Melamed famously called a liability rule,[23] one that would establish a discernible cost for the government to impose restrictions on property. And insofar as the government is acting as a well-intentioned democratic agent of the people, these costs will be accounted for in our delegated public policy choices.

Scholars looking closely at the takings clause have not investigated in much depth the consideration, if any, the framers of this clause gave to how takings would supplement or complement the use of the police power. As Harry Scheiber reminds us, eminent domain was hardly used until well into the nineteenth century and at a time when government regulation of private property under the police power was already well established.[24] Coming to modern times, takings is a blunderbuss, a generally difficult mechanism for the government to accomplish policy goals. First, it is expensive, demanding after all just compensation to implement a particular strategy. Second, it is politically costly, as state governments have found in the two decades following the Court's Kelo decision.[25] Many states have acted to restrict the scope of "public use" in order to limit the effective use of eminent domain.[26] Somewhat curiously, post-Kelo property rights advocates have spent much less capital in efforts to narrow the scope of "public purpose" in state constitutions or in other ways to limit through constitutional amendment or statutory design the use of the government's police power to control the use of private property. Takings politics touches a third rail of democratic politics and even if we could imagine that carefully tailored use of eminent domain to improve public health, safety, and general welfare could well supplement the use of the police power for this same purpose, it is hard to see that the present state of politics and public opinion would countenance its use for such ends. Whether or not this is an all-considered accurate rendering of the matter, the police power seems like a more domesticated version of government interference with private property and so bold efforts to limit it, in the same way that eminent domain has come to be limited by legislatures, the people directly, and courts, have been rather muted.

The structure and strictures of takings doctrine contribute to a failure in imagination and in creativity in regulating. Because it is an express constitutional power, it tempts lawmakers to address social problems associated with the use or misuse of private property by this one-size-fits-all technique of confiscation. Calabresi and Melamed usefully describe this method as creating a liability rule and, as such, moving the government to a more attractive strategy than if they were left only with a property rule, something that would track the police power controversy divide between an acceptable and an unacceptable deployment of official power to disturb the dominion of the property owner. But laying in the background of this view of the cathedral is the big question of whether the property-torts interface is the only or the best modality to look at this issue of social need and governmental strategy.

Here is another view – perhaps more of a snapshot – of the cathedral: We could imagine that the government's interest in prohibiting a certain use of private land, and in this prohibition reducing the economic value of that property by a meaningful (in the Lucas sense) amount, does not warrant the big step of changing owners. Because the government is hemmed in by regulatory takings doctrine, it has little choice in the matter. Moreover, the incentives for owners to implement the government's objectives (which, after all, might include, as in Berman v. Parker, destroying their own property to meet a common welfare requirement) are muddled. They might be willing to oblige the government's interest, but the incentives to hold out – which is, in essence, the very reason for having an eminent domain power at all – are too great. What if the government, instead of being required to transfer money from the public fisc to this private owner through just compensation could make the decision to restrict the owner's prerogatives through its general police power without a duty of compensation? However, and this is the key to all this, there would be a public fund made up for the express purpose of ameliorating the impact of government's intrusions on private property rights. This fund would be administered by public authorities – perhaps citizens deputized to carry out this role as a volunteer on behalf of the community. The availability of funds would soften the blow to property owners differently affected, but would neither oblige the government to pay the market value of the property nor always oblige the government to pay anything. The fund would be a mechanism for spreading losses. This is a view of the same cathedral that Calabresi and Melamed looked at in the explicit sense that this bears some analogy to how compensation schemes work, at least in a world where this social insurance scheme is not configured as a strict entitlement whose access is equivalent as exactly as possible to the loss suffered. Rather, it is a way of spreading the costs of losses, and avoiding litigation, in order to create a practical mechanism to enable progress that comes from the private or public sector undertaking necessary actions while also accounting for the impact on liberty and property.

This somewhat half-baked idea undertakes to look at how regulation that is in a sense a mash-up of two distinct regulatory regimes – takings and the police power – might accomplish valuable social goals without the 100 years' worth of problems that Mahon and its progeny have levelled on us.

NUDGES

One of the most prominent forms of alternative regulatory strategy is, at its heart, a sort of admixture of traditional economic thinking and behavioral psychology. Stemming from the pathbreaking work of Daniel Kahneman and Amos Tversky[27] and articulated elegantly in important work by Cass Sunstein and Richard Thaler, it is the use of so-called "nudges."[28] Nudges involve informal methods derived from close attention to the decision environment (what they call the "choice architecture") to get individuals to engage in beneficial ways without edicts or even economic incentives. Nudges are easy and cheap. According to Sunstein and Thaler, they can have, in some settings, equivalent effectiveness as traditional methods of regulation, but without the coercion and its attendant costs.

Many nudges are used to facilitate healthy human behavior, such as the inclusion of healthy food snacks at eye level in the grocery store and near the cash register. Setting default options for certain purchases, such as, for example, electric cars or other products that have social benefit, is an example of a valuable nudge. The gamification or creation of opportunities for simple competition in a setting where folks need encouragement to take important civic action, like voting, is a nudge used in various settings. Those involved in so-called design theory can assist – that is, nudge – certain behaviors through the layout of a store or any environment in which certain patterns of behavior are preferred. Ultimately, various nudges, used presently or still to be conjured up, trade on the insights of behavioral psychology and track what Kahneman and Tversky called System 1 thinking and also the use of heuristics.[29] Nudges are not dissembling, but they do take the opportunity for how individuals use mental shortcuts to reason and are deployed to change behavior and therefore change results. They are paternalistic, insofar as they assume that professional designers can improve on human decision-making by taking steps to influence – some might say manipulate – the choice architecture in order to produce certain outcomes. But it is libertarian in the fundamental sense that it does not decree action but, instead, creates conditions that ultimately redound to the benefit of individuals.[30]

In the settings in which the police power would be applicable, it is not obvious how nudges would replace traditional or contemporary models of regulation. However, it is easier to see how they would complement regulatory strategies. Consider the example of environmental protection at the local level. Creating defaults that would result in greater uses of safer, rather than less safe, appliances and other common instruments would help augment more interventionist strategies. Some of the regulation that aims to improve morals, for example the efforts to encourage better treatment of animals, could be augmented, or in some instances even supplanted, by nudges. Pictures of animals in distress is a homely example of a nudge and its use. More imaginative techniques might involve various commitment devices for, say, weight loss and also other important goals. Indeed, a company called sticKK exists to help create and enforce "behavioral contracts" to help nudge individuals toward the realization of their goals.[31]

In comparing regulatory approaches, tax scholar Brian Galle sees advantages, interestingly enough, in both command and control regulation and in nudges.[32] As to the former, he notes that "[s]ticks are, except in unusual circumstances, the more efficient tool for reining in the social overproduction of some negative-externality-laden good. Sticks earn the government money, while carrots drain the treasury, wasting hard-won tax revenues."[33]

*

One of the key messages in this chapter's discussion of regulation and regulatory alternatives is that the police power, precisely because it typically undergirds a significant public authority to compel action and to utilize the mechanisms of the criminal law and law enforcement to implement public goals, should be evaluated always to see if there are less draconian alternatives to command-and-control regulation. Some of the alternatives discussed above involve the continuing use of the police power or else governmental power that is at least as heavy-handed (as with the taxation power). Others are more gentle in that they seek to accomplish good policy ends with less interventionist means. It is impossible to generalize in any sensible way about whether one of these approaches is better than another. Not only are circumstances which call for some measure of governing different from one another, but in the usual run of cases it may be best for the government to use a combination of regulatory techniques, rather than something off the shelf. The old saying that "if one has a hammer, everything then looks like a nail" is apt here. In our commitment to good governing, we should be ever on the lookout for mechanisms and techniques that accomplish our ambitious goals with the best bang for our buck and the least intrusions on our freedoms and peace of mind.

RETURNING TO EXPERTISE AND DEMOCRACY

A challenge that we have raised at different junctures, sometimes more abstractly and other times in the context of particular examples, is how to balance the government's reliance on expertise and expert decision-makers in undertaking its regulatory strategies with our commitment to democracy and democratic choice. We learn much from a combination of our long, complex history as a republic, from theories from great minds of the past and present who have looked at the matters of decision-making in the policy arena, an arena made up of both politics and principle, and also at the practice of both expertise and democracy. Ultimately, the best choice is not either/or, but a calibrated yet evolving combination of democratic choice and reliance on evidence-based strategies that benefit from experts utilizing their expertise. An interesting conclusion that derives from the so-called Dunning–Kruger effect is pertinent here. This effect reveals that those with insufficient information (or, as the hypothesis often is framed, an overall lack of pertinent skills) tend to overestimate their skills and, as the saying goes, don't know what they don't know. Simultaneously, experts will often underestimate their knowledge and skill, a result perhaps of the laborious work of examining data and chasing down the vast amount of information and research that they would want in order to become truly confident in their analyses and conclusions.[34] To the extent that the Dunning–Kruger effect has real resonance, we should be cautious about pure democracy, given that those lesser skilled citizens will always outnumber others. Choices made through democratic decisions, even if we can introduce some meaningful elements of deliberation, can be problematic, and we should attuned to these problems and on guard against relying inordinately on such decision-making tactics. However, we should be cognizant of the holes and flaws in what experts would tell us – not so much because data and evidence cannot be trusted, but because the translation of facts about the real world by those entrusted with expertise over certain facts can be biased in various unconscious ways.

All of this is to say, as many have said before, that expert decision-making (frequently the *sine qua non* of bureaucracies and bureaucratic choice) and unmediated democracy are imperfect methods of making and implementing policy. We need to be vigilant about the flaws in both methods and think constructively about how to balance these modes of making policies and exercising power with one another and how best to capture the advantages of both modalities.

This enduring challenge is important to consider in the context of the police power, as we have described it here. In its origins, the police power was synonymous with the legislature's plenary power. We had a sense that our elected representatives would make the essential choices, both big and small, about how to regulate certain activities in order to promote health, safety, morals, and the general welfare. This system was by design a means of making decisions based upon the will of the people (democracy) and the best assessment of the situation and its needs (expertise, perhaps here in the Burkean sense of the term). Over time, however, we saw the police power being delegated to other authorities, including governors, local governments, administrative agencies, and other contraptions of governance. And so the exercise of this power was in the hands of an assembly of institutions, each speaking in the name of the government and thus on behalf of we the people. We are unlikely, happily enough, to go back to a world in which the legislature makes all or even most of the policy decisions under the police power. Therefore, we must attend to these difficult, but not intractable, issues of democracy and bureaucracy, of government by both passion and reason, a combination that worried Madison and, later, Abraham Lincoln, but has become ingrained, if not inherent, in our multifaceted political process. Continuing attention to the evolving operation of the police power in modern and future America will give us a vantage point to see how these decision-making modes can combined into a sufficiently mobilized whole that good governing becomes our entrenched approach to constitutional stability and successful constitutional performance.

NOTES

1. See generally Andrei Shleifer, "Understanding Regulation," 11 *Euro. Fin. Mgt.* 439 (2005).
2. See, e.g., Richard Posner, "Theories of Economic Regulation," 5 *Bell J. Econ. & Mgt. Sci.* 335 (1974).
3. See the various examples in Maxwell L. Stearns & Todd Zywicki, *Public Choice Concepts and Applications in Law* (2009).
4. See Thomas McGraw, *Prophets of Regulation* (1984).
5. For a good, comprehensive discussion of the concept, see Daniel H. Cole & Peter Z. Grossman, "When is Command-and-Control Efficient? Institutions, Technology, and the Comparative Efficiency of Alternative Regulatory Regimes for Environmental Protection," 1999 *Wisc. L. Rev.* 887 (1999).
6. See Bruce A. Ackerman & Richard B. Stewart, "Reforming Environmental Law," 37 *Stan. L. Rev.* 1333 (1985). See also Bruce Yandle, "Emerging Property Rights, Command-and-Control Regulation, and the Disinterest in Environmental Taxation." https://link.springer.com/chapter/10.1007/978-1-4615-1069-7_12.
7. See, e.g., Rena I. Steinzor, "Reinventing Environmental Regulation: The Dangerous Journey from Command to Self-Control," 22 *Harv. Env. L. Rev.* 103 (1998).
8. Wallace Oates, "The Net Benefit of Incentive-Based Regulation: A Case Study of Environmental Standard Setting," 79 *Amer. Econ. Rev.* 1233 (1989).
9. For an especially interesting exploration of incentive-based regulation in the context of regulating cigarettes, see Jon D. Hanson & Kyle D. Logue, "The Costs of Cigarettes: The Economic Case for Ex Post Incentive-Based Regulation," 107 *Yale L. J.* 1163 (1998).
10. See, e.g., Bruce A. Ackerman & William T. Hassler, *Clean Coal/Dirty Air* 121–28 (1981) (arguing for greater reliance on "ends-oriented" environmental regulation and less on "means-oriented" regulation); Office of the Vice President, *Improving Regulatory Systems: Accompanying Report of the National Performance Review* 24 (1993) ("Performance standards are generally preferable to prescriptive or design standards because they give the regulated industry the flexibility to determine the best technology to meet established standards.")
11. Jon D. Hanson & Kyle D. Logue. "The First-Party Insurance Externality: An Economic Justification for Enterprise Liability," 76 *Cornell L. Rev.* 129 (1990).
12. See generally Arthur C. Pigou, *The Economics of Welfare* (4th ed., 1932).
13. On Pigouvian taxes, see Gregory Mankiw, "Smart Taxes: An Open Invitation to Join the Pigou Club," 35 *E. Econ. J.* 14 (2009).

14. See William J. Baumol, "On Taxation and the Control of Externalities," 62 *Am. Econ. Rev.* 307 (1972).
15. See Jonathan S. Masur & Eric A. Posner, "Toward a Pigouvian State," 164 *U. Penn. L. Rev.* 93 (2015).
16. An assumption vigorously critiqued in Victor Fleischer, "Curb Your Enthusiasm for Pigovian Taxes," 68 *Vand. L. Rev.* 1673 (2015).
17. Louis Kaplow & Steven Shavell, "On the Superiority of Corrective Taxes to Quantity Regulation," 4 *Am. L. & Econ. Rev.* 1, 7–10 (2002).
18. See, e.g., Lily Batchelder et al., "Efficiency and Tax Incentives: The Case for Refundable Tax Credits," 59 *Stan. L. Rev.* 23, 47–48 (2006) (discussing the benefit of uniform subsidies).
19. See Lee Fennell, "Willpower Taxes," 99 *Geo. L. J.* 1371 (2011).
20. David A. Weisbach & Jacob Nussim, "The Integration of Tax and Spending Programs," 113 *Yale L. J.* 955 (2004).
21. Ibid., at 958.
22. For an interesting recent discussion of the connection between regulation and wealth redistribution, see Daniel Hemel, "Regulation and Redistribution with Lives in the Balance," 89 *U. Chi. L. Rev.* 649 (2022). See also David A. Weisbach, "Distributionally Weighted Cost-Benefit Analysis: Welfare Economics Meets Organizational Design," 7 *J. Legal Analysis* 151, 154–58 (2015).
23. Guido Calabresi & Douglas Melamed, "Property Rules, Liability Rules and Inalienability: One View of the Cathedral," 85 *Harv. L. R.* 1089 (1972).
24. N. Scheiber, "Public Rights and the Rule of Law in American Legal History," 72 *Cal. L. Rev.* 164 (1984).
25. See Ilya Somin, *The Grasping Hand: Kelo v. City of New London and the Limits of Eminent Domain* (2016).
26. See ibid., at 107.
27. See, e.g., Amos Tversky & Daniel Kahneman, "Judgment under Uncertainty: Heuristics and Biases," 185 *Science* 1124 (1974).
28. See generally Cass Sunstein & Richard Thaler, *Nudge: Improving Decisions about Health, Wealth, and Happiness* (2008).
29. See Daniel Kahneman, *Thinking, Fast and Slow* 67 (2013).
30. See generally Russell Korobkin, "Libertarian Welfarism," 97 *Calif. L. Rev.* 1651 (2009); Jeffrey J. Rachlinski, "The Uncertain Psychological Case for Paternalism," 97 NW. U. L. Rev. 1165 (2003).
31. www.stickk.com/.
32. See Brian Galle, "Tax Command ... or Nudge? Evaluating the New Regulation," 92 *Tex. L. Rev.* 837 (2014).
33. Ibid., at 851. See also Brian Galle, "The Tragedy of the Carrots: Economics and Politics in the Choice of Price Instruments," 64 *Stan. L. Rev.* 797 (2012).
34. On the Dunning–Kruger effect, see "Why Can We Not Perceive Our Own Abilities?" *The Decision Lab*. https://thedecisionlab.com/biases/dunning-kruger-effect.

Conclusion

The reward for reaching the end of a long book should be a short conclusion, and so the concluding words here are brief.

The police power in the American states was designed to become, and has indeed become, the fulcrum of regulatory choice in our republic. It is a power inherent in state constitutionalism, sometimes made explicit in the documents and other times merely assumed as a central feature of what it means for government to have authority to act on behalf of its sovereign people and to the betterment of the people's welfare.

There has been no practical reason to define it in clear and coherent ways, and despite scholars' and judges' efforts over more than two centuries, a one- or two-sentence definition remains elusive. Nonetheless, the contours of the power, its scope and its purpose, can be and have been shaped by many years of judicial interpretation and also close scrutiny by commentators. In older times, there were efforts to get at the beating heart of the police power in a holistic way; and so many cases from the states and, more rarely, from the Supreme Court aspired to give meaning to this general power. In more contemporary times, it would seem that this quest has been largely abandoned. The police power is defined most commonly in consideration of a particular dispute, the question always being: "How far can the government go in regulating X or Y?" Usually this has been accompanied by a consideration of a constitutional right that is put up against the police measure in order to determine whether the government has transgressed on an individual's right under either the national or the state constitution. But the quest is ultimately the same: To articulate the powers of government to protect our health, safety, morals, and welfare – its essence and its purpose – and to likewise figure out when this power has gone too far and must be reigned in by our understandings of what the constitution requires.

Given all that we know about the American legal system, we should be surprised that these questions will ultimately be answered, for better or worse, by courts in adjudication. And so the place to look for a comprehensive understanding of the scope of the police power will be the large body of cases in which the police power has been implicated. The value added of a deep analysis of the police power as here in this book, is that one can look at these legal decisions alongside a broader account of the power, focusing on why it is such an instrumental part of our scheme of American constitutionalism, how it evolved, what structural considerations go into its use and appropriate limits, and, finally, how it can be used by responsible governments to address some of our super-wicked problems.

The use of the phrase "good governing" to describe the overall aim and objectives of the police power is intended to have two separate meanings: First, it refers to the common good that the power is meant to facilitate, this as part of our overarching, albeit dynamic, constitutional objectives; and, second, it refers to the ambition that we have a government that works, that does its best to truly protect us from threats to our health and safety, the preservation of community morals that we can agree upon as twenty-first-century Americans committed to equality and inclusion (among other commitments, to be sure), and to the general welfare. We should expect our leaders to govern well and for the common good.

Index

abortion
  Dobbs v. Jackson Women's Health Organization, 141
  morals regulations for, 141
  Roe v. Wade, 145–46
Adams, John, 38
Adams, Willi Paul, 93–94
administrative bureaucracy and power, delegation of
  anti-administrativist movement, 135, 192, 266
  expertise in, 188–93
  Major Questions Doctrine, 191–92
  New Deal policies and, 189, 190
  under nondelegation doctrine, 188
  skepticism of, 190–91
  special purpose authorities, 189–90
administrative law, 197–98
  police power and, 251–53
Administrative Procedure Act (1946), US, 116, 262–63
adult entertainment, moral regulation of, 143
  judicial evaluation of, 144
Affordable Care Act, US, 268, 269–70
Agins v. Tiburon, 214, 215–16
alcohol and drug consumption, moral regulation of, 140, 144, 148
Ambler Realty Co. v. Village of Euclid, 118–21
amendments, to constitutions. *See also* Constitution, US
  to state constitutions, 74, 125
animal welfare laws, 150
animus, legal, 244–48
  equal protection doctrine, 245
  against LGBTQ+ populations, 247–48
anti-administrativist movement, 135, 192, 266
anti-commandeering doctrine, 265
arbitrariness, 242–44
  inclusiveness and, 244

  proceduralist review of, 243
  salus populi principle, 244
  sic utere principle, 244
  synoptic review, 243
Articles of Confederation, in US Constitution, 21, 22, 47
  federalism under, 51–52
assisted suicide, 241–42
Austin, Benjamin, 76
authoritarianism, concerns about, 310–13

Baker v. Carr, 249
Banner, Stuart, 67
  on natural law, 81, 82–83, 73
Barbier v. Connolly, 90–91
Barnett, Randy, 96, 125
Barron, David, 182–83
Barron v. Baltimore, 69, 222, 264
Baumol, William, 321–22
Bentham, Jeremy, 68
Berman v. Parker, 134, 152, 218, 325
Bernick, Evan, 96, 125
Bill of Rights, 69–70, 81–82, 201
  in Delaware, 23
  morals regulation and, 145–46
  natural rights in, 223–24
BiMettalic v. State Board of Equalization, 210–11
Binford v. Sununu, 159
Blackstone, William, 76
  British legal philosophy and, 68
  on police power, 45–46, 60
"boundary picking," 108–9, 201
Bowers v. Hardwick, 142, 146
Brady, Maureen, 79
Brandeis, Louis (Justice), 72, 111
Brennan, William (Justice), 98–99
Brick Presbyterian Church v. Mayor of New York, 56–57
Briffault, Richard, 180

333

Brown, Adam, 32
Brown v. Maryland, 26, 53
Buchanan v. Warley, 114
Buck v. Bell, 114
Bullman-Pozen, Jessica, 183, 275
Burger, Warren (Chief Justice), 166
Bush, George Herbert Walker, 135
Bush, George Walker, 135
Buttetieg, Pete, 304

Calder v. Bull, 69, 152
  judicial review and, 221
Campbell, Jud, 203–4, 207, 234, 229, 230
Cardozo, Benjamin (Justice), 201
Carpenter, Daniel, 189
Cedar Point Nursery v. Haddid, 11, 216
Champion v. Ames, 140–41
Charles River Bridge v. Proprietors of Warren Bridge, 70
Chevron v. NRDC, 266
citizen safety. *See* public safety policies
The City of Cleburne v. Cleburne Living Center, 202, 243
City of Erie v. Pap's A. M., 143
The Civil Rights Cases, 289
Claeys, Eric, 120
classical legal thought, 96
Cleveland Telephone Co. v. City of Cleveland, 99
Clinton, Bill, 135
command-and-control regulations, 322
Commentaries on the Laws of England (Blackstone), 45
Commerce Clause, 140–41
common good constitutionalism, 186–87
common goods, zoning laws and, 120–21
common law
  development as legal theory, 80
  judicial intervention and, 30, 31–32, 179
  judicial review and, 69
    state constitutions and, 30–32
  private property law and, 69–70
  sic utere principle in, 55
  state constitutions influenced by, 30–31, 55–64
    judicial intervention and, 30, 31–32
    judicial review and, 30–32
  zoning laws and, 122
Commonwealth v. Alger, 58–60, 79–80
Commonwealth v. Tewksbury, 250–51
Conchatta v. Miller, 144
consent principles, in state constitutions, 22–24
  evolution of, 23
  good governance and, 23–24

Constitution, US. *See also* Bill of Rights; Contract Clause, in US Constitution; rights, individual, in US Constitution
  Articles of Confederation, 21, 22, 47
  federalism under, 51–52
  Commerce Clause, 140–41
  Eminent Domain clause in, 65
  First Amendment
    during Covid-19 pandemic, 160
    free speech and, 203–5
    individual rights under, 202–5, 206–7
    morals regulations and, 143
  Fourteenth Amendment, 70–71, 109–10, 226–29
    Due Process Clause of, 146
    original meaning of, 96
  interpretation of, 81
  judicial review in, 81–82
  Ninth Amendment, 226–29
  political strategy and, 48–51
  public meaning of, 48–51, 77
  purpose of, 48–51
  Reconstruction amendments, 264
  salus populi principle and, 289
  Second Amendment, 206–7, 298–300
  state constitutions influenced by, 2–3
  Supremacy Clause in, 53
  Tenth Amendment, 51–52, 54, 226–29
constitutional avoidance canon, 250
Constitutional Convention, 22, 26
constitutionalism
  administered, 134–35
  British, 29
  common good, 186–87
  laissez faire, 84–87
  The Slaughterhouse Cases, 95
  libertarian, 86–87, 142
  republican tradition of, 47–48
constitutionalism, American, 2–3
  classical liberal theory and, 28–29
  criticism of, 47–48
  federalism and, 276–78
  interpretive method for, 81
  public meaning of, 48–51
  purpose of, 48–51
  strategic approaches to, 48–51
constitutions. *See* state constitutions, state constitutionalism and
contestation of rights, 229–31
Contract Clause, in US Constitution, 65, 82
  eminent domain under, 65–66
  liberty of contract, 103
  morals regulations and, 142
  restriction of state regulatory authority and, 68

private property under, 65–66
property rights under, 69–70
state authority under, 65–66
contract rights
　during Lochner era Supreme Court, 88–95
　police power and, 43
Cooley, Thomas, 42, 95, 126, 180–81
Cornell, Saul, 205–6
countermajoritarian mechanisms
　during Lochner era Supreme Court, 86–87
　during Progressive era, 100
　state constitutions as, 32–33, 101
Covid-19 pandemic
　due process during, 210
　First Amendment and, 160
　Jacobson v. Massachusetts, 159
　police power and, 158–62
　public health regulation during, 158–62, 169–70, 308–10
　　First Amendment protections, 160
　　legal reasoning for, 160–61
　sic utere principle and, 286–87
　state constitutional power during, 5
　scope of, 160
　separation of powers, 175–76
culture wars, 149–50
Cushman, Barry, 108–9

Dartmouth College cases, 63–64
De Mortibus Maris (Lord Hale), 71–72
Declaration of Independence, 18
Declaration of Rights, in Pennsylvania state constitution, 20
Delaware
　Bill of Rights, 23
　state constitution in, 29
delegation. *See* administrative bureaucracy and power, delegation of; nondelegation doctrine
democracy, 327–29
　state constitutions and
　　legislative supremacy in, 25
　　representative democracy and, 24–25, 93–94
DeShaney v. Winnebago County, 305–6
Devlin, John, 175
Devlin, Lord, 142
Dillon, John, 181, 196
disclosure regulations, 320
discrimination cases
　Plessy v. Ferguson, 7, 71, 74, 91–94, 289
　　Harlan dissent in, 92–94, 244–45
　Yick Wo v. Hopkins, 92
District of Columbia v. Heller, 205, 299–300
Diver, Colin, 243

Dobbs v. Jackson Women's Health Organization, 141, 224
Dubber, Markus, 7, 60, 310
due process, 208–11
　during Covid-19 pandemic, 210
　restriction of state regulatory authority and, 68
Due Process Clause, of Fourteenth Amendment, 146
Dunning–Kruger effect, 328
duty of public care, 186
Dworkin, Ronald, 142
dynamic federalism, 270–76
　education policies and, 272
　health policies and, 272
dynamic police power, 270–76

early legislative policies, in US, 67–68
　common law traditions and, 68
　natural law principles and, 67–68
　positive law and, 68
　purpose of, 68
　sic utere principle in, 68
　statutory lawmaking, 67
education, right to, 228
education policy, 272
Eisenstadt v. Baird, 145–46
Ellickson, Robert, 153–54
Ely, John Hart, 249
Emergency Powers of the Governor Act of 1945 (Michigan), US, 176
Emerson, Blake, 186
eminent domain
　under Contract Clause, 65–66
　Holmes on, 102
　Horwitz on, 128
　jus publicum principle and, 101–5
　Pennsylvania Coal v. Mahon, 86, 101, 102–4, 128
　　Kohler Act and, 103
　　takings law and, 103–4
　police power and, 101–5
　during Progressive era, 101–5
　property rights and, 214–15
　salus populi principle and, 152
　in urban settings, 152
Eminent Domain clause, in US Constitution, 65
The End of Liberalism (Lowi), 190
environmental protection policies, 300–2
　Flint water crisis and, 301
　new governance traditions, 300–1
environmental racism, 300
equal protection, right to, 208–11
　animus and, 245
Erie Canal, construction of, 65
Ernst, Daniel, 188, 197–98

Euclidean zoning, 118–21
executive powers, in state constitutions, 19, 201
   unbundled executive power, 174
expertise, 327–29
   in administrative bureaucracy and power, 188–93
   skepticism of, 190–91

Federal Communications Act, US (1934), 262
Federal Communications Commission, 88
Federal Trade Commission Act, US, 262
federalism, federal power and
   American constitutionalism and, 276–78
   Articles of Federation, 51–52
   Brown v. Maryland, 53
   dynamic, 270–76
      education policies and, 272
      health policies and, 272
   expansion of, 270
   Gibbons v. Ogden, 52
   McCulloch v. Maryland, 53
   during New Deal era, 263
   New York v. Miln, 53–54
   opportunistic, 272–73
   over commerce issues, 54–55
   police power and, 51–55
      conceptual approach to, 261–62
      dynamic, 270–76
      expansion of, 262–66
      Major Questions Doctrine, 266
      national, 266–70
      salus populi principle and, 265–66
      principal-agent formulation, 273–74
      "separate spheres" analysis of, 270–71
Federalist Papers (Hamilton and Madison), 105
   infrastructure in, 64–65
   state constitutionalism in, 18, 22, 36, 230
Feinberg, Joel, 142
Field, Stephen (Justice), 211
Finnis, John, 142
First Amendment
   during Covid-19 pandemic, 160
   free speech and, 203–5
   individual rights under, 202–5, 206–7
   Lochnerism and, 11
   morals regulations and, 143
Fishkin, Joey, 109–10
Fiss, Owen, 124
Fleming, James, 167
Fletcher, George, 142
Fletcher v. Peck, 69–70
Flint water crisis, 301

Food & Drug Safety Act, US, 262
Forbath, William, 109–10
Forbes' Case, 80–81, 250–51
formalism, 96
Foucault, Michel, 7, 310
Fourteenth Amendment, 70–71, 109–10, 226–29
   Due Process Clause of, 146
   original meaning of, 96
Frankfurter, Felix (Justice), 72, 204
Franklin, Ben, 26
Freund, Ernst, 42, 60, 87, 114, 188, 197–98
   on localism of police power, 181–82
   on police power, 138
Friedman, Barry, 305, 306–7
Friends of Danny Devito v. Wolf, 159
Frug, Gerald, 182–83

gambling, morals regulation of, 140–41
Gardner, James, 2–3
George, Robert, 142
Georgia Lactation Consultant Practice Act, US, 237
Gerken, Heather, 183, 271, 275
Gestle, Gary, 20, 220
Gibbons v. Ogden, 52, 264–65, 308
Gillman, Howard, 90, 109–10, 125
Gluck, Abbe, 271
Godkin, Edwin, 106
Goldberg, Suzanne, 139
Goldberg v. Kelly, 212
Gomillion v. Lightfoot, 249
Gonzales v. Raich, 267
Gorsuch, Neil (Justice), 178–79, 308–9
governance structures. *See also* regulatory governance; *specific topics*
   analysis of, 331–32
   authoritarianism concerns and, 310–13
   as control mechanism, 310–13
Grad, Frank, 137
Granger laws, 71
Great Britain
   constitutionalism in, 29
   legal philosophy and thought in, 68
   US colonies' relationship with, 18
Great Society, 11
Gregory v. Ashcroft, 265
Griswold v. Connecticut, 145–46
guns and firearms, regulation of, 297–300
   District of Columbia v. Heller, 205, 299–300
   New York State Rifle & Pistol Ass'n v. Bruen, 205, 298–300
   public opinion on, 298
   Supreme Court and, 298–300
Gunther, Gerald, 241

Index

Hale, Lord, 71–72
Hamilton, Alexander, 22, 201, 272–73. *See also* Bill of Rights; *Federalist Papers* (Hamilton and Madison); rights, individual, in US Constitution
Hand, Learned, 201
Harlan, John (Justice), 90–91, 241, 242
    Plessy v. Ferguson dissent, 92–94, 244–45
harm principle, 139–40
Hart, H. L. A., 142
Hart, Henry, 251
Hartog, Dirk, 196
Hawaii Housing Authority v. Midkiff, 152
health care, right to, 228
health policies, 272
heuristics, 326
Hohfeld, John Wesley, 197–98
Holmes, Oliver Wendell (Justice), 72, 97–98, 201
    on eminent domain, 102
home rule mechanisms, for police power, 181–82
Honore, Tony, 142
Horwitz, Morton, 81, 103, 122, 128
    on eminent domain, 128
housing policies
    access and affordability mechanisms, 291–96
    zoning laws and, 291–93
        construction prohibitions under, 292
        criticism of, 294
        NIMBY movement, 293
        YIMBY movement, 293, 294
Hulseboch, Daniel, 36
Hunter decision, 180–81
Hurst, J. Willard, 8, 61–62
hyper-localism, police power and, 183–84

Illinois Central Railroad v. Illinois, 100
imperium in imperio concept, 181, 182
In re Abbott, 159–60
In re Tahiti Bar, 144
incentive-based regulations, 320–21
individual rights. *See* rights, individual, in US Constitution
infrastructure
    in Federalist Papers, 64–65
    modern examples of, 163
    Novak on, 64
    police power and, 64–67
    during Progressive era through massive public investment, 87–88
    as public policy, 64–67
    public rights to, 64
    Scheiber on, 65
    wealth inequality and, 302–5
initiative lawmaking, 106

International News Service v. Associated Press, 97–98
interpretation, judicial
    legal canon for, 250–51
        of constitutional avoidance, 250
        during Legal Process era, 251
        for police power, 250–51
        presumptions in, 250–51
Interstate Commerce Act, US, 262–63
Issacharoff, Sam, 249

Jacobson v. Massachusetts, 94–95, 114, 159, 308
Jefferson, Thomas, 28, 38
Jew Ho v. Williamson, 113
judicial intervention
    in common law traditions, 30, 31–32
    individual rights and, 203
    during Lochner era Supreme Court, 86–87
    state constitutions and, 31–32
judicial review
    Calder v. Bull and, 221
    in common law traditions, 30–32, 69
    establishment of, 68–72
    individual rights and, 221–23
    Marbury v. Madison, 30–31, 221
    self-dealing and, 249
    state constitutions and, 30–32
    in US Constitution, 81–82
jus publicum principle, 69–70
    eminent domain and, 101–5
    during Lochner era Supreme Court, 106–7
    nuisance laws and, 61
    during Progressive era, 100
    public rights and, 63

Kahn, Alfred, 319
Kahneman, Daniel, 326
Kelo v. City of New London, 71, 152, 218
Kendrick, Leslie, 246
Kennedy, Anthony (Justice), 146, 147, 245
Kennedy, Duncan, 96
Kohler Act, US, 103
Kovacs v. Cooper, 134

labor laws
    National Labor Relations Act, 88, 262
    under National Labor Relations Act, 88
    during Progressive era, 88
laissez faire constitutionalism, 84–87
    Lochner era Supreme Court and, 84–87, 107–11
    police power and, 107–11
    The Slaughterhouse Cases, 95
land use regulations, police power and, 153
lawmaking. *See* early legislative policies, in US

Lawrence v. Texas, 146, 245–46, 247–48
Lawton v. Steele, 113
Lee, Sophia, 134–35
Legal Process era, 251
Legal Realism movement, 108
legislative powers, of states, under state constitutions, 19
legislative skepticism, 73
  initiative lawmaking and, 106–7
  jus publicum principle and, 106–7
  during Lochner era Supreme Court, 105–7
  during post-Reconstruction era, 93
  during Reconstruction era, 86
LGBTQ+ populations
  animus against, 247–48
  Bostock v. Clayton County, 247–48
  Lawrence v. Texas, 146, 245–46, 247–48
  moral regulations and, 149–50
  Obergefell v. Hodges, 147–48, 247–48
  Romer v. Evans, 147, 245–46, 247–48
  United States v. Windsor, 247–48
liability rule, in takings law, 324
liberal theory, American constitutionalism and, 28–29
libertarian constitutionalism, 86–87, 142
liberty of contract, 103
  restriction of state regulatory authority and, 68
liberty rights, 28–32
  presumption of liberty, 193–94
The License Cases, 60, 70, 89
Lincoln, Abraham, 329
Linde, Hans, 98–99
Lindsley v. Natural Carbonic Gas Co., 115
Lingle v. Chevron, 217
Liquormart v. Rhode Island, 144
Little Rock v. Arkansas, 169
localism, of police power, 180–84
  arguments for, 183
  disadvantages in, 183–84
  home rule mechanisms, 181–82
  hyper-localism, 183–84
  imperium in imperio concept, 181, 182
  in nineteenth century, 181–82
  origins of, 180
  skepticism of, 184
Lochner era, for US Supreme Court, 255–56
  conceptual approach to, 84–87
  contract rights during, 88–95
  countermajoritarian elements during, 86–87
  individual rights during, 201, 204–5
  Jacobson v. Massachusetts, 94–95, 114
  judicial intervention during, 86–87
  jus publicum principle during, 106–7
  laissez faire constitutionalism and, 84–87, 107–11

  legislative skepticism during, 105–7
  Mugler v. Kansas, 89–91, 93–94, 125, 131–32
  Munn v. Illinois, 8, 71, 72, 74, 89, 131–32
  Plessy v. Ferguson, 7, 71, 74, 91–94, 289
    Harlan dissent in, 92–94, 244–45
  property rights during, 88–95
  regulatory takings law, 86
  state-building during, 84
  zoning laws and, 118–21
Lochner v. New York, 84, 107–8
Locke, John, 224–26, 235
Londoner v. Denver, 210
Lowi, Theodore, 190
Lucas v. South Carolina Coastal Council, 214–15
Lutz, Donald, 3, 18
  on consent theory, 23

Madison, James, 18, 28, 38, 272–73. *See also* Bill of Rights; *Federalist Papers* (Hamilton and Madison); rights, individual, in US Constitution
  on tyranny, 203
Major Questions Doctrine, 191–92
  federalism and, 266
  police power and, 266
majoritarianism. *See* countermajoritarian mechanisms
Mansfield & Swett v. Town of W. Orange, 119, 121
Marbury v. Madison, 30–31, 69
  judicial review and, 221
Marshall, John (Chief Justice), 52, 267, 297
Marshfield, Jonathan, 164, 177–78
  on nondelegation doctrine, 178–79
Marvin v. Trout, 140–41
Massachusetts, Contract Clause in, 65–66
Masterpiece Cakeshop v. Colorado, 245–46
Matthews v. Eldridge, 212
McCormack, Bridget, 178–79
McCulloch v. Maryland, 53, 269
McQuillin, Eugene, 180
Members of the Medical Licensing Board of Indiana, et al. v. Planned Parenthood Great Northwest, 224
Merrill, Thomas, 213
Michelman, Frank, 213
Michigan
  Emergency Powers of the Governor Act of 1945, 176
  Flint water crisis, 301
  nondelegation doctrine in, 176–77
Mill, John Stuart, 139–40
Minnesota Rate Case, 131–32
Mississippi, zoning laws in, 130
morals regulations

Index

for abortion, 141
for adult entertainment, 143
  judicial evaluation of, 144
for alcohol and drug consumption, 140, 144, 148
through animal welfare laws, 150
under Commerce Clause, 140–41
criminalization of sex work, 148–49
culture wars and, 149–50
First Amendment and, 143
for gambling, 140–41
harm principle and, 139–40
individual liberty and, 141–42
  Bill of Rights and, 145–46
  libertarian constitutionalism and, 142
  liberty of contract and, 142
legitimacy of, 142–43
against LGBTQ+ populations, 149–50
Mill on, 139–40
Novak on, 138–39
police power and, 138, 150–51
public indecency statutes, 166
for public safety, 145
under Restatement (Second) of Torts, 145
scope of, 139–40
sic utere principle and, 139–40, 142–43, 144–45
in state constitutions, 137
origins of, 137–38
Mugler v. Kansas, 89–91, 93–94, 125, 131–32
Muller v. Oregon, 108–9
Munn v. Illinois, 8, 71, 72, 74, 89, 131–32

Nachbar, Thomas, 258
National Complete Streets Coalition, 297
National Labor Relations Act, US (1935), 88, 262
national police power, 266–70
National Pork Producers Council v. Ross, 265
natural law
  Banner on, 81, 82–83, 73
  police power and, 73
natural rights, 58, 78, 81, 223–26
  in Bill of Rights, 223–24
  Locke on, 224–26, 235
  police power compared to, 227–28
  property and, 73
Nebbia v. New York, 84–85, 108–9, 237
Nedelsky, Jennifer, 24, 126
negative rights, 220
New Deal, 11, 134–35, 262–63
  administrative bureaucracy under, 189, 190
  federalist expansion during, 263
  Second New Deal, 262
New Hampshire
  lack of chief executive in, 20
  state constitution for, 82–83

New Jersey
  state constitution of, 136
  zoning laws in, 119–20
New York
  Forbes' Case, 80–81
  state constitution for, 201
New York State Rifle & Pistol Ass'n v. Bruen, 205, 298–300
New York v. United States, 261
Newsom, Gavin, 271
NFIB v. Sebelius, 269–70
NIMBY movement, 293
Ninth Amendment, 226–29
nondelegation doctrine, 176–79
  administrative power limits under, 188
  Major Questions Doctrine and, 191–92
  Supreme Court support for, 191
Novak, William J., 42
  on morals regulations, 138–39
  on police power, 7–8, 76, 122
  on positive rights, 236
  on rights to public infrastructure, 64
  on *salus populi* principle, 58, 125–26
  on state constitutional rights, 220
nudges, 326–27
nuisance laws
  jus publicum principle and, 61
  moral nuisance, 145
  police power and, 79
  public infrastructure and, 79
  Restatement (Second) of Torts, 145
  sic utere principle and, 56, 57
Nussim, Jacob, 322

Obergefell v. Hodges, 147–48, 247–48
occupational licensing
  police power and, 157–58
  Uniform Bar Exam and, 158
O'Connor, Sandra Day (Justice), 146–47, 217–18
Oklahoma, state constitution of, 136
"On Participation" (Pitkin and Shumer), 184
O'Neal, Emmett, 105
opportunistic federalism, 272–73
originalist interpretations, of state constitutions, 164

Paine, Thomas, 203, 223
Parmet, Wendy, 169–70
patria potestas, 45
Pearson, Susan, 84
Penn Central case, 214, 215–16, 233
Pennsylvania
  Declaration of Rights, 20
  state constitution in, 29

340 Index

Pennsylvania Coal v. Mahon
  eminent domain and, 86, 101, 102–4, 128
  Kohler Act and, 103
  takings law and, 103–4, 128
People ex rel LeRoy v. Hurlbut, 180–81
People v. Adams, 159
The People's Welfare (Novak), 7–8, 76
  public morality in, 138–39
performance-based regulations, 321
Pigovian taxes, 321–22
Pildes, Richard, 249
Pitkin, Hannah Fenichel, 184
Planned Parenthood v. Casey, 146–47
Plessy v. Ferguson, 7, 71, 74, 91–94, 289
  Harlan dissent in, 92–94, 244–45
Poe v. Ullman, 241
police power. *See also* federalism, federal power and; localism, of police power; *salus populi* principle; *sic utere* principle; *specific cases; specific topics*
  Blackstone on, 45–46, 60
  Brick Presbyterian Church v. Mayor of New York, 56–57
  Brown v. Maryland, 26
  in *Commentaries on the Laws of England*, 45
  Commonwealth v. Alger, 58–60, 79–80
  conceptual approach to, 1–11, 158–62
    analysis of, 331–32
  contract rights and, 43
  as control mechanism, 45–46
  Covid-19 pandemic and, 158–62
  early legislative lawmaking as influence on, 67–68
  eminent domain and, 101–5
  expansion of, 10
  federalism and, 51–55
  Fourteenth Amendment and, 70–71
  Freund on, 138
  general welfare protections and, 55–64
  Gibbons v. Ogden, 52
  historical development of, 45
  history of, 3–5
    role of Supreme Court in, 3–4
  as household management, 46
  infrastructure and, 64–67
  judicial interpretation of, 250–51
  laissez faire constitutionalism and, 107–11
  The License Cases, 60, 89
  litigation over, 4
  morals regulations and, 138, 150–51
  national, 266–70
  natural law and, 73
  natural rights compared to, 227–28

  Novak on, 7–8, 76, 122
  nuisance laws and, 79
  obscurity of, 178–79
  occupational licensing and, 157–58
  during post-Reconstruction era, 88–95, 124
  practical purpose of, 6–7
  private property and, 101
  property rights and, 43
  public health regulation and, 158–62, 169–70
  public works and, 64–67
  during Reconstruction era, 72–75
  regulatory takings doctrine, 104–5
  salus populi principle and, 62, 63, 152
    federalism and, 265–66
  The Slaughterhouse Cases, 70–71, 90, 125
  as social control mechanism, 46
  state constitutions and, 72, 228
    as core component of, 2
  structural approaches to, 5
  in urban settings, 151–57
    eminent domain issues, 152
    for land use regulations, 153
    for tenant protection, 155
    zoning laws, 153–56
  Vanderbilt v. Ames, 63
  "wicked problems" and, 193
  zoning laws and, 121–22
police power national, 266–70
political rights, 213
political skepticism
  state constitutions and, 18, 25–28, 36–37
  Wood on, 26, 86
popular sovereignty, through state constitutions, 22–24
  constitutional structure, 125
  good governance and, 23–24
  in post-revolutionary era, 23
positive rights, 226–29
  Novak on, 236
  public safety policies and, 306
  right to education, 228
  right to health care, 228
  sic utere principle and, 228–29
Post, Robert, 3
post-Reconstruction era. *See also* Lochner era, for US Supreme Court; Progressive era
  administrative policy during, 87–95
  collective welfare policy, 93
  legislative skepticism during, 93
  national legislation policy during, 87–95
    expansion of, 88
    for police power, 88–95, 124
    in Supreme Court cases, 88–95
  property rights during, 93, 211

reasonableness standards during, 111–16
unreasonable statutes during, 93
Pound, Dean Roscoe, 197–98
power, structuring of, 193–94
Precautionary Principle, 288
preemption, 269–70
presumption of liberty, 193–94
Primus, Richard, 279–80
private law
    public law compared to, 9
    sic utere principle in, 55
private property law
    in classic common law traditions, 69–70
    under Contract Clause, 65–66
    police power and, 101–5
    during Progressive era, 98–99, 127
    under state constitutions, 37, 38
privilege-no right, 197–98
proceduralist review, of arbitrariness, 243
Progressive era. *See also* Lochner era, for US Supreme Court
    administrative policy during, 87–95
    Bureau of Animal Industry, 88
    countermajoritarian instruments during, 100
    eminent domain during, 101–5
    Federal Communications Commission, 88
    jus publicum principle during, 100
    labor laws during, 88
    massive public investment during, 87–88
    national legislation policy during, 87–95
        expansion of, 88
        for police power, 88–95, 124
    in Supreme Court cases, 88–95
    private property rights during, 98–99, 127
    property rights during, 211
    public trust doctrine, 100
    public welfare policy during, 185, 186–87
    reasonableness standards during, 111–16
    salus populi principle during, 63
    sic utere principle during, 63
    takings law during, 101
Progressivism, 47–48
property, definition of, 103
property rights, 211–18. *See also* private property law; zoning laws
    Agins v. Tiburon, 214, 215–16
    under Contracts Clause, 69–70
    eminent domain and, 214–15
    freedom to use, 56
    International News Service v. Associated Press, 97–98
    The License Cases, 60, 70
    during Lochner era Supreme Court, 88–95
    during modern era, 212–13

natural rights and, 73
Penn Central case, 214, 215–16, 233
police power and, 43
political rights and, 213
during post-Reconstruction era, 93, 211
during Progressive era, 211
reconfiguration of, 211–12
salus populi principle and, 215
under state constitutions, 28–32
    private property protections, 37, 38
takings cases, 214–15, 216–18
Pruneyard Shopping Center v. Robins, 216–17
public choice theory, 318–19
public health regulation
    during Covid-19 pandemic, 158–62, 169–70, 308–10
    First Amendment protections, 160
    legal reasoning for, 160–61
    Little Rock v. Arkansas, 169
    police power and, 158–62
public indecency statutes, 166
public interest, 72
public law, private law compared to, 9
public meaning, of constitutions, 48–51, 77
public purpose requirement, 106
public rights, 28
    jus publicum principle and, 63
public safety policies
    citizen safety and, 145, 296–97
    as positive right, 306
    reimagination of, 305–8
public trust doctrine
    during Progressive era, 100
    public welfare policy and, 185
    state constitutions and, 28
"public use"
    eminent domain and, 13
    in takings cases, 11
public welfare policy, requirements of, 185–88
    common good constitutionalism, 186–87
    cost-benefit analysis of, 186
    development of, 185
    as duty of public care, 186
    during Progressive era, 185, 186–87
    public trust doctrine and, 185
    salus populi principle and, 288–91
    Vermeule on, 186–87
public works, police power and, 64–67

Raffensberger v. Jackson, 237–39, 257
Rakove, Jack, 36–37, 201
Randolph, Edmund, 26
ratemaking authorities, 131–32
rational choice theory, 32

Rawls, John, 167–68
Reaching our Sisters Everywhere (ROSE), 237
Reagan, Ronald, 135
reasonableness standards, 240–42, 260
　judicial review and, 240–41
　during post-Reconstruction era, 111–16
　during Progressive era, 111–16
Reconstruction amendments, 264
　salus populi principle and, 289
Reconstruction era. *See also* post-Reconstruction era
　legislative skepticism during, 86
　police power at end of, 72–75
Redish, Martin, 204
regulatory governance. *See also* takings law
　administered constitutionalism and, 134–35
　anti-administrativism and, 135
　conceptual approach to, 283–85
　intervention techniques
　　classic models, 318–21
　　command-and-control regulations, 322
　　disclosure regulations, 320
　　incentive-based regulations, 320–21
　　performance-based regulations, 321
　　taxation, 321–23
　modern approaches to, 133–36, 162–63
　New Deal policies, 134–35
　nudges in, 326–27
　　heuristics and, 326
　public choice theory, 318–19
　public faith in, 135
　rights revolution and, 136
　at state level, 134–35
　　growth of, 134–35
regulatory takings doctrine, 104–5
　Lochner era Supreme Court, 86
Rehnquist, William (Chief Justice), 267
Reich, Charles, 212
Renton v. Playtime Theatres, 143
representative democracy, 24–25, 93–94
Restatement (Second) of Torts, 145
right to education. *See* education, right to
right to health care. *See* health care, right to
rights, individual, in US Constitution, 68–72. *See also* property rights; *specific rights*
　in Bill of Rights, 69–70, 81–82, 201
　in Delaware, 23
　morals regulation and, 145–46
　natural rights, 223–24
　"boundary picking" and, 108–9, 201
　Campbell on, 203–4, 207
　conceptual approach to, 200–8
　contestation of, 229–31
　definition of, 229–31

due process, 208–11
　during Covid-19 pandemic, 210
　restriction of state regulatory authority and, 68
　to equal protection, 208–11
　expansion of, 202
　federal power and, 201
　under First Amendment, 202–3, 206–7
　　during Covid-19 pandemic, 160
　　free speech, 203–5
　　Lochnerism and, 11
　　morals regulations and, 143
　judicial intervention and, 203
　judicial review and, 221–23
　during Lochner era of Supreme Court, 201, 204–5
　during modern era, 230–31
　natural, 58, 78, 81, 223–26
　　in Bill of Rights, 223–24
　　Locke on, 224–26, 235
　　police power compared to, 227–28
　　property and, 73
　negative rights, 220
　original forms of, 201
　political, 213
　positive, 226–29
　　Novak on, 236
　　public safety policies and, 306
　　right to education, 228
　　right to health care, 228
　　sic utere principle and, 228–29
　salus populi principle and, 204, 207
　under Second Amendment, 206–7
　under state constitutions
　　form of, 219–21
　　function of, 219–21
　　individual rights in, 219
　as trump of federal power, 207–8
rights revolution, 136
Roberts, John (Chief Justice), 233, 247, 269–70
Rodriguez, Cristina, 183
Roe v. Wade, 141, 145–46
Romer v. Evans, 147, 245–46, 247–48
ROSE. *See* Reaching our Sisters Everywhere (ROSE)
Rossi, James, 63–64
rule of law, 188–93

Sacks, Albert, 251
safety policies. *See* public safety policies
salus populi principle, 9, 10
　arbitrariness and, 244
　eminent domain and, 152
　individual rights and, 204, 207

Novak on, 58, 125–26
police power and, 62, 63, 152, 288–91
   federalism and, 265–66
   during Progressive era, 63
   property rights and, 215
   public welfare and, 288–91
   Reconstruction amendments and, 289
   zoning laws and, 117–18, 119
Sanders, Anthony, 223
Sassen, Saskia, 182–83
Sato, Sho, 182
Sax, Joseph, 216–17
Scalia, Antonin (Justice), 174–75, 205
Schad v. Mount Ephraim, 143
Scheiber, Harry, 8, 42, 72, 238, 324–25
   on infrastructure construction, 65
Schleicher, David, 292
Schmitt, Carl, 51
Schragger, Richard, 182–83
Schwartzman, Micah, 246
Second Amendment, 206–7, 298–300. *See also* guns and firearms, regulation of
Second New Deal, 262
Securities & Exchange Acts, US, 262
Seifter, Miriam, 175, 198
self-dealing, 248–50
   judicial review and, 249
   skepticism of, 249–50
self-enforcing equilibrium, 32–33
"separate spheres" analysis, of federalism, 270–71
separation of powers, in state constitutions, 88, 166, 173–79
   during Covid-19 pandemic, 175–76
   nondelegation doctrine, 176–77, 178–79
   of plenary power, 174
   statutory interpretation of, 176
   unbundled executive power, 174
sex work, criminalization of, 148–49
SFFA v. Harvard, 209
SFFA v. U. North Carolina, 209
Shapiro, Martin, 165
Shaw, Lemuel (Justice), 106–7
Sherman Antitrust Act, US, 262
Shill, Gregory, 296–97
Shoked, Nadav, 184
Shumer, Sara, 184
sic utere principle, 69–70, 285–88
   arbitrariness and, 244
   Brick Presbyterian Church v. Mayor of New York, 56–57
   in common law, 55
   during Covid-19 pandemic, 286–87
   damage and, 286
   in early lawmaking, 68
   morals regulations and, 139–40, 142–43, 144–45
   nuisance laws and, 56, 57
   positive rights and, 228–29
   Precautionary Principle, 288
   in private law, 55
   during Progressive era, 63
   tort law and, 91, 286–87
   Vanderbilt v. Adams, 57
skepticism
   of administrative bureaucracy, 190–91
   of expertise, 190–91
   legislative, 73
   during Reconstruction era, 86
   of localism of police power, 184
   political
      of state constitutions, 18, 25–28, 36–37, 86
      Wood on, 26, 86
   of self-dealing, 249–50
   of zoning laws, 156
Skowronek, Stephen, 262
The Slaughterhouse Cases
   laissez faire constitutionalism and, 95
   police power in, 70–71, 90, 125
Smart America, 297
Smith, Adam, 45
Smith, Henry, 213
social control, through police power, 46
Sotomayor, Sonia (Justice), 247
Souter, David (Justice), 242, 266–67
special purpose authorities, 189–90
Spencer, Herbert, 204
state constitutions, state constitutionalism and. *See also specific states*
   amendments to, 74, 125
   British constitutionalism and, 29
   common law traditions and, 30–31, 55–64
      judicial intervention, 30, 31–32, 179
      judicial review, 30–32
   conceptual approach to, 137
   consent principles in, 22–24
   evolution of, 23
   good governance in, 23–24
   Constitutional Convention, 22, 26
   as countermajoritarian mechanism, 32–33, 101
   during Covid-19 pandemic, 5
   scope of constitutional powers, 160
   democracy and
      legislative supremacy, 25
      representative, 24–25, 93–94
   executive powers under, 19, 201
   failure of, 2–3
   Federalist Papers and, 18, 22, 36, 230

state constitutions, state constitutionalism (cont.)
  good governance through, 3, 32–35
    consent principles and, 23–24
    as project, 34–35
  individual rights in, 219
  legislative powers under, 19
    limits on, 26–27
    separation of, 88, 166
  length and stability of, 32
  Major Questions Doctrine and, 191–92
  modern developments in, 136–51, 162–63
    governance strategies, 137
    morals regulation, 137–38
    positive rights, 136–37
  morals regulations in, 137
    origins of, 137–38
  Novak on, 220
  objectives of, 2, 3
  originalist approach to, 164
  police power and, 72, 228
    as core component of constitutions, 2
  political strategy and, 48–51
  popular sovereignty through, 22–24
    through constitutional structure, 125
    good governance and, 23–24
    in post-revolutionary era, 23
  property rights and, 28–32
    private property protections, 37, 38
  public meaning of, 48–51, 77
  public rights and, 28
  public trust doctrine and, 28
  purpose of, 17–18, 48–51
  reform as constitutional reset, 25–28
    through skepticism, 86
  renaissance for, 98–99
  representation and, 24–25
    democracy and, 93–94
  during revolutionary era, 18–22
    active governance as goal of, 20, 201
    colonials' connection to Great Britain, 18, 29
    constitutions as instruments of governance, 21
    early framers of state constitutions, 18–20, 21
    political legacy of, 21–22
  right to liberty, 28–32
  separation of powers in, 88, 166, 173–79
    during Covid-19 pandemic, 175–76
    nondelegation doctrine, 176–77, 178–79
    plenary power, 174
    statutory interpretation of, 176
    unbundled executive power, 174
  skepticism of, 18, 25–28, 36–37
    Wood on, 26, 86
  structure of, 25–28
    popular sovereignty through, 125
  subordination in, 22–24
  Tarr on, 18, 29, 36, 41, 266
    on changes in state constitutions, 136, 220
  theories for, 2–3
    political, 63–64
    rational choice theory, 32
    US Constitution as foundational influence on, 2–3
state regulatory authority, restriction of
  through due process, 68
  through liberty of contact, 68
State v. Reid, 206
state-building, during Lochner era Supreme Court, 84
Stevens, John Paul, 146
subordination, in state constitutions, 22–24
Sunstein, Cass, 248, 288, 326
Supremacy Clause, 53
Supreme Court, US. *See also* Lochner era, for US Supreme Court; *specific cases*
  gun regulation and, 298–300
  history of police power and, 3–4
  Major Questions Doctrine and, 191
  nondelegation doctrine and, 191
  during post-Reconstruction era, 88–95
Sutton, Jeff, 31, 137, 181–82, 219
synoptic review, of arbitrariness, 243

takings law, 230, 323–26. *See also specific cases*
  liability rule, 324
  during Progressive era, 101
  property rights and, 214–15, 216–18
  "public use" in, 11, 71
Taney, Roger B. (Chief Justice), 60, 70
Tarr, Alan, 18, 29, 36, 41, 266
  on state constitutional changes, 136, 220
taxation, 321–23
  Pigovian taxes, 321–22
Taylor, Frederick Winslow, 189
tenant protections, police power and, 155
Tenth Amendment, 51–52, 54, 226–29
Terminiello v. Chicago, 202–3
Texas v. Johnson, 202–3
Thaler, Richard, 326
Thayer, James Bradley (Justice), 201
A Theory of Justice (Rawls), 167–68
Thomas v. Smith, 121
Thorpe v. Rutland & Burlington Railroad Co., 63–64
Thurlow v. Massachusetts, 140
Tiebout, Charles, 274
Tiedeman, Christopher, 42, 100, 125–26
Tomlins, Christopher, 7, 80, 310

tort law
    general welfare protections under, 55–64
    Restatement (Second) of Torts, 145
    sic utere principle and, 91, 286–87
transportation policies, 296–97
    National Complete Streets Coalition, 297
    Smart America, 297
Tribe, Laurence, 108
Trump v. Hawaii, 247
Trustees of Dartmouth College v. Woodward, 82
Tversky, Amos, 326
tyranny, Madison on, 203

Uniform Bar Exam, 158
United States (US). *See also* Constitution, US; constitutionalism; New Deal; state constitutions, state constitutionalism and; Supreme Court, US; *specific states*; *specific topics*
    Administrative Procedure Act, 116, 262–63
    Affordable Care Act, 268, 269–70
    Bureau of Animal Industry, 88
    culture wars in, 149–50
    Declaration of Independence, 18
    Federal Communications Act, 262
    Federal Communications Commission, 88
    Federal Trade Commission Act, 262
    Food & Drug Safety Act, 262
    Interstate Commerce Act, 262–63
    Kohler Act, 103
    National Labor Relations Act, 88, 262
    Securities & Exchange Acts, 262
    Sherman Antitrust Act, 262
    Voting Rights Act of 1965, 290
United States Dep't of Agriculture v. Moreno, 244–45
United States v. Lopez, 261, 265
United States v. Morrison, 261, 266–67
United States v. Windsor, 247–48, 265
urban blight, 153
Urofsky, Melvin, 127
US. *See* United States (US)

Vanderbilt v. Adams, 57
Vanderbilt v. Ames, 63
Vattel, Emer de, 45, 310
Vermeule, Adrian, 63–64, 186–87
vested rights, 65, 96
Village of Belle Terre v. Boraas, 153
Virginia
    state constitution in, 23
    zoning laws in, 121

Virginia v. Black, 203
Voting Rights Act of 1965, US, 290

Waldron, Jeremy, 207–8
Washington v. Davis, 209
Washington v. Glucksburg, 241–42
water law doctrines, 100
wealth inequality, infrastructure and, 302–5
Weber, Max, 189
Weingast, Barry, 59
Weisbach, David, 322
West Coast Hotel v. Parrish, 84–85
Whiggish political theory, 139–40
White, G. Edward, 44
White, Ted, 77, 108–9, 201, 238
Whitmer, Gretchen, 176
Wickard v. Filburn, 267
"wicked problems," police power and, 193
Williams, Robert, 26, 137
Williamson v. Lee Optical, 237–38, 255–56
Wilson, James, 38
Wisconsin Legislature v. Evers, 176
Wood, Gordon, 18, 20, 24–25, 26, 86

Yick Wo v. Hopkins, 92, 202, 244–45
YIMBY movement, 293, 294
Young, Ernie, 272–73, 274

Zackin, Emily, 227, 229
zoning laws, 117–22
    Ambler Realty Co. v. Village of Euclid, 118–21
    Claeys on, 120
    as common good, 120–21
    in common law tradition, 122
    early establishment and regulation of, 117–18
    Euclidean, 118–21
    housing policies and, 291–93
        construction prohibitions and, 292
        criticism of, 294
        NIMBY movement, 293
        YIMBY movement, 293, 294
    during Lochner era Supreme Court, 118–21
    Mansfssield & Swett v. Town of W. Orange, 119, 121
    in Mississippi, 130
    in New Jersey, 119–20
    police power and, 121–22
    salus populi principle and, 117–18, 119
    skepticism of, 156
    Thomas v. Smith, 121
    in urban settings, 153–56
    in Virginia, 121

Printed in the United States
by Baker & Taylor Publisher Services